Dog Catalog

DOG CATALOG

BY DON MYRUS

MACMILLAN PUBLISHING CO., INC.
NEW YORK

COLLIER MACMILLAN PUBLISHERS
LONDON

Macmillan Publishing Co., Inc.
866 Third Avenue, New York, N.Y. 10022
Collier Macmillan Canada, Ltd.

Library of Congress Cataloging in Publication Data
Myrus, Don
   Dog catalog.
   Bibliography: p.
   Includes index.
   1. Dogs. I. Title.
SF426.M97   636.7   78-17134
ISBN 0-02-588230-9

Editorial and Design Associates
Claire Romanof—associate editor
Lorraine Froehlich, Spida Grean and Richard Benjamin Romanof—editorial assistants
Julius Vitali—researcher
Joseph Hass—photographic printer
Irwin Wolf—design consultant

First Printing 1978

Printed in the United States of America

To Hazel Sawtelle Abrams and Irving Dietz

1
The Attachment   1

2
So You Want to Get a Dog   15

3
The Well-Mannered Life   33

4
Providing for the Dog   47

5
Dog News & World Report   71

6
Showing   89

7
Judging   109

8
Hunting, Racing, Fighting   119

9
Working—They Don't Do It for the Money   137

10
Fantasy   155

11
Art Work   183

12
My Dog Has Fleas and Other Matters
Physical, Sexual, and Psychological   215

13
Beware of Dog and Dogs Beware   235

A.K.C. Breeds Illustrated   254

A Select Bibliography   265

Index   271

Photograph by Peter Simon

ACKNOWLEDGMENTS

Jeanne Fredericks, Macmillan Publishing Co., Inc., for her insight and receptivity, and Patricia Cruz, American Kennel Club judge and *Newsday* dog columnist, for her expert advice and helpful introductions, and to the following for their generous cooperation:

Laddie Carswell and Robert Clyde, professional handlers; Patricia Coblentz and Kathy Ouwel, Museum of American Folk Art; Walt Chimel, Gaines Dog Research Center; Teresa Gannon, Axiom Market Research; Douglas D. Greathouse (Major, USAF), Chief, Military Dog Studies Branch; John T. Marvin, President, Dog Writers' Association of America; William White Parish, Esq.; Robert Reynolds, President, National Dog Groomers Association; Barbara Royer, Carnation; Louis A. Salerno and family (Doberman owners); Willard Turnbow, Food and Drug Administration, Department of Health, Education and Welfare; Caroline Thompson, Director, Special Projects, American Society for the Prevention of Cruelty to Animals; H. Edward Whitney, Long Island Rare Breed Association.

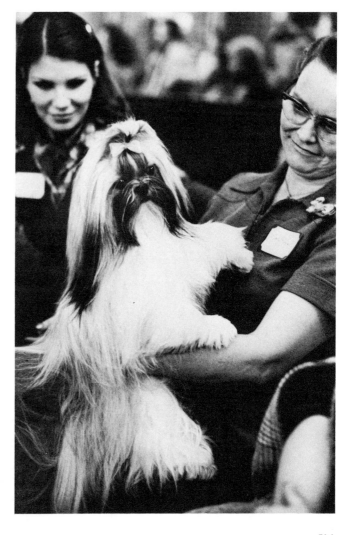

1

THE ATTACHMENT

THE CANINE CONNECTION

SOMETHING OF VALUE
  by Sarah Hawkes

WILD DOG
  by John Clayton

SPENDING TIME TOGETHER

MAN'S FAITHFUL FRIEND
  by Vladimir Hulpach

Opposite page: Peter Simon—photographer-author of Moving On, Holding Still; Decent Exposure; Carly Simon: Complete *(she is his sister); and* Reggae Bloodlines—*hugs his dogs near his home at Gay Head, Martha's Vineyard.*

The Canine Connection

Dogs aren't human, but in many ways they might as well be.

A science fiction writer, intending to startle, might describe a world without children . . . or dogs. For people look at dogs and see much that is human. People act accordingly: they make doghouses and dog clothing and even jewelry to be worn by dogs; they develop special drugs and practice veterinary medicine to cure dog illnesses; they even inter and sometimes enshrine dogs.

Many dogs achieve a human role: they get talked to. And many owners believe that, in the process, com-

The Chihuahua, a breed perfected in the U.S., is the descendant of a ninth-century Mexican Taltec Indian dog, the techichi, and a small hairless Asian dog carried across the Bering land bridge to America. Chihuahuas like their own kind (and people), but not other breeds. (Photograph by Daniel O'Toole; courtesy of the FDA)

munication takes place. A dog's expressions are interpreted and articulated—out loud—and often a dog is expected to listen to aspirations, troubles, oral meanderings. (A person walking a dog, supposedly just the two of them alone, can bring a smile to an eavesdropper.)

People breed dogs, train them, groom them, handle them, judge them (having entered them in competitions to win colored pieces of ribbon and silver bowls).

In our time hunting with dogs, except in rural areas, is uncommon—but many people continue the activity in the symbolism of sport and in the exercises and drills of pointing, flushing, and retrieving that are part of dog shows and trials. People also arrange for dogs to race each other and even to fight each other (and, of course, people bet on the results).

Some exotics even eat dogs, as did the Aztecs centuries ago.

. . . mostly people "have" dogs to enjoy them and to cherish the company they keep.

Then there are those who observe and report dog affairs in newspapers, magazines, and books—whole publishing houses are devoted exclusively to the literature of dogs. Others are involved with dogs as actors in the theater, film, and on TV, often to sell products—both the people and the dogs doing the selling.

There are those who study dogs in the wild to understand their predatory function, while some are deeply concerned about dog waste and its effects on urban ecology.

Some people spend time and energy hating dogs, and a few unfortunates live in constant fear of them.

But mostly people "have" dogs to enjoy them and to cherish the company they keep.

Something of Value

by Sarah Hawkes

The changed status of many middle-class dogs since World War II—from taken-for-granted mutts to cherished select breeds.

Through the late eighteen-hundreds and into the early nineteen-hundreds packs of strays ran loose on city streets and were systematically rounded up and killed, often shot. Frequently, dogs went mad, and the daily papers were filled with reports of their savage attacks.

The American pit bull terrier, whose antecedents are disputed, now is kept mostly as a household pet, although some are known to have been used as fighting dogs and some to hunt boars. The breed, which can range from 40 to 125 pounds, needs lots of exercise. It is recognized by the United Kennel Club. (Photograph by Don Myrus)

Though people died of the dread hydrophobia, muzzle and leash laws enacted in many areas of the U.S. were heatedly protested by some as the greatest possible cruelty to animals. By far the great mass of Americans kept mongrel mutts of one variety or another, let them run loose, breed indiscriminately, and subsist as best they could on table scraps and forage.

For the rich it was different. They had long treated their pets with care and attention and, perhaps, with affection. But according to Thorstein Veblen, the motive was less lofty. In *The Theory of the Leisure Class*, published in 1899, he said of the dog, because

he is an item of expense, and commonly serves no industrial purpose, he holds a well-assured place in men's regard as a thing of good repute. The dog is at the same time associated in our imagination with the chase—a meritorious employment and an expression of the honorable predatory impulse. . . . The commercial value of canine monstrosities (the "grotesque" breeds), such as the prevailing styles of pet dogs both for men's and women's use, rests on their high cost of production, and their value to their owners lies chiefly in their utility as items of conspicuous consumption.

2

And consume the rich did:

The Morgans and the Rutherfords imported, bred, and showed "the breeds."

In July 1911 Mrs. A. Dupont imported six Sealyham terriers from Great Britain, the first of their kind to reach the United States. She valued them at three hundred thousand (pre-World War I) dollars.

In 1907 Mrs. Alan Sheppard is reported to have raced across the U.S. in a special train to try and save the life of her Maltese "poodle" and, when her efforts proved unsuccessful, announced plans to build a monument in the pet cemetery in Hartsdale, New York. Two years later Dr. C. L. Dana, writing in *Medical Record* magazine, described a condition he designated as zoophil psychosis—a passion for animals that "amounts to a disease attacking morbid lovers of pets."

A noted sufferer from the "disease" was the twentieth-century Englishman T. H. White, author of *The Once and Future King*, who, upon the death of his Irish setter, wrote: "I died last night. All that was me is dead, because it was half her. She was wife, mother, mistress & child."

The dog, as hero, was adored, praised, marveled over. Amazing loyalty to master was frequently reported in the press. The husky, Togo, leader of a sled team that carried diphtheria serum 560 miles in 127 hours from Nena to Nome in 1925, preventing an epidemic, wound up taxidermically stuffed in Yale's Peabody Museum. Another sensation occurred when Admiral Byrd's glorious sled team was serenaded in the far reaches of the Antarctic, over the radio, by a "dog chorus."

Meanwhile the average dog, the mutt, rarely saw a veterinarian. He wandered free, mated, fought, strayed, scratched his fleas, succumbed to distemper or rabies or any number of other ills.

Then something happened. When, exactly, or why is a matter of conjecture, but the free and supposedly easy life enjoyed by all those "lucky dogs" began to change. Though some may think back with nostalgia to a time when man and dog had more freedom of sorts, it is clear that the dog, at least, is far better off today than ever before.

The change became evident during World War II.

The boy who marched off to fight often left at home a mongrel who, in the tension of war, was revaluated as the cherished companion who had walked the boy to school, kept him company through lazy summer afternoons of fishing, followed him through his rounds of chores, hunted, played, and even slept with the boy.

Those who waited at home took pains to see that the dog would be there to greet the "boy." Families, with a sentimentality made the stronger by their guilt of non-participation in the war, gave new value to Spot, Duke, Prince, King as a link to the absent warrior.

Other things happened, too. Wartime advances in medical technology benefited dogs as well as people; information about the value of good nutrition became widespread. Later, the postwar affluence of the fifties and sixties was extended to the family dog, who became more and more often a purebred and costly possession to be valued and protected.

Sarah Hawkes is a novelist with a special interest in mythology and social history. She is one of those people who cherish both dogs and cats.

Craig Francisco and his Rottweiler. Campaigning Roman legions used dogs to herd livestock. As the cattle were consumed, the dogs were left behind—being named after the various conquered towns and later developing breed distinctions. The Rottweiler went farther than any other Roman cattle dog—to Rottweil, in Germany. (Photograph by Spida Grean)

Wild Dog

by John Clayton

A prize-winning short-story writer tells the poignant history of a once-wild dog who came to a "civilized" end.

A woman friend of mine found Lucky in the Santa Cruz Mountains, and she tamed him by placing chunks of meat closer and closer to her cabin until finally she could coax him to her with her voice and stroke his brown fur. He was heavy-muzzled and broad-chested, and I liked to think of him as a noble wild beast. But there was, paradoxically, my human need to civilize him.

I saw Susan also as wild. The two of them running across a hilltop campus lawn, Susan barefoot, her long blond hair loose behind her. Oh, they were very impressive, the two of them, both wild. Or she'd drive off on a back road with Lucky surging alongside, 20, 25, even 30 miles an hour for short stretches. Amazing for a big collie-shepherd-husky. Running, head high and pumping, the fixed concentration of a human runner on his face. Refusing to give up. And so I poured my human meaning into Lucky. Wild dog. Susan's wild dog.

She thought of him as *her* dog. "If I couldn't take him with me," she said to me once, "I think I'd have him put to sleep." But that was mostly gesture, for when it came to leaving him to move in with a lover who wouldn't have the dog—well, she left him: left him with me.

And didn't see Lucky for two years. By then she was no longer with her lover—saw me for an afternoon in New York, and by then Lucky was *my* dog. When she came in, he barked and barked—it was his only dog-fault—then sat by my chair. "Lucky," she crooned to him, "baby. Hey, Lucky." He went over for a pet the way he would, then turned away and curled up at my feet. Then, suddenly, he sat up and whimpered and started barking at us both. Finally he went over to Susan and put his paws on her lap and stared into her eyes and licked her face and smelled her up and down. We were laughing, both of us, but underneath I felt frightened that he wouldn't stay with me, thought of Jack London's *Call of the Wild* and figured I was, of the two of us, more the representative of civilization. But then we said good-by and I called "Lucky—come here!" And he came.

We were good friends by then. When I was building my house and had to sleep on the floor of my office for a month, Lucky slept next to me and kept at bay the loneliness and spooks all night in a deserted office building. And when I hiked in the woods Lucky ran along, plunging, with his amazing sense of fully expressed honest power, into the brush, charging back across the trail to make contact, then into the brush on the other side. When he smelled deer he went mad, wailing and howling—but he never caught a deer, never brought home a rabbit or squirrel, and I still wonder what he ate in the Santa Cruz Mountains.

All he ever caught were skunk and porcupine. "Jesus Christ not again," I'd yell, and he'd put his muzzle to the ground and walk sideways knowing what was coming. Two cans of tomato paste in a bucket of warm, soapy water, wash him down with a scrub brush while he stood for it like a stoic—unless I let go for an instant and he was off into the woods until morning. Tomato paste and a hosing down, then I'd jump back to avoid the spray as he shook off his lion hair. "Now stay *out* of here!" And he'd slink off.

Porcupine was worse. I took him to the vet the first time, $10 to knock him out, pull out the quills, keep him overnight. After that I did it myself, holding him, petting him, calling him a dumb goddamned ignorant poor old beast and pulling out the quills with a pliers. What I remember best is Lucky's courage. I knew, even as I yanked, that if it had been me, I'd have been screaming. But Lucky hardly made a sound. He didn't pull away. He stood high, as if I were grooming him, only once in awhile trembling and letting out a tiny highpitched sound from the back of his throat.

He was very brave and, hunter or no, very wild. A ferocious fighter, he was *my* wildness, my courage. Myself, I'm no fighter, and I dislike machismo in relations with men or women, yet not-so-secretly I admired Lucky, loved to see him take on a dog bigger than himself, a big black Lab, a Great Dane. Once he attacked a trained shepherd and bled a hell of a lot, but mostly he could get away with it. Huskies are dangerous fighters, but he demolished huskies. Once he wiped out an Irish wolfhound, biggest of all dogs, but to be honest, I have to add that the wolfhound was a timid, soulful, civilized creature with a delicate stomach.

Myself, I'm no fighter, and I dislike machismo in relations with men or women, yet not-so-secretly I admired Lucky, loved to see him take on a dog bigger than himself, a big black Lab, a Great Dane.

I loved to watch him start a fight. He wouldn't bark, he'd growl, very low in his chest, and he'd walk s-l-o-w up to the other dog like a gunfighter, and about this time I'd say "*No*, Lucky," in as serious a tone as I could manage. "Come on, Lucky, act your age" (because if the vet was right when Susan found him and he was seven then, by the time he came to me he was ten, and he fought all through his early teens). Lucky would back off a moment, then close in, sniff ass, circle in the usual dogdance, then seem to move off, tail wagging, satisfied.

John Clayton and Lucky. "If he was ferocious, he was also terribly gentle, a real baby, coming up with adoration in his eyes, staring into mine, wanting to be petted." (Photograph by Laura Clayton)

As the other dog—I'm remembering a big, black Lab on the commons in Amherst, Massachusetts—came after him, suddenly Lucky would pivot, leap up, teeth bared, growl turn to wild barking, and heave against the other dog and top him, topple him, roar and snap but never do damage, and I'd be trying to grab his tail and pull him free. "Goddammit, Lucky!" but secretly letting him act out my own macho stuff.

Terrible! I remember how I really had to face up to that. I was walking through the University of Massachusetts campus with a friend, a feminist. Lucky was walking alongside, sniffing the earth, then head up, listening, then plunging forward, and I called "Lucky!" —knowing he'd smelled male dog. And there was this little black cocker spaniel up ahead and I roared "LUCKY!" and for once he listened, pulled up short, slunk back. I said, "Good *girl,* Lucky," and my friend guffawed until I had to laugh too. So much for my support of the women's movement!

I'm sad, thinking of how I used this dog, expressed my own power secretly through him; and when I felt worthless, kicked him off the bed or out of the house or cursed him for being wet and muddy on the rug and hated him, and when he'd look up at me with devotion, snap my fingers and tell him to *Get* down under the goddamn table. I think I slowed him down, I think I

gave him a human sense of shame, and I'm sorry. I regret not letting him be whatever dog he was outside my human metaphors. He was wilder than my human sense of wildness—and much more complicated. If he was ferocious, he was also terribly gentle, a real baby, coming up with adoration in his eyes, staring into mine, wanting to be petted. Wonderfully joyful when my children would come out for the weekend, he would bark and whine and tremble with what I guess was love.

He stayed powerful and lived long. Every day he ran behind my car or ran in the woods, and when he was fifteen and sixteen and cataracts began forming visibly on his eyes and he walked with stiffness and he couldn't hear to bark at footsteps on the gravel driveway, he was still a "noble, wild beast." That metaphor—nobility: like a lion, like a warrior knight—never left him. He ran behind the car more slowly, and finally he had to walk and I'd slow down to pick him up. He fought less, and when he fought, mostly lost. It hurt to see him lose a fight and once, against a St. Bernard, get his eyelid split open and his ear chewed bloody. It was no pleasure to see him fight now, bravely as ever, watch the two dogs leap up on hind legs and swirl and then the thud of Lucky on his back, trying to right himself.

He ran less in the woods and slept more, old dog in the shade of a tree. Sometimes his stomach gave out on him and he barfed up his dinner, but always as close to the front door as he could get, and always he went around afterward sad and ashamed. There is a wonderful vet in the Connecticut Valley, Dr. Katz, and when Lucky was about seventeen, he examined him. "He's in good shape, real good shape. He should make three, four more years."

But old dog, one hot afternoon he squirmed under the VW to keep cool; he'd never done that before. Middle of the afternoon I went out to the car to drive down to the post office. I felt irritated—hadn't been able to work well—wasn't seeing much, got in the car, looked over my shoulder, started to back out of the driveway. The car rose up a hump; I jammed on the brakes—a goddamned rock?—rolled forward, heard a noise, got out to look: Lucky was trying to squeeze out again. Howling, but too softly, rhythmically. I picked him up, his body had spasmed into stiffness. I picked him up and drove him to Dr. Katz, trying hard not to feel anything —guilt, regret, pain.

But he didn't die. Nothing broken, shock to the system, keep him a couple of days. Tough old dog.

Then his kidneys went. Old dog, body poisoning itself now, not much chance. "I'll put him to sleep tonight. Let's give him whatever chance he's got."

My wife—wife I'd met after I'd lived two years with Lucky—she cried; my nine-year-old boy cried. I held back. We waited for the vet's call.

But he didn't call. Next day he told us, "He's fighting back. He's really making it. His kidneys are functioning again."

He held on and we went to visit him. I had a hard time, because I'd been the one to run him over and because I couldn't stand seeing him in a hospital, hooked up to an intravenous feeder, muscle tone slack, hair falling out, thinner beneath all that fur than we'd ever realized. We went up to his cage. His eyes were glassy; he didn't know us.

The next day, shaved in places, tubes still in him, he looked at us and his eyes seemed to make contact; he thumped his tail a little. It went on for nine days, until Lucky was stronger again, no tubes now. He stood up when we came and knew us. "Noble, wild beast," I said, rubbing him down in the old way. On that night his lungs filled up and he died.

They gave him to me in a plastic bag; I put it inside a cardboard carton and carried him to the car, the same car. I feared the stink of his death and kept the windows open. Home, it took too little digging to make a hole for him at the edge of the garden, he was so slight. We planted flowers.

Well, he was seventeen years old. I miss him. I still reach down to pet him or suddenly imagine I see him in the shadow of the couch. It hurts me that I killed him. It hurts me more how he died, a wild dog to die such a civilized death, stuck with tubes and needles, dying behind cage bars in a hospital. And to know that I'd caged him long before by humanizing him—*my* dog—so much: my speed, my power, my courage, my nobility, my self-hatred, my aging, my tenderness. Whoever Lucky was, he was his own dog.

John Clayton is a writer of fiction and Associate Professor of English at the University of Massachusetts in Amherst. His stories have been reprinted in a number of anthologies and in Best American Short Stories *and the* O. Henry Prize Stories. *He has published a number of essays on modern literature and a full-length critical study,* Saul Bellow: In Defense of Man. *He is now at work on a novel,* Time Exposure.

A PUZZLING ARRAY OF MASTERS

A dog's world is a helpless satellite of a man's world. A dog has a puzzling array of masters: the romping friend of children, the guardian of the blind, the trained sentry of the armed forces and department stores, the hard-working employee of the sheepherder, the manicured exhibit of exhibitionists, and the accepted member of so many families.

—Edited and excerpted from Jack Gould's New York Times *review of the TV documentary "It's a Dog's World," produced by Alan Landsbury and telecast on N.B.C. November 25, 1966. © The New York Times Company. Used with permission.*

Spending Time Together

A selection of photographs: walking, jogging, taking the dog for a ride. It is the simple pleasures of companionship that cement the bond.

The First Dog heels on command of the First Girl. (Photograph courtesy of the White House)

Unlike most cats, dogs love to travel—especially in cars and trucks. Dogs are for going along. (Photograph above by Peter Simon)

Just what qualities dogs share with humans is not clear. A sense of humor? Maybe. Tolerance, certainly, and that makes companionship possible. (Photograph at right by Philip Minicozzi)

Walking-the-dog. *There is no activity quite like it, a routine obligation for all sorts of weather. But it is also that category of duty that satisfies. Surely no one dies of boredom who has a dog to walk on a beautiful country road or busy city street. As for dogs, hardly any are known who can resist getting out.* (Photograph at left by Peter Simon)

"A man's dog stands by him in prosperity and poverty, in health and in sickness." From Vest's Eulogy on a Dog. (Photograph by Bill Owens from his book, **Working: I Do It for the Money.** Used with permission.)

Dogs such as these massive Great Pyrenees, when kept as pets, take a tremendous amount of care, feeding, and exercising. (Photograph by Daniel O'Toole; courtesy of the FDA)

This old man and his dog are a pleasure to contemplate.
Mr. Valentin Zacharov has two, which he separately
takes for long walks. (Photograph by Don Myrus)

Man's Faithful Friend

by Vladimir Hulpach

An American Indian tale that draws the moral, no man ever *need be alone who has a dog.*

Much sleep had passed in the Lost Valley, many times had Wahu watched the migrating flocks of geese and listened to the thundering hooves of the vast bison herds.

Merciless time had carried everything away on its wings. All that was left were the long shadows slowly settling on the silent countryside. Only they understood the old Indian, and it was with them that he conversed every evening before the stars came out above the camp.

One evening, when the shadows were longest, they brought him a message from the great Manitou himself.

"Yet it was he who loved you best . . ." he heard the voice of the Great Spirit coming from the distance.

"The Great Spirit awaits thee: prepare for thy journey, prepare for thy journey," they whispered. "Make thy farewells, Wahu, make thy farewells!"

"Who is there for me to take leave of?" said Wahu, smiling sadly. "My sons and daughters have long since left for various corners of the earth, and the people here will be only too glad to see me go."

The old man rose to his feet. Picking up his battered paddle he walked slowly down to the river.

The silvery mist was already rising from the water when Wahu pushed off for the last time in his canoe. There was nothing now to keep the boat from sailing down the calm river toward the Eternal Hunting Grounds.

And yet, had only the old Indian turned to look back, he would have seen someone running along the river-bank, his eyes full of sorrow.

But Wahu saw no one. Entrusting his canoe humbly to the current, he was carried away faster and faster all the time. And as it was borne swiftly toward the Thunder Rapids, the soft, melancholy melody of Wahu's deathsong sounded above the great roar of the waters.

But someone else had in the meantime thrown himself in the river and was now likewise being carried into the vortex of the tumbling waves.

Wahu fell deeper and deeper, a deafening din drowning all other sounds, until he at last came to rest on a surface as white as milk.

"This is the White River," he thought. "Now I shall soon be there."

Just then he saw in front of him two rocks like a huge gateway, and a bay in which the waves lapped gently in unending succession.

The old man allowed his canoe to drift to the white bank, where he got out. He had not even taken a good look around when the rocks stood apart and two handsome warriors came out, their headdress giving off a silvery sheen.

"We are the guardians of the Eternal Hunting Grounds," said the first warrior. "We have been expecting you."

"But why do you come alone?" asked the second.

"I no longer had anyone to look after me, much less to accompany me on this voyage," Wahu replied.

"In that case, who is it gazing at you from out of the water, his eyes filled with sorrow?"

Wahu turned round abruptly, to find that he was being watched by the most faithful pair of eyes he had ever seen.

"Why, it's my dog! My dog!" he whispered, deeply moved. And he went down to the White River and took his faithful four-footed friend in his arms.

"I would never have thought of him," he said aloud.

"Yet it was he who loved you best . . ." he heard the voice of the Great Spirit coming from the distance.

Thus it was that the old Indian and his only friend entered the Eternal Hunting Grounds, treading the path along which no one ever returns.

Reprinted from American Indian Tales and Legends *by Vladimir Hulpach (translated by George Theiner), with illustrations by Miloslov Troup (London: Paul Hamlyn, 1965. Distributed in the U.S. by Leon Amiel Publisher).*

DOG STAYS IN BOAT

A Federal grand jury indicted Cyril E. LaBrecque for manslaughter, charging that he refused to throw his eighty-pound, eleven-year-old Labrador retriever, Happer, overboard to make room for two desperate crewmen clinging to the gunwales of a lifeboat after LaBrecque's schooner sank.

At the trial in May 1974 in the U.S. District Court, Camden, New Jersey, Captain LaBrecque testified that had he thrown Happer into the sea, the boat would have capsized and that in any case he couldn't have lifted the animal.

The jury found LaBrecque not guilty.

Slick Jack, a purebred smooth fox terrier, at age six weeks, moments before leaving the litter. (All photographs of Slick Jack by Don Myrus)

2

SO YOU WANT TO GET A DOG

THE PUPPY JOURNAL
  by Claire Romanof

FIRST AID FROM THE AMERICAN
  KENNEL CLUB

ENGLISH COCKER
  by Kate Romanski

IS A SIBERIAN HUSKY FOR YOU?

GOOD ADVICE

TWENTY-ONE WOLVES?

THE GROUPS

"We talked to him, petted him, let him nap in our laps and sleep in our beds until he'd grown up a bit and felt happy on his own."

The Puppy Journal

by Claire Romanof

An intimate account of deciding on a breed, searching for a litter, choosing and then raising the pedigreed dog named Slick Jack. Also a practical guide that includes information about breed selection and early care.

There is an almost universal human response, usually of delight and pleasure, at the sight of infant animals. Only slightly less than human infants but more than kittens and colts, a puppy most consistently evokes kindly emotions—maternal, paternal, nurturing, and protective. Because the dog breeds are so numerous, varied, and distinctive, a sense of the miraculous and wonderful is often especially acute in the presence of a perfect little dog.

Our Scottie was beautiful—a black/brindle of fine conformation (form and structure) and impressive lineage. He possessed all the terrier bustle and intensity, and he had a wonderful self-important Scottie dignity and a certain aloofness with outsiders—he never would tolerate the touch of a cooing stranger. To watch him rush, blunt legs scrambling, across a field after a squirrel (he never did catch one) was a true delight. Bathed, groomed, clipped, plucked, and brushed he was—like his father before him—magnificent. But the time it took!

He was sickly all of his eight years and he was also epileptic, a condition that necessitated his being given a pill twice a day, every day, without fail, always.

Often, he radiated a discontent that we never did quite fathom. He would lie, four short legs out, straight,

square head resting on front paws, looking up at us from under authoritative, bushy brows. His eyes were accusative, it seemed, and demanding, and a little sad. He always made one feel that he wanted more.

In the middle of a particularly cold winter he began to shiver every time he got out-of-doors, and he would wet, on occasion, in the apartment or more often in the elevator on his way out.

The diagnosis was a kidney infection; he didn't respond to antibiotics and in a couple of weeks he was dead, euthanized when he became incontinent, constantly feverish, and too weak to do anything much.

We missed him terribly and grieved and were reluctant, too soon again, to give our affections to another of his ilk.

But the time did come, after a couple of years and knowing full well what we were getting into, that we decided to have another dog. So delighted were we with the decision that we became at once impatient, intense,

". . . we can't imagine how we could have gotten along without him."

16

desperate. We had to have our pup at once!

Resist any impulse to rush out and quickly acquire a dog. Though temperamental and physical characteristics of individual dogs of the same breed are much alike, the breeds are very different, one from another, in more than just outward appearance. There are people who can tell you almost exactly what to expect of a particular breed so that you can determine in advance its appropriateness for you. With a mixed-breed dog, though, you're completely on your own.

We purposefully avoided department store "kennels," pet shops, shelters, and pounds, where we could be tempted into a precipitous act, and began a reasoned research and discussion program. In our house we turn first to books. We also talk a lot. How to arrive at the best dog for a suburban family of four—two adults and two good-size boys, all of whom are around a lot but usually busy? Noisily, a few things were quickly proclaimed.

> We wanted a small dog that didn't need too much exercise but one large enough to hold its own with three cats, yet not obliterate them.
> We wanted a huge, rough-and-tumble dog who could keep pace with a jogger, a cyclist, a swimmer, a skier, whatever.
> We wanted a short-haired, smooth dog that didn't need clipping or stripping or cutting or too much grooming and washing.
> We wanted a lush, soft, woolly, cuddly beast.
> I wanted a Maltese, an elegant little lapdog, but I was loath to admit it. When pressed, which I was, I reverted to the familiar and was ready to embrace a Scottish terrier.
> That we wanted a purebred male was all that was certain.

So we read books about dog behavior, psychology, and development, looked at pictures of the AKC breeds, wrote to the secretaries of the parent clubs of the breeds in which we were interested for official descriptions, histories, and referrals. We wrote, too, to local breeders and handlers of good reputation, and we went to dog shows. We tried to keep in mind that no matter how appealing a dog looked, a suburban house is probably not the best place for a Siberian husky who might embarrass one by eating the neighbor's cat, and that someone must spend twenty to thirty hours a week keeping an old English sheepdog groomed for the show ring.

Deciding that you want a dog and of which breed is one thing; finding one may be quite another, unless you're willing to chance a purchase from a retailer (pet shop or department store). We were not. Such dogs are often bred and kept in the most appalling conditions by puppy mills where the only concern is profit and the merchandise has to be moved before it grows too big to appeal. Young dogs shipped long distances at a sensitive age can be so traumatized by the experience that they

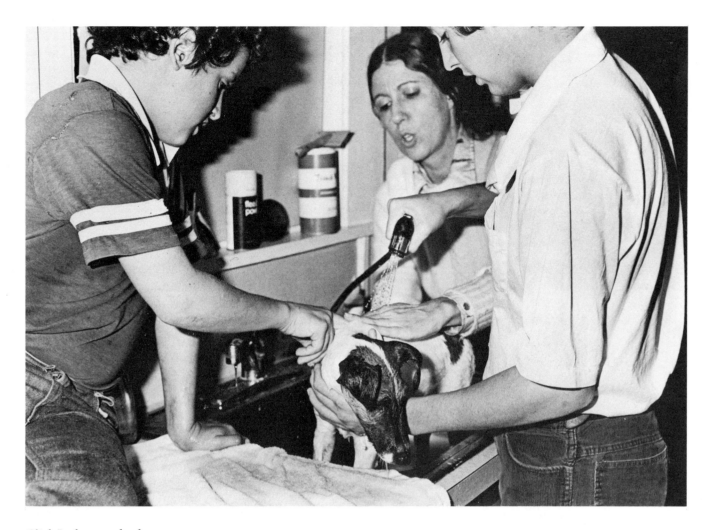

Slick Jack gets a bath.

never recover emotionally; they also become very susceptible to disease. Such a pup may be seriously ill before it ever leaves the store, and sick or not, a pup that has spent the sixth to the tenth week of its life—the time during which its ability to socialize develops—in a kennel with only minimal human contact will always be more dog-oriented than people-oriented. If during some or all of this impressionable time a puppy has been alone in a pet shop cage, it will not be socialized either to dogs or to people and is likely to be timid and neurotic in various ways.

Though there may be some decent mass-market kennels and pet shop operators, we found none willing to say anything informative about the source of their merchandise. It's best to avoid them completely even if you are given a health guarantee or AKC papers. AKC registration has nothing to do with quality, health, or breeding techniques, nor is it a guarantee that you could show the dog later. Even though purebred, a badly bred dog may have physical faults that would disqualify it from the show ring.

After we made our decision, it took weeks and many phone calls to find a puppy of the breed we wanted. We were put in touch with professional terrier handlers in our vicinity, who in turn put us in touch with the owner-handler of a male who had sired a litter. At the time the pups were three weeks old. Three weeks later, at the earliest possible moment, we went to get him.

In a warm and pleasant room of the breeder's home, close to the sounds and smells of family life, in a large wood-and-wire, paper-lined pen, were three fat, smooth

---

If you balk at having a puppy in bed (many do), then put the puppy's bed close to yours so that your presence can be literally sensed—heard, seen, smelled.

---

fox terrier puppies. Two were black-and-white, and the third (ours) had tan markings. He was the most active, outgoing, busy, and curious of the litter—qualities we were looking for. Some lifelong personality traits are already obvious at six weeks; sociability is one of them.

We left the breeder's home carrying the pup, a receipt, a certificate of pedigree prepared by the breeder, including AKC registration numbers of sire and dam and written information about the inoculations he had

Slick Jack went into a home of four people and three cats. Two of the cats ignored him, but the youngest, Thor, adopted him as a playmate.

had, when he was wormed, and his eating habits. The AKC litter registration form that we would need to register the pup had not yet been processed and would follow later.

With the exception of a good puppy food and a light collar and leash, almost any normal home can well supply a puppy's initial needs, but there are some wonderful things—toys and beds and bowls and coats and brushes—that make life easier and a lot more fun. [See Chapter 4, "Providing for the Dog."]

Volumes of advice have been written about how to start off the right way with a new puppy. Mostly, it's good advice—keep calm, speak softly, provide a private place for it to get away from it all. But we rejected the

advice to leave our pup alone with a hot water bottle and ticking clock (to imitate a heartbeat) on his first night away from the security of his family nest. We believed, then, and do more so now, that physical, sensual comfort gives a pup a better temper. We talked to him, petted him, let him nap in our laps and sleep in our beds until he'd grown up a bit and felt happy on his own.

If you balk at having a puppy in bed (many do), then put the puppy's bed close to yours so that your presence can be literally sensed—heard, seen, smelled.

Slick Jack, our smooth fox terrier, is of an old breed—stylish, with a certain handsome elegance of manner and appearance. He's of modest size, 17 pounds and 15

The 6 A.M. walk.

Ed Beckmann, top right, is the Director of the Problem Puppy School. All puppies are a problem to someone. Slick Jack behaved as puppies will—uncivilized, demanding, raucous, and silly. Slick Jack learned from Beckmann everything a dog should know—to sit, to wait, to lie down, to walk with a person, not to grab trouser cuffs, and to eliminate out of doors. Slick Jack would concentrate intently and wag his tail a mile a minute when being taught. Physical correction was never used, nor were voices raised. Here Ed Beckmann explains to Noah—one of Slick Jack's family—how training is to progress.

Slick Jack, who is tan and white, had two littermates, both black and white.

inches high. He requires little grooming. At six months Slick Jack is lively, intelligent, independent, and feisty. He's companionable, not too delicate for a wrestle, and a faster runner than anyone in the household. He's outgoing and sociable, enthusiastically greeting visitors at home and total strangers on the street, and he's exuberantly active, two traits that may not appeal to everyone. Konrad Lorenz in *Man Meets Dog* [see index] cautions that the fox terrier is not the breed for nervous people. He personally dislikes the overly sociable dog, which he describes as emotionally immature. We, on the contrary, don't need to claim Jack's exclusive affection and adoration. We delight in his delight in the human race, and we can't imagine how we could have gotten along without him.

Claire Romanof has been deeply involved with writing and books for over twenty years. She's also been fascinated by dogs. Slick Jack is the second pedigree she's owned. The first was a Scottish terrier, predictably named Macduff.

Slick Jack, just short of four months, maturing nicely.

First Aid from the American Kennel Club

Besides an avuncular "buyer beware," the breed organization of the United States does provide helpful advice about how to locate the dog you want. AKC explained.

People who go to the trouble (and it can be trouble) of buying a purebred dog almost always go one more step and register that dog, at modest cost, with the American Kennel Club. The litter registration form goes off to AKC headquarters in New York, and about two weeks later the "papers" come back, completed.

For the great majority of owners of purebred dogs, this is their only contact with AKC. The registration form finds its way into the family file drawer along with birth certificates, diplomas, and the like. Each year more than a million dogs are registered, and the fees involved support the bulk of the AKC's ten-million-dollar budget.

Besides registering dogs—certifying that a particular individual has a pedigree, that its antecedents can be identified and its roots traced back for generations—the AKC engages in a variety of activities that don't generate much income but do provide the prestige that makes registration a must for owners of purebred dogs. Here's how it began.

In 1873 the world's first kennel club, known simply as The Kennel Club, was founded in England under the patronage of the Prince of Wales. It has been the model for all other such clubs, including the American Kennel Club, founded a year later.

The AKC is a nonprofit organization that furthers the interests and enhances the well-being of purebred dogs. To this end AKC establishes and enforces uniform rules and standards for dog shows throughout the U.S. Though it has no legal authority, AKC has power, which its founders and early members knew a great deal about. Though AKC was (and still is) composed of the elected delegates from member clubs across the country, the organization was for many of its early years dominated by a group of wealthy, important easterners. Many of them also belonged to the extraordinarily prestigious New York-based Westminster Kennel Club, which is still a bastion of wealth and social elitism. A Rockefeller was elected president in 1977.

Through the acquisition of delegate proxies and the exercise of conservative decisions by its Board of Directors, the AKC remained pretty much the same—an exclusive club for special people—until after World War II. Then, in the fifties and sixties, AKC's reputation for scrupulous, if rather crotchety, integrity touched with a certain snobbish glamour, appealed to the upwardly

mobile, newly affluent, and recently leisured American dog owner. The dog population grew, the dog sport grew, and the AKC grew. Here's how it works today.

The AKC *is* its roughly four hundred-member clubs —breed clubs, all-breed clubs, obedience clubs, etc.— each of which elects a delegate to exercise a vote in the larger organization. These delegates are the legislative body of the AKC. They make the rules and elect the Board members from among themselves. The Board formulates policy.

Each individual club has a secretary whose name and address (along with the name of the delegate) is published quarterly in the club magazine, *Pure-Bred Dogs—*

If you want to buy a purebred dog, obtain from the American Kennel Club the name and address of the current secretary of the appropriate parent breed club. (These clubs often have "American" as part of the name.) The secretary will send you a pamphlet containing information about the origin and purpose of the breed, its history in the U.S., characteristics of temperament and personality, special needs that a potential owner should take into consideration, and the official breed standard, which is a description of the physical properties of an idealized representative of the breed.

The pamphlet will also list handbooks, magazines, and newsletters available, and these in turn will contain information about kennels and breeders and special breed events.

To learn about breeds other than those 122 recognized by the AKC, see the index for rare breeds and other American registries. See bibliography for lists of breed periodicals.

American Kennel Gazette. When you want to buy a dog, the place to begin is the secretary of the American parent club of the breed in which you are interested. And AKC will be delighted to tell you how to make contact.

AKC now has almost five hundred employees. A few are field representatives scattered across the country, but most work at the New York office. What do all these people do?

They register purebred dogs, maintain the Stud Book, publish the *Stud Book Register,* license or sanction some eight thousand dog events a year, assign stewards to oversee them, license about twenty-four hundred judges, publish the results of dog events in the *Gazette,* maintain records of the results of the shows going back to the beginning, license new clubs, run film, printing, microfilm, and publishing departments, manage seminars and media shows, collect dog art, and maintain a twelve-thousand-volume library.

Every day ten to twelve thousand pieces of mail are delivered to AKC, of which eight to nine thousand are applications of one kind or another. There are at AKC some fifty different form letters, but even so about three hundred personal letters are dictated every day. And the telephone department answers five hundred calls a day.

It takes two weeks for a puppy's registration form to be processed through AKC. When applications, with breeder's litter registration form, are received at the club, they are screened for obvious errors or omissions, which about 20 percent have. Those that are correct are then put through a computer to check for mistakes in names, ages, condition, and AKC registration numbers of the sire and dam. If all is as it should be, information about the new registrant is fed into the computer by two different people, who in effect catch each other's errors. There is again another computer check, and an error analysis sheet is printed out if need be.

AKC's IBM 370 computer handles about a million new registrations a year, printing out eleven thousand lines of type a minute. Until 1970 there was no computer at AKC—all work had to be done by hand and all records were kept in seemingly endless rows of files and record books. Now the histories of twenty million dogs are stored and can be traced electronically. The show performance records and registrations are not crossmatched. The puppy mill product and the most knowledgeably bred, carefully nurtured potential champion both receive exactly the same piece of paper from AKC's computer, and that's why AKC distributes this warning:

> There is, unfortunately, a widely held belief on the part of the general public that "AKC" or "AKC papers" and quality are one and the same. This is not the case. AKC REGISTRATION IN NO WAY INDICATES THE QUALITY OF A DOG. A registration certificate indicates only that the dog is the product of a registered purebred sire and dam of the same breed. Quality in the sense of "show quality" is determined by many fac-

tors, including the dog's health, physical condition, ability to move, and appearance. Breeders trying to breed show stock are attempting to produce animals closely resembling the word description of perfection contained in the breed standard. Many people breed their dogs with no concern for the qualitative demands of the standard for their breed. When this occurs repeatedly over several generations the animals, while still purebred, can be of extremely low quality in terms of the standard for their breed.

By establishing and rigidly maintaining standards of excellence for dogs and by recognizing the people who aspire to meet those standards in breeding, handling, and showing of dogs, the American Kennel Club makes it possible for a pet owner to have and cherish a sound, healthy, and well-bred purebred pup.

For information contact The American Kennel Club, 51 Madison Avenue, New York, NY 10010.

HOUND   SPORTING   NONSPORTING

TERRIER   TOY   WORKING

American Kennel Club purebred dog classifications

The whole point is that dogs are specialized marvels—each breed having been developed to satisfy a specific human need and not merely for visual variety. But along with physical and temperamental specialization, almost every breed has developed certain hereditary disorders. Some of the larger breeds are susceptible to hip dysplasia, some smaller dogs to dislocation of the knee joint. Thirty different breeds of all sizes suffer from hereditary retinal disintegration (night blindness), which leads to total blindness. The Great Dane is subject to heart and kidney disease and has a very sensitive tail that is easily injured. Boston terrier pups almost always must be delivered by Caesarean section because their heads are too large to allow a natural birth. This sort of information about a particular breed is never volunteered by retailers and rarely by breeders. It's wise to do some detective work so that the dog you get will be a healthy one, and you'll understand what you're getting into. (Illustration by Jill Miriam Pinkwater—hereafter so cited; reprinted from *Superpuppy* by Jill and Daniel Manus Pinkwater [New York: Seabury Press, 1977])

English Cocker

by Kate Romanski

Compounded confusion of nomenclature clarified.

There has been a lot of erroneous information published about English cockers over the years, due probably to the confusion in terminology by the layman, a situation that has not been helped by the American Kennel Club or the American Spaniel Club.

Originally there was only one breed of cocker spaniel both here and in England. As time passed, the breeders in the U.S. began to develop a cocker of a different type from the traditional English type. There was enough difference by the mid-1930s that the English Cocker Spaniel Club of America was organized to preserve the true cocker spaniel. The members of the ECSCA pledged to breed only from cockers tracing directly back to English bloodlines without any infusion of American blood.

It took ten long years of careful research into pedigrees to find out which dogs could be considered pure English, but in time the AKC did recognize the dogs as the English cocker spaniel, retaining the name cocker spaniel for what had become in reality the American cocker spaniel. So now we have the confusing situation of the cocker spaniel in Great Britain and all over the world being termed the "English cocker spaniel" in the AKC Stud Book, whilst the cocker spaniel of the AKC Stud Book is known in Great Britain and all over the world as the "American cocker spaniel"!

. . . the old-fashioned American cockers were not so far removed in breed type from the English cocker as they are today.

To confuse one further, over the years the American cocker has developed into a definite show-type dog, but there are also the old-fashioned, pet-type American cockers that on occasion have been mistaken for English cockers (or, in some not-so-ethical cases, sold as ECs) because the old-fashioned American cockers were not so far removed in breed type from the English cocker as they are today.

This is all very mixed up to someone who knows nothing about the two breeds and their history. For further information see the *American Cocker Review*, 202 S. Clovis Ave., Fresno, CA 93727. The ECSCA Review is sent to all club members, but may be subscribed to by anyone interested in the breed for eight dollars per year. The address of the English Cocker Spaniel Club of America is P.O. Box 223, Lake Pleasant, MA 01347.

A useful handbook on the breed sells for five dollars postpaid. It is available from Virginia Benson, 701 Morningview Ave., Akron, OH 44305.

AKC WANTS YOU TO KNOW

If . . . you buy a purebred dog that you are told is eligible for registration with the American Kennel Club, you are entitled to receive from the seller an application form that will enable you to register your dog.

If . . . the seller cannot give you the application, you should demand and receive full identification of your dog in writing, signed by the seller, consisting of the breed, the registered names of your dog's sire and dam, your dog's date of birth, the name of its breeder, and, if available, its AKC litter number.

Don't be misled by promises of "papers" later.

Demand a registration application form or proper identification as described above. If neither is supplied, DON'T BUY THE DOG.

A pamphlet on the subject is available from the American Kennel Club.

Is a Siberian Husky for You?

Breeders of pedigreed dogs are somewhat unusual among business people, being choosy about their customers. If you fit any of a half-dozen categories, you're advised to stay away from the Siberian.

Interested in buying a Siberian husky? Then you've already heard how marvelous they are. We think you should also be told that they do have their shortcomings and may not make the ideal pet for everyone who is attracted to them.

Siberians are a gregarious lot and need the company of other dogs or of people at all times. If you work all day or have room for only one dog . . . *don't buy a Siberian.*

While capable of strong affection for his family, the Siberian husky is also very friendly with strangers. So, if you want the fierce loyalty of a one-man dog . . . *don't buy a Siberian.*

The Siberian husky is not a watchdog, although those ignorant of his true nature may be frightened by his appearance. If you want a dog with aggressive guard-dog instincts... *don't buy a Siberian.*

At least once a year Siberians shed their coats. If you don't mind fur all over the house and in the very air you breathe, then, fine. But if you value neatness at all times, then... *don't buy a Siberian.*

Siberian huskies have a natural proclivity for digging holes in backyards. If you take great pride in your landscaping efforts... *don't buy a Siberian.*

Of all the shortcomings to be found in a Siberian, the most dangerous is its tremendous desire to run. But the very first dash that a puppy makes across the road could be his last run, anywhere. A Siberian, for his own protection, should be kept confined or under control at all times. If you are one of those people who think it is cruel to kennel a dog, then . . . *don't buy a Siberian.*

Of all the shortcomings to be found in a Siberian, the most dangerous is its tremendous desire to run.

We just happen to believe that any dog is better off in a proper kennel than running loose all over the countryside. Yes, a kennel dog is missing a lot in life: the chance to be hit by a car; the fun of being dirty, full of burrs, and loaded with worms; the opportunity of being attacked by other dogs; the joy of being sick on garbage and infested with disease; the pleasure of being tormented by mean kids; the thrill of being shot in a farmyard; and finally the great comfort of never knowing where he belongs or how to behave. We don't want to see any Siberian become a tramp.

From a pamphlet published by the Siberian Husky Club of America.

Good Advice

If you are the sort who likes to know what to do before taking on a fifteen-year commitment or "what might have been" if you had chosen differently, here is a selection of helpful books. They were submitted by English-language publishers, and they are in print and available. Besides books of puppy care and comprehensive guides, there are also books for kids—with their own brand of wisdom—both the cute and the more sophisticated.

Do you really want to get involved with a dog? These books may help you to decide.

Man Meets Dog ($2.50; New York: Penguin Books, 1953), by Konrad Lorenz, is a wonderful look at the nature of the domestic dog (Lorenz calls them "the animal with a conscience") and of man, with much personal information about the author's own pets.

The Mind of the Dog ($13.50; New York: Arno Press, 1973; reprinted from a 1936 edition), by F.J.J. Buytendijk, is an early psychological/scientific study of the nature of the dog, infused with the author's phenomenological philosophical attitudes—for instance, "The dog's eyes are speaking to us. They are a testimony: they utter the hidden and the inexpressible—melancholy, fidelity, love and understanding. Is this true, or is it mere poetic fancy?"

Understanding Your Dog ($7.95; New York: Coward, McCann and Geoghegan, 1972), by Michael Fox, discusses in detail the body language of dogs, the development of puppies, physically and emotionally, the meaning of their play, and the effects of environment on their social adjustment.

Why Does Your Dog Do That? ($7.95; New York: Howell Book House, 1967), by Göran Bergman, is a compact, scientific examination of dog behavior based on personal experience.

Dog Behavior, The Genetic Basis ($4.95; Chicago: University of Chicago Press, 1965), by John Paul Scott and John L. Fuller, synthesizes nearly twenty years of dog research done at the Jackson Laboratories in Maine. The authors have written the definitive book, on which most later popularizations are based, dealing with the effects of behavioral development, heredity, and environment on dogs. The experiment was begun with five breeds—wirehaired fox terrier, American cocker spaniel, Basenji, Shetland sheepdog, and beagle—which were mated and crossed in various ways and backcrossed to produce animals like the "ancestral" pure breeds with which the experiment was begun. The methodology of the experimentation is meticulously detailed right down to floor plans for puppy nurseries, dog runs, and test mazes. The conclusions the authors reach are of importance to human and animal geneticists, to dog breeders, and to pet owners.

Some Swell Pup ($5.95; New York: Farrar, Straus and Giroux, 1976), by Maurice Sendak and Matthew Margolis, poses the very significant question, "Are you sure you want a dog?" In comic-book cartoon drawings and dialogue balloons, the book lets you know how horrid a pup can be before it's been civilized. Like many of the best children's books, this one will be appreciated by grownups.

These will help you pick a breed.

The Modern Dog Encyclopedia (Harrisburg: Stackpole Books, 1956), edited by Henry Davis, is a good overview of dogs. It includes black and white photographs of AKC recognized breeds.

The Encyclopedia of Dogs ($25.00; New York: Thomas Y. Crowell, 1973), by Fiorenzo Fiorone, is a large and beautiful work of impressive scope compiled with the assistance of the Federation Cynologique International and thirty-five member clubs. There are photographs in color of all recognized American, European, Asian, and African breeds, most in action. Physical characteristics and history of each are given.

What do you do for a dog who's been used to company all his life and now must be left alone for long stretches?

The Pocket Encyclopedia of Dogs ($6.95; New York: Macmillan Publishing Co., Inc., 1975), by Ivan Swedrup, offers excellent color illustrations and information on the history, care, psychology, breeding, showing, traveling, licensing of the various breeds. AKC and Kennell Club of Great Britain classifications are used.

The Complete Dog Book ($7.95; New York: Howell Book House, 1975), the official publication of the American Kennel Club, is the authoritative book in the U.S. for anyone having to do with purebred dogs. There is a photo, history, and official standard for each recognized

Books for dog shoppers and dog owners.

breed and for the AKC miscellaneous group. The book also tells how to register, train, groom, feed, breed, and care for your dog.

The Dell Encyclopedia of Dogs ($2.45; New York: Dell Publishing Co., 1974), by Lou Sawyer Ashworth and Irene Kraft, offers 619 entries from "abdomen" to "zygoma" (the cheekbone of a dog) and includes "virtually all breeds currently recognized throughout the world" coded by country of recognition.

The Hamlyn Guide to Dogs ($5.95; London: Paul Hamlyn, 1974), by A. Gondrexon-Ives Browne, has color illustrations and a brief description of 341 dog breeds, arranged according to function or work performed.

Dogs, Pets of Pedigree ($9.95; New York and London: Drake, 1975), by Suzanne Troy, has good photos of eighty popular breeds in color, most showing adult dogs with a pup of the same breed.

The American Dog Book ($14.95; New York: E. P. Dutton, 1976), by Kurt Unkelback, covers the American-developed breeds—Alaskan malamute, black-and-tan coonhound, Nova Scotia duck tolling dog—American Kennel Club breeds, Canadian Kennel Club breeds, and some of the rare breeds. (As a matter of interest, a tolling dog makes a great spectacle of itself to arouse the curiosity of ducks in its vicinity. When they come by for a closer look, they make easy targets for the hunter. The dog then retrieves.)

Toy Dogs ($9.95; North Pomfret, Vt.: David and Charles, 1977), by Harry Glover, is an absolute delight. The text and black and white drawings by the author are charming, photos by Diane Pearce, very compelling. The author explains that, from the beginning, toy dogs were meant to be amusing companions. "It is essential that a toy dog should have the ability to amuse—not by performing tricks, as this is the province of the trained poodle of circus and stage, but by playing the games which are natural to it. If a large dog tries to catch its tail and falls over, it is grotesque. . . . The same act performed by a pug at several times the speed, with the quickness of recovery . . . becomes a most entertaining spectacle."

The Uncommon Dog Breeds ($8.95; New York: Arco, 1975), by Kathryn Braund, gives history, photo, breed standard, and club list for twenty-five rare breeds.

The Complete Puppy & Dog Book ($14.95; New York: Atheneum, 1977), by Norman H. Johnson in collaboration with Saul Galin. Dog books intended to guide the reader through the stages of a dog's life and to answer questions concerning care, feeding, and training usually have an early section devoted to what dog breed is best for what type of person. Among the categories covered in this book is "Your Temperament." The idea is that a placid person should have a placid dog. Old Sleepy Joe—the plant night watchman—should get himself a hound, not a terrier, and since Joe barely earns a subsistence living, he should acquire a beagle, which

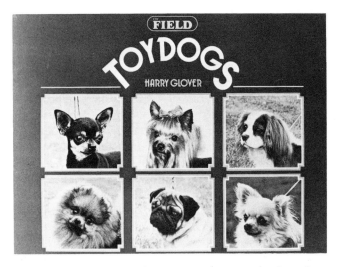

when full grown at eighteen pounds eats a lot less than a black-and-tan coonhound of sixty pounds.

The authors' attitudes about children and dogs seem to be relaxed, as long as the dog is not of the tiny breeds. "Breeds like most spaniels (especially the springer), most of the hounds (particularly the basset and beagle) and working dogs (boxer, bullmastiff, Great Pyrenees, Newfoundland, collie, old English sheepdog, Rottweiler, samoyed, schnauzer) as well as sporting dogs (retrievers, setters) will take pummeling, pinching, pulling and pushing without showing any displeasure."

Dogs should be compatible with the climate. Here again canine adaptability makes for a lack of serious concern except where extremes are involved. Moreover, "short-nosed breeds (Boston terrier, bulldog, English toy spaniel, French bulldog, Brussels griffon, pug, boxer, Pekingese) are generally subject to upper respiratory conditions, and a damp climate is not good for them— although most do adapt."

And, of course, you should have a little, quiet dog in an apartment; a big, vigorous dog belongs on a farm.

As for sex, males, unless fixed, have a tendency— sometimes absolutely a compulsion—to mate, and this drive can cause problems—fights, wandering, general nervousness if frustrated. Females, on the other hand, are doting, less independent.

Once you've decided on the breed and are about to bring your puppy home one or both of the following care books will be helpful.

Superpuppy ($9.95; New York: Seabury Press, 1977), by Jill and D. Manus Pinkwater, is a super book, full of sensible, practical advice and information presented in a clear and pleasant style. Excellent illustrations.

The Good Dog Book ($9.95; New York: Macmillan Publishing Co., Inc., 1977), by Mordecai Siegal, is something else. Besides general care information there are some unusual entries—canine meditation, weight watching, care of the elderly ("Life Begins at Eight"), and some great games for kids and dogs—tug-of-war, I'm gonna get you, and "shnuf," which the author describes

this way: "Tilt your head back in an exaggerated manner and snap it forward with a pretended sneeze. It seems to amuse all dogs. Some dogs will even sneeze along."

Also noted:

That Hilarious First Year ($2.50; Caldwell, Idaho: Caxton Printers, Ltd., 1971), by Bea Boynton.

Maxwell Riddle's Complete Book of Puppy Training and Care ($6.95; New York: Coward, McCann and Geoghegan, 1971).

Practical Guide to Dogs ($10.00; London: Paul Hamlyn, 1975), by Kay White and Joan Joshua, is exactly what it proclaims itself; includes good color photographs.

Now That You Own a Puppy ($2.95; New York: Frederick Fell, 1975), by Joan Tate.

How to Bring Up Your Pet Dog ($4.95; New York: Dodd, Mead, 1972), by Kurt Unkelbach.

The New Dog Owners Handbook ($5.95; New York: Howell Book House, 1972), by J. Hajas and P. Sarkany, is a how-to book of captioned illustrations.

All About Small Dogs in the Big City ($8.95; New York: Coward, McCann and Geoghegan, 1975), by Anne Seranne, emphasizes forty of the smaller dogs.

How to Raise a Dog in the City and in the Suburbs ($1.95; New York: Simon and Schuster, 1938; revised, 1972), by James R. Kinney and Ann Honneycut. The authors have a way with words. In a section called "Don't Buy a Grown Dog," for instance, they say, "Dogs have an uncanny memory and loyalty for their first loves. They may pretend to like you, but secretly they are always comparing you unfavorably with their former master, who was (invariably) a much nobler person, with a much finer home, and a classier dresser . . ." Besides good information about dogs, handily phrased, there are incomparable Thurber drawings.

Need a name? Here are some good sources.

Please Don't Call Me Fido ($1.95; New York: Berkley Publishing, 1977), by Carolyn Boyce Johnes, includes more than a thousand names and their derivations, meanings, and associations. For example, Luca is the name of actor James Caan's American pit bull terrier (and also of a hit man in *The Godfather*) and there is Colle, the dog in Chaucer's "The Nun's Priest's Tale." Also Lassie, Strongheart, Rin Tin Tin, and a lot more.

Chinese Names for Oriental Dogs ($6.95; Fairfax, Va.: Denlinger's, 1975), by Will C. Mooney. Because Chinese is the basic language of the Orient, the author advocates the use of Chinese names for dogs of Oriental origin.

The Chinese language is not written in phonetic form, so the Chinese words included in this book have been Romanized according to the Modified Wade-Giles System—more widely used today than any other system of Romanization.

The twelve hundred English words listed, and their Romanized Chinese equivalents, include words commonly used in naming dogs and words that English-speaking persons usually associate with the Orient. Also, there are lists of numbers, seasons, the months, days of the week, words relating to time, jewels, trees, shrubs, flowers, colors, birds, and family relationships.

This book will help you to name your Pekingese, Shih Tzu, Lhasa Apso, Chow Chow, Pomeranian, Siberian husky, Samoyed, American Eskimo (spitz), Tibetan or Japanese spaniel, Tibetan terrier or mastiff, Mexican hairless, Chinese crested dog, or one of the other Oriental breeds appropriately.

Pet Names ($7.00; New York: Scarecrow Press, 1962), by Jean Taggart, lists traditional names for dogs, arranged by country of origin and geographic locale—northern dogs, British dogs. An appropriate name for a Newfoundland, a northern water dog, might be Aegir, god of the sea. Baron means strong man and is suggested for a retriever, while Pye is proper for a spotted dog.

Here is good advice for kids about pups and dogs.

A Closer Look at Dogs ($2.95; New York: Franklin Watts, 1975), by David Cook and Valerie Pitt, succinctly outlines the history and development of the domestic dog and compares it to its relatives—jackals, coyotes, and wolves. The dynamics of the wolf pack is explained, as is how the pet dog, in its many varieties, came to be. Attractive color illustrations, diagrams, and charts.

Dogs, Best Breeds for Young People ($5.95; New York: Harcourt Brace, 1969), by Wilfred S. Bronson, is an especially interesting book because the usual history, selection, and care advice is augmented by lots of useful tidbits of information not found in most books for children. For instance, when threatened by a hostile dog (the signs of hostility, not always what one might think them to be, are described), the author cautions the child not to run. "Stand your ground as calmly as you can. Hold your hands against your chest and face him, turning as he turns to go behind you. Look him always in the eye and say friendly things in a gentle voice." The "stay" command might work on a dog that has had any training at all. Ever wonder why some dogs roll in smelly things? ". . . in the old days a wild dog rolled in something that stank in order to conceal his own smell from wary game he wanted to sneak up on. Today's tame dog has no such purpose, but the stench from a long-dead thing sets up an age old impulse." Why some dogs "hunt" cars, why males scent-mark their "territories," and why dogs "wolf" down their food are some of the interesting bits of information that make this a delightful book.

Dogs and Puppies ($4.47; New York: Franklin Watts, 1976), by Jane Rockwell, is a very good simplified look at the dog, including its origin and history, anatomy

and body language, and choosing, caring for, training, and feeding a pup. Concludes with an explanation of the AKC groups. Illustrated with black-and-white photographs and drawings.

What Is Your Dog Saying? ($7.95; New York: Coward, McCann and Geoghegan, 1977), by Michael Fox and Wende Devlin Gates, explains body language and other doggy behavior mostly in a question-and-answer format. Why is your dog more aggressive on leash than off? He's protecting you. What do you do for a dog who's been used to company all his life and now must be left alone for long stretches? Get him a pet of his own—a kitten or a box turtle or just leaving the TV on might work. There's lots more of these and Dr. Fox's guide to choosing a dog, in chart form, is excellent.

A Puppy for You ($6.95; New York: Charles Scribner's Sons, 1976), by Lilo Hess, tells how to get one and what to do when it's brand new. Good large photographs in black-and-white complement the text for young readers.

My Dog, Your Dog ($5.95; New York: Macmillan Publishing Co., Inc., 1978), by Joseph Low, makes an important point: A dog, like the little girl in the nursery rhyme, can be very, very good—or horrid. Delightful pastel drawings and succinct text compare a good dog and a bad dog who, in the end, are found to be one and the same and much loved, despite lapses in decorum.

Twenty-One Wolves?

A dog census from 1877 shows Newfoundlands most populous, and, among the least, something called a "duf."

The annual report of the New York City Permit Bureau for 1877 shows that 11,991 licenses to keep dogs were issued in that year. The classification of the breeds is as follows: Newfoundland, 1,132; Spitz, 1,603; Scotch terrier, 872; Skye terrier, 514; bull terrier, 21; Maltese terrier, 4; terrier, 412; black and tan, 2,146; red and tan, 2; mongrel, 2,234; bull, 452; mastiff, 52; Prince Charles, 3; King Charles, 54; Prince Albert, 1; Spaniel, 129; setters, 390; pointers, 106; poodle, 505; greyhound, 159; bloodhound, 285; hound, 131; Indian hound, 1; wolfhound, 1; foxhound, 1; Italian greyhound, 2; shepherd, 103; fox, 123; Esquimaux, 52; Pomeranian, 7; St. Bernard, 71; coach, 211; Japanese, 3; Chinese, 9; Maltese, 4; wolf, 21; pinscher, 2; Dandy Dinmont, 8; retriever, 7; pug, 60; box, 4; behill, 1; hunting, 4; duf, 1; Yorkshire, 1; French, 1; Gallup, 1; German, 1; Dutch, 1; gazelle, 2; corsette, 1; sorner, 2; Mexican, 3; Irish Colly, 1; brindle, 1; African fox, 1; Siberian, 2; Poland, 1; Brazilian, 2; Russian, 1; Spanish, 2; rat-catcher, 1; Ulm, 1; and Lararach, 2.

The Groups

Hound, sporting, nonsporting, terrier, toy, and working dogs. (Photographs by Don Myrus)

William and Nancy Schmitz at home with two of their bull terriers, which they breed. (Bull terriers are representative of the terrier group.)

Robert DeNigris, a bartender in the Gatsby country of Long Island, keeps in touch with the outdoors all year round because his Doberman likes and needs the exercise. (Doberman pinschers are representative of the working dog group.)

Arlene Ward: *"I started about fourteen years ago. Have we been successful? The fluffy miniature white is a champion and was the ninth ranking dog of the breed in 1977. Besides the dogs, I have a husband and two daughters; the girls are already involved in junior show-manship. (Miniature poodles are representative of the nonsporting group.)*

Patricia Proctor: *"Why am I doing this? A hobby. Why are we joint owners of the poodles? Well, through a mutual friend I heard that Arlene needed help in groom-ing and showing, so we decided to get things going. We don't own all the dogs jointly. The Dalmatian is mine; he's about to be a show dog."* (Dalmatians are repre-sentative of the nonsporting group.)

Don Sturz and his family own eight golden retrievers, one standard poodle, and one German wirehaired pointer. Here he is shown with his wife and son and two of their goldens.

"During the week I am a Nassau County police detective, and on week-ends a professional handler. My son, Don, was the top junior handler picked by Kennel Review *magazine in 1975 and my daughter, Janet, won the same award in 1976. My wife, Marilyn, fin-ished a champion and has a working certificate for a dog in the field. She really does the paperwork, now."* (Golden retrievers are representative of the sporting dog group.)

Sunny Shay's Ch. Shirkhan of Grandeur won best American breed in show and best in show at Westminster in 1957, and she was named best owner, breeder, and handler. In 1977, after fire destroyed her kennel, Roger Rechler offered her the facilities of the kennel built under his outdoor swimming pool. He is an industrial and office building developer, an art collector, and an Afghan enthusiast. (Afghans are representative of the hound group.)

"I never liked Pekes but Doris has—ever since she was six years old, she says. When our neighbor decided to go on a long cruise, he asked us to take his Peke. Pekes can't swim very well. Their legs are too short and their coats weigh them down. They quickly sink. We took the dog for him, but it was just another dog to me. That is, until one day the Peke and I were in the front yard when a big, black mutt came by—looking fierce. The Peke took after him, snarling and snapping. I admired a dog that could be so small yet so fearless. From then on I became interested in the breed."—George Owen. (Pekingese are representative of the toy group.)

In The Butterfly Lions ($13.95; New York: Viking Press, 1978) novelist Rumer Godden describes her own lifelong involvement with Pekingese and elegantly draws their history in the West where Queen Victoria's love of the breed brought them to popularity and the East where Queen Victoria's contemporary, Tzu-hsi, the powerful Dowager Empress of China, continued an ancient adoration of the dog. Pekingese, according to legend, took form when a lioness "yielded to the delicate caresses of a butterfly and ever afterwards have to be as brave as lions and dainty as butterflies." A beautifully written and illustrated book.

SOME BOOKS, A LITTLE DIFFERENT

Dog lovers who are history buffs will find it difficult to resist the two-volume *Dogs, Their History and Development* by E. C. Ash ($28.50; New York: Benjamin Blom, 1972, first published in London in 1927). In the introduction the Duchess of Newcastle says that the work contains a "fund of historical detail and a collection of unique illustrations, from the first of every known variety down to the best species of today."

Chapters include "Dogs in Ancient Religions, Folklore and Legend" and "Early Authorities" who go back to 443 B.C. "The Dog in English History" includes the Laws of Howel the Good, from the tenth century. A quote from the chapter on ancient Chinese dogs is notable: "Dogs may be classified in three: hunting dogs, watch dogs and edible dogs. The latter is the same as cow, very tame."

De Canibus Britannicus—written in Latin by John Caius in 1570 and translated to *Of Eng-lishe Dogges, The Diversities; The Names, The Nature and The Properties*—may be considered the first book devoted exclusively to dogs. Caius presents three types in minute detail: High Bred, Country, and Mongrel. The major source of information about dogs for 200 years, the work, translated by A. Fleming in 1576, is now available in a facsimile edition ($7.00; Norwood: Walter J. Johnson, 1969).

Also noted:

The Criminal Prosecution and Capital Punishment of Animals (London: C. P. Evans, 1906), by William Heiniman.

Your Dog's Horoscope (New York: Harper & Brothers, 1947), by Dorothea C. Pratt.

Our Puppy's Baby Book ($3.95; New York: Howell Book House, 1961). Available in either pink or blue, it has spaces for dates and pedigree and for photos taken at various stages of development. You can record a paw print and keep a feeding chart. Not essential, but fun.

Standard poodle in Malibu, California, taking the hurdles in response to hand signals. (Photograph by Vincent Tajiri)

AKC rules of the behavior game and an explanation of the point system that means getting ahead.

3

THE WELL-MANNERED LIFE

OBEDIENCE TRIALS

MY LEASH LAW PROBLEM
by Safford Chamberlain

CIVILIZED CANINES
by Ed Beckmann

HOW ANIMALS ARE TAUGHT
THEIR TRICKS

THE DOG GROOMERS

Although centuries old, obedience trials came into prominence when the American Kennel Club established them in the 1930s as tests of dog behavior.

Now, to compete, a dog must be purebred and at least six months of age. It must be registered with the American Kennel Club or be part of an AKC-registered litter. While spayed or castrated dogs cannot compete in conformation classes, they are allowed in obedience trials because it is performance that counts and not whether the dog is able to reproduce its kind. Blind or deaf dogs may not compete.

Obedience trials are divided into classes or grades of competition. Beginners compete in the Novice Classes A and B. When a dog has won passing scores of 170 or more at three shows under three different judges, it has earned the title of Companion Dog and is entitled to a C.D. after its name.

Next are Open Classes A and B. After it has won passing scores at three shows in these classes, it gains the title Companion Dog Excellent, or C.D.X.

Utility Class competitions follow. Three scores of passing or better earns the title U.D. This is the highest title a dog can win except for a T for Tracking. The ultimate title then is Utility Dog Tracking, or U.D.T.

Tracking tests are not held at dog shows, since they must be run out-of-doors and in areas that are usually not designed for spectators.

A perfect score in each class is 200, and a passing score is 170. But no dog can qualify for a "leg" toward its title unless it has scored more than 50 percent of the points allowed for each exercise of the competition.

There are six exercises in Novice competition. If a dog made a perfect score in five of these but scored zero in the sixth, it could have a total score of 170 or more, but still would not qualify for a "leg" toward the title.

Novice and Open Classes are divided into A and B. The difference is roughly that between an amateur and a professional. In Novice A and Open A the dog must be handled by the owner or a member of his family. Novice B and Open B exercises are identical with Novice and Open Class A. However, professional handlers and trainers and others can show the dogs.

A judge must score a dog zero for any exercise that it fails to perform a principal part of upon the first command. He must severely penalize the dog if it fails to complete any exercise. He'll take off points if the dog is

Photograph by Vincent Tajiri

sluggish, fails to give its handler its attention, or is sloppy in its work. Any dog that relieves itself in the ring cannot make a qualifying score. The judge is required to give credit in scoring for a dog's willingness and enjoyment while performing an exercise.

In the Novice Classes A and B points for perfect performance are:

Heel on Leash 40
Stand for Examination off Leash 30
Heel off Leash 40
Recall 30
Long Sit (1 minute) 30
Long Down (3 minutes) 30
Maximum Total Score 200

The heel on leash is designed to prove that the dog has been taught to walk quietly at the side of its owner,

never getting tangled up, and to sit when the owner stops.

In the stand for examination the judge touches the dog's head, body, and hind quarters. If the dog sits during or before the examination, shows shyness or resentment, or if it growls or tries to bite, it will get zero and be disqualified. Slight movements of the feet, or moving after the examination, will bring lesser penalties.

The judge is required to give credit in scoring for a dog's willingness and enjoyment while performing an exercise.

The heel-free lesson proves that the dog will obey when free of the leash.

34

In the recall the dog stays where left until called and responds promptly to the handler's command, "Come."

In the Novice Classes during long sit and long down the handlers remain in the ring, away from their dogs, one minute for the sit, three minutes for the down.

The Open Classes are for dogs that have passed all of the Novice requirements. No dog can enter these classes unless the American Kennel Club has awarded that dog the official Companion Dog (C.D.) title.

Dogs can be handled in the Open B Class by anyone. A feature of this class is that dogs that have won their Companion Dog Excellent (C.D.X.) and Utility Dog (U.D.) titles may continue to compete in Open B.

Points for a perfect performance in the Open Classes are:

Heel Free	40
Drop on Recall	30
Retrieve on Flat	20
Retrieve over High Jump	30
Broad Jump	20
Long Sit	30
Long Down	30
Maximum Total Score	200

These exercises are similar to the Novice Class events. The Utility Class is for dogs that have won the C.D.X. title.

Points for a perfect performance in Utility are:

Signal Exercise	40
Scent Discrimination—Leather Article	30
Scent Discrimination—Metal Article	30
Directed Retrieve (of glove)	30
Directed Jumping	40
Group Examination	30
Maximum Total Score	200

In the signal exercise the dog is required to obey only hand signals, rather than vocal commands.

The directed retrieve is designed to test the dog's response to his handler's hand signal directing it to one of three gloves placed widely apart in the ring. The judge specifies which glove to retrieve.

In the directed jump the dog is sent away from the handler, stops and sits on command, and jumps as directed. In the group examination the dogs are left standing near each other. The judge will examine each dog individually, as in a regular show ring, while the owners are some distance away. The dog must not show any fear or resentment of this. It must not move out of position until handlers are back in place.

A tracking test cannot be conducted at dog shows, either indoors or outdoors, since it requires room. Courses have to be plotted out days ahead and laid well in advance.

This final test is designed to prove that the dog could be used to search out and find some object, locate a child or other person lost in the woods, or follow the trail of a criminal.

Edited and reprinted from the Ralston Purina Company's booklet, Obedience Trials.

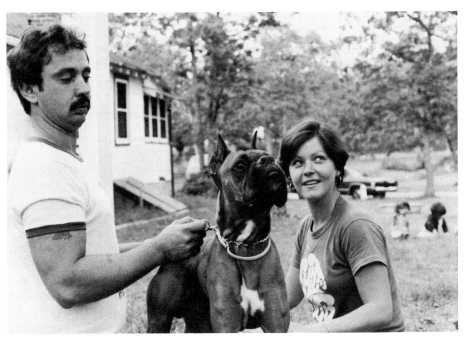

"Rocky is full-grown now. He was a gift from Danny's grandfather. He cost $260. I like him so much, I am thinking of getting a female and raising them. The kid can do anything and be safe."—Daniel Moleti with boxer, Rocky, and his wife, Eileen. (Photograph by Don Myrus)

My Leash Law Problem

by Safford Chamberlain

The author is torn by conflicting sentiments—a desire to obey the law and to do right by his neighbors, on the one hand, and to satisfy what he imagines is his dog's urge to bound freely about and his own sense of nostalgia, on the other. After considerable contemplation he reluctantly concludes that South Pasadena ("ten miles by freeway from the Los Angeles City Hall") is no place to play home on the range.

For the record, I love my dog. However, I do not love walking him. Possibly there are those who will see these two attitudes as flatly contradictory. These people may as well stop reading now, for we have nothing in common. On them has descended the dog's own mantle of nobility and devotion to duty. On me, alas, has descended the mantle of the willful and habitual violator of the South Pasadena leash law.

Anyone ignorant of this law will be obligingly informed of it by the nearest South Pasadenan. I learned of it the first time I ventured out with my half-breed puli, Gus.

A word about this animal. According to the dog books pulis are both intelligent and strong-willed. I have concluded that this means they respond brilliantly to commands, but only when there's nothing more interesting to do. In this Gus is the true child of his mother, a pure-bred puli. His father, a winsome English sheepdog, seems to have contributed mainly reinforcement of Gus's sheepherding instincts. Gus classifies walking organisms into two categories, dogs and sheep. Dogs are things one either mates with or fights, depending on how they smell. Sheep are the other things with legs, around which one runs in circles while barking and lunging playfully at their ankles.

People, of course, fall into the sheep category. So it was that on my first excursion into the suburban streets of South Pasadena Gus joyfully bounded up to give the sheep treatment to a stout, florid-faced lady with the hectic light of hysteria in her eyes. She let me know about the leash law in no uncertain terms. So, in those early days, did several others. One was a rather remarkably hostile young man who, finding himself herded, responded like a matador, snapping his jacket in Gus's face. Another was a macho-type karate expert who threatened to deal Gus a lethal kick in the head. Yet another was a man who told me he would shoot Gus with his .44 Magnum the next time Gus chased his cat.

At first I didn't believe them about the leash law. Having grown up in an era when dogs got some respect, I thought all this talk about a leash law was just hysterical or paranoid raving. A visit to the police station brought me face to face with modern suburban reality.

The leash law, I found, was a very thorough ordinance. "No person," it stated, "owning or having control of any dog shall cause or permit the same to be or to run at large upon any street, lane, alley, court or other public place, or upon any private property, other than that of the person owning or having charge or control of such dog, in the city, unless such dog is restrained by a substantial chain or leash not exceeding six feet in length."

There it was. It was not immediately clear to me how my dog could be both running at large and restrained by a substantial chain or leash. Still I discerned a general intent to keep him, in his unattached natural state, out of every street, lane, alley, court, yard, lot, or other earthly expanse whatsoever except what I happened to own myself, which was a house on a 50-by-150 foot lot.

This was more than a little disturbing. Light-years ago, in the pre-World-War-II days when I was a growing lad in South Pasadena, the idea that the only good dog was a leashed dog would have been barely intelligible. Streets, lanes, alleys—these were their preemptive lounging areas. Cars drove around them. For adventure they had the whole range of uninhabited hills that separate South Pasadena from Los Angeles. Uninhabited, that is, except for skunks, possums, jackrabbits, gopher snakes, coyotes, and yes, at least one herd of actual sheep.

On summer nights I could sit with my dog in the weeds of an uninhabited hilltop and hear, from the playground below, the band that played for dances on the tennis courts and, from the hills in back of me, the howls of coyotes.

Ah Gus, that were paradise enow for thee, you barbarian!

But no more. As that rare creature characterized, in the words of Lord Byron, by "beauty without vanity—strength without insolence—courage without ferocity—and all the virtues of man without any of his vices"—as the noble friend of man and poets you possessed yourself of the lanes and alleys of South Pasadena; and even now a vestige of the old respect survives in that section of the dog ordinance granting you a free license tag if you have been "honorably discharged or released from service in the armed forces." Pale reflection of past glory! During World War II army recruiting sergeants came to town seeking dogs to "disarm enemies, carry messages and supplies, detect saboteurs, and tend the wounded"! But now—now, poor rejected thing, you are required by law to go about on the end of a leash.

Beyond this, public notices proclaim that you are banned from parks and football fields, even on a substantial chain or leash. Hidden householders spy on you from behind drawn blinds to see that you do not profane their ivy. Civic-minded citizens write guest editorials for the town weekly indignantly complaining that "a dog's 'calling card' is rather distasteful, especially if stepped in," and city councils declare it a dog owner's responsibility to retrieve said calling card within five minutes after deposit.

How does it happen that Gus's excretions are thus so officially denounced? Obviously the root cause is that universal evil, population growth. Although South Pasadena still has its Carnegie library and enough big wooden houses and quiet shady streets to attract moviemakers looking for old-time small-town atmosphere, the town has slowly succumbed to urban pressures. Ten miles by freeway from the Los Angeles City Hall, bounded on one side by the big city and on the other sides by major suburban centers, its population has gone from fourteen thousand in 1940 to twenty-four thousand in 1974. By modern standards that's not astonishing, but it has happened without any increase in area, and the effect has been like that of the closing of the frontier.

With the filling up of the hills, there is no place for dog or man to go to get away from the neighbors. I used to be able to walk two hundred yards from my parents' house and be in coyote country. On summer nights I could sit with my dog in the weeds of an uninhabited hilltop and hear, from the playground below, the band that played for dances on the tennis courts and, from the hills in back of me, the howls of coyotes. In 1943 the coyotes were numerous enough that the city still, as in the past, hired a professional hunter to clear them out. Now not only that hill but all the other hills between it and Los Angeles are built up, and I have nearly forgotten what a coyote howl sounds like.

Another cause for the leash law, originally, was a concern for public health. The law was enacted the same year the coyote hunter was last hired, in 1943, apparently in response to pressure from county health officials faced with a significant increase in rabies. Probably there was a connection between the coyotes and the rabies, and it may be that since the coyotes have gone, that public health issue has also sunk into irrelevance. But it doesn't really matter. Dogs are clearly regarded by some as nuisances in a city that is 66 percent more crowded.

This situation poses a problem for the dog owners. Those who are like me, and I suspect that many are, find themselves torn between sympathy for their dogs, obligation toward their neighbors, and fear of the law.

Of course the proper conduct is to attach the substantial chain or leash and walk the dog every afternoon when you get home from work, dutifully scooping up his calling card as soon as deposited. If you're lucky, there will be a vacant lot or two where you can let him run. In a lax mood you might even let him frolic for a moment on the library lawn.

Sometimes I behave as I ought to, and it must be said that devotion to duty has its compensations. For example, the elderly lady who was mugged and robbed of the brown paper bag in which she regularly collected her dog's droppings must have experienced a satisfactory feeling when contemplating the mugger's moment of discovery.

Still, it is hard to do right. Normally I wait till midnight and let the dog sneak out the front door, hoping that for half an hour there will be nobody on the street for him to herd and incidentally, if they happen to be strangers, to frighten out of their wits. Gus of course thinks the whole block is his personal sheep farm, and too often for my complete happiness I am to be seen in the wee hours, barefooted and bathrobed, intervening in the roundup of neighbors on their front walks.

So far they have been very understanding. Nevertheless this whole situation has a foreseeable end. It is dawning on me that I am not suited to be a dog owner in an antidog environment, and that after Gus there should be no more dogs until I can retire to a sheep farm in Australia.

Safford Chamberlain, a former newspaper reporter, teaches writing and literature in the Los Angeles college system. His own writing has appeared in PMLA, Down Beat, The Realist, *the* Los Angeles Free Press, *and the* California Socialist.

A FABLE OF AESOP—EATING THE BREAD OF IDLENESS

A man trained one of his two dogs to hunt and kept the other as a house dog. The hunting dog complained bitterly because, whenever he caught any game in the chase, the other was given a share of it. "It is not fair," he said, "that I should go out and have such a hard time of it, while you do nothing and live well on the fruits of my labour."

"Well, don't blame me," said the other dog. "It is the master's fault; for he did not teach me to work myself, but only to eat what others have worked for."

It is the same with children. They cannot be blamed for being lazy if their parents bring them up in idleness.

Civilized Canines

by Ed Beckmann

People shouldn't kick dogs or beat them with sticks (or with anything else, for that matter); they shouldn't even shout at their dogs. However, when a dog has a loudmouthed but otherwise even-tempered owner, the dog can be expected to adjust. Lord knows, dogs are adaptable enough.

There are ample books on the way dogs should behave and a legion of small businesses set up to serve. The following analysis is by the "love-praise-reward" practitioner Ed Beckmann, director of the New York Academy of Dog Training and of the Problem Puppy School, and author of Love, Praise and Reward: The New Way to Teach Your Dog.

What is a dog trainer? Well, it appears to me there are dog trainers everywhere. Under the taxi driver's cap is an experienced dog trainer, and even your dentist while drilling his way to your root canal will cheerfully advise you as to the best way to housebreak your dog. If you've consulted with several other dog trainers such as Aunt Millie, the milkman, and the paperboy and are more confused than ever, consult a professional.

Good professional teachers are hard to find, and the ways and means of professionals vary a great deal. However, there are some things you can be sure of: If you pay a fee, you can demand a realistic, humane teaching program with clear goals; if you follow the rules, you can look forward to positive results. Check credentials, quiz the trainer, challenge theories with good common sense and humanity.

One problem with housebreaking your dog is the obvious by-product and its disposal. In today's society ecology and a clean environment are of more and more importance. I recommend two methods. The first is for those who let dogs use the yard or an outside run. Bury a bottomless trash can in the ground. Put the feces into the can, add liquid enzyme waste treatment, then cover. I usually stick a bug repellent to the cover in the summer to discourage flies. The enzyme can be procured from any good pet supplier. A preconstructed device, called Doggie Dooley, is available from Huron Products, 555 Moore Ave., Bellevue, OH 44811.

Then there is Doggie Cleanup, a portable container designed for fast disposal. Each unit contains a cardboard scoop and cardboard container. Each is folded compactly for convenience. Unfold the Doggie Cleanup, scoop into the container, cover, and dispose. Doggie Cleanup is available from Edmar Pet Supplies, P.O. Box 1422, New Rochelle, NY 10805.

In teaching a dog to be obedient, leashes and collars are not only unnecessary but actually distracting to the dog's concentration. As with any teaching program we humans have experienced, a dog's teaching program can be fun, oppressive, or even cruel. If your attitude is that your dog wants to please, it really doesn't matter whether the dog jumps all over you for love or sits excitedly waiting for you to come to give love. Then dog teaching can be fun. But if your attitude is that your dog is following some basic instinct to dominate you and is constantly trying to get the best of you on the ladder of pack dominance, then obedience training can become oppressive and possibly cruel.

There is absolutely nothing wrong with the use of food in teaching a dog, as long as the food isn't used as a bribe. To avoid bribing is very simple. Use the food to initiate your dog's teaching, but remember to praise and to love when the task is completed. Dogs thrive on affection and praise. After awhile affection and praise will be enough. Take a special treat (I use cheese or bologna) and hold it out toward your dog. If he leaps forward to snatch it, quickly withdraw your hand—up and away. Repeat this until he realizes that leaping gets him nowhere. Hold the treat out toward the dog's mouth. As he reaches toward it, raise the treat over his head and downward. His natural tendency will be to sit. When he does, praise him lavishly and give him his treat. Repeat this procedure several times. Cheerfully say the word "sit." Do not harshly command or repeat the word. Remember, instant success is not required. Don't take the matter too seriously. Be calm and have fun!

To us, a jumping dog can be annoying and possibly harmful. To the dog, jumping is a natural expression of love and excitement. What a horrible shock it is for a dog when he expresses his love in this fashion and gets a knee thrust into his stomach or is screamed at or even flipped over on his back! One of my solutions is to remove the dog's motivation for jumping. Simply, but with perseverance, every time he leaps up, withdraw your hands up and away. Turn away. Do not push him off; let him get off himself. As soon as he is off, immediately pet and praise him. If he begins to jump again, quickly withdraw. It won't take long for him to get the idea.

The method works for tricks, too. An example is getting your dog to sit up. Have him sit, then praise and reward him, and quickly bring out a treat. Bring it just a few inches over his head—just high enough so that he can't jump but must raise his body and front legs off the ground. Immediately praise and give him his reward. Repeat this procedure a few times daily, slowly increasing the length of time he sits up before you praise and give him a treat.

For general training there are four avenues one can take:

    1. Private training. A trainer comes to you and works with you and your dog in the home environment. This is the most desirable way.

    2. Group classes. Attractive because of low costs—twenty-five to fifty dollars, with from five lessons (one a week) to twelve lessons (two a week). Training is generally poor and prolonged compared to private training, but I believe group training is more desirable than kennel training.

    3. Kennel training. Owner and family do not participate; convenient, but I believe the education of a dog is too important to leave to the pros alone.

    4. By book. The most common complaint I've heard about dog training books is that the variety of methods borders on chaos.

Here is some help in evaluating recent dog-training books.

City Dog ($7.95; New York: E. P. Dutton, 1975), by Richard A. Wolters. I remember a blind date. The idea of possibly meeting Ms. Right dazzled through my mind—part Marilyn Monroe, part mother, great cook, and of course filthy rich; love at first glance. Alas, when I arrived, I discovered that well-meaning friends had set me up with an old flame.

In teaching a dog to be obedient, leashes and collars are not only unnecessary but actually distracting to the dog's concentration.

When I began to read this book, I had a similar anticipation. Revolutionary, rapid method, never reprimand a dog unless you are sure he knows what is expected of him. A fantastic and worthwhile discussion and step-by-step puppy testing procedure. These are some of the things that enticed me. But as in my youthful experience with romance, Wolters quickly brought me back to standard procedures and concepts—those found in many dog training books. And mostly he relies on the command/correct/praise approach. The photographs, by the author, are excellent in both their dramatic and instructional value.

Dog Training My Way ($5.95; New York: Stein and Day, 1972), by Barbara Woodhouse, offers a training method of domination. Ms. Woodhouse believes that a dog somehow thrives on it. She would have trouble with me, I'll tell you, because I can't imagine dragging a shy, young dog through the streets, jerking him by the leash.

How to Train a Watchdog ($5.95; Blue Ridge Summit, Pa.: Tab Books, 1975), by Bruce Sessions, discusses in detail the selection and training of a guard dog. How-

Ed Beckmann, dog trainer and author of Love, Praise and Reward: The New Way to Teach Your Dog *(New York: Coward, McCann and Geoghegan, 1978) and his dogs. (Photograph by Alex Wasinski)*

ever, it disturbs me that the book seems intended to teach the average person how to train a watchdog.

One of the most serious problems facing people in their relationship with dogs is the problem of the biting dog. Mr. Sessions may be unleashing thousands of unskilled owners and, possibly, some unbalanced, sadistic people in the training of attack dogs.

Leave guard dog training to the highly skilled professionals, I say.

How to Train Your Dog in Six Weeks ($8.95; New York: Frederick Fell Publishers, 1976), by Bill Landesman and Kathleen Berman, is an approach to training different categories of dogs—normal, overfriendly, high-strung, aloof, shy, fear-biter, aggressive. In addition to obedience, the authors discuss breed selection, puppy training, and problem control.

Procedures are fairly common, and methods are rather mechanical and impersonal. The correction techniques are excessive and possibly harmful.

The authors argue that punishing corrections to effectively train dogs keeps them from being turned over to a pound or abandoned. They proclaim hitting to be cruel, and offer their nonhitting but harsh method as a somehow humane approach. Teacher rationalization, I say.

The Liberated Dog ($9.95; New York: Holt, Rinehart and Winston, 1977), by Matthew Margolis with Julie Grayson, is Mr. Margolis' fourth dog training book. It is described as "the ultimate discipline of off-leash control." The heart of the method is the corrective jerk—followed by praise. Command your dog, and if he doesn't listen properly, use the corrective jerk. All corrective jerks are preceded by a sharp "no!" The "ultimate control" off-leash is done by extending the length of the leash to a fifteen-foot clothesline and then progressing to a hundred-foot fishline. These aids are needed to administer the corrective jerk. This concept of training is based on the most common attitude toward training a dog—that you must teach the dog you're master with a do-it-or-else approach.

My experience is that as long as a dog is attached to you by such disciplinary umbilical cords, there will be good response. But too many dogs learn No-Leash, No-Correction—No Listen.

The Natural Method of Dog Training ($3.95; New York: M. Evans, 1963), by Leon F. Whitney, D.V.M., an effective and easily understood book that will certainly get your dog trained. The concept of teaching a dog without force is one I subscribe to fully, and many of the methods used by Dr. Whitney for teaching dogs have proven themselves in my own work.

But the emphasis here is on conditioning according to experimental work done with animals, and there seems to be a very clinical attitude. This is the only way I can understand Dr. Whitney's sometimes frightening procedures in dealing with problem behavior. Isolating a dog in a closet doesn't sound very natural to me.

Obedience Class Instruction for Dogs ($10.95; New York: Macmillan Publishing Co., Inc., 1971), by Winifred Gibson Strickland, who is obviously a very well-informed dog trainer. This book rates high on my list for any serious trainer or obedience club. But it is not thorough enough or clear enough for the home trainer or do-it-yourselfer. Ms. Strickland's statement, "The trainer who resorts to violence to train dogs is nothing more than a sadistic bully who is satisfying his ego by brutally forcing dogs to obey him," is worth remembering and perhaps should be posted on the walls of kennels and training classrooms everywhere.

Paul Loeb's Complete Book of Dog Training ($6.95; Englewood Cliffs, N.J.: Prentice-Hall, 1974), by Paul Loeb. I once received a call from a woman with real fear in her voice. She had received a dog as a gift and now the dog was after her and her children, trying to bite them, keeping them trapped in rooms. They had finally lured the dog into the basement and fed it by pushing food through a slightly ajar door with a stick, which the dog also attacked.

I arrived at her home to evaluate the problem. I went out back to the basement window, wiped away the dirt, and peered in. To my surprise I saw a five-pound, floppy-eared puppy. I went into the house and opened the basement door. Out bounced a playfully barking, harmless little dog.

It developed that the woman had no experience with dogs and had passed her fears on to her children—simple playful behavior was turned into a fiendish assault.

Loeb's book sets this kind of tone. It is a fine example of how *not* to train your dog. His understanding of canine behavior seems based on a belief that the dog is out to get you at every turn.

Loeb makes much of such mundane activities as staring, proclaiming that if you turn your eyes away first from a dog's gaze, you have submitted to its will. Begging at your table is also to be considered an aggressive act. "Naturally, the place aggression should be nipped is in the bud, which in your dog's case could be whining." According to Loeb "it's the rough equivalent of a pleased giggle but at the same time it is a pleading noise, a means of making you feel sorry for him, a manipulative gesture." To deal with aggressive behavior one is advised to be ever-vigilant—never let the dog get the edge.

Recommended methods include throwing a boot at a dog, dropping telephone books, hitting, or dabbing vinegar and Tabasco sauce in its mouth.

There is an authoritative tone in this book which to the unknowledgeable and inexperienced could be believable. There are better and more humane ways to teach dogs. I suggest you stay far away from this one of unnecessary suffering and punishment.

Toward the Ph.D. for Dogs ($14.95; New York: Harcourt Brace Jovanovich, 1975), by Robert J. Martin and

Napoleon A. Chagnon, is intended to offer an individual a complete guide to training, from novice through utility, using the AKC regulations as a guide. Unfortunately, the authors are obviously more interested in expediency and obedience degrees than in the welfare of dogs. Their use of the word "correction" is synonymous with punishment. If getting your dog a title is important to you, and if the dog has a personality that can withstand rough handling (and if you don't mind "bopping it on the nose") this is a clearly written book.

21 Days to a Trained Dog ($6.95; New York: Simon and Schuster, 1977), by Dick Maller and Jeffrey Feinman, is a basic approach to training that teaches the dog obedience without any physical force—bravo! The idea is to wait until the dog performs naturally and then to use spoken praise. In this manner the dog is taught complete obedience. Maller calls his method "operant conditioning"—a novel and interesting method, but one he hasn't worked out far enough for all purposes. For instance, Maller is unable to teach a dog to heel using his operant conditioning. And he reverts to such old-fashioned procedures as the knee-in-the-chest method for jumping up. Also, I believe he's wrong in his idea that a dog must be purposely starved to perform for food. My dogs, at any rate, do flips for a piece of cheese even after eating as well as any dog can.

Understanding Your Dog, A New Approach to Training ($7.95; North Pomfret, Vt.: David and Charles, 1977), by Peter Griffiths, offers information concerning the domestication of the dog that is fascinating for someone who wants to learn more about the natural history of dogs and how it relates to training. A flaw, though, is the comparison of wild dog relationships with the interrelationship between man and his pet dog. A dog can tell the difference between a man and a dog and will relate differently to each. It is a wonder to me that experts don't study the relationship between man and dog and their reactions and use the findings as the basis for training. Comparing floppy-eared Fido to a wolf is like comparing a jet-setter to Neanderthal man.

The Pearsall Guide to Successful Dog Training ($9.95; New York: Howell Book House, 1973), by Margaret Pearsall; Milo D. Pearsall, technical advisor. My own approach to teaching dogs—love, praise, and reward—is based on motivating the dog to work with and to help the trainer. Within the framework of competitive obedience (for showing) and the use of leash and choke collar, the Pearsalls offer the most positive and forward teaching approach I've read. It is based on teaching us to understand training from the dog's point of view. One of the most difficult things for a good trainer to achieve is a feeling in his human students of the dog's personal involvement in the training program. This book does just that, and it is a must for those who want to teach complete obedience, novice-through-utility procedures.

If I were giving gold stars, I'd empty the box here.

Treat a puppy nicely and the treatment will be reciprocated by the dog, which is an essential condition where children are involved. (Photograph by Peter Simon)

How Animals Are Taught Their Tricks

From an article in Scientific American *at the turn of the century we learn that teaching dogs the alphabet is not quite what it seems, although "memory" is a factor to be considered.*

The training of animals—teaching them to perform all sorts of entertaining tricks—is a task that requires perhaps a special talent on the part of the trainer.

The first thing every dog must learn is his name. Select a short, sharp-sounding name, and stick to it.* Never call him anything else. If you have several dogs, the name is taught on the same principle. Divide their food; then, placing a piece on the ground, call each in turn by his name, and give him the food when he comes to it. Send the others back if they come forward out of their turn. By and by they will learn that a certain name is always associated with a certain dog. Ramble among the dogs, and call out one of their names every now and then. If the right dog comes to you, reward him with a piece of cracker. Pay no attention to the other dogs. They will learn very soon, and the first great lesson—dependence and obedience—will have been learned.

The next thing is to teach him to go and get any object called for. Place a glove on the floor; then say to the dog, "Fetch the glove," putting the accent on the last word. Then, when he has done this several times, place a shoe on the floor, and teach him to fetch this in a similar manner. Now place both objects on the ground and teach him to fetch either one, as asked for—rewarding him when he brings you the right one, rebuking him when he fetches the wrong, which you take from him and replace. He will soon learn to distinguish the articles; then a third may be substituted, and so on until a number are on the floor. You should then go into the next room, taking the dog with you, and send him in to fetch any article you mention. After a little time he will bring you the right one every time.

Next teach him differences in color. Place a red object on the floor and a blue one beside it. Teach him to fetch the article called for as you did before, being careful to reward him every time he brings you the right handkerchief. Then put down a green object, a purple, a yellow one, and so on; until finally the needed array of colors can be placed for selection.**

Next, he should be taught the articles of furniture—table, chair, etc. He must go to each one as you call out its name. Finally, combine some of the previous commands: "Place the glove on the chair"; "Get the handkerchief and place it on the table," etc. At first this should be said very slowly, and only half the command repeated at once; but the halves of the sentence may be gradually blended together, until you can say it as you would to any individual, and the dog will obey your command.

To a certain extent, also, dogs may be taught the letters of the alphabet, the numbers of spots on cards, large dominoes, etc. The method of training them is simply one of constant repetition. Cards bearing the letter or number are placed in front of the dog. The letter or number is called out aloud at the same time the dog is shown which one it is. After several trials he will select this one when it is called for and disregard the others. This once learned, the next letter is taught in like manner, until a large number are recognized by the dog, and he is able to pick out any of them at will.

It must be admitted, however, that most feats of this character, as performed in public, are the result of some trick rather than any marvelously elaborate training on the part of the dog, which would be necessary if these feats were genuine—granting them to be possible at all. As a matter of fact, most of these apparently marvelous feats are based on a very few cues, given to the dog at the appropriate time, to which he has been taught to respond in a simple manner. A few examples will make this clear.

The dog watches his master's eyes, and when his master glances in any direction—at a card, for example—the dog can follow his glance . . .

Many of these feats are performed by means of a cue word, in just the same kind of way as "mind-readers" entertain and puzzle their audience. As soon as this word is given—it may be in the course of a sentence—the dog knows that he is to perform a certain action. It is not necessary for him to understand the whole of the sentence; only one word in it. As soon as that word

*Expert trainer Ed Beckmann of Problem Puppy school couldn't. agree less. He reasons that a short, snappy name like Spot can confuse a puppy when he hears a common word like "not" or "hot," etc.; much the same, he feels, a puppy called Lear might be confused by the command, "Come here." Konrad Lorenz, although not writing about puppies in this context, believes that dogs can hear subtle differences in articulations. In *Man Meets Dog* Lorenz mentions three Alsatians (German shepherds) called Harris, Aris and Paris. "On command from their master, 'Harris (Aris, Paris), Go to your basket,' the dog addressed and that one only would get up unfailingly and walk sadly but obediently to bed."

** This whole business is indeed a real trick since dogs are thought to be color-blind. It is possible that the anonymous writer of this item was himself the victim of deception—gullibly succumbing to the trick of trainer-manipulation of dogs by cue words or eye movements. Interestingly, both techniques are described a little farther on in the article.

is caught, the action is performed. Each action corresponds to a certain cue word. Again, there is the method of training by the use of the eyes. The dog watches his master's eyes, and when his master glances in any direction—at a card, for example—the dog can follow his glance and pick out the card in turn. Or the dog may be told to bark a certain number, in which case the dog watches his master's face closely and simply barks until the eyes, or some movement, tell him to stop. He does not have to know that he barks nine times. All he has to know is that he must go on barking until he is told to stop by his master's signal; the trainer is the one who does all the counting.

There are certain stage tricks which depend very largely upon the dog's memory, however—such as picking up a numbered card, and the like. The cards are arranged in a row, and the trainer stands in front of the row in which the card rests. A string is attached to the dog's neck. First, the dog is trained to go to the row of cards nearest the trainer; then, if he is inclined to pick up one too near, a slight pull on the string is given, pulling the dog up to the required number. The trainer stands at a certain distance from the table in these tricks; if close to the table, the dog knows it means card one; if farther away, card two; if still farther, card three. By care in training, the dog can be taught to pick out any required card without in any way knowing the number written upon it. When the dog has been taught to pick up any card by means of this code, the trainer may appear to make it far more complicated by causing the dog to add, subtract, multiply, divide, etc. All that is necessary, of course, is for the performer himself to do the sum, mentally note the position of the card giving the answer, and indicate this card to the dog by means of some hidden code.

In the same way horses can be made to stamp out any desired number, tell the date of a coin, etc., simply by pawing the ground until the trainer gives them the signal to stop by means of some secret sign, unnoticed by the audience.

Edited and reprinted from Scientific American, *September 11, 1911.*

TINY TREATS FOR TRAINING

Many types of food make an excellent reward for your dog's good behavior. We have found that a thumb-sized piece of American cheese works quite well, as does a slice of banana. But after laborious testing our experts have discovered the perfect tidbit, a slightly rank, warm chunk of liverwurst—Jones Farm brand preferred.
—*Richard Benjamin Romanof*

The Dog Groomers

The well-mannered dog is often well groomed by skilled, trained professionals. Here is a rare photographic glimpse of groomers' seminars and demonstrations in Atlantic City. Plus reviews of dog-grooming books.

The Standard Book of Dog Grooming ($14.95; Fairfax: Denlinger's, 1975), by Diane Fenger and Arlene F. Steinle, is a good book if you want to do your own grooming or understand what the professional groomer should be doing to your dog, or if you aspire to become a professional groomer.

Grooming equipment and its proper use, canine anatomy, and external parasites are discussed. The breeds are divided into groups according to coat textures and lengths and techniques of grooming—scissored, parted, stripped, feathered, etc. There are black-and-white photographs and diagrams throughout.

How to Trim, Groom and Show Your Dog ($5.95; New York: Howell Book House, 1975), by Blanche Saunders, is directed at the show groomer. There are twenty-one diagrams covering all breed types.

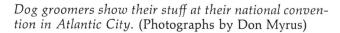

Dog groomers show their stuff at their national convention in Atlantic City. (Photographs by Don Myrus)

The Complete Poodle Clipping and Grooming Book ($9.95; New York: Howell Book House, 1969), by Shirlee Kalstone, tells how to groom the most popular dog in the U.S. Besides diagrams and information about equipment and how to use it, there are directions given for fourteen different basic poodle clips, each of which has several different variations. There is the Miami Clip and the Summer Miami Clip, the New Yorker Clip, the Bolero New Yorker, and the Fifth Avenue New Yorker.

Grooming and Showing Toy Dogs ($14.95; Fairfax: Denlinger's, 1976), by Peggy A. Hogg and Dr. Robert J.

Berndt, is a comprehensive and practical text designed as a manual for the dog show exhibitor of toy breeds. Both authors of this book are experts. Peggy A. Hogg is a professional handler who has shown winning dogs at Westminster for two successive years; she also handled the number-one toy dog in the United States in 1972. Dr. Robert J. Berndt is licensed to judge a number of breeds, including several in the toy group. Illustrated with photographs and line drawings, and treating each toy breed individually, this book includes detailed advice for both novice and professional handlers.

TYPICAL TIPS FOR GROOMING

Grooming is not a difficult craft to master given certain prerequisites—a reasonably steady hand, a reasonably even temperament (the dog must not sense anxiety), and the realization that hair once clipped grows back again so that no clip is irrevocable. And you need a guide either in the form of a veteran or one of the numerous books available.

From books you'll learn such as the following:

The poodle's face may be clipped clean or left with a moustache. Poodles shown in the breed ring in the puppy, English saddle or continental clips must have clean shaven faces. On all other styles, a moustache is optional. You simply select the style you like best.

The face is always clipped with the dog in a sitting position, facing you. Each time your dog fusses and tries to move during the clipping, immediately put him back into place. Firmly command him to sit, then start clipping again. He will soon understand what is expected of him.—*The Complete Poodle Clipping & Grooming Book.*

And for grooming spaniels:

Clip the ear, starting from the top and going as far as the natural fold. Clean the hair off to this point outside and inside the ears. The hair on the top of the head, from the outside corners of the eyes to the top corners of the ears, is left longer to give the appearance of more stop. Scissor around the edges of the ears carefully, going with the grain of the hair. Always have the scissors pointing away from the dog. Use the thumb and forefinger to hold the edge of the ear, and scissor next to the fingers. Then the ear leather will not be cut.—*The Standard Book of Dog Grooming.*

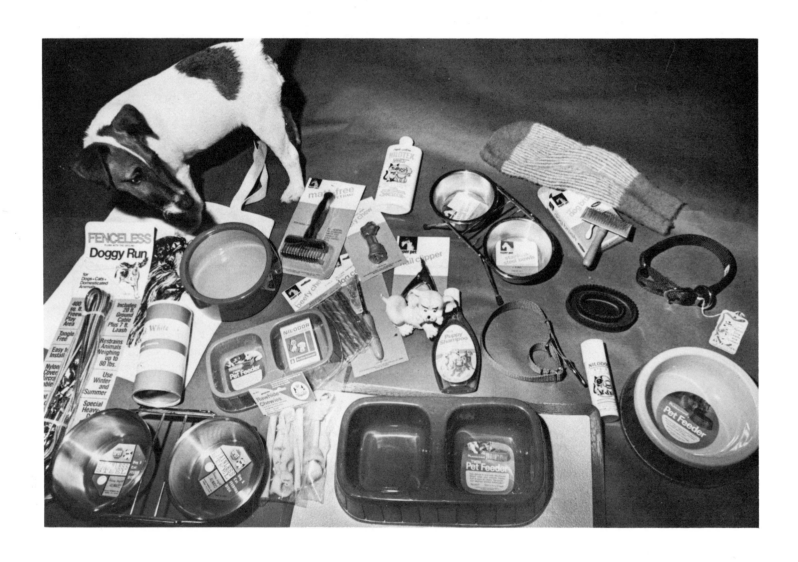

4
PROVIDING FOR THE DOG

AL
by Janice Johnson Roomkin

MY EXPERIENCE WITH RUSSIAN
WOLFHOUNDS
by C. M. D'Enville

WALL STREET GOES FOR THE
DOGS
by Abner A. Layne

CARNATION SUPPORTS FOUR
HUNDRED DOGS, AND THEY
ARE SAID TO EAT PRETTY
WELL

DID YOUR DOG EVER ASK,
"WHAT'S FOR DINNER?"

THE BEST FOOD FOR DOGS
by James Watson

DOG FOOD: THE FEDS' POSITION

A STATISTICAL ABSTRACT OF
DOG OWNERSHIP IN THE
U.S.A.
compiled by Richard Benjamin Romanof

DOG CARE IN BRIEF

DEATH WITH DIGNITY
by Maxwell Riddle

RESTING IN PEACE

WANT TO GET A TERRIER TO
CHICAGO? A ST. BERNARD
TO PARIS? HERE'S HOW
by Frank Filippelli

THEY'LL GET IT FOR YOU
WHOLESALE, OR MAIL ORDER
IS BEST
by Georgia Kufeld

Al

by Janice Johnson Roomkin

Al.

*The care and feeding of Alexis Petruska Vladi-
mir Johnson-Roomkin, and the good life in city
and suburbs. Moral: For runners it is a borzoi.*

The most distinctive quality of a borzoi is its shape.
Long, spindly legs support a hunchbacked body and
pointed nose. It's an improbable anatomy that is bound
to draw comment and induce confusion. Once an old
woman berated me for starving my "collie." A small boy
in Chicago asked the logical question, "That dog got
any camel in 'im?" One either loves or hates the shape.

I met my first borzoi in 1965 while on a skiing holiday
in Boyne Mountain, Michigan. As I sat by a fire to warm
my toes, I came nose to nose with what I later learned
was a borzoi—tall, sleek, and like the snow outside,
dazzling white. I remember that trip as the one in which
I got two frostbitten toes and fell in love with borzois.

Students at Smith College weren't allowed to keep
dogs in campus housing in 1965, although things may
have since changed. The borzois in my life at that time
were owned by a favorite professor and his wife who
gave me some hands-on experience with the breed and
imparted insights they had gathered as owners of a
borzoi kennel.

It was not until June 1970 that I was able to get my
own borzoi. Against the protests of my friends and
family I set out to buy a borzoi with money I had set
aside for this purpose years before. I was still in my last
year of graduate school at the University of Wisconsin.
Despite an uncertain future, I felt I could wait no longer.

My husband Myron, who grew up in a petless home,
had reservations. He argued that all dogs bark too much
and long-haired dogs are the worst because their hair
falls out as they bark. I maintained that, while that
might be true of other dogs, the borzoi did neither. I
lied. Though our dog rarely barks, and then only at in-
truders, he does howl at sirens, violins, and the theme
of the NBC evening news. When a borzoi howls, people
listen, especially in the middle of the night. And after
seven years our borzoi has molted enough to make a
good-size sweater.

The borzoi is not the easiest breed to own. They take
dedication, as Alfred A. Knopf, the publisher, once
learned. He chose the name Borzoi Books and the running hound as his colophon. In keeping with an image
that had brought him great success, he purchased two
borzois to live in his Park Avenue apartment. He soon

gave up on the idea, however, after finding the exercise
routine too demanding and the shed hair too abundant.

Myron and I visited several kennels and saw many
puppies, none of which looked anything like they would
grow into a majestic animal. They were shorthaired,
awkward, and small with long ratty tails; the borzoi of
my dreams was furry, perpetually swift, and large.

Maybe that's why I bought Petruska, a one-year-old
dog with dark-red markings. But Petruska could not
adjust to life outside the kennel and turned out to be a
sickly dog. Heartbroken, I gave her up.

A few months later I had recovered enough to try
again. I bought a ten-week-old puppy and named him
Alexis Petruska Vladimir Johnson-Roomkin (plus assorted meaningless—to me—kennel names for AKC
registration). Myron picked him out from among his
littermates. Alexis was less frisky than the others, more
curious. Like the others, he was incredibly awkward for
such a stately breed.

Al, or, as his friends call him, "Big Al," grew about
one inch each week in his first year to a shoulder height
of thirty-three inches. We kept a chart of his height on
the kitchen wall along with the date. I still wonder what
the next tenant thought we were recording with those
pencil marks. To aid his growth, we gave him plenty of
food, vitamins, and large quantities of calcium. My
father, who had once kept packs of hunting hounds, had
a theory that a puppy should have dry food available at
all times. This, he felt, bred good eating habits and emotional security. We still maintain the practice, and I
honestly don't know if it works or not.

Like most hounds, Al is highly intelligent but equally
obstinate. To our surprise he was housebroken in one

day, never damaged our property or furniture, and is very loyal. But try to get him to come immediately when off leash; it's when he's good and ready. This despite a ten-week course in obedience training. The simple fact is that he prefers the company of four-footed creatures to ours, and we've learned to accept it.

Each time Bellow published a new volume, we'd run to read whether our dog had made it into print.

One trick he learned on his own is how to cajole or extort food from strangers. At the dinner table, notwithstanding our efforts, he positions himself so that he is visible but not obvious. Over the years he has learned to identify the easy marks. He stares, he begs, and sometimes even sits with his front legs crossed waiting to be rewarded. But all at a proper distance. Some people, like my mother-in-law, can't eat a mouthful when the dog is in the room. Others plan their meals around the thought of leaving this starving, skinny dog some scraps. But once you learn that Al is a "con artist" and that his skinniness is hereditary, you begin to strike back. Our cleaning lady used to tell us how Al forced her to eat standing in a corner until she learned to turn on the vacuum cleaner to frighten him while she ate. Lunch wasn't quiet, but she didn't go hungry.

The borzoi is a vision of fashion, art deco grace, and vodka ads. It is thought that borzois should be seen in public at one end of an elegant leash with a fashionably attired long-legged beauty at the other. The reality of a powerful running hound belies this picture. I am neither long-legged nor do I walk Al in anything resembling fashionable attire. The rule in dog walking is functionalism, especially in winter—sheepskin coat, stocking hat, six-foot L. L. Bean scarf, and Canadian arctic sheepskin-lined boots. Rainy days are met with high rubber boots and an old army rain poncho. Pleasant days in spring and summer are welcomed with a variety of jogging clothes pared down for the higher temperatures.

The borzoi is clearly not your once-around-the-fire-hydrant stroller. He likes to run, especially in inclement weather. His silky undercoat insulates him well from the coldest temperature. We adhere to the ritual of three walks a day—one being a two-mile jog, or rather, I jog while Al simply walks quickly. All this dog walking takes time, however. Friends and neighbors begin to worry whether you truly work for a living. One neighbor, in fact, after seeing me walk Al for the third time that day, was convinced that my marriage was in trouble. No one, he reasoned, could spend that much time with a dog and have a satisfactory home life, too.

As a member of our family, Al has been uprooted all too many times. We have moved seven times in as many years, and this has caused problems. Life in Madison, Wisconsin, was quiet and friendly for dogs and people.

Al and Janice Roomkin.

In those days Al enjoyed playing with other dogs, running through woods, and swimming in lakes. He was a big small-town dog.

When we moved to Hyde Park in Chicago, a period of readjustment was needed. Our first apartment was very small. Al took to chewing on wooden pencils as an expression of his frustration. When we moved to larger quarters four months later, the pencil chewing immediately stopped.

As an inner-city community, Hyde Park has a problem with crime, especially street crime. The openness of the young dog from Madison did not fare well in this environment. Nasty encounters with street-wise dogs left Al with a few scars and highly suspicious of all four-legged creatures. As far as people were concerned, Al's size and lean-and-hungry look gave me the courage to take those evening walks. In fact I affectionately thought of him as the "Monster of the Midway." Twice he ran off nude men who, for reasons I don't want to know, were out for an evening sortie.

Hyde Park is also an intellectual community and the home of the University of Chicago. Al was well regarded in the new apartment building. Howling at sirens was tolerated and even enjoyed by some. Often tenants invited him to ride the passenger, rather than the freight, elevator. Dog walking around the new apartment was interlaced by brief encounters with the

Al and Myron Roomkin. (Photographs of Al *et al.* by Charles Maxey)

worldly and the renowned, most of whom, I am happy to report, do take time to notice an attractive dog. One of our illustrious neighbors, Saul Bellow, developed a certain affection for Al. Each time Bellow published a new volume, we'd run to read whether our dog had made it into print.

Then we moved again, this time to the vicinity of Northwestern University. Al now runs in a forest preserve along a bridle path. He is again a happy dog, happy at chasing along a bridle path in a forest preserve. And, of course, he's always happy to be eating—whether the small birthday cake my Aunt Alice makes or the free Baskin-Robbins birthday ice cream cone we won for him once.

In addition to our many moves, we've had to do a lot of traveling.

On his first car trip of any distance I gave Al a tranquilizer. In losing the coordination of his body, he placed the blame on a stranger traveling in the car and snapped at her. On the return trip, with the same passenger, the untranquilized dog was a perfect gentleman, lying down on the back seat, as he always has since. He has never been tranquilized again.

The decision to travel with the dog influences our choice of cars. We only consider four-door models with generous back seats. Enroute to our destination we stop every three hours for exercise. Fellow travelers slow to gape at the creature trotting along the median strips.

Without exception we have found hotels and motels generous. (Of course we make reservations for him in advance.) We always warn maids to expect a large dog,

and whenever possible we have the room made up during his morning walk.

Kenneling is sometimes unavoidable and is always traumatic. Alexis recognizes the smell and sounds of the kennel and becomes visibly tense. He stands close and stares with pleading eyes. As he is taken away by some strange handler, he manages one last pitiful glance in our direction.

Because of our guilt, I have always taken pains to examine the kennels beforehand. Cleanliness, space, availability of water, personal attention, and quietness of the facility are all considered. Our first choice presently for Al is a "luxury kennel." It is called a "pet motel" and is so convincing in appearance that on our first visit Al pranced up to the door, as is his custom at all Holiday Inns. He now knows better. Even with its piped-in stereo music and biscuit breaks, he does not enjoy the carpeted "imperial suite" we rent for him. The report card, which is filled out daily by his "valet," evaluates toilet habits, eating habits, personality, and physical appearance. He does not eat well, but consistently rates an "excellent" in personality. All this would seem more ridiculous were it not for the fact that it was Al's veterinarian who recommended the kennel initially.

Borzoi people stick together. To be walking a borzoi, or to allow that one has ever owned one, admits you to the club. While those who indicate curiosity about the breed are politely tolerated, owners are openly embraced. Once an elderly woman approached me and hugged me. She told me about her happy childhood complete with two white borzois and how everything, including the dogs, was lost in the Depression.

On the other hand, with the "professional" owner, opening comments generally include an attempt to establish bloodlines and to evaluate pedigree, kennels, sires and dams, and points toward championship. The more casual owner, who chooses not to show, is more concerned with eating habits, shedding, and whether or not yours would be a suitable mate for his borzoi.

Though never choosing to go into the show ring, I have been tempted to take Al coursing. A weekend club races borzois and other hounds not far from my home. I went so far as to purchase a racing muzzle. Unfortunately, it could not be returned. A thousand rabbits could have run in front of Al, but he still would have been more concerned with removing the muzzle than chasing prey. He is a racetrack dropout, a victim of refusing to keep his mouth closed.

Janice Roomkin is a graphic arts instructor, a graduate student in architectural business administration, and a world-class fencer.

GONE TO THE DOGS

—In 1959 a three-year-old black dachshund named Mozart was the beneficiary of the seventy-thousand-dollar estate of the late Mrs. Clara Sammis Cole. Income from the estate was directed to go to "one who would give loving care to Mozart."

—Superior Court Judge Ward J. Herbert of Newark, N.J., ruled in 1964 that eighty-three-year-old Mrs. Geraldine Rockefeller Dodge (niece of John D. Rockefeller and widow of Marcellus Hartley Dodge) could, in spite of her guardians, continue to feed her forty-nine dogs fifty thousand dollars' worth of choice-cut meat each year.

—The great railroad historian Lucius Beebe in 1966 left fifteen thousand dollars of a two-million-dollar estate in trust to care for his St. Bernard, T-Bone Towser II.

—Eleanor E. Ritchey, an oil heiress, died in 1968 leaving a hundred and fifty dogs and four and one-half million dollars. Five years later, after litigation by relatives—near and distant—a Florida appellate court determined that Auburn University's School of Veterinary Medicine could receive the bulk of the estate, but only after it carried out Ms. Ritchey's directive to find a good home for each of her pets. Auburn alumni were asked to rise to the challenge and take in the eighty remaining dogs.

My Experience With Russian Wolfhounds

by C. M. D'Enville

Janice Roomkin's successful experience of keeping a borzoi in an apartment and later in a suburban home, and of taking it out for daily "walks"—one being for only two miles—results from the breed's relative inactivity in modern times. Just how much living space a borzoi could use in the early nineteen-hundreds is described in this piece on Russian wolfhounds—then the name of the breed.

We have had all kinds of dogs around the place, from a little shivery black-and-tan with eyes that bulged like a boy after his Thanksgiving dinner to a big, tawny St. Bernard, who in spite of his formidable appearance had about as much sense and courage as a calf. My hat is off, however, to the Russian wolfhound as the real thing in dogs.

A friend of mine sent me a pair of them from Texas, and a month's experience with them taught me that my preconceived notions about dogs certainly did not apply to them.

First, they were so gentle. I had always thought that to own a dog raised to kill wolves for a living would be like making a companion of a caged lion. It is said that a wolf, if given a start of two hundred yards, will be overtaken by the wolfhound in the next six hundred yards and quickly dispatched by a nip behind the ear. This ear-nipping tendency seems to be instinctive in wolfhounds. Even the puppies at play will spar with each other for the "ear hold," quite unlike other dogs such as terriers and setters, which try to get a grip on each others' paws or hindquarters.

As household pets I found wolfhounds to have uniformly the most gentle dispositions I have ever seen in dogs. They would submit to almost any amount of teasing by other dogs and children, with no further remonstrance than to retire with dignity and judgment to the seclusion of their kennel.

In the morning, when I unchained them for their morning run, the difference between wolfhounds and the rest of the dog world that I had met was most apparent. The only comparison I can think of is greased lightning. My house faces on a twelve-acre field abandoned to a growth of daisies and goldenrod. In spite of its size this lot proved utterly inadequate to the buoyancy and exuberance of these dogs. These were off and back again, up and down the field in the twinkling of an eye, one minute to appear like a couple of white objects in the distance and the next as flashes of white rushing by like the wind. Hardly the conventional picture of a wolfhound standing meekly by the side of some Russian princess!

. . . at night they gave out the most weird and awful sounds I have ever heard from a dog—not a howl or a bark but some kind of wail, like the cry of a lost soul.

On one or two occasions at night they gave out the most weird and awful sounds I have ever heard from a dog—not a howl or a bark but some kind of a wail, like the cry of a lost soul.

Twice they got loose, and each time were gone three days. When they came back, they were much bedraggled and sad of eye. How far they had been, I'll never know. Even yet I hear stories of their passing by from neighbors who live six or eight miles away. It was that sad cry and the flash of white—and in one case leaving in their wake a pig with a torn ear and jowl, and a half-dozen dead chickens, which I settled for—that were most remembered.

If ever there was a Dr. Jekyll and Mr. Hyde among dogs, it is the wolfhound. He is as mysterious as a Sherlock Holmes story. When I moved to town, I sent my dogs back to Texas, not because I had not become attached to them but simply because my morning horseback ride of ten miles was cut out, and I couldn't give them the exercise they needed. My opinion is that the wolfhound is par excellence the dog of the open country. To keep him under any other conditions is cruelty to him and a source of trouble to his master.

Reprinted from Country Life in America, *September 1909.*

Wall Street Goes for the Dogs

by Abner A. Layne

While you are providing for your dog, your dog and his kind are fabulously enriching an entire industry. Here is an analysis of that market by the editor of Standard & Poor's Fixed Income Investor.

Any business that sells $3 billion worth of anything a year will attract Wall Street's attention. If it's a steadily growing business, it will receive the Street's approbation—and its admiration if it's a high-profit business.

On all counts pet-food producers win the hearts of Wall Street's bird dogs, the stock analysts.

Pet-food producers topped $2.8 billion in retail sales in 1976, and by now the figure is without doubt over $3 billion. That's more than we humans spend on our own cereals. In fact, it's nearly as much as we spend on books.

And the business, growing like a healthy puppy, keeps fooling the forecasters. About six years ago, when pet food was a fairly new but respectable $1.4 billion industry, the optimists among forecasters predicted about 70 percent growth to $2.4 billion in sales in 1977. Even the most optimistic didn't foresee the actual rise to $3 billion, 114 percent growth. In investment terms that's 13 to 14 percent growth compounded annually. Not many industries do that well or that consistently.

But best of all, from the Street's point of view, is that it's a high-profit business. The industry would win a smile from frosty J.P. Morgan himself. While profit (before taxes) in the human food processing industry is a boring 3 percent, some lines of pet food can, on occasion, top 50 percent. Exciting? Yes, indeed. Profits like that make the corporate mouth water. So, starting from an industry of mostly small producers fifteen years ago, the pet-food industry has gained a stature and profile typical of most big industries.

For one thing, there is a standout giant leader—a General Motors, a U.S. Steel so to speak. In pet food, it's Ralston Purina, whose pet-food sales, now nearing $1 billion, are nearly equal to the total sales of the next three producers in the hierarchy of size—Carnation, General Foods, and Quaker Oats. The top four are followed at a distance by a second tier—Liggett Group, Heinz, and Mars (the privately owned candy maker).

Abner A. Layne, author of Wall Street Goes to the Dogs, *has been a financial writer and editor for twenty years. He discovered the investment potential of pet foods when he began feeding two cats—Henri IV and Schroder. Recently he fed two bitches, Sappho and Lolita, as a house and dog sitter on a Caribbean island. He says:*

"Two feedings a day of dry food, mixed with water, out of an unbranded fifty-pound sack. The dogs loved it, whatever it was. A most satisfactory experience. As for the cats, they have yet to like more than half of any can, sack, or container of any brand you care to name." (Photograph by Donald W. Newton)

After the big seven comes a pack of smaller producers, which all together sell about $660 million worth of pet foods.

The war for sales and bigger shares of the market is fierce and fought with the most sophisticated advertising weapons that high profit margins can buy. The score that distinguishes victor from vanquished is kept in dollar shares of market, tons of food sold, and price per pound received. In 1976, for example, 45.5 percent, or $900 million of dog-food sales, was in the category of dry foods. Ralston Purina (they're far and away the biggest in the dry food sector) sold $528 million in that category. Sales for their six brands were at an average of 28.7 cents per pound. That was about 1.9 cents more than the industry average of 25.8 cents per pound.

Those two added pennies made a big impression on the Street. Ralston Purina's tonnage multiplied by the pennies meant an extra $35 million in profits. (Production costs don't vary much from company to company.)

Another battle in the pet-food war is fought in the aisles of the neighborhood supermarket. With five cents of every customer's dry grocery dollar going for cat and dog food, the supermarket manager makes sure that those products get adequate and often prominent space for display—on average, 60 yards of shelving to hold the boxes, bags, cans, and cartons of pet food.

Importantly, recession hardly dents the luxuriant growth of pet-food sales. In 1975, when humans spent 10 percent more dollars for vittles, we were, considering inflation, only buying about the same quantity as in 1974. However, we ponied up 14 percent more to feed our pets. And the extra growth is not because of an explosion in the pet population. To be sure, between 1964 and 1974 pets in hand, on laps, under foot, and just around grew by some 50 percent to 65 million. But during the same decade retail sales of pet food grew by 250 percent.

While profit (before taxes) in the human food processing industry is a boring 3 percent, some lines of pet food can, on occasion, top 50 percent. Exciting? Yes, indeed.

Impelling the meteoric rise in pet-food sales was an explosion in advertising dollars. For example, Alpo's dog-food sales in 1964 were given a $1.5-million advertising push. By 1969 the push was up to $5.75 million, nearly four times as much. Another example: In 1974 Ralston Purina was spending $152 million on its fifteen brands —ten times as much as ten years before. In fact, all pet-food manufacturers together spent $21 million in 1965 on network commercials to promote their products. Ten years later that figure was $273 million, more than ten times as much.

53

Such statistics impress investment advisers mightily. They like an industry that sells aggressively, especially when there's proof that buyers respond to advertising as enthusiastically as pet owners do.

Indeed, the pet-food industry grew mightily in the past decade and a half. But analysts don't make a living just by looking back. They prognosticate. And here's how the future looks:

Competition. There's going to be a rough-and-tumble fight for space on supermarket shelves. Pet food is just not going to be quite as profitable on a linear-foot basis as some other categories of food. Coffee, for example, now has such a high retail value that it's bound to grab away more shelf space in accordance with the grocer's rule-of-thumb which equates display space with sales in dollars. Up to now pet-food shelf space has been growing faster than any other category, with the possible exception of soft drinks. But tonnage per linear foot has been slowing down, and the analysts look for less shelf space for pet food. That will mean even harder competition for the shrinking space.

Population. The rate of growth of the dog population will be about the same as human household formations, 2.2 percent a year. According to some experts, however, bigger dogs will constitute an increasing proportion of the dog population, so dog-food production tonnage will grow at 3.5 percent a year. Other experts disagree. Dog-food consumption will grow, they say, but only at about 1.2 percent a year over the next five, down about a half a percentage point a year compared with the previous four. But they're unanimous on one point: Dry dog food will be the fastest growing subcategory.

New products. The next five years will see an avalanche of new products, partly as a result of competition and partly as a result of owner concern. Marketing men call this "segmentation of the market by end-user characteristics." So far we've seen special foods for the obese dog, the dog that's well past his prime, and for puppies at various stages of development. You can depend on marketing men to come up with more special market segments, from pregnant bitches to neurotic breeds that need pacifiers.

Naturally, the next five years will see changes in the ranking of producers too. Here's how they'll fare in the five years ahead:

Ralston Purina. In 1978 the company will hit $1 billion in pet-food sales. As the top producer now in dry foods, it can't improve its share of the market much. Probable strategy: Try for more share of sales in urban markets, where dry food hasn't done too well up to now. Best potential boost: As meat prices get higher, dry foods will sell better than ever.

Carnation. As number two it tries harder, putting out a major new product every year. It has launched a new semimoist dog food on the national market. Company should be first in growth. Probable strategy: More new products. Worst fear: Zooming meat prices will handicap Carnation, which has only 40 percent of its sales in dry foods.

General Foods (Gaines is a subsidary). Most of its sales are semimoist dog food. It is vulnerable to Ralston Purina and Carnation inroads in this category. However, it's not going to surrender the number-three spot without a fight, and its latest innovation—a semimoist food for dogs of various age classes—got a good reception in the marketplace.

Quaker Oats. The company has been losing market share because of its heavy reliance on canned dog food. Recently, however, it successfully introduced a product expressly for the part of the market that likes to mix dry food with moist or canned food or table scraps. The introduction was costly, and profits could suffer.

Liggett Group. This company is heavily dependent (75 percent) on Alpo, the best known of the all-meat canned dog foods. The company could have problems if meat prices go up with a surge, but recently it did introduce a new dry dog food.

Heinz. Bottom of the publicly traded major list in sales, and mostly in cat foods. However, it is making a new effort to grow and to take a bigger share of the market.

The rest of the pack. Good news and bad news for them. Good news: Dry dog food is attracting price-conscious customers. Bad news: Image-conscious customers are moving to buy higher-priced canned foods and semimoist foods. That is not good for the smalls, which are most dependent on dry foods.

On the whole, the next five years will be good ones for most pet-food producers, but not as good as the past five have been.

DEDUCT YOUR DOG

Of course you can deduct dog expenses for your dog who earns money, or equivalent value (best-in-litter, for example, or as a stud).

Blind people may deduct the purchase price of a seeing-eye dog and all costs of upkeep as a medical expense.

Watchdogs are deductible, but 100 percent can only be taken off if the dog watches 100 percent of its time and does not serve also as a pet.

A dog killed in an accident may be listed as a casualty loss—the first hundred dollars, however, is not deductible.

Carnation Supports Four Hundred Dogs, and They Are Said to Eat Pretty Well

How the second-largest dog-food manufacturer has gone about creating and testing its products for almost fifty years.

In 1932 twenty purebred Scottish terriers moved into quarters at Carnation Farms in the state of Washington. Today the corporation's kennels house four hundred purebred dogs of seven breeds.

These figures represent the phenomenal growth of the pet food industry in the past half-century, and the intensive research in canine nutrition that has supported that growth.

Commercial pet foods began appearing on the market in the 1930s. All of the early products were dog foods (cat rations came much later) and all were supplements —biscuits, kibbles, or meals designed to be mixed with table scraps or other foods. One of the first of these prepared products was a dry mixture of meat meal and gruel grains manufactured by Albers Milling Company. Called Husky Dog Food, the Albers product was packed in burlap bags and shipped to Alaska, where the owners of sled dogs mixed it with fish for their hard-working draft animals.

Shortly after the merger of Carnation Company and Albers in 1929, the two companies set out to formulate a complete ration for dogs. The two major characteristics of such a food are nutritional adequacy and taste acceptability. So for their first tests of a new pelleted food, researchers used an assortment of stray dogs rounded up in Seattle and housed in a makeshift shelter. Then Scottish terriers, at that time one of the most popular breeds in America, were substituted because they happened to be favorites of Carnation's president, E. H. Stuart.

A dog enjoys a little variation in diet but doesn't actually need it, and can be maintained on a single diet for a lifetime. Carnation executives report that dogs have lived in vigorous, good health on a diet of Friskies dry ration, and others on canned Friskies, for twelve to fourteen years. It is said that none have ever shown signs of nutritional deficiencies.

The company does state that dogs are so miscellaneous and they live in so many different environments that no single food can be suitable for all. Much of the variety in dog foods is designed to meet these differences in physique, temperament, and living conditions.

The dogs of Carnation Farms, Carnation, Wash.

Did Your Dog Ever Ask, "What's for Dinner?"

Dog owners as gourmet cooks and their dogs as finicky eaters; a food critic's flavor test; Terri McGinnis' recipe for dog biscuits.

All but the most naive or neurotic dog owners know that if it comes to eating or starving, a dog will eat. What people really worry about, then, is whether a dog *likes* what he is served. And among those persons conditioned to feeling important only if they can cook up something palatable, the idea that a dog might be as easily satisfied by a handful of processed, dried, nutritionally sound food is anathema. A dog (never much of a fool anyway) realizes the human concern and, given the chance, will stick his or her nose up at any opportunity—turning away from a bowl of kibble and knowing that a more delicate morsel, lovingly prepared, will be handed down.

Our dogs are extensions of ourselves . . . of our own pretensions . . . often of our own neuroses. But they can also add piquancy to our lives. Through them one can be delightfully foolish, happily self-indulgent—luxuries only people can afford, but that dogs somehow seem to understand. The household pet exists to serve master or mistress. If you get your kicks serving Quiche Lorraine to your puppy, so be it.

For flavor variety and color add liver powder (found at health food stores)—3 tablespoons; or . . .

An example of the ridiculous-raised-to-the-sublime occurred when Raymond A. Sokolov reported in the family-food-fashion-furnishings section of *The New York Times* about his personal taste test of a half-dozen or so different dog foods. Involving his experience as a food editor, he rated them on a star system.

Mr. Sokolov found that a product named Ground Chuck needed seasoning but nevertheless was worth three stars on his four-stars-for-best scale. (Nothing got four.) Milk-Bone Biscuits received three stars, too. (He ate a second biscuit spread with butter.) Prime, which was chicken-flavored and tasted like cake, was worth two stars, as was Medallion, which had a strong meat flavor to its chunks.

Critic Sokolov gave one star each to Purina Dog Chow, Recipe (a beef and egg dinner), and to the lamb chunks called Laddie Boy. He found Top Choice, Gaines Meal, and Alpo Horsemeat chunks unworthy of even one star. Worst of all was Daily All-Breed, which the human taster of dog food found to have a "strong, mysterious odor." He couldn't eat it, much less digest it.

Did you ever really think about dog biscuits? Well, Dr. Terri McGinnis has. This lady offers on page 56 of her *Dog & Cat Good Food Book* (San Francisco: Taylor & NG, 1977) this recipe:

DOG BISCUITS

  1 *cup all-purpose flour*
  1 *cup wheat flour*
½ *cup wheat germ*
½ *cup powdered dry milk (or soymilk powder)*
½ *teaspoon salt*
  6 *tablespoons margarine, lard, chilled bacon fat,*
     or other shortening
  1 *egg*
  1 *teaspoon brown sugar*

1. Combine white flour, wheat flour, wheat germ, powdered milk, and salt in a bowl. Cut in shortening until mixture resembles corn meal.
2. Beat the sugar with the egg, then stir in the sugar-egg mixture. Add water gradually as necessary to make a stiff dough (approximately ½ cup). Knead on a floured board until dough is smooth and pliable. Then roll out ½ inch thickness and cut with a cookie cutter (bone or cat shapes are appropriate).
3. Bake at 325 degrees F. until lightly browned (about 30 minutes). Makes about two dozen biscuits.
4. For flavor variety and color add liver powder (found at health food stores)—3 tablespoons; or dried vegetable flakes—1 tablespoon; or mashed or pureed cooked green vegetables or carrots—1 cup. Add these flavor ingredients following the sugar-egg mixture and adjust water addition to the dough accordingly.

Whip it up and give it the Sokolov test.

The Best Food for Dogs

by James Watson

Long before the laboratory study of carbo-hydrates and vitamins, owners tried hard to provide good nutrition. Here is dog-raiser Watson's view, including his "one absolute rule" of "thorough cooking." He wrote in 1908.

Nearly every large kennel now relies to some extent upon one or other of the several makes of dog biscuits. We have good evidence that the demand for this convenient form of food has grown very much of late years in that there is a greater number of firms engaged in supplying the needs of dog owners, whether of small or large kennels. Usually in large kennels biscuits form the morning meal. For the main meal of the day, given in the evening, food is cooked and fed cool or cold. Stale bread mixed with soup or meat, or mush made of various condiments in which meat is either mixed and cooked together or the mush subsequently mixed with the soup and meat, forms this main meal of the day. It may also consist of broken biscuits, dry or soaked in water or soup, with or without added meat. So, it will be seen, there is a variety of methods for feeding.

No matter what the material is of which the mush is made, there is one absolute rule which must be followed, or the dogs will soon get out of shape—that is, thorough cooking.

The fact is that there is milk and milk.

Whatever meat you get, have it clean and sweet. Kennels in a farming country can generally procure a cow or horse, and so long as the meat keeps sweet it is all right. With city kennels meat is an item that tells. Country kennels also get milk at a cheap rate, as a rule, and it should be known by all dog-fanciers that exhibitors of rabbits are strong believers in milk for putting a polish on the coat of their exhibition animals, so when procurable it may well be added to the kennel bill-of-fare.

There has perhaps been more discussion as to milk for dogs, particularly puppies, than anything else in the dietary line. Some hold that milk is a fruitful source of worms in puppies. The fact is that there is milk and milk. Warm milk from the cow is a very different thing from cold skim milk, and even the best cow's milk is radically different from the milk of a mother dog.

In place of weakening the cow's milk it should be enriched, either by concentration in the way of boiling and thus evaporating the water, or by adding eggs. It is remarkable how closely eggs and bitch's milk agree in analysis, being practically the same with the exception of the lack of sugar in eggs.

Only about a third of the quantity of ordinary milk one would give a puppy is needed when concentrated milk is used.

Edited and reprinted from Country Life in America, *May 1908.*

"Tuo-Tuo, our dog, is a very expensive household pet. It costs 30¢ a day to feed him—that's $109 a year—and $13 a month to have him groomed—that's $155 a year—not including the vet bill. We spend over $350 a year, but we don't care. We love him." (Photograph by Bill Owens, *Suburbia*. Used with permission.)

Dog Food:
The Feds' Position

A primer, which if followed, should make you happy and keep your dog well nourished.

It's quite possible to maintain and rear dogs on proteins solely of plant origin. But in practice it's wise to include some animal protein, both to make the food more acceptable to the dog and to round out the types of amino acids supplied by different protein sources. Animal-source protein does not mean the consumer must buy meat or choose canned products; the ingredient list on most dry-type foods, for instance, reveals that meat meal or meat derivatives have been used in the formula.

Other sources of good protein for dogs are eggs, milk, and cheese. However, they may not always be digested well and can pose other problems. Except for pregnant or nursing or very young animals, eggs may provide too rich an addition to an otherwise well-rounded diet. But if eggs are being added, they should always be cooked, because raw egg white destroys the essential nutrient biotin. Raw yolk is safe, but it doesn't provide the protein.

Many owners feel they should give their dogs a dish of milk. After a dog has been weaned, he rarely needs milk, and older dogs may not be able to digest it well. Milk can produce diarrhea.

Cheese is a good protein source and is often used for rewards or snacks. The usual dog food cannot, because of economics, include high levels of cheese in the formulations. Cheese is used primarily as a flavoring agent in a few dog foods. Owners who feel a cheese flavor is desirable may simply grate a bit on top of the regular food.

Animal by-products can be some of the most nourishing ingredients in dog foods. Regulations have specified what can and cannot be contained in by-products. Permitted are lungs, livers, spleens, kidneys, brains, stomachs, intestines, and fat and lean trimmings. Not allowed are intestinal contents, hooves, bones, hides, and horns.

The major difference between dog food and food prepared for humans is that entirely different sources of ingredients may be used for the two products. Meat and bone meal derived from animals that have died other than by slaughter are commonly used in dog foods but not in human foods. Because of high cooking temperatures, however, the products should not pose a health problem.

Nutritionally, canned foods are generally not superior to dry types of food. Palatability is a decided plus factor for the canned ration. But many generations of animals have been raised on "complete and balanced" rations of both types of foods.

"Many, if not most, dog foods contain cereal grains as a part of the total formulation." From Dog Food, The Feds' Position. (FDA photograph by Daniel O'Toole)

For dogs, dry food products are easily accepted. Commercial products are generally well formulated. The crunchy texture of dry food is appealing to most dogs and helps to clean teeth. Dry food is also easily digestible and produces firm stools.

Owners who wish to switch from canned to dry food can usually do so easily by mixing the dry food with progressively smaller amounts of the canned food they are trying to phase out. Abrupt switches are possible, but may result in the first couple of meals being turned down. However, when really hungry, a dog will eat—and eat all its needs over about a twenty-minute period. Continued refusal could be a sign of illness.

Relatively new and popular are the semimoist pet foods, packaged in individual servings. Although some animals seem to thrive on them, others find them indigestible. These products often have a high percentage of sugar, and since some dogs do not easily tolerate sucrose, diarrhea or vomiting may result. For maintaining product stability and preventing spoilage in this special packaging, a variety of nonnutritive additives are required.

In choosing among moist, semimoist, or dry food, what's listed on the label should be the consumer's main guide. Here the shopper finds what percentage of protein, fat, fiber, and moisture are present; often ash and certain minerals are also part of the guaranteed analysis.

The presence of animal fat increases palatability for most dogs. Some owners whose pets have dry skin problems have found it beneficial to add one to two teaspoons of safflower or corn oil to the food. The advantage of the oil, as opposed to animal fat, is the presence of linoleic acid, which is essential for normal skin and coat development. Linoleic acid can also be purchased from pet stores in concentrated form.

Fiber provides some bulk and is usually present naturally in small amounts—around 5 percent for pet food.

Many, if not most, dog foods contain cereal grains as a part of the total formulation. These, like their all-meat counterparts, may also qualify as "complete and balanced" dog food rations.

One term consumers often misunderstand is "ash," which is really mineral content. It came to be listed as ash because, when the food is tested for the percentage of minerals present, it is baked at high temperatures, and what is left—the ash—is the mineral content, which does not burn up.

Calcium and phosphorus are the major nutrient minerals present in ash, and may also be listed in the guaranteed analysis.

On ingredient listings the consumer's best bet is to look for a wide variety of ingredients. Although one may not recognize the value of some of them, variety itself can be an indication that a manufacturer has tried to round out the types of protein and fat sources and the vitamin and mineral content. Whatever is listed first is the ingredient most prevalent in the product; what is listed last is present in the smallest quantity. So the order of the listing helps to size up the product.

Grains, legumes, and meat and bone meal are important sources of a variety of nutrients; they usually appear first in the ingredient list of dog foods. Fats and dairy products formulated to be acceptable to the dogs are also of high value. No substance may be added that is not shown to be safe, and no indigenous substance may be present at levels ordinarily harmful to health.

Many dog owners today feel their dog needs a vitamin or mineral supplement besides his regular food. But when regular diets supply all the vitamins and minerals in amounts known to be needed by the animal, supplements are unnecessary. They can be harmful if overused unless food intake is low due to illness.

Edited and reprinted from HEW Publication No. (FDA) 76-2060 *written by Jane Heenan.*

Nutrient Requirements of Dogs ($4.75; Printing and Publishing Office, National Academy of Sciences, 2101 Constitution Avenue, N.W., Washington, D.C.). Statements on nutrient requirements are accompanied by descriptions of the common signs of deficiencies. The tables include nutrient requirement values that provide for adequate nutrition of both growing puppies and adult dogs. The report states as a "general belief" that "prolonged intake of high-protein diets can be harmful to dogs."

Trade publications include *Petfood Industry* (Garden State Building, Sea Isle City, NJ 08243) and *Pets/Supplies/Marketing* (1 East First Street, Duluth, MN 55802).

A Statistical Abstract of Dog Ownership in the U.S.A.

compiled by Richard Benjamin Romanof

The greatest percentage of dog owners is found in the Southeast, 21 percent, and the smallest in New England, 4 percent.

18 percent of families with three or more dogs have an annual income of less than $5,000, while only 10 percent of families owning three or more dogs have an income over $25,000.

92 percent of dog owners are whites and 8 percent are blacks or others.

45 percent of high school graduates own dogs, while 40 percent of college graduates are dog owners.

34 percent of childless households contain dogs, and 9 percent of families with children 12 to 17 own three or more dogs.

The lowest percent of dog ownership, 8, occurs in households in the $8-$10,000 range.

69 percent of one- or two-person households have no dogs, and 10 percent of five-or-over-person families own three or more dogs.

27 percent of single people and 50 percent of married people own dogs.

61 percent of women who read *Hustler* own dogs.

The most popular soap opera among women owning dogs is "The Young and the Restless."

32 percent of women owning three or more dogs watch "Happy Days."

Nearly five times as many women owning one dog are in the audience of "The Wonderful World of Disney" than are women owning three or more dogs.

Dogs in the South have more fleas, ticks, and mange than dogs in any other region. There are more dog owners there.

The favorite type of music of dog owners whose pets suffer from ticks is country music.

The favorite early-evening news show of people whose dogs suffer from mange is the NBC Nightly News.

Only .9 percent of owners of three or more dogs read *Rolling Stone* magazine.

Make of all this what you will.

From Target Group Index 77, published by Axiom Market Research Bureau, Inc., 420 Lexington Avenue, New York, NY 10017.

Dog Care in Brief

Succinctly presented common-sense information about food and water, grooming and handling, housing, health, the facts of life.

Dogs are individuals, and their food needs differ. A grown dog does well on one meal a day, while a puppy should have food more often. It is a good idea to feed on a regular schedule. Most commercially produced dog foods provide a balanced diet. Do not give your dog raw eggs, and do not give adult dogs milk. Do not give your dog any bones, such as chicken, which can splinter and lodge in the throat or digestive tract. Always have fresh water available.

Never pick up a dog by the legs, as this can cause serious injuries. Bathe the dog periodically and dry with a towel to prevent colds. Combing helps remove dirt particles, prevents hair balls, and distributes oil. Clip out mats and burrs. Make certain your dog does not have fleas or ticks, which can cause serious illnesses. All dogs need exercise.

Outdoor dogs need a warm house, free of drafts, as well as some shade. The doghouse should be elevated to keep out water and dampness. Never confine your dog where he cannot reach adequate shelter.

Puppies need shots to prevent infection, and these should be given soon after weaning. Watch for signs of illness or internal parasites, loss of appetite, lack of interest, rough, dull coat, or discharge from nose or eyes. Take the dog to a veterinarian when these occur. Many cities and counties have license, leash, and rabies vaccination laws. Know and obey these laws. Never dump or abandon a dog.

Millions of dogs are killed each year because they are unwanted. There are simply no homes for them. Do not let your dog contribute to this needless suffering. Have your female dog spayed and your male dog neutered. You will have a happier, better pet.

The Animal Protection Institute (P.O. Box 22505, Sacramento, CA 95822) provides a bookmark on which is stated this essential information.

Oster shears.

Advanced Animal Aids, 2924 Main Street, Dallas, TX 75226, makes beds, pads, and "apartments" (enclosed beds) for dogs in a variety of quilted, patchwork designs that are warm, practical, and exceptionally handsome.

The ultimate luxury—a doggy water bed from Johnson Pet-Dor, 8809½ Shirley Avenue, Northridge, CA 91324; also from Johnson, the Pet-Dor is available in a range of sizes.

Carrying cases from Alco, 601 West 26th Street, New York, NY 10021 are sturdily and attractively designed.

61

Car comfort for the dog who's often on the road making the show circuit or for the occasional weekend traveler, the Kennel-Aire crate (from Kennel-Aire, 725

North Snelling Avenue, St. Paul, MN 55104) and the Safari version (Safari Kennel Products, 51 Sullivan Street, Westwood, NJ 07675).

Most dog foods, like Milk-Bone biscuits, are available in supermarkets and grocery stores. Others, specifically formulated for particular nutritional needs and minimal waste, are available through suppliers of pet products.

For pamphlets available from Carnation write 5045 Wilshire Boulevard, Los Angeles, CA 90036; from Gaines, 250 North Street, White Plains, NY 10625.

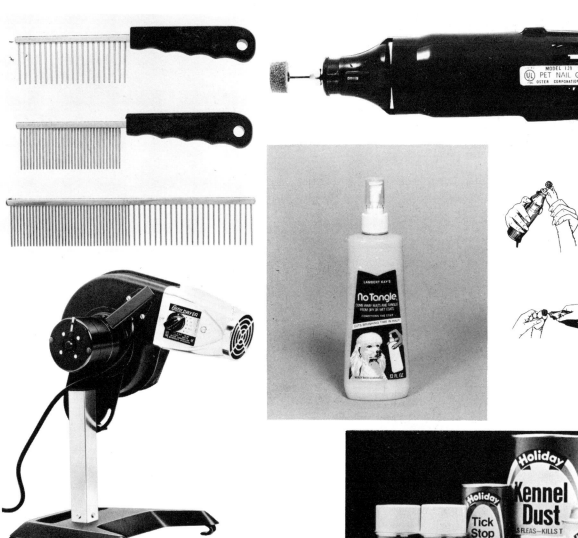

There are lots of things to help a dog feel fresh and smell sweet, including Lambert-Kay's No Tangle (767 Fifth Avenue, New York, NY 10022); a collection of external preparations including cologne from Holiday (Box 148, Topeka, KA 66601); hair dryer from Oster (5055 North Lydell Avenue, Milwaukee, WI 53217); and a nail groomer from Oster, plus a variety of combs from Safari.

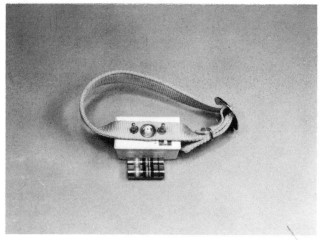

For noisy barkers, try a nonshocking collar that contains a tiny microphone sensitive to a dog's bark only. A buzzing vibration set off in the collar by the barking will distract the dog from whatever caused it to bark in the first place. From Thomas Instruments, 3750 Wheeling Street, Denver, CO 80240.

Dinner bowls—ceramic and plastic—can be simple or ornate. Toppet (Box 446, Richboro, PA 18954) and

Rubbermaid (147 Akron Road, Wooster, OH 44691) are representative.

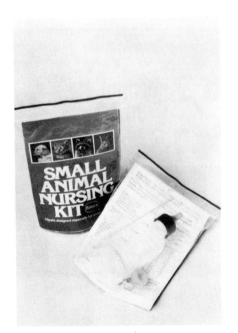
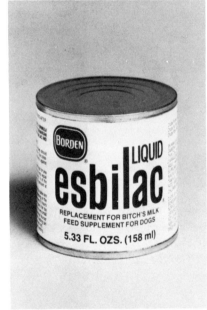

For the orphaned or rejected pup there's Borden's small animal nurser—bottles with specially designed nipples—and Esbilac, a replacement for bitch's milk. For later,

there's a special puppy weaning formula. Borden, 5100 Virginia Beach Boulevard, Norfolk, VA 23501.

There are mink coats and jewel-studded collars for dogs, but nothing quite so chic as Rufio's T-shirts from J. P. and Moonlight, Ltd., 101 West 12th Street, New York, NY 10011. Rufio, a miniature poodle, models Laura Nadworny's original exclusives designed especially for the canine physique. Rufio's T-shirts come in four sizes and range from reasonably warm to frivolous throw-ons. (Photograph by Jamison)

San-Away from NBS, Route 1, Huntsville, OH 43324, shown at left, helps to deal with waste.

There are many wholesalers of pet products that are available in stores and through catalogs.

The Model Label of 817 Harvard Ave., Sunnyside, CA 94087, makes an airy pallet for a dog to relax on. Whether or not it surpasses a water bed, it seems at least as appealing as a box spring and better, any day, than an old rug.

A SIMPLE KENNEL BED

The best kennel bed or rest for a dog is a square, wooden, traylike box, raised slightly from the floor by strips of wood nailed to the bottom.

In kennels that are open on one or more sides, something more than an open box is needed for shelter. In such cases the box should be a high one, fitted with a hole in front, to admit the dog, and a flat lid that, when closed, forms a bench upon which the dog can lie. The bottom of the entrance hole should be several inches from the bottom of the box, to keep the bedding from working out. Such a house within a covered run is a great comfort to a female with whelps, because the interior provides a warm nest for the puppies, while she can get out of their reach when they worry her too much by jumping onto the flat bench formed by the lid.

Edited and reprinted from *Country Life in America*, September 1909.

Death With Dignity

by Maxwell Riddle

The renowned dog writer and all-breed judge describes an inevitable end—in this case one that came with dignity, close to the hearth.

When she was about a year old, the big Great Dane, Nibs, had some terrible attack whose nature could not be certainly diagnosed. She suffered severe joint pain. If one tried to lift her head, she screamed in agony. She could not make her legs work in unison.

One veterinarian said she would die. Another said that, although he did not know what the illness was, he would try to save her life. He did, and she lived happily and without pain for five years.

However, she still lacked complete muscular coordination, and this occasionally put her back in the veterinary hospital. She liked the doctor but had to be dragged into his hospital.

Last week she returned to us very weak and with what could only be termed "bed sores." For a day or so she gained strength. Then the muscular trouble returned. She had great trouble rising, and even more trying to lie down.

Sunday she could not get up at all and she ignored food. It is amazingly difficult to get a hundred-and-fifty-pound dog to its feet. But we were able to do so twice, and to get her outdoors. But the second time she collapsed in the snow and seemed content to stay there.

We got her back into the living room and then tried to face our decision. One dare not make a decision on the basis of his own convenience, but upon questions of the dog's suffering and her chance to get well.

I called the veterinarian. At his end I could hear the Browns-Giants football game.

"Will you come after the game?"

When he came, he offered to help me move her to the barn, but I said no.

I sat on the floor and put her head in my lap, speaking gently and stroking her neck and ears, as the fluid was injected into the big leg vein.

Gradually the great head sank lower into my lap, and the neck muscles relaxed. Breathing stopped so gently it was hardly noticeable, but I continued to stroke her neck until the last body tremor had ceased.

Beneath the heavy snow the ground is unfrozen. Near the sheep pasture there's an area of briars and swamp, where dogs like to snuffle for rabbits. Generations of the dogs of Ryedale lie there. And now, Nibs.

Resting in Peace

Maxwell Riddle buried his dog in "an area of briars and swamp, where dogs like to snuffle for rabbits." For those who want a more formal setting, there are some four hundred canine cemeteries.

Hartsdale Canine Cemetery offers you complete interment services, including transporting your pet to the cemetery, attractive caskets, burial vaults, and a wide assortment of quality monuments, memorials, and headstones. Annual flower care is available, consisting of appropriate arrangements in spring, summer, and fall. Endowment plans for perpetual care are also available. These funds provide everlasting care for your pet's burial place. Should you have any questions or desire further information, please do not hesitate to call our office or visit our cemetery. Hartsdale Canine Cemetery, 75 North Central Park Avenue, Hartsdale, NY 10530—(914) 949-2583

It's easy to take a cheap shot at pet cemeteries. Yet when you consider that a dog is around for a dozen or so years, often as the most devoted and obvious of companions, then one shouldn't be surprised, shocked, or in anyway amused if that dog is mourned upon death and buried with what stands for honor in our society.

If you don't have a south forty or even a decent plot of ground to call your own (and your dog's), and if you're not scientifically oriented enough to give the carcass over to the veterinarian for autopsy, then you can usually take it to the local humane society for disposal.

There are more than four hundred pet cemeteries in the United States . . .

Or you can buy a grave site.

There are more than four hundred pet cemeteries in the United States, and while some are marginal operations, many are not. "America's First Animal Burial Ground" was established in 1896 in Hartsdale, N.Y. Interments there now start at about two hundred dollars. Among other notables, John Barrymore, Kate Smith, Gene Krupa, and Joe Garagiola have pets there.

The largest pet cemetery, opened in 1972, is the fifty-acre Bubbling Wells Pet Memorial Park overlooking the Napa Valley in California. It's divided into the Garden of Honor (for police dogs killed in the line of duty), the Garden of Gentle Giants (for St. Bernards and great Danes), and the Gardens of Companionship and Devotion. Bubbling Wells also has a "farm burial area" of mass graves containing over forty thousand animals.

At Hartsdale there is the War Dog Memorial in tribute to the dogs of World War I, and at the Bide-A-Wee Pet Memorial Park in Wantagh, N.Y., there is a memorial to Sarge, an army hero of the World War II K-9 Corps. Also at Wantagh is the cocker spaniel, Checkers, who once was so prominently mentioned on TV by a then Senator Richard M. Nixon.

Six out of ten American households own pets, and though only about 2 percent of these eventually reach a pet cemetery, animal graveyards scattered across the country are visited by a steady flow of people extending to dogs the rituals and ceremonies that make dealing with death possible for them.

AUTOMATED KENNEL, PATENT NUMBER 3,718,120

Modern Animal Care, Inc., of Fort Lee, New Jersey, has patented an automated kennel, called Inn the Dog House, that allows a single attendant working from a control panel to care for many dogs at the same time.

Each dog is housed in a fiberglass compartment, is given an outdoor run every day, and is directed back inside by cushioned arm panels. The compartments are automatically cleaned and supplied with fresh food and water and are under twenty-four-hour television observation.

AUTOMATIC DOG WASHER, PATENT 4,056,078

Handwashing may become a thing of the past for dogs, as it largely is now for cars. Clem and Antoinette Blafford of Brooklyn, New York, have figured out a patentable way to wash a dog automatically. The animal's body is placed in a compartment, where it is sprayed with soapy, then clean water. The head of the dog is not in the compartment and remains dry. A second enclosure then holds the dog's body while it is blown dry with heated air.

One thinks of the wax-extra when getting the car washed. Will there be a flea-rinse option?

Want to Get a Terrier to Chicago? A St. Bernard to Paris? Here's How

by Frank Filippelli

The manager of World Wide Pet Transport tells what his company will do and for what price—$627 for the St. Bernard.

To move a fox terrier from New York to Chicago, we would pick up the dog from his home on whatever day the owner wishes; board until the owner has relocated to Chicago; supply the required veterinary health certificate and veterinary rabies vaccination; supply a properly sized airline-approved travel kennel; arrange for a nonstop flight booking to Chicago; deliver to either JFK or LaGuardia Airport; and finally, meet the dog on arrival in Chicago and deliver him to his new home.

An estimate of the charges for such a trip:

Pick up from residence in New York	$25.
Two nights boarding @ $5.00 per night	10.
Veterinary health certificate	15.
Veterinary rabies vaccination	15.
One #200 travel kennel	31.
Delivery to JFK or LaGuardia Airport	25.
Airfare to Chicago, Ill.	30.
Transfer in Chicago from airport to residence	25.
Handling of all arrangements	15.
TOTAL	$191.

A St. Bernard going from San Francisco to Paris would fly nonstop to New York City, be met on arrival at JFK, boarded overnight and go on nonstop to Paris the next day.

An estimate for the St. Bernard:

Transfer dog from residence to San Francisco Airport	$ 25.
One #600 travel kennel	79.
Veterinary health certificate	15.
Veterinary rabies vaccination	15.
Airfare to New York City	120.
JFK Airport pickup	25.
One night boarding	8.
Delivery to JFK Airport	25.
Airfare to Paris, France	300.
Handling of all arrangements	15.
TOTAL	$627.

The above move would be a door-to-door service. The owner may obtain any part of our services or the complete move.

The owner may obtain any part of our services or the complete move.

All the airfare rates are established by either the actual weight of the dog and kennel combined or by the volume weight (dimensional size of kennel), whichever is greater. The rates do not vary from airline to airline.

World Wide moves about two thousand animals a year, purebreds, show champions, and pet mixed breeds among them.

PET MOVERS

World Wide Pet Transport
96-01 Metropolitan Avenue
Forest Hills, NY 11375

Flying Fur Pet Travel Service
310 South Michigan Avenue
Chicago, IL 60604

Pet Transportation Service
2239 Taraval Street
San Francisco, CA 94116

WINTERIZING

During a recent particularly bitter winter, dog clothing—long an optional item of fashion—became de rigueur in the minds of many owners.

Not only was the cold to be feared, but irritation in the form of dog skin acne was caused by rock salt thrown on roads and walkways to dissolve the seemingly omnipresent ice.

Sales in dog garments for inclement weather boomed: water-repellent, pile-lined coats in New York City ... matching sweater-coat-boot sets in Virginia ... fleeced-filled denim coats in Connecticut ... rhinestone-studded pet sweaters in Michigan.

But as every mother knows, the presence of a warm, heavy coat doesn't assure the absence of the common cold. In this case, what's true for children is true for dogs.

To bring relief to suffering dogs, a veterinarian in Rochester, N.Y., resorted to prescribing decongestants—his favorite being Contac capsules. We wouldn't give anything like that, though, to a dog without consulting our veterinarian first.

They'll Get It for You Wholesale, or Mail Order Is Best

by Georgia Kufeld

Almost everything a dog could ever require or desire—from toys to medications—is pictured, described, and priced in catalogs that are available for the asking. Some companies accept phone orders and credit cards. All ship nationally and internationally.

The Dog's Outfitter, Inc., is a wholesale distributor and sells to the professionals in dogs only by mail order. We do not sell retail at all, but of course we will welcome anybody's business as long as it conforms to our catalog shipping terms, which are basically wholesale terms.

In the business of pet supplies there is a curious middle area that is neither wholesale nor retail but is called professional. Breeders, exhibitors, handlers, groomers, vets, trainers, etc., are all considered professionals, and our catalog gives them this price structure although some items are priced at the dealer's wholesale price and some items are priced below the dealer's wholesale.

Georgia Kufeld, president of the Dog's Outfitter, a mail order pet products supplier.

In a letter to the editor from Georgia Kufeld, President, The Dog's Outfitter, Inc., Box 509, Glen Cove, NY 11542, no phone orders, mail order only.

Good catalogs are also available from: The Kennel Vet Corporation, Box 68, Uniondale, NY 11553 (516) 292-0430; Animal Specialties, Box 531, Camden, NJ 08101 (800) 257-8351.

Traveling with your pet, rather than shipping it, can be delightful if you know what to expect. Some airlines and steamship companies provide helpful literature, including interstate and international health, quarantine, and inoculation requirements. Three excellent do-it-yourself guides are Touring with Towser *from the Gaines Dog Research Center, 250 North Street, White Plains, NY 10625;* Have Dog, Will Travel *from Nabisco, East Hanover, NJ 07936; and* Travelling with Your Pet *from the ASPCA, 441 East 92nd Street, New York, NY 10028, which operates an Animalport at Kennedy International Airport, catering exclusively to animal air travellers.*

69

Photograph by Peter Simon

5

DOG NEWS & WORLD REPORT

INTERNATIONAL ROUNDUP

AN ALMOST EXTINCT BREED:
THE CHOLLIWOCH
by Frederick Franck

FORTY MEMORABLE MORSELS &
TOUCHING TIDBITS
by Richard Benjamin Romanof

THE CHINESE SHAR-PEI—HEIR
TO THE PEKINGESE? THE
CHOW?
by E. T. Linn

WIREHAIRS AND NONWHITES,
NORWAY'S PUFFIN DOG,
HUNGARY'S NINE
INDIGENOUS BREEDS, AND
THE SOCIÉTÉ CANINE
DE MONACO

THE FRENCH TAKE THEIR DOGS
EVERYWHERE—AND
SERIOUSLY

DOGS OF EUROPE—Personal Report
by Maggie McCall

CLOSE ENCOUNTERS

THE FAMOUS: DOGS & PEOPLE

IMPORTED DOGS
Letter from the AKC

NOTES FROM THE WHITE HOUSE

A survey of dog matters which includes these items: Italy—free dog bones from butcher shops; Great Britain—members of Parliament race a greyhound; Monaco—whiskers and ears left untrimmed; Japan—foundation prays for departed animals; Taiwan—fragrant meat eaten; South Africa—plan to slaughter dogs for fur coats stopped; Northern Ireland—blasts caused canine neurosis; Soviet Union—three-dog limit; and Germany—in Gergweis dachshunds outnumber humans.

The Fédération Cynologique International, in Thuin, Belgium, is the controlling body of some of the world's most important kennel clubs in such countries as India, Peru, Japan, the Union of South Africa, Cuba, Monaco, Mexico, Poland, and Chile, as well as clubs in most western European countries. Though the American Kennel Club is not a member of the Federation, it recognizes many of the same clubs for purposes of registration in the United States of imported, purebred dogs.

(For information about how to register an imported dog contact the American Kennel Club, Foreign Registration Desk, 51 Madison Avenue, New York, NY 10010. And see the pamphlet *AKC Special Registry Services*.)

As national political and social characteristics vary amazingly, so, too, do attitudes about, and regulations concerning, dogs.

Japan

In 1969 Mrs. Richard Haeberle, Jr., an American breeder and exhibitor of boxers, was the first woman in Japanese dog-show history to act as a judge, and there's been only one other since. Mrs. Haeberle returned to Japan at the invitation of the Tokyo Kennel Club in 1977 to evaluate 140 dogs in the Boxer Club of Tokyo specialty. "The congenial attitude of the boxer enthusiasts toward each other was commendable," she said. "No apparent tension, dissension or envy was evident," something that can't always be said of Americans in the "doggy business." There are dog handlers in Japan, Mrs. Haeberle went on to explain, but very few large kennels. The show boxers are principally house dogs. "Their quality and condition of coat were excellent and their feet were to be envied—just beautiful. The ears are chopped much later (between three and four months) in Japan than our boxers, and they're done extremely well. As any breeder knows, care of the ears after they've been cut is of utmost importance. The Japanese are very precise people." The boxer ranks tenth among popular breeds in Japan. The Pomeranian is first. Japanese prefer miniature dogs in white to all others.

In 1972 the Tama Dog and Cat Memorial Park of Tokyo announced completion of its new two-story memorial building, in which the ashes of pets and their owners could rest together forever. The cemetery, operated by Jikeiin, a Buddhist foundation set up to offer prayers for the souls of departed animals, was said to be the first such service offered anywhere in the world.

Taiwan

In the same year, 1972, an intense debate raged in Taiwan over the sensitive subject of "fragrant meat," the standard euphemism there for edible dog. Enthusiastic devotees maintain it is an unparalleled cold weather tonic (it's eaten mostly in winter) and a restorer of sexual vigor.

Eating dog has always been common in Taiwan, especially among those of Cantonese origin, but one had to patronize small, back-alley establishments that were illegal because they relied primarily on dognappers for supplies. The public debate began when the first full-size "fragrant meat" restaurant opened on a major thoroughfare and displayed large, prominent signs advertising its speciality. The restaurant's owners maintained their own "ranch" with a licensed staff veterinarian and had hopes of exporting canned dog meat to other areas of Asia. (In Hong Kong, where there are few strays, dognapping has been a problem. There the dog is often valued more for its gastronomical qualities than for its companionable personality.)

Under the headline LET THEM EAT SNAKE (which they do, too) an English-language Taiwanese newspaper ranted against the sale of dog meat as offensive to pet owners while the restaurant's manager insisted, from personal experience, that dog meat was effective as a tonic for the elderly, as an aid to relief from stomach trouble and rheumatism, and as a great "body warmer" in winter. He did concede, though, that dog meat's efficacy as a stimulant to sexual potency might simply be a superstition.

Dog meat was a common food throughout ancient China and is still highly regarded in modern times, especially in the South. A story is told, supposedly true, about Li Huang-chang, an eminent nineteenth-century Chinese official who, on a visit to London, was presented with a prize pedigreed dog. A few days later Viceroy Li's hosts received the following note.

"As I am advanced in age I usually take little food. Therefore, I have only been able to take a very small portion of your delicious meat, which indeed has given me great gratification."

South Africa

"I love dogs," said a Johannesburg resident. "I just want to make better use of them." Kennel clubs and the SPCA of South Africa rushed to prepare petitions as disbelief turned to horror. A Mr. Smit planned to breed and slaughter dogs to make fur coats.

Northern Ireland

The pet dogs of Belfast, Northern Ireland, showed all the signs of nervous strain that the people were feeling as years of constant explosions took their toll. Dogs often ran away in panic or were deserted as people left home in haste because of terrorist activity. The Ulster Society for the Prevention of Cruelty to Animals reported a significant increase in the number of strays received during periods of violence. Though the most disturbed dogs were sedated once they reached the shelter, many continued to be nervous, cringing at the slightest sound, or vicious and unmanageable from fear.

Italy

Sometimes, on the Festival Day of St. Francis of Assisi, the patron of small animals, stray dogs romp free in Rome spared, temporarily, from the dog-catcher's snare. The Society for the Protection of Animals will arrange a festival meal of tripe for the cats, who for generations have inhabited the Colosseum, the Forum, and other historical ruins while veterinary patrols promote free bones for dogs from butcher shops.

Great Britain

In England, while Member of Parliament Clement Freud, a grandson of Sigmund, hawked dog food on the telly with a baleful bloodhound called Henry, seven other MPs jointly owned a racing greyhound.

Conservative Godfrey Langdon said, "Whether he wins or loses he will give us valuable experience in the greyhound world that will be useful in discussing the subject in the House of Commons."

The dog, named Back-Bencher, won four out of six starts.

When Scotland Yard's Commissioner ordered British policemen to stop seeking new homes for the dogs and cats of people they had sent to prison, the Chairman of Britain's Canine Defense League threatened to invoke an 1867 law prescribing six months in jail for anyone maliciously harming an animal. The law would be invoked against policemen or the Commissioner himself if necessary, the Defense League announced.

Monaco

Mrs. Rose Radel of New Jersey, the owner of miniature pinscher Champion Repeage's Toma, was the only person to take her dog to Europe to campaign in the summer of 1977. Upon her return she said:

"Dogs were allowed everywhere—in buses, in the parks, shops and restaurants where they were delighted to have them. . . . Benching in Monte Carlo is absolutely magnificent: the setting is a lovely formal garden bordering on the sea. Colorful slender ribbons were distributed to be worn by the exhibitors or on the dogs' leads, and we received written evaluations from the judges in San Remo and Nice. . . . Professional handlers are practically nonexistent there, and most people show their own dogs. Exhibiting is casual, and there's no trimming of whiskers or cleaning up ears on miniature pinschers.

"We were greeted by a bouquet of roses from Princess Antoinette of Monaco," Mrs. Radel went on to say. "Princess Antoinette has miniature pinschers, vizslas, Canaan dogs, and pharaoh hounds in her kennels." (See the index for information about rare breeds, including Canaan dogs and pharaoh hounds.)

Soviet Union

The Russians have vigorous requirements in their dog sport. In trials for working dogs, for example, both dogs and men are expected to run a course the size of three football fields, clear hurdles, scramble over high walls, climb up and down staircases, and otherwise comport themselves as if they were boots in the United States Marine Corps.

And becoming a judge in the Soviet Union is no snap either, according to Pamela Cole of New York, whose mother is a judge in the United States.

To apply for a license there, one must have trained and shown at least three dogs in both conformation and obedience and must have studied for one year by attending lectures and receiving instruction from senior judges. If approved, one spends another year in actual ring work as an apprentice. Only then is one named a junior arbiter.

For a dog to be designated a champion, it must excel at "work"—obedience diplomas are required for German shepherds, field trials for gun dogs, and even basic obedience for toy breeds (sometimes referred to as "room" or "decorative" dogs) before they are allowed to be shown in the conformation ring.

Ms. Cole attended a Moscow Kennel Club Show (there are five official regional clubs in the U.S.S.R. which honor each other's registrations) and reported all the dogs she saw to be in top condition and well-fed. The standard daily diet for an adult German shepherd was one pound of meat, one of fish, a half-pound of cottage cheese, an egg, porridge, and macaroni. A dog-food industry does not seem to have taken hold in Russia.

Dogs are popular and allowed in all housing in the Soviet Union, though city families are restricted to no more than three. Breeding is strictly controlled. Breed club members meet periodically with geneticists, who plot out breeding programs for the coming year. Besides breeds shown in the West, a visitor to Russia will see several small native breeds similar to the toys and larger, uniquely Russian breeds such as the West Siberian laiker (which means "barker"), the Estonian greyhound, and the Charney terrier, a large, curly-haired dog developed from the crossbreeding of Airedale, Rottweiler, and giant schnauzer.

The AKC does not include the Soviet Union on its current list of recognized foreign registries, so these, or even the more familiar Soviet-bred varieties, won't be seen in the United States in the near future.

Germany

Not the case with the dachshund, though, which is among the ten most popular breeds in the United States. Dachshunds are exported in sizable numbers from Gergweis, a town ninety miles from Munich, which is referred to as the Dachshund Capital of the World. In Gergweis, where more than one thousand dachshunds outnumber the human population two to one, an enterprising innkeeper, in an effort to attract tourists, advertised "dachshunds per hour"—a free dog to walk around with during a stay in Gergweis. The same innkeeper also features dog beds in each guest room, and he will prepare a special menu for a guest's dog on request.

United States

Meanwhile, back in the U.S.A., the CIA is developing secret materials that could temporarily disable guard dogs at foreign embassies; the Shawmut First National Bank and Trust Company of Massachusetts is handing out dog biscuits to customers' pets at drive-in windows; the Jersey Shore Bank issues Lolli-pups to pups; and in 1977 the American Kennel Club elected a woman, Nan Aylings, to its board of directors. She had joined the AKC staff in 1949 as a registration clerk, and then worked her way up to become the first woman board member.

And finally, Max Donovan, an apparently normal New Yorker, supposedly worked for a Wall Street brokerage firm, received a salary, and paid bills and taxes. He turned out to be a schnauzer.

An Almost Extinct Breed: The Cholliwoch

by Frederick Franck

The personal involvement of a man with a marvelous and rare breed of dog—its acquisition, customs, eating habits, and social significance.

There he lies, stretched out on the pure, precious Bukhara rug I got out of Uncle Alfred's estate, watching me write.

Women fall for him instantly. He has gentle, melancholy eyes, sometimes with a glint of what one could mistake for humor. He is impressively male, weighs eighty pounds, and is superhirsute—brushy black coat with tan chest, belly, and eyebrows. I can't go anywhere without people stopping me:

"He *is* beautiful! What a dog! Never saw one like that! What kind of a dog is he?"

We have a certain standing in this town, and I intend to maintain it.

"He is a cholliwoch, Mrs. van Nostrand."

"Golliwog, huh? What is a golliwog?"

"No! Cholliwoch. It is Gaelic, guttural 'ch,' as in *chutzpah*! Cholliwo*ch*, see! Of course you've never seen one . . . a cholliwoch is an Orkney sheepdog. You know the Orkney Islands, northwest of Scotland? Well, that is the home of this kind of dog. He is probably the only one this side of the Atlantic."

"That's the kind of a dog I wouldn't mind having! I'm Scotch-Irish myself, on my mother's side. Must be expensive . . ."

"That's not it. Cholliwochs are quite rare, see, nearly extinct. Actually they can't be exported."

"So how did you? . . ."

"Well, that *is* a long story; if you want to hear the whole story . . ."

"Sure I want to hear the whole story. He *is* gorgeous! How did you get him?"

"To be frank, connections. It's not what you know, it's who you know, right? I always wanted a cholliwoch. And last year we got this Christmas card from friends in Scotland who have three of them. They happen to have a summer place in the Orkneys. I graduated from Edinburgh, you know, Royal College of Surgeons, so I have a lot of friends in Scotland. Oh, wait a minute, I happen to have the card in my pocket. Look! Here, you

Frederick Franck and Brush. (Photographs of Dr. Franck and Brush by Lukas Franck)

see, that is Ann and her husband Denys and their cholliwochs. . . . The guy on the steps is Sir Ian Mackenzie, you know, the Master of Hounds of the Musselboro hunt, with their third cholliwoch, Froufrou. She got the Grand Prix—'Meilleure Chienne' (Best Bitch) or 'Chienne Parfait' (Perfect Bitch)—at the Cannes Festival last year. So I dropped a line to Ann, you know, the Duchess of Musselboro (I hate to sound as if I'm name dropping), and there followed a lot of transatlantic calls, for she and Denys had a hard time with the Orkniks. They resented having one of their cholliwochs exported. Well, to cut a long story short, we went to get him at Kennedy just four weeks ago, him and a big crate of food besides. He is quite a gourmet.

"Now I want to tell you, I didn't realize it at the time, and, mind you, I am crazy about him and so is my wife, but there are some drawbacks to cholliwochs. They are worth the trouble, though, know what I mean?"

"What do you mean, there are drawbacks?"

"In the first place they have car-phobia. For the last four weeks we have been trying to get him into the car.

Matter of fact, Betty, all cholliwochs have that. On the island he comes from there is just one car, a very old Rolls, belongs to Derek, you know, the Earl of Sconekirk. So the dogs are not used to cars—crazy about buggy rides, though—and terrific on the moors for grouse shooting. In fact, they are the ideal dog for both town and country."

"That so? So what do you do about the car-phobia?"

"Well, as long as there is life there's hope, as we doctors say. For the time being we stay home a lot."

"And what are the other disadvantages?"

"They are not really disadvantages, just ethnic peculiarities. One is he doesn't bark when people come into the yard or even into the house. Ann wrote: 'They are a taciturn breed, and in that respect they are very much like all of us Scots.' And that is a fact. He only barks briefly, but very loud, when we go out, as if he wants to say: 'Is this trip necessary?' Helen and Otto, next door, say he stops barking very quickly, is no bother like that yapping son of a bitch across the road. 'Sure,' I say, not surprised! 'Our friend the Duchess calls cholliwochs "a taciturn breed." ' The other thing is the diet. That *is* a problem, but I am licking it! He only eats biscuits and haggis, you know."

"I don't know what haggis is, but dog biscuits you can get at any A & P."

"Well, let's take the biscuits first. I don't mean *dog* biscuits. He wouldn't even look at *dog* biscuits. He only eats MacVittie & Price Scottish Oatmeal Biscuits. That's why Ann sent a whole crateful! They *are* good biscuits, no question, and imitated a lot. Try them. They are ideal with cheese, especially Stilton."

"So, when you run out of those biscuits, what do you do?"

"No problem! No problem at all! You can get them at Bloomingdale's in the gourmet section and there is another shop on Madison Avenue, you know, a couple of blocks from Brooks Brothers. No, that is no problem, the haggis is the problem, or *was* a problem, I should say."

"What do you mean haggis? What the hell is haggis?"

"No, Betty, don't tell me you don't know what haggis is! Why, it is the national dish of Scotland! At the drop of a hat they feed you haggis—the better classes, I mean.

Brush, a cholliwoch.

The haggis is carried in on a huge silver dish by the cook or butler or whatever they have, and followed by this guy in kilts who plays the bagpipes! What is it made of? Sheep innards, it is made of! Sausagelike, but whitish."

"What does it taste like?"

"Now, how can you describe a taste? Very special. It does take getting used to, but by the time I graduated I really liked it. I am still crazy about it. It gives me nostalgia for Scotland."

"I thought you people were vegetarians."

"That's right, but at the time I hadn't been converted yet. But vegetarian or no vegetarian, try and find sheep innards in this town! But as you say, now we are vegetarians, and I've licked the problem. We are now making a very creditable mock-haggis out of tofu—you know, soybean curd. Sure! You get it in health food stores or in Chinatown. We eat it a lot. It's one hundred percent protein! It has practically no taste, but you spice it and you can give it any taste you like. So I make a mixture that tastes exactly like haggis. I don't want to bore you with the recipe in detail, but let me tell you he doesn't know the difference! He loves it! Has no idea it's not sheep innards! Now, excuse me! Gee, I am already late for my dentist's appointment. Give my best to the kids. Sorry I've got to run."

I always wanted a cholliwoch. . . . So I dropped a line to Ann. You know, the Duchess of Musselboro.

"With a diet problem like that I'd think twice about getting a cholliwoch. Still, if I ever see one in this country. You never know! There may be a couple around somewhere, who knows?"

"Funny you should say that. Before I run off I have to tell you that the day after he arrived at Kennedy, we passed the dog pound. You know Charley Brown, the vet? He works there, so we stopped in to make an appointment for his shots. So we walk into that animal shelter, as they call it, and what do I see? You could have knocked me down with a feather. In one of those cages next to some nasty kind of pregnant chihuahua-mutt—a cholliwoch!

" 'Where the hell did you find *that*, Charley?' I asked."

" 'Funny critter, huh?' said Charley. "They picked him up on the Turnpike, I guess. The perfect genetic riddle! Part shepherd, probably part Airedale, and a bit of collie. Maybe a pinch of schnauzer in him, too—who knows? But he doesn't want to eat nothing. Nothing! Tomorrow we'll put him to sleep."

" 'Dr. Brown,' I said firmly, 'this is a cholliwoch (*ch* as in *chutzpah*; it is Gaelic), and nobody here is going to put a cholliwoch to sleep!'

"So we paid two dollars and lifted him into the car. As soon as I got home I put through a call to Ann.

" 'Ann,' I said, 'this is an incredible story!' So I told her.

" 'Oh, I *am* so relieved, I am so relieved,' I heard her sigh across the Atlantic. Nobody sighs like Ann. 'You know, there is considerable unrest in the Orkneys. They accuse Denys of having spirited away one of the last male cholliwochs to America, of all places! It might cost him his political career. Oh, I am so relieved, Federico! Now be a dear and send the dog back immediately; be an angel, Federico! Just send him airmail collect. And could you add a short note of appreciation for lending you a cholliwoch for the Greater New York Dog Show? Yes, yes, do, on your own letterhead! That will be splendid. Thank you. Denys will be overjoyed! Tata!' "

Frederick Franck was born in Holland and holds doctorates in medicine, dentistry, and fine arts. He was for three years on the staff of Albert Schweitzer's legendary jungle hospital in Lambaréné. Besides a dog, he has a cat, eight chickens, ten doves, and two ducks.

Forty Memorable Morsels & Touching Tidbits

by Richard Benjamin Romanof

Journalists have long been fascinated by dogs. Here are some stories going back to 1902.

Dogs: Dangerous drunk. March 24, 1902.

Greyhound travels 1,500 miles from Montana to Oakland, California, to find its owner. February 7, 1906.

Forty-two spectators at dogfight, New York City, plead guilty. March 11, 1909.

Letter notes dog license is $2, marriage license is $1. Asks if dog is worth difference. January 22, 1910.

First arrest made under Montclair, New Jersey, law which forbids dogs to bark after 9 P.M. August 2, 1910.

Dog fanciers doubt as many rabid dogs exist as claimed by New York City Health Department: say dogs tagged as mad are merely thirsty. December 24, 1911.

Dog's crossed eyes straightened with glasses. April 30, 1926.

Germany called upon by France to replace 26,000 dogs stolen in war. December 17, 1919.

Newfoundland dog swims to shore with lifeline from stranded ship, and ninety-two passengers and crew are safely landed. December 17, 1919.

Lafayette College students asked to discontinue bringing dogs to classes. April 7, 1922.

Paris College of Psychiatry professor says dogs are insincere. January 25, 1924.

France—Shortage of wheat crop starts fight against the feeding of white bread to dogs. September 25, 1924.

Collie, sentenced to life imprisonment at Thorston prison, released on parole. October 27, 1924.

Texas boy found guilty of cruelty to a dog ordered by judge to write "Vest's Eulogy of a Dog" five hundred times. January 11, 1925.

...dogs tagged as mad are merely thirsty.

Paris police arrest gem thief who had trained dog to bite off anklets. February 23, 1925.

Flea-proof—Department of Agriculture finds dog that fleas will not stay on. June 7, 1925.

Berlin city fathers vote for increase of dog tax to support opera. September 3, 1925.

Irish setter rescues boy from sinking into quicksand in Park Avenue excavation. September 22, 1925.

Rags, war mascot, to enter show in 106th Infantry Armory, Brooklyn. October 9, 1925.

Rags denied entrance owing to uncertain pedigree. October 10, 1925.

Rags will have his own show at reunion of First Division. October 16, 1925.

Bond Street, London, opens beauty shops and rest rooms for dogs. December 29, 1925.

Dogs' right to bark at night goes to high court in Toulon, France. January 21, 1926.

Francie, black-and-tan pet, arrives from Paris clad in hooded cape with handkerchief and kid gloves; has complete wardrobe costing $4,000 yearly. March 25, 1926.

Canada—Price of huskies soars as result of failure of snow motors. February 14, 1926.

France—Dog bites tax assessor. Court upholds dog. May 2, 1926.

Premier Poincaré cheered for clemency to man who sent dead dog in diplomatic pouch. December 10, 1926.

Dogs permitted to ride in Paris motorbuses on payment of fare. January 12, 1927.

Poodle outruns BMT train from Canal Street to Queensboro Bridge Plaza. February 6, 1927.

Earl of Berkley unable to support pack costing $30,000 a year. October 27, 1927.

Dog barking into telephone brings rescue to woman when attacked by masked man. November 27, 1927.

Idaho team faces 150 miles hard sledding with medicine for boy. December 7, 1927.

Polish language quiets man's dog who had bitten three persons. January 8, 1928.

Train flagged by dog, saves owner when he is overcome on railroad track. February 1, 1928.

Dog swims eight hours in flooded cellar after fire. March 12, 1928.

Pomeranian in Seattle, threatened with operation to remove bark, is trained to keep quiet. April 10, 1928.

Divorced couple share custody of chow dog. September 29, 1928.

Fellow (dog) shows Columbia University psychology class he understands 400 words. November 11, 1928.

Ginger, double for Rin Tin Tin, dead. October 15, 1929.

Denmark forbids Pavlova's dog, Duke, to enter without a passport. April 21, 1930.

Edited and reprinted from the New York Times Index, *1902 to 1930.* © *The New York Times Company. Used with permission.*

The Chinese Shar-Pei— Heir to the Pekingese? The Chow?

by E. T. Linn

There are approximately seventy-five or so shar-pei in the U.S. The Linns have gotten in on the ground floor and are helping the breed to become known.

We became interested in the Chinese shar-pei after reading an article in *Dog Fancy* magazine in 1976. We were already breeding and showing Siberian huskies. After receiving more information and studying it, we decided we would like to add the shar-pei as our second breed.

The thought of getting in on the ground floor and helping the breed to become known was an exciting prospect.

We were not disappointed. The breed is a nice medium size, and the temperament is lovely. After living with the shar-peis for almost a year, we are even more sold on them.

They can be bouncing clowns or lovely, dignified companions. They are affectionate, yet the ideal watchdog. They are a loyal family dog. When strangers come, they sound the alarm and are ready to bark it up if need be. A simple reassurance from the family and they are calm again, ready to make friends. Their intelligence is outstanding, and they are very quick and eager to please.

Though of medium size, they are powerhouses. It is a very well-muscled breed, in spite of its wrinkled appearance. There are some shar-peis who retain their many wrinkles into adulthood, while others seem to grow into a lot of this extra skin. They all retain the wrinkles on the head and across their shoulders.

There are now approximately seventy-five or so of the breed in the United States. The majority are found on the West Coast, but many are appearing in the East now, where they are placed in the nonsporting group. In our opinion it is a working breed.

"We were not disappointed. The breed is a nice medium size and the temperament is lovely."—E. T. Linn speaking of the Chinese shar-pei.

The word *shar-pei* means "dog with a sandy coat." The breed existed for centuries in the southern provinces near the South China Sea; its origin is believed to be Dah Let in Kwun Tung Province. Ceramic statuettes and figurines modeled after shar-pei have been traced back to the Han Dynasty (206 B.C. to 220 A.D.).

The shar-pei has also been called the Chinese fighting dog, and about one in fifty were actually used for fighting in organized dog fights. If they did not demonstrate fighting or guarding ability early in life, they were slaughtered and eaten.

They can be bouncing clowns or lovely, dignified companions.

The breed almost became extinct after 1947, when Mao Tse-tung ordered all dogs destroyed. Their beautiful skin was made into ladies' coats, and their flesh was eaten by the very poor.

The first shar-pei imported into the United States was Jones Faigoo in 1966. His Chinese breeder was Chung Ching Ming. The first real effort to save the breed came in 1973, when an issue of *Dogs* magazine had an article and pictures from Matgo Law in Hong Kong, who pleaded for help to save the dog from extinction. "Who knows?" wrote Mr. Law. "If we can ship some of our dogs to your country, they may someday become as popular as the Pekingese or the chow. We can only hope." Over two hundred replies came in from interested Americans; however, there were very few dogs to import. Ernest Albright, one of the first to receive these dogs, immediately saw the potential of this breed and started an endless program of research, letter writing, and promotion.

The shar-pei come in colors of fawn, light fawn, cream, and black. Coat types are the very short, bristly, harsh horse coat and the brush coat, which is near one inch in length and stands off from the skin at ninety degrees over the wrinkles. There are three types of tails—the short, which almost looks as if it has been docked, the medium, and the long, which curls in a complete circle.

The skin is very loose with profuse wrinkles, especially on puppies. The skin tightens up over the lower half of the body as a pup matures, with full size being reached at six to eight months.

The tongue has the distinction of being either all blue-black or flowered, meaning one with spots of various sizes.

Because of the profuse skin above the eyes the dogs have to be watched closely for any turning or rolling in of eyelashes, which can irritate the cornea. But this condition is treatable with little effort.

The head displays a blunt muzzle, even more so in the males. Also, there is very little stop between nose and skull, and the head, observed directly from the front, reminds one of a hippopotamus or sea lion. The ears, small and triangular, lay tight to the head and point toward the eyes.

The average size is eighteen to twenty inches at the shoulder, with weight between forty to fifty pounds. Overall balance is very important.

Shar-pei puppies housebreak themselves at a very early age. Their average life-span in China is twelve to fourteen years, with the oldest known shar-pei living to be eighteen.

For more information write Linn's Chinese Shar-Pei, Route 6, Box 398, Asheville, NC 28803.

Wirehairs and Nonwhites, Norway's Puffin Dog, Hungary's Nine Indigenous Breeds, and the Société Canine de Monaco

In this, the age of the satellite-relayed telephone call, a letter of inquiry doesn't always get answered—advanced technology developing bad manners—but when a reply does arrive it is often of great interest. Here's what we've found out from distant places.

Our correspondent from the Union of South Africa, R. M. Murchie, reports that contrary to the differentiation in the United States, smooth fox terriers are much more populous than the wire variety—302 to 195 in 1977. Other designations are as carefully made. A breakdown of the staff of the Kennel Union of Southern Africa shows white people—eight women, one man—and nonwhite (all women)—one Asian, four Moslems, and six coloreds. It is further stated: "There is no racial discrimination of any kind in the Kennel Union."

The Norsk Kennel Klub has ten thousand members. Its director, Bjørn Stang reports that Norway is unique in breeding the lundehund, or puffin dog. Other breeds, raised for the hunting of hares, are the dunker, hygenhund, and haldenstøver.

The Magyar dog organization has some twenty-seven thousand members with fourteen training schools. There are nine breeds of Hungarian dogs recognized by the Fédération Cynologique Internationale.

From Budapest we learn: "Some of these breeds can be traced back to the animals the nomadic Magyars brought with them from Asia and Eastern Europe, when they settled the Carpathian basin about a thousand years ago. Our dog breeders export a great many of these nine breeds, mostly puli, komondor, and Hungarian vizslas."

The Norsk Kennel Klub has ten thousand members. . . . The Magyar dog organization . . . twenty-seven thousand.

The secretary of the Société Canine de Monaco writes, "We organize one big championship show a year with the national and international champion titles on offer. We coordinate the Société Canine Internationale de la Méditerranée (International Dog Week of the Mediterranean) during which are held a championship show at Nice (France) and one at San Remo (Italy) as well as our own. The three towns are at about a half hour's distance by car from each other so the week is a great success, attracting very good quality dogs from all over Europe with the possibility of achieving a championship faster than otherwise (three different countries, three different judges and so on)."

A DIVING DOG

A canal boat captain, P. H. Hanley, has one of the most remarkable dogs in the state. He is extremely fond of being in the water and is a noted diver, as evidenced from the following account.

A piece of wood and a piece of iron tied together were thrown overboard and to them was attached a nineteen-foot line with which to haul up the dog when he had recovered the articles. He gathered himself up in the style of a man or a frog when entering the water, and after being under for a long time appeared with the wood and iron in his mouth and was hauled on board the boat, hanging by his teeth to the wood attached to the rope. He has only one known rival at this business, the latter being a Newfoundland dog owned at Verplanck's Point on the Hudson. Hanley's dog is a brindle bulldog.

Edited and reprinted from the *Ellenville* (New York) *Journal*, July 1878.

The French Take Their Dogs Everywhere—and Seriously

The French, as might be expected, are a special case. Not always friendly to human outlanders, they go out of their way to give the silver-service treatment to dogs.

Until 1974, when passenger, and consequently pet, service was discontinued on the *Paquebot France*, a dog crossing the Atlantic could spend time in one of thirty-two carpeted, stainless-steel kennels that were set on the sun deck's port side. There were exercise runs decorated with lampposts and fire hydrants and special elegant menus printed for "M. and Mlle. Chien."

Now, except for a select small number of small dogs that may be carried in the passenger cabins, it's the bag-

Dog at lunch in Paris. (Photograph by Ellen Count)

gage hold of an Air France jet, the only amenity of which seems to be pressurization.

The dog who used to travel *on* the *France* could make its way *through* France with the help of the Guide Mi-Chien, a directory of hotels and restaurants that warmly welcome canines. This is a more civilized approach than that taken by the Guide Michelen, which only indicates establishments that will not accept dogs with a drawing of a dog's head with a slash through it, an unpleasant way to tell the tale.

But most hotels and restaurants in France do accept dogs. Rarely, while dining, one sees a dog, lap-held, sharing its master's meal. Usually dogs sit polite and quiet beneath tables, enjoying occasional nibbles passed from above and sips of water from pretty bowls always set on saucers, sometimes even on lace doilies, by accommodating restaurateurs.

Some hotels ask a small nightly fee for dogs, but most allow them to stay with their masters at no charge. The legendary Paris Ritz, a bastion of comfort and luxury, provides cashmere blankets for guests' pets.

Dogs are seen everywhere in France—at museums and galleries, supermarkets and movies, at hairdressers and dentists, and also at church.

IN DOG FANCY, EVEN THE WRITERS HAVE A CLUB

The Dog Writers' Association of America, Inc., was founded in 1935. Today, it includes one hundred and eighty writers spread across the United States—newspaper columnists, authors of dog books, dog book publishers and editors, magazine publishers and editors, and freelance professional writers. A yearly competition for excellence in dog writing results in awards presented at an annual banquet held in New York City over the Westminster Kennel Club weekend in February.

The Association also sponsors the Dog Writers' Educational Trust, which gives scholarship grants to worthy young people who desire to further their education in professions that are dog-oriented, such as veterinary medicine and animal husbandry.

The secretary of both organizations is Mrs. Sara Futh, Kinney Hill Road, Washington Depot, CT 06794; president is John T. Marvin of 3 Blythewood Road, Doylestown, PA 18901.

Dogs of Europe—Personal Report

by Maggie McCall

A look at the Continent and at Great Britain reinforces some stereotypes and comes up with a few surprises.

The largest dog show in the world, Cruft's, takes place in London. Continental Europe, however, has been rapidly catching up in both breeding and ownership of dogs. If one used the star system to rate countries for dog interest and ownership, the cast would read, in order of primacy, England, West Germany, France, Italy, and the Benelux countries.

England is generally the number-one exporter of pedigreed bitches for breeding—almost every Yorkshire terrier bred in Germany has an English "mum"—and the high standard of the English breeder keeps profits rolling in from this lucrative business.

England is the only country in Europe that demands a six-month quarantine for any dog entering the country. This includes the prize-winning pedigreed dog as well as the family mongrel, and the owner assumes all costs. The very excellent reason for this strict regulation is the fear of rabies, a disease that elsewhere has reached almost epidemic proportions in the last few years.

Leash laws seem to be strictly enforced in the large cities in England; the local law in small towns and villages seems to turn a blind eye when the neighborhood canine corps take a stroll along the green. Dogs are still used to herd sheep, and the greyhound is trained as a racing dog; among the most popular breeds are the Afghan, whippet, and poodle.

If you want to start a riot in Switzerland, drop four gum wrappers on the street and talk loudly. If they haven't taken you away by this time, let your dog off the leash.

According to one Member of Parliament there is more mail regarding animal protection (especially antivivisection) than on any other subject of national interest or importance.

Surprisingly, many Germans—having stereotyped themselves as disciplinarians—don't much train their dogs. For example, there is the great Dane who lives in the neighborhood. Six-foot-two on his hind legs, one hundred thirty pounds of friendly puppy, this Apollo of

dogdom is owned by a little old lady who *should* wear tennis shoes. The poor creature can be seen running the mile in ten, as she clings desperately to the heavy chain attached to the puppy. We suggested a Western-style saddle, with horn, but we don't think she heard us.

Germans take their dogs everywhere. It's the only place we've lived where we have to check the guest list for pets. We weren't aware of this practice when we dined at the local gasthaus and were a bit unnerved when we found the grandson of Rin Tin Tin seated on the floor at the next table. The dog was well behaved and quiet until some poodle puppy, high on sauerkraut and beer, slipped its leash and attacked. Within three seconds we were overrun with dogs—from under the tables came cockers, dachshunds, and assorted mongrels. Peace was eventually restored, but eating out in Germany has never been the same for us since.

The most beloved dog in Germany is the German shepherd; the most currently popular is the Yorkshire terrier; however, lack of space for the shepherd and high cost for the Yorkshire keep their numbers down. The poodle, dachshund, and the cocker are the top sellers.

Germans generally prefer pedigreed dogs to mongrels and purchase directly from a breeder. The pet shops and independent animal farms (not breeders) have been criticized for selling sick animals for very good profit and have been exposed in the country's largest-selling magazine.

Owning a dog in Germany can be expensive. In addition to purchase price, food, grooming, shots, and general paraphernalia, the license costs thirty-five dollars a year and the bite insurance another forty-five dollars annually. There is no quarantine law, but all dogs entering Germany—and all the other European countries—must have proof of shots against rabies and distemper.

There are laws, however, regarding how much space you must have in your home before you are allowed to own a large animal. Leash laws are strict in reverse order to the laws in England. One does see loose dogs in the city, but if a dog is loose in the woods—even if the owner is in the area—the dog may be legally shot by the forest master. There is really no public park, wood, or beach where dogs are legally permitted off leash, so most Germans join clubs and train and exercise their animals on the club premises.

Many of the larger breeds are trained as guard dogs, but these local clubs also train in general obedience and for shows. Guide dogs are trained in special centers throughout the country; so far these centers have not started training for the deaf, but it is fairly certain they will as soon as the American programs get into full swing.

The French follow close on the heels of the Germans, but prefer the smaller breeds.

Italy breeds one of the finest boxers in the world, along with the lesser known Mastino Napolitano. Dog ownership in Italy is confined to the upper-middle and high-income groups. This is true in Spain, too, which is famous for its prizewinning poodles. Both these countries are fairly lax on leash laws—except in the high-income areas—and one sees many muzzled animals.

The Italians still enjoy the promenade, and they are such spiffy dressers and amusing talkers that a favorite pastime is people-watching at an outdoor café. Rome's Via Veneto is a lively spot. One day we picked a good seat, ordered, and were soon treated to one of the most hilarious episodes outside of a Chaplin rerun. Walking toward us was an elegantly turned-out man, just about five feet tall, swathed in Gucci, Pucci, silk, mohair, and glove leather. He was walking a magnificent, haughty Afghan almost as tall as he was.

Traffic in Italy is always hectic, but lunch-hour traffic is quadraphonic cacophony. The cars got a bit tangled and had to slow down—in Italy this is a signal for every driver to lean on his horn. Every driver did, and the Afghan went wild. She shot up in the air, pulled at the leash, quivered, completely lost all her previous sangfroid, and collapsed at her master's feet. He had strong words for the offending honkers and not less than fourteen significant gestures. Then he bent down and attempted to lift Her Majesty. He spoke passionately to her, attempting to convince her that those filthy cars would never come near her. Eventually, when he did manage to lift her into his arms, she was deadweight. The poor short fellow staggered down the street, arms outstretched, with half an Afghan on the port side and half on the starboard. One needs very little money for entertainment in Italy.

There are few breeds of dogs that strike terror in the hearts of grown men like the Doberman. I've known Dobermans that really suffered emotionally as a result of people running in fright as they neared. Most Doberman owners contend this is the direct result of the Hollywood wartime propaganda films and demand their day in court. The British Doberman, however, doesn't have this problem. If clothes make the man, it is possible that ears make the dog (fierce). The British don't allow ear cropping, so Dobermans, with lovely flopping ears become, if not altogether sweet looking, at least approachable.

The Swiss are orderly people . . . their houses are orderly, their children are orderly, their streets, their bank accounts and their dogs are orderly. If you want to start a riot in Switzerland, drop four gum wrappers on the street and talk loudly. If they haven't taken you away by this time, let your dog off the leash.

We were resting our tourist feet in a park in Zurich one very hot afternoon when we heard a woman scream. In any other country this could mean rape or robbery. In this case her large German shepherd had slipped his leash and took off in a wild dash for the ornamental fountain. He jumped in, executed some of the fancier Olympic free-style strokes, drank half the fountain dry, and avoided any attempts to remove him by the simple dog-expedient of shaking his wet coat at approaching strangers. I was really thrilled to be a witness at what was probably the most disorderly act performed in Switzerland during this century.

The small Benelux countries—Belgium, Holland, and Luxemburg—are keen on the large breeds such as St. Bernard, standard poodle, Picard, and the Belgian shepherd. The paperwork involved in importing a dog to Belgium can be a very complicated and teeth-gritting experience.

The dog salons all over Europe are big business, as are the manufacturers of dog clothes, leashes, toys, beds, foods, and the thousand and one things that pampered pets seem to require to maintain proper social status. Unfortunately, Europeans have never bothered about "curbing" their dogs, and you walk the streets at your own risk.

For the most part, the dogs of Europe are pampered, protected pets and status symbols.

Maggie McCall is a consumer affairs writer for Off Duty *magazine in Frankfurt, Germany. She is a former reporter for the* San Francisco Chronicle.

Close Encounters

At the Bar del Lupo in Civitella Alfedena, a village at the edge of the quarter-million-acre Abruzzo National Park, just ninety miles east of Rome, one can sip an apéritif and watch a half-dozen or so wild wolves move, aloof and beautiful, through a five-acre fenced enclosure.

These wolves are among the last of their species—there are about fifteen Apennine wolves in the Parco Nazionale d'Abruzzo, about one hundred in all of Italy—which the government is trying to protect and preserve.

It is hoped that the accessibility of beast to the view of man will engender a certain respect, if not actual affection, among the farmers and shepherds of the area, and that this will in turn ensure the wolf's survival in its natural habitat.

Not long ago anyone who killed a wolf would proudly display the pelt and accept the gratitude of his neighbors. Now the wolves are protected, and the Italian government provides an indemnity to farmers for livestock lost to them.

The Apennine is smaller and more delicately muzzled than other European wolves. There are reddish-brown highlights in its grey fur and a dark stripe running down each foreleg.

For information about the park and surrounding villages write to: Direzione; Parco Nazionale d'Abruzzo; Via Livorno, 15; 00162 Rome, Italy.

The Famous: Dogs & People

Humanizing effects of dogs on their masters and mistresses—specifically: Carl XVI Gustaf of Sweden, Franklin D. Roosevelt, Lyndon Baines Johnson, and the Dowager Duchess of Marlborough (née Gladys Deacon):

Not even a king can be irreligious. Carl XVI Gustaf of Sweden, even as you and I, walks his dog. (Swedish royalty is refreshingly unpretentious.) Thus a most remarkable event occurred one night in December 1976. The king's dog, a black Labrador named Ali, was sniffing along when he came upon an unconscious woman lying in the walkway. The king rushed the woman to shelter, sounded the alarm, and worked to revive her. The woman, a Chinese visitor to Sweden, recovered, and word of the episode spread throughout the world, as can be imagined. But, alas, all was not praise. It seems that Moslem leaders protested—Ali being a holy name and Moslems not being particularly fond of dogs anyway.

King Carl now calls his dog Charlie, and Sweden's supply of oil from the Near East is assured.

More famous than the King Carl–Ali/Charlie relationship was that which existed between President

---

THE BURTONS AND THEIR FOUR DOGS AT DOCKSIDE

The British six-month quarantine has been in effect for almost sixty years, causing hardship for innumerable visitors—but also keeping the British Isles one of those few places in the world free of the dread rabies disease. Among those not permitted to be with their dogs on British soil for the quarantine period were Richard Burton and Elizabeth Taylor. The year was 1968, and the then still-married couple managed to work in London making movies (he, *Where Eagles Dare;* she, *Secret Ceremony*) and still get to live with their dogs. No laws were violated.

By the simple expedient of spending a great deal of money—more than twenty-five hundred dollars a week—the Burtons lived on board a 120-foot, 200-ton white yacht at a dock in the Port of London with their two Pekingese and two Lhasa Apsos.

Franklin D. Roosevelt and a Scottie named Fala. The president was a picturesque figure with his flowing black cape, his jauntily set fedora, his long, thin cigarette holder, and his constant companion, Fala. Never before or after was there a more dignified dog. Fala even came off well next to that other great showman of the time, Winston Churchill.

President Roosevelt was not above using Fala to advantage. During his fourth presidential campaign opposition leaders charged that a United States naval vessel had been sent to the Aleutian Islands to pick up Fala after a presidential trip there. (It was wartime.) Expressing indignation but not attempting to mask a slyly, humorous tone, the president retorted: "Republican leaders have not been content with attacks on me, or my wife, or my sons. No, not content with that, they now include my little dog, Fala. Well, of course, I don't resent attacks, and my family doesn't resent attacks, but Fala *does* resent them. . . ."

(Fala died in the spring of 1952—two days short of his twelfth birthday. He was mourned by millions.)

The king's dog, a black Labrador named Ali, was sniffing along when he came upon an unconscious woman lying in the walkway.

A president who had considerably less luck with his dog-related public image was Lyndon Baines Johnson. LBJ, who was reported to love dogs, made the mistake of pulling the ears of one of his beagles in public. Traphes Bryant, presidential kennel keeper, related the incident in his book *Dog Days at the White House* (New York: Macmillan Publishing Co., Inc., 1975):

> Yes, I was there the day the president picked up his little beagle, Him, by the ears. . . . What the president was trying to do was please the photographers by getting the dogs to do a trick. [There were two beagles, Him and Her.] Lyndon Johnson was such a tall man he had to bend way over even to get near a beagle. So he was bending over and just took hold of Him by the most convenient handle, his ears, probably thinking of some Texas story about a farmer lifting his dog that way. Even when he heard the yelps, the president didn't realize that anything was wrong. He just matter-of-factly explained that pulling their ears was good for the dogs, and that everyone who knew dogs liked to hear them yelp.
>
> What the president didn't remember, or know, is that you can only try this lift-'em-by-the-ears trick with a puppy. Old-time farmers and hunters start to pick up a pup by the ears and if it yelps, they stop and pick up one that doesn't. Puppies are light, but grown dogs have more weight than their ears can comfortably support. . . .
>
> After LBJ's goof, the White House was flooded with mail. Some defended the president, most condemned him. Reporters around the world were going to dog experts to poll their opinions on beagle ear-pulling. Veterinarians were anti-president on the matter. So were the National Beagle Club, the American Kennel Club and the American Society for the Prevention of Cruelty to Animals.

The glittering world of aristocracy, immense wealth, fame—even notoriety—doesn't mean much to dogs. When, as is sometimes the case, that world palls in its splendor, it can be dogs (and sometimes cats) that seem to have lasting value, seem to be satisfying where all else has failed.

An illustrious example of all this was the Dowager Duchess of Marlborough, who spent the last four decades of her life living simply in an old-fashioned farmhouse surrounded by dozens of Blenheim spaniels in the Oxfordshire village of Mixbury. The duchess might have given up a lot in her removal from society, but not one of the glorious ties to the Marlborough past. It is Blenheim spaniels that appear in those famous Gainsborough portraits of the Marlborough family.

Incidentally, the duchess, who died at the age of ninety-six, was a great beauty in her time and before her marriage at the age of forty the rage of La Belle Epoque. She was intimately involved with the artists Edgar Degas and Auguste Rodin, the writer Anatole France, and the poet Rainer Maria Rilke. Marcel Proust said of her, "I never saw a girl with such beauty, such magnificence, such goodness and charm." Prince Wilhelm of Germany lost his heart to the woman born Gladys Deacon. The prince gave her a ring from the crown jewel collection, and it was his father, the Kaiser himself, who intervened to get it back.

Yet in the long autumn of her discontent—estranged from her husband—it was those Blenheim spaniels that gave her comfort.

A FABLE OF AESOP— KNOW YOUR LIMITATIONS

A man owned a Maltese spaniel and an ass. He made a habit of playing with the dog, and whenever he dined out, he used to bring back something to give it when it came and fawned on him. The ass was jealous, and one day it ran up to its master and frisked around. The master received a kick that made him so angry that he told his servants to drive the ass off with blows and tie it to its manger.

Nature has not endowed us all with the same powers. There are things that some of us cannot do.

Old English bulldogge being recreated by David Leavitt, who uses old print as his standard. (Photographs by David Leavitt)

Imported Dogs

Letter from the AKC

How the club handles the accrediting of pedigrees of a foreign registry body.

In our pamphlet entitled AKC Special Registry Services dealing with imported and domestic dogs, you will note our lists of registry organizations whose pedigrees may be acceptable in support of applications to register imported dogs in AKC's Stud Book, or to enroll an imported dog for breeding purposes only.

The accrediting of pedigrees of any foreign registry body is a matter that is determined by the AKC Board of Directors. Any action taken by our Board in this respect is based on a number of factors. One of the most important considerations is the availability to us of the published Stud Book records of the organization in question.

The official export pedigree certificates issued by most foreign registries are acceptable for dogs imported into the U.S. provided the pedigrees meet our requirements for completeness, and provided we have some knowledge of the registration practices of those registries.

In a letter to the editor from Marianne G. Goldstein, Manager, Foreign Registration Department, American Kennel Club.

Canaan dog. Also known as the pariah dog, and closely related to the Afghan, Ibizan, Saluki, and Basenji. (Photograph by Judith K. Ardine)

For information about this breed, write Greater Swiss Mountain Dog Club, Carinthia-R.3 6210N 700E, Lafayette, IN 47905. (Photograph by C. Adrian)

Notes from the White House

An illustrated account mentioning Amy, Grits, Benji, Sandy, and JB, plus the ubiquitous sniffer shepherds.

Not all visitors to the White House are the two-legged kind. This last year the president's daughter, Amy, and her friendly dog, Grits, have been host and hostess to Benji the Wonder Dog and Sandy, who works in *Annie,* as well as a few VIP dogs that have distinguished themselves in sports, such as Frisbee-playing and obedience.

If Mrs. Carter is known as the First Lady and Amy is known as the First Child, it would follow that Grits would be known as the First Dog.

Sandy came from an animal shelter in Connecticut. Saved by the bell. He has an understudy, Arf, in case he misses a curtain call. Both Sandy and Benji were big hits when they visited the White House. They would be invited back anytime, with or without handlers.

Chip and Caryn Carter have a black dog named JB. We do not know what JB stands for.

There are a couple of bomb-sniffer shepherds here with the Executive Protection police. They wear identification tags with name and picture just like human staff members. This is the first time dogs have been on the police staff at the White House, and just like the Secret Service, they are members of the Treasury Department.

The Dalmatian, a dog of reserved temperament, was once seen with roving bands of Romany gypsies. The breed, whose origins trace back to Dalmatia, is best known as a coach dog—its speed, endurance, gait, and affinity for horses suiting it well. Called the English coach dog, plum pudding dog, and firehouse dog, the Dalmatian would clear the way for a high-riding, horse-drawn vehicle or run along under its axles. Dalmatians are born white, spot later, and require no clipping, docking, or cropping and little grooming.

6

SHOWING

THE FANCY

THE BEAUTIFUL ONES

THE HANDLERS

LOVING A DOG: A LITTLE
    SENTIMENT, A LOT OF SENSE
Book Review

THE WELL-GROOMED ONES ARE
    DOGS
by Red Smith

THE CORDED POODLE

ORGANIZING THE UNORGANIZED
by Ed Whitney

ONE MAN'S NEW BREED—
    BRINGING THE LITTLE LION
    DOG TO AMERICA
by Robert Yhlen

PORTUGUESE WATER DOG

HOW A NEW BREED ACHIEVES
    RECOGNITION
Note from the AKC

SHOWING PUREBRED DOGS
Book Reviews

The Fancy

"Collectively (usually with the), all those who pursue or are enthusiastic over, any particular act, practice, or amusement; also the object of their pursuit or attachment. . . . The fanciers of animals, esp. birds and dogs."

By permission. From *Webster's New International Dictionary* © 1959 by G. & C. Merriam Company, publishers of the Merriam-Webster dictionaries.

In all parts of the country, all year long, on every weekend there are dog shows. The attraction? Pleasant competition and an appreciation of good breeding. Here

Harold Goodman arrives at the Long Island Rare Breed Show with his Neapolitan mastiffs. (Photograph by Don Myrus)

The Beautiful Ones

The color and excitement of the dog sport as photographed at both the classic Westchester and the novel Long Island Rare Breed Association shows.

As Indian summer belies autumn's natural character, so occasionally in very late August or early September there occurs a day when the temperature falls, the wind blows briskly, the sky takes on a beautiful but ominous cast, and the leaves themselves seem to assume a golden hue. There is a tang in the air. October is previewed. It's grand to be outdoors and vigorous. One strides forth, breathing deeply.

On just such a day—Saturday, September 11, 1977—

the Westchester Kennel Club held its Sixtieth Annual Dog Show. If anything, the setting surpassed the weather. Lyndhurst is a sixty-seven-acre, nineteenth-century estate set on a bluff overlooking the Hudson at Tarrytown, New York, at that point where the river reveals itself to be the most majestic in North America. The last private owner of Lyndhurst was the robber baron and railroad magnate, Jay Gould. Now it is part of the Trust for Historic Preservation.

As the exhibition tents billowed in the breeze, their blue and gold stripes flashing, some three thousand dogs (3,247, to be exact) were showing before venerable judges, from 8 A.M. to 7 P.M. The dogs had been clipped and plucked, bathed and scented, brushed and combed —with hair spray and, some suspect, tint. They were among the very finest of pedigreed animals to be seen anywhere in the world.

And seen they were—by about ten thousand people

(no exact count for the humans). The spectators seemed mostly to be "just folks," not especially well groomed and certainly not of the preening sort. There were far more jeans than twill trousers and skirts; yet there were a number of participants who gave a certain cachet to the event—a sort of gentry elegant in the way of the rich who attend lawn parties. The spectacular was being held for the purpose of selecting the best dogs from among the very good . . . of breed, of group, and of the whole event itself, the last being that prize known as "Best in Show."

Among the AKC's 122 recognized breeds there is the rigid, large, shorthaired pointer; the fluffy, showy, little Pomeranian; the Irish wolfhound (tallest of the breeds), and the dachshund (long, smooth, or wirehaired). An amazing diversity, and possibly confusing to the first time dog-show visitor. But it takes no more than a good look at the show catalog and a few hours' observation to realize that what at first seems chaos and random rushing about is quite simply an orderly, categorized, ritualized beauty contest.

Soon after the grand Westchester affair, in a schoolyard a few hours' drive away, the Long Island Rare Breed Association held its Second Annual Match. Westchester was somewhat smart, even sophisticated. Un-

pretentious would best describe most of the exhibitors of the forty-five animals at the Long Island event.

Some of the dogs—Neapolitan mastiffs and American pit bull terriers—have a certain utilitarian attractiveness, since a frightening visage can certainly be useful to a fighter. One wouldn't want to meet a Swinford bandog in a dark alley, either. Others—the Australian shepherds, specifically—possess a beauty that one is quicker to accept: slender heads and long, slim bodies with flowing hair—the look of the collie.

Outside of this show world there are those creatures variously called mongrels, mutts, and curs—creatures about which there is ambivalence. George Bernard Shaw wrote: "I like a bit of a mongrel myself, whether it's a man or a dog; they're the best for every day."

Even dog fanciers recognize that the promiscuously mixed *can* be lively and also intelligent and beautiful— random chance having its benefits. The problem is in the word *can*. It is a truism among dog breeders to say that one is never certain what one will get in the most carefully controlled breeding situation, so why gamble further? Why pick a puppy mutt and never know, until perhaps too late, how it will grow up?

Obviously, prudent men and women don't take chances; they keep pedigrees.

All the spaniels, pointers, and setters come from the same progenitor, thought to have been Spanish. Spaniels were first separated into two groups —land and water. The land spaniels, depending on individual size, were called either cockers or springers. Cocker spaniels were the smallest members of a litter, good for hunting woodcock. The larger springers were used, as their name

indicates, to spring game for gunners. There are ten AKC-recognized spaniel breeds, though the Brittany spaniel is really a pointer and the Irish water spaniel is a retriever. Shown left, with the longer curtain, is the cocker spaniel; right, is an outstanding example of the English cocker spaniel.

Originated in the Sinai and developed in Afghanistan, the Afghan hound reached the U.S. in 1926 and gained popularity very slowly. Bred to hunt leopards and to course rabbits and gazelle in mountainous terrain, the breed today is an unequaled hurdle racer.

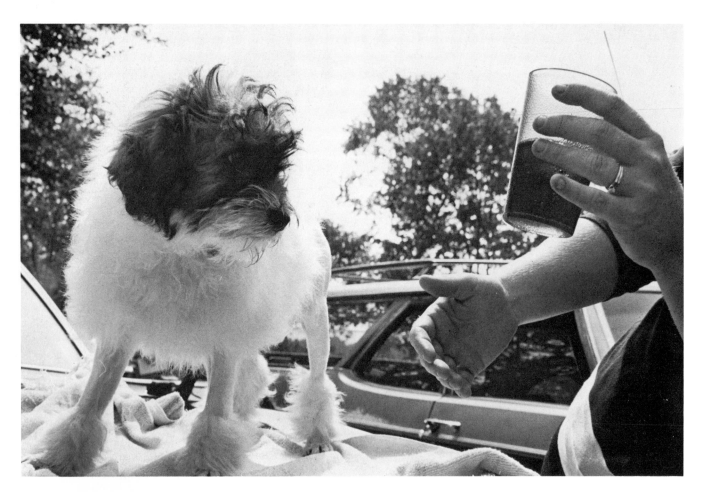

Little lion dog. (Photograph by Don Myrus)

The Handlers

Who they are, what they do, how much money they make.

Almost anybody can show a dog. Occasionally even an inexperienced handler will win big. To be fairly certain that a good dog is presented in its very best form—in full bloom, as they say—takes years of experience and hours of dedicated, hard work. Since some people can afford to maximize their odds, they turn to the professional handlers, who, as pros always have, work for the money. There are some two thousand licensed handlers.

(Handlers admitted to AKC-sponsored shows were licensed by the AKC until 1977, when a court ruled the practice illegal. Now anyone may handle. But reputation still does count.)

A well-reputed handler—who is for dogs what trainer, jockey, and groom are for horses—can be expected to earn $20,000 a year. Others, more ambitious, better organized (perhaps), willing to make bigger in-

---

You can lease a dog when it is in full bloom, win with it, and then return it when its showing life is ended.

---

vestments in breeding and in assistants to help around the kennel and on the road, have been known to take in $200,000 a year. How much of that they actually get to keep is, besides themselves and the IRS, anybody's guess.

The career of a show dog averages five or six years—generally starting on the "campaign trail" at about three years of age. A dog can't be shown until it's six months old, when it may compete in puppy class events at AKC licensed shows.

Handlers prefer that a puppy reach twelve to sixteen weeks of age before deciding whether it has a chance of winning championship status. How long and, therefore, how much it will take for any particular dog to gather sufficient points depends not only on the dog's anatomical features, but on its personality and on the competitive climate—whether or not a particular breed has a large number of top contenders at any given time.

Any owner who retains a handler can expect to spend a minimum of one thousand dollars, and some spend fifteen times that amount before a dog can be called "champion." Poodles cost more than boxers because poodles cost more to groom.

Bob Clyde of Lindenhurst, New York, who is in his late thirties, has been in the dog game since his early teens. "In those days I could work for eighteen hours at a stretch. Often I'd be grooming at two in the morning. I just can't do that anymore, although now I can strip in

an hour what used to take three."

Besides a thriving kennel in which they breed Welsh terriers and wirehaired fox terriers, and in which dogs of other owners are boarded, Mr. and Mrs. Clyde raise their seven children, a house dog, and a house cat. When a litter of twelve-week-old Welsh terriers was shown to a potential buyer, the showplace was first the kitchen and then the dining room, as the puppies scampered about. A dozen children reached down to pet the animals during a birthday celebration. "In the summer there are two birthdays a month around here."

Some breeders express shock at the idea of *their* champion-stock puppies being introduced to a family with young children . . . or one with cats. The Clyde household would seem to be ample evidence that all any young dog needs to be well adjusted is care and atten-

A judge must evaluate a dog's gait. To make the best impression, handlers have developed styles reminiscent of ballet choreography. Note the grace of this handler and the absorption of the vizsla—a pointer-retriever introduced to the U.S. by Hungarian emigrees in the wake of World War II. (Photograph by Don Myrus)

Bob Clyde, professional handler, at grooming table with welsh terriers. (Photograph by Don Myrus)

Sunny Shay and one of her champion Afghans. Her lavishly appointed kennel has a tile-lined grooming alcove with a built-in drier. (Photograph by Richard Benjamin Romanof)

tion, and the more people the better.

A half-dozen miles away, in Amityville, Laddie Carswell has a slightly smaller kennel, where he keeps the sporting dogs he shows. An older man than Clyde, Carswell has been a kennelman/handler/breeder since the Depression, which forced him out of law school.

"Actually the Depression began for my family in 1928. I had to take a job, and I went to work in Chicago for Mr. Moser of the Moser Business College for Women. He had a kennel with a hundred and fifty dogs. Marshall Field furnished it. They paid me $10,000 a year then, which would be the equivalent of about $100,000 now, but, of course, there just isn't that sort of money going into private kennels now. There just aren't many private kennels, and the ones that still exist are comparatively small."

The reason for the demise of the large private kennel is the same as the reason there aren't many large estates: higher taxes, especially graduated income taxes and escalating property taxes. Also the IRS no longer allows the rich to write off all the costs of their kennels year after year, as it once did. Now if a kennel loses money for five years, the IRS terms it a hobby and permits no deductions.

Clyde and Carswell make most of their current income from handling other people's dogs.

Fees vary. Some handlers charge as little as $30 per dog per show (and there are part-time novice handlers trying to break in who charge nothing).

Laddie Carswell usually handles twenty-five dogs and receives thirty-five dollars each time he shows one. Clyde has twenty to thirty "accounts." His fees are:

$35 . . . . to show
$15 . . . . bonus for winning best of breed
$40 . . . . bonus for winning best in group
$50 . . . . bonus for winning best in show

Thus, a Bob Clyde-handled dog, if it wins best in show, would cost its owner $140. And since it is not unknown for a dog to win thirty best-in-show awards in its career, such a dog would cost its owner forty-two hundred dollars just in the handler's fees.

Why do it? What is the motivation for a dog owner?

To breed a dog or to select a dog from another breeder's litter is to take a chance, to make a statement, to conspire with the fates. Will the puppy selected develop true to expectation, following the optimum form? Will the owner have picked the best, trained best, handled best, selected just the right show to enter, even— played politics best? Or, if the owner puts the dog's fate in the hands of a handler, did the owner choose the right handler?

In short, choosing a dog and showing it add up to a

Handlers with their charges at the Westbury Kennel Association show.

The winner of the 1963 Westminster Kennel Club show was the English springer spaniel Ch. Wakefield's Black Knight. The handler is Laddie Carswell, who now has a kennel in Amityville, New York. He has been a kennel-man / handler / breeder since the Depression. "They paid me ten thousand dollars a year then, which would be the equivalent of about one hundred thousand dollars now, but, of course, there just isn't that sort of money going into private kennels now." (Photograph, above, by Evelyn Shafer; left, by William Brown)

sporting proposition. That's why dog news is reported in the sports' sections of the newspapers.

It is certainly not a financially sound activity—not for owners anyway, unless they win big—say a best-in-show at Westminster. Then the financial returns can be immense. Otherwise, only for handlers, kennel owners, accessory and food manufacturers can dogs be a lucrative business.

For most dog owners showing is a hobby, a social activity, a competitive outlet. The prize money is nil, the trophies, by any standard, of limited aesthetic value. But the thrill of winning and the status it brings results in hundreds of thousands of people participating in shows each year, all over the world.

As might be expected, the dog sport has its oddities. It's perhaps not surprising that some owners buy into already-established dogs—blue chip investments, so to speak. You can lease a dog when it is in full bloom, win with it, and then return it when its showing life has ended. In this way one would never even have to touch the dog that wins the cup—not if a handler does the showing. Nor does one have to care for and train puppies or be responsible for old dogs.

Both Clyde and Carswell observe that great champions seem born to the role—that is, they are natural troupers. Once they get a taste of the show circuit, they seem to thrive on it. When their careers end, they seem disappointed, seem to suggest that, more than anything else, they'd like to be back showing off their stuff on the weekends.

Handlers aren't always the quintessence of calm, cool professionalism. Occasionally a dog comes along with whom a handler develops a special rapport. The two begin to function as a perfect team. When such a dog loses, handlers have been known to go "temporarily bananas," according to Bob Clyde. "Then it's not a matter of money or professionalism but of pride, of love." The pressure on a handler to win can become too much.

Another occupational hazard is severe bursitis and arthritis, especially for terrier handlers.

But old handlers, like old generals, never die. Yet, they don't fade away either. They become judges.

Loving a Dog: A Little Sentiment, a Lot of Sense

Book Review

A good book for the practical, "tweedy" set is *Especially Dogs . . . Especially at Stillmeadow* (Philadelphia: J. B. Lippincott, 1968), by Gladys Taber. It is one of those "best-loved" books that could be excerpted in the *Reader's Digest*. That is to say, it is accurate, pleasantly phrased, and very easy to read.

Mrs. Taber's father, "Papa," serves as a foil for a sentiment that is frequently in danger of oversweetening the anecdotes. He is somewhat idiosyncratic but lovable in his gruff, bumbling way. As there is no fervor to match the faith of the converted, we are led to believe that he, who initially resists a dog and then succumbs, is forever smitten.

> He dug a grave down by the river at the edge of our land and buried Timmie by himself. . . . Papa never spoke Timmie's name again until I wrote him that I wanted to get a puppy, and then he said if I betrayed Timmie's memory by getting another dog, I should understand I couldn't bring it in the house. No interloper was going to live under the same roof.

Of course, the young Gladys does get a puppy, and the reader learns how to go about the process, but not to worry if "love at first sight" overturns all the advice that should have been taken. Mrs. Taber is not hysterical about the rules. One feels that the dogs in her life probably have had a very good time—not overprotected or smothered with affection, but cared for.

She seems to think that keeping a dog clean has something to do with driving fleas away. But it is a harmless sort of error since cleanliness has other virtues. As for cleaning, here's her method:

> If you use the bathtub [to bathe a dog], you have to clean the bathroom, which is a chore at any time. In warm weather, I take the Irish to the lawn with a pailful of warm water, the shampoo, a scrub brush, and bath towels. I use the hose for rinsing, then towel the coat dry. If I am lucky, two young neighbors drop by in their bathing suits and I sit idly and watch.

The book is full of handy tips nicely served up. And the author is not preachy. For example, on the subject of selection: "I have known a few women who spent more time choosing a dress than in picking out a puppy, without stopping to consider that the dress will last a short time, while a dog will be a part of their lives for years."

The chapter "Show Dog" gives a fine glimpse of a professional handler—in this case Art Baines. One day Art came to test out Mrs. Taber's dog.

> He gaited her around the yard. He ran with an easy flowing step and Holly skimmed lightly behind him, so lightly her paws did not seem to crush the grass blades. Both of them were grinning. A thoroughbred racehorse is beautiful to see, but a thoroughbred Irish has the grace of a bird in flight. When he drew up and put his hand before her muzzle and she stopped, she stood with head lifted, plume straight out, and forelegs straight as a die."

Mrs. Taber insisted that Art could only have Holly for the actual shows. That meant she had to rush off before every weekend to meet up with the handler who was, of course, also showing other dogs. Art drove a Cadillac, and owner and handler made frequent hair-splitting highway rendezvous.

> We spent most of our time commuting to places near and far to meet Art and deliver Holly or meet him and get her back. He was on the northeastern circuit, and it seemed to cover everything but Nevada and California. We met him at seven in the morning forty miles from home. We met him outside Danbury at noon. We met him at eleven at night at some crossroads near a village not even on the map.

Eventually the phone call came; Art announcing the championship. Predictably, the owner of Ch. Still-meadow Hollyberry Red had a good cry. Understandably, as you read Mrs. Taber's recounting, you might too.

The Well-Groomed Ones Are Dogs

by Red Smith

America's foremost sports columnist goes to Westminster.

Ch. Ziegfried von Silber Wald, a giant schnauzer, was hurling imprecations across the aisle at Ch. Bourbon von Silber Wald, who cursed back.

This was in the bench area in Madison Square Garden, which provided slum housing Monday and yesterday for something like three thousand contestants in the Westminster Kennel Club's annual show. Dogs waiting to parade before the judges and dogs whose posing was finished sat, stood, crouched, snoozed, shivered, and shouted in cages stowed and sometimes stacked in little wooden cubicles set side by side in seemingly endless rows, while people shuffled through the congested aisles to ogle and exclaim over one hundred-odd breeds from affenpinschers to Yorkshire terriers, from bichons frises to Shih Tzu. Many dogs shared their stalls with people, and it can be stated as law that in the Westminster show, which is to performing pooches what the Palace used to be to vaudeville, the dogs are better groomed than their owners.

In the bench area strict segregation is the rule, with beagles side by side in this row of stalls and bloodhounds occupying separate but equal quarters over there.

AKC-SANCTIONED MATCH SHOWS

Often incorrectly called puppy shows (because puppies as young as two months may be entered), a match show is sanctioned by AKC but does not provide winners with points toward a championship. Besides puppies, older dogs also participate in sanctioned matches, but champions of record and in some instances dogs with major points toward the championship do not. Judges at match shows are approved by AKC. Sanctioned obedience matches are also held.

AKC CRACKS DOWN ON HAIR SPRAY

The Board of Directors of the AKC took umbrage in late 1977 about a phenomenon widely known and long practiced at dog shows everywhere in the United States: cosmetic manipulation of show dogs through the use of hair sprays and lacquers. The AKC arbiters now feel that cosmetics falsify the quality of the coat and that their use in the show ring is, therefore, to be considered highly improper and grounds for ruling a show dog "Excused—foreign substance—unable to judge coat texture."

At a dog show grooming area items include scissors, combs, brushes, cotton-tipped sticks, mineral oil, shampoo, hair conditioner, hair spray. As for schnauzers, they are of three types: miniature, standard, and giant. Miniature and standard were ratters, and the giant was a cattle drover and guard in German breweries. (Photograph by Richard Benjamin Romanof)

Here a woman in pants worked with clippers and hair spray on her black poodle. There a Great Pyrenees gazed incuriously back at spectators staring at him. He looked like a polar bear, and he wore a black bib because his kind tends to drool.

Mastiff Alley looked like the shed row at Belmont, for these creatures are approximately the size of two-year-old horses. Some years ago, when Mrs. Marie A. Moore was trying unsuccessfully to breed a champion from the great race mare, Gallorette, as many as a dozen or two mastiffs ran loose on her farm at The Plains, Va. If a visitor didn't get kicked by a horse, he was a mortal cinch to be trampled by a dog. The Hound of the Baskervilles was a mastiff—"Mr. Holmes, it was the footprint of a gigantic hound"—and in all the years Mrs. Moore bred the variety, she was never troubled by a Baskerville.

Many dogs had bylines on their cages. "Ch. Benhil's Shenanigans" read the nameplate over a huge black Newfoundland deep in sleep. Equally deep in the stall beside him was a small American creature in blue jeans. There was no way of telling whether it was male or female.

There were black Scotties looking like half of a whisky ad, Dalmatians seeming out of place so far from

any firehouse, asthmatic bulldogs, and many pale-eyed Siberian huskies.

Snatches of conversation were overheard. "No," said an uncommonly ample woman, "it had nothing to do with showing. I was allergic to the dandruff."

When primped and fluffed for the show ring, old English sheepdogs have something in common with ferryboats, in that it is difficult to see which is the bow and which the stern. Here was one just resting on the bench, however, and he could look back at his visitors because a silver barrette held the hair out of his eyes.

If there are any clients unfamiliar with the akita, he looks like a sled dog, with an expensive coat of brown and black and a curly tail. Locked in a cage with one of these was a woman's handbag and camera. The Belgian tervuren has a sharp nose and an aristocratic manner. A Bernese mountain dog, black with brown points, lay beneath a sign identifying him as the property of Mrs. Robert Redford, Sundance, Utah.

While crowds moved through the bench area like wet cement, judges were at work in the show rings. Herman G. Cox of Fort Worth was laying a practiced eye on soft-coated wheaten terriers. He wore horn-rimmed glasses and a waistcoat embroidered with dogs of many colors. Wheaten terriers, like cowboys, wear chaps.

Judge Cox would clasp a dog's head between his hands and gaze into the terrier's eyes. He would run hands over shoulders, back, and hindquarters, step back wearily, and stand with chin cupped in hand. With the faintest of hand signals he would direct the handler to

walk the dog, trot in a circle, halt, and pose. A two-hundred-pound adult skipping in a circle looks plain silly.

Spectators were jammed around an adjacent ring where Great Danes were working. After each Dane did his stuff, there was applause. From still another ring came shouts of approval as Edd Embry Bivin, also of Fort Worth, picked a miniature schnauzer to become a ch. Judge Cox worked on and on.

It was growing late, but the crowds in the bench area didn't diminish. A woman with an old English sheepdog on a tight leash shouldered through an aisle crying a warning: "Watch out, she's in season." To right and left, dogs howled, all candidates for best of opposite sex.

Illustration by Jill Miriam Pinkwater

The Corded Poodle

The look of the poodle when kept naturally, and why it is not much anymore.

A peculiarity of the poodle's coat is that it must be kept constantly brushed out, or it will twist up into little cords that increase in length as the new hair grows and clings about it. The unshed old hair and the new growth entwined together thus become distinct, ropelike cords that, unless cut off, will in time drag on the ground and interfere with the dog's freedom of movement. A few owners admire these long cords and keep them tied up in bundles on the dog's back, but this is about as unsightly an arrangement as can be conceived.

Corded poodles are very showy and attract a great deal of attention . . .

Corded poodles are very showy and attract a great deal of attention, but they have lost their popularity with many fanciers because of the difficulty in keeping them clean enough to have in the house. The coat must be oiled from time to time to keep the cords supple and to prevent their breaking off, and since the coat cannot be brushed, the only way to keep the dog clean is to wash him, which with the poodle is a long and laborious process.

Also it takes hours for the coat to dry, during which time the dog must be kept in a warm room or he will catch cold. The result is that most corded poodles, unless they chance to be owned by someone who can give them more care and attention than most people have time to bestow, have coats that are dirty and somewhat smelly.

At one time it was thought that the corded and noncorded were two distinct breeds, but it is now generally accepted that the coat of every well-bred poodle will develop cords if allowed to do so.

WESTMINSTER AND CRUFT'S, PRESTIGIOUS DOG SHOWS

The Westminster Kennel Club Show, held in New York every February, has been described as the world series of American dogdom. Cruft's Dog Show, held in London every February, is the British equivalent. Started in 1891 by a dog biscuit salesman, the show rights were sold in 1938 by Charles Cruft's widow to The Kennel Club. Entries at Cruft's include only former champions or those who have, during the preceding year, achieved first or second place at championship shows. To win at Cruft's is really winning.

Organizing the Unorganized

by Ed Whitney

"Rare breeds" explained concisely.

What is a rare breed? There are many breeds that are not recognized by the American Kennel Club, but for one reason or another are recognized by foreign kennel clubs. Some of these breeds have been around for centuries. All must have a well-organized pedigree (registration or "Stud Book"), and their owners must ultimately be interested in having the breed recognized by the AKC.

Why do people get involved with rare breeds? First and foremost, they have fallen in love with the individual dog and breed. They also have the pride of being the first one on the block to own one. In addition, there is the possibility of achieving recognition for helping to get a breed established in this country. Individuals may become involved because of the relaxed competition and fun at dog shows. They also have the challenge of being personally involved in trying to save an endangered species, utilizing current breeding philosophies or theories. Finally they may be just a little "crazy."

Breeds in the Long Island Rare Breed Association—a national group—are the Neapolitan mastiff, Portuguese water dog, Chinese crested, Xoloitzcuintli, Canaan dog, Finnish spitz, little lion dog, Chinese shar-pei, Australian shepherd, Tibetan mastiff, plus the Tibetan spaniel and the Cavalier King Charles spaniel, the latter two also having AKC miscellaneous classification.

. . . they may be just a little "crazy."

The Long Island Rare Breed Association, 111 New York Avenue, Smithtown, NY 11787, welcomes inquiries.

Fine dogs engender the enthusiasm of both sexes, all ages, and every economic station. Here is Marilyn Dziedziech with her very impressive Neapolitan mastiff. (Photograph by Spida Grean)

Kathy Robinson and her Tibetan spaniel. In 1977 the breed became eligible for AKC Miscellaneous Group competition. The lamaseries of Tibet once were guarded by these little dogs, but most often the Tibetan spaniel was a pet and companion. The first of the breed to be officially imported into the U.S. arrived in 1967. (Photograph by Don Myrus)

The Neapolitan mastiff, said to be a re-creation of an ancient Roman guard dog, made its debut in 1946 in Naples, achieving there the recognition of the Ente Nazionale della Cinafilia Italiana, the AKC of Italy. In the U.S. it is shown at rare breed shows.

102

One Man's New Breed— Bringing the Little Lion Dog to America

by Robert Yhlen

Lady and little lion dog of the seventeenth century were among the works of art studied by Robert A. Yhlen to establish a modern standard for the breed.

The author, who says "zodialogically I am a Leo" and "I have been intrigued with lions" since childhood, perhaps expectedly took an interest in the very rare little lion dog. Here's how he brought it to America, encouraging the breed to prosper.

I have been asked, many times, how I became involved with the little lion dog. Well, it started in 1971; I read in the *New York Times* an article about the Cruft's Show in England. A dog which had been very rare was making a comeback and was being shown for the first time. The breed was the lowchen, or petit chien lion, as it originally was called. Someone was bringing a few of them back to the U.S. after having seen them at Cruft's. My interest was spurred by the article for several reasons; zodialogically I am a Leo, and back into my childhood, I have been intrigued with lions. I was interested in seeing just what this little "lion" looked like and started pursuing the task of trying to obtain as much information as I could by locating the dogs which were brought into the U.S. and by writing to the English breeder. My attempts led to many frustrations; the task was no easy one. The little lion dog completely eluded me. The more I looked for information, the less I found. One thing I knew—there were not many of them and acquiring one would prove difficult. Through the English breeder, I finally obtained a picture of the dog and the name of the couple who brought the little lion dog into the U.S. I visited with them to satisfy my curiosity and I was hooked; the dogs were, as their name implies, little and lionesque. Out of that meeting, a lasting friendship began with Jane and Charles Cook, whose honesty and intelligence added to my growing commitment to the little lion dog. Through Jane, I acquired Cluneen Dana (Pinkie), the first little lion dog in the U.S., and also the first two of her puppies. Together, the Cooks and I have put a club together and informed the AKC of the little lion dog.

I had already been involved with two other breeds— obedience work with the German shepherd and showing the Afghan hound. I enjoyed working with them, and when bringing in another breed, I had to decide if I was over-dogged—too many dogs and not enough time, money or energy for them. Well, it took quite some time to work out all the dilemmas I created for myself, but as I threw myself into the little lion dogs, the answers worked themselves out and slowly the little lions took over. My decision was to actively pursue the little lion dog.

There were not many other people as interested or involved with the breed as I, so I had to house many of the dogs myself to learn what these little guys were all about. I could not call on other breeders or buy a book on the breed, as one could do with a standard AKC breed. I had to learn myself about conformation, coat colors, character, and growth, as well as how trainable they were, and if they were good lap dogs. As it turned out, they are feisty and active, healthy and trainable. The breeding program and learning process would take longer

Bob and Carole Yhlen and their little lion dogs. For information about the breed, contact Jane R. Cook, RR 1, Box 171 A, Madford, NJ 08055.

than I had expected. Unlike the larger breeds, which have eight to ten puppies per litter, these only had three to five.

News articles about little lions were beginning to appear and something wonderful was getting started—rare breed dog shows. Requests started coming to me for puppies and a waiting list developed. It was on a first-come, first-served basis. People were asking for show quality this, color that, and I started to assist with imports, trying to help as much as I could.

I saw that this breed, like all others, had its problems. I had to select, from my stock, which to breed and which to cull. I saw in them a chance not often given—to bring a breed back to its original appearance and prominence. In trying to discover the dog's history, I went through old books and works of art by Europeans of the fourteenth through seventeenth centuries. While in Spain, my wife and I poured over countless lithographs and gravures in antique stores. The origins of the breed are steeped in antiquity. The dogs are thought to have been the result of combining two ancient toy breeds, the Teneriffe, which is the modern bichon frise, and the Bolognese.

The little lion dog, or petit chien lion, originated in France, according to the Federation Cynologique Internationale. The dog was a genuine lap dog and drawing-room pet of the Florentine nobility, but it was not until the mid-1900's that their survival was insured. A Belgian woman realized that there were only a few little lion

dogs left and collected all she could. Before she died, she passed her stock on to a close friend in Germany. From those few dogs—forty in 1967, in the entire world—the breed is enjoying a comeback. In Europe and in England, within the last three years, they have been shown in their own breed classes. The dogs reached the U.S. in February 1971 and the Little Lion Dog Club of America was established shortly after. There are now fifty-eight little lion dogs registered with the club.

(For information, contact Little Lion Dog Club of America, 31 Byram Bay Road, Hoptacong, NJ 67843.)

TAKING RICKY'S RAP

A classic case of a man's devotion to his dog occurred in southwestern Virginia in the early 1960s.

Jim Laing paid a one-thousand-dollar fine and spent seven days of a four-month sentence in jail. He got out early only because the governor commuted the contempt-of-court sentence.

Mr. Laing had not only refused to give up his German shepherd, Ricky, for execution but wouldn't tell of his whereabouts. Ricky had killed a neighbor's ewe.

104

Portuguese Water Dog

A prime example of a rare breed.

One of the many breeds not registered with the American Kennel Club is the Portuguese water dog. A flyer circulated by the breed club in America, in somewhat archaic prose, notes:

> In bygone times this race existed everywhere along the coasts of Portugal. Today, owing to modifications in the fishing systems used, the race has become restricted practically to the province of Algarve. A swimmer and diver of quite exceptional qualities and stamina, this dog is the inseparable companion of the fisherfolk to whom it is of great utility not only during fishing but also as a guard to defend their boats and property. Whilst his master is fishing the dog is attentive, and should a fish escape (from hook or net), he jumps voluntarily into the sea to retrieve it, diving under water if necessary. It also swims out to retrieve any broken net or loosened rope end. These animals are also employed as couriers between boat and land, or vice-versa, even when the distance is considerable.

One of the notable characteristics of this swimming dog ("well-balanced, robust, and well muscled") is that its feet are webbed—the membrane between the toes is of soft skin well covered with hair.

Pamela Schneller, secretary of the Portuguese Water Dog Club of America, 233 West Islip Road, West Islip, NY 11795, reports that currently there are about one hundred and fifty of the dogs in the world, most in the United States.

Ed and Barbara Whitney, breeders of Portuguese water dogs at their Spindrift Kennels (111 New York Avenue, Smithtown, NY 11787), state that prices of the dogs are three hundred and fifty dollars, with the pick of the litter five hundred dollars.

The Portuguese water dog is a webfooted relative of the poodle, the Kerry blue terrier, and the curly-coated retriever. (Photograph by Raymond Picone)

OLD-FASHIONED REMEDY— THE SULPHUR DIP

In behalf of the sulphur dip there is no harm in stating the homely information that it is highly beneficial to the human skin and hair. Once I overheard a charming lady whispering to a kennelman a request for a bottle of his decoction the next time he mixed it— before the dogs had reached the tank. It appeared that she was annoyed at times with a feverish scalp and dandruff. Observing the coats of the dogs, she secretly tried the dip and found a relief she had not obtained from a hairdresser's attention. Needless to say, she made the application in the privacy of her boudoir at night and passed through the odorous stage before she appeared to her friends.

The hair of all animals is a vehicle of germs. So are fleas, lice, and flies. Drive the whole army away daily.

—Edited and reprinted from *Outing*, June 1907.

Photograph by Peter Simon

How a New Breed Achieves Recognition

Note from the AKC

Getting into the Stud Book.

The admission of a new breed to our Stud Book has in recent cases been the result of work that has extended over quite a period of years. The circumstances surrounding each new breed are always somewhat different. However, we would expect to find a club that had been organized for the advancement of the interest of the particular breed in question. It would be a specialty club, one of whose primary functions would be to keep

---

We would want to know that the dogs had been purebred for a good many generations . . .

---

a Stud Book for the breed. Our correspondence with such a group would probably extend over a period of eight to ten years or more. We would want to know that the dogs had been purebred for a good many generations, that accurate Stud Book records had been kept on them, that there were a good many specimens of the breed in the country (well up into the hundreds, at least), and that they were owned by a good many different people in various parts of the country who were seriously interested in breeding and exhibiting them in AKC shows, as well as registering them in the AKC Stud Book.

In a letter to the editor from Pamela Mathews, American Kennel Club.

SOVIET DOGS

There are about 50,000 pedigreed dogs in Moscow. The most popular breeds are the Asian ovcharka, Laika, boxer, and Doberman pinscher.

Favorite names are those of the space dogs: Ugoljok (Blackie), Veterok (Breezy), Laika (same as the breed name, Barker), Bielka (Squirrel), Strelka (Little Arrow), Pestrushka (Piebald), and Chernuska (Little Black Fellow).

Showing Purebred Dogs

Book Reviews

A Quick Guide to Standards for Show Dogs ($1.95; Garden City: Doubleday, 1972), by Maxwell Riddle, contains concise descriptions of standards, faults, and reasons for disqualification for the AKC breeds. Written to be easily understood and designed to travel well, it is the best book available for the handler and dog show visitor. Includes a photo of each of the 122 recognized breeds and of those in the miscellaneous group.

Secrets of Dog Show Handling ($8.95; New York: Arco, 1972), by Mario Migliorini, is a practical how-to book.

How To Show Your Dog and Win ($6.90; New York: Franklin Watts, 1976), by Kurt Unkelbach. Though written as an introduction to the dog sport for young people, this is the best, clearest, and consequently most interesting explanation of the world of the fancy. It demystifies the procedures and point systems of the breed ring, obedience trial, and junior showmanship competition. The latter began in 1929 as "Children's Handling" to keep the kids who went to dog shows with their parents busy and out of trouble; it was continued in order to nurture new generations of handlers. In 1950 the name of the sport was changed to "Junior Showmanship," and in 1971 the AKC established nationwide standards and regulations. In junior showmanship competition judges are not concerned with the quality of dogs in the ring—it is handlers only who are being judged. Children ten through sixteen may compete. Includes fine photographs.

Junior Showmanship ($4.95; Fairfax: Denlinger's, 1969, 1975), by Alice J. Boyer, offers step-by-step advice and instruction, including what to wear in the ring. The detailed diagrams of ring movement patterns are large and easily understood, and the photographs are interesting. Complete AKC junior showmanship regulations and a sample junior showmanship judge's application (for those seventeen or over) are included.

A Dog by Your Side ($6.95; New York: Charles Scribner's, 1977), by Lilo Hess, is a good introduction for the youngest readers to the show world. Kennels, breeding, grooming, the AKC groups, show point systems, and judging standards are explained.

7

JUDGING

A SPECIAL BREED: THE
   ALL-BREED JUDGE
by Maxwell Riddle

THE GREAT BENCH SHOW

THE FOX HUNT THAT ALMOST
   WAS—THE SECOND
   WESTMINSTER

MORE BORZOIS BY FAR IN
   U.S.A. THAN IN U.S.S.R.

WINNING POINTS—THE AKC
   WAY TO CHAMPIONSHIP

THE UNITED KENNEL CLUB

QUICK-STUDY BREED QUIZ

JUDGING
   Book Reviews

". . . every good judge has to recognize at a glance whether a dog is right or wrong . . . a priceless gift acquired by long and painstaking study."—Tom Horner, English judge. (Photograph opposite by Don Myrus)

A Special Breed: The All-Breed Judge

by Maxwell Riddle

A review, with extended comments, of Tom Horner's Take Them Round, Please.

Tom Horner, the English dog judge, has written a very wise book—*Take Them Round, Please* ($8.95; North Pomfret, VT: David and Charles, 1977), which calls to mind judging experiences of my own, sacred and profane, funny and embarrassing.

Now, right off, he says: "Judging is a demanding task but most rewarding; with luck and a bit of skill it can

"How many athletes have to do one hundred to three hundred full knee bends in a day?"

109

Maxwell Riddle, famed international all-breed judge, after selecting a flat-coated retriever as best in group. The breed was developed from the Labrador retriever and St. John's Newfoundland. (Photograph by Stephen Klein)

Judge Edd Embry Bivin of Fort Worth, Texas, at work during a Westminster Kennel Club show at Madison Square Garden. There is a point system of physical evaluation of dogs by judges. A Pekingese, for example, could receive as many as ten points for a perfectly shaped skull, five for its ears, even five points for its expression. A dog that had a total one hundred conformation points would be a flawless example of the breed, identical to the official standard. Besides, such a dog would need a certain style best described as star quality. (Photograph above by Don Myrus)

Judge Riddle gives a Best in Group to a beautiful English setter on its way to Best in Show at the San Luis Obispo Kennel Club event in 1969. The English setter was once expected to crouch low, to set, and to point out game. Modern setters just point. (Photograph left by Joan Ludwig)

turn the most ordinary person into someone in demand as a judge all over the world. To travel at other people's expense is the best way I know to see the world—much better than joining the Navy."

I agree, except I don't think Tom Horner is a most ordinary person, and I also have a higher opinion than that of myself. But Tom is wrong on one point. Very few American dog judges are ever going to see the British Isles at other than their own expense. It is true that I have had my expenses paid to judge in Britain. But then I have also been asked to judge and have been told that my lodging, but not food or liquor, would be paid for two nights at a second-class hotel.

Tom suggests that if you want to learn to judge, you should sit at ringside and write your own critique of each dog as the judge proceeds. Then compare yours with the critique the judge writes for *Dog World* or *Our Dogs*.

Now come on, Tom! If you sit at ringside, you are going to be engaged in conversation with others whether you like it or not. You'll hear all about the judge's sex life, who bought him his last case of whiskey, or her those orchids. And, of course, you'll learn that in any case the judge is a nincompoop who doesn't know one end of a dog from the other.

Tom does make a point that most exhibitors and ringsiders forget:

> Judging is a responsible and exhausting business. It calls for a considerable degree of knowledge, discrimination, integrity, tact, a good memory (stewards cannot always be relied upon), and physical stamina. The mental effort entailed in sorting out a large entry is no small item, nor is the amount of exercise involved to be underrated.

How right he is! Show me a banker or factory manager who has to make so many hard decisions in a single day. And how many athletes have to do one hundred to three hundred full knee bends a day!

When he says "stewards cannot always be relied upon" he is referring to something that doesn't happen in America or Canada. In Britain and many other countries dogs are entered in three or four classes. (Over here this is unusual.) So British ring stewards are expected to put the new class dogs in front and then to line up the others in the order in which they finished in the previous classes. Sometimes they make mistakes, and sometimes the judges forget.

I remember the time when the chief steward broadcast over the public address system: "The American judge has just given the challenge certificate to the dog which took second in the open class."

I remember also the comment of my steward, an all-breeds judge himself. I had said that I had read the rules and they said the judge could reverse himself if he felt he had made a mistake.

"*. . . there are thousands who will tell you that you have to be born with it (an eye). And they'll tell you that they were (and you weren't and haven't got it.)*"—*Maxwell Riddle.*

"Yes, we have that rule," he said. "But I never heard of anyone being damn fool enough to do it."

Horner writes:

> Knowledge, decisiveness, integrity and the rest of the necessary qualities are useless without one vital possession—an "eye for a dog," which is the ability that every good judge has to recognize at a glance whether a dog is right or wrong, good, bad, or indifferent. A priceless gift, without which no one can make a real success of judging, it is acquired by long and painstaking study of anatomy, breed standards, high class dogs and poor ones. . . .

Shucks, Tom. Maybe that's the way you got your eye for a dog, but there are thousands who will tell you that

111

"Judging is a responsible, exhausting business. It calls for a considerable degree of knowledge, discrimination, integrity, tact, a good memory . . . and physical stamina."— Tom Horner. (Photograph by Don Myrus)

you have to be born with it. And they'll tell you that they were (and you weren't and haven't got it). I remember one judge who had given himself the honor of being born with it. All I ever could determine was that he had an eye for women, and women with fat purses. At least that went for all of his five wives, except the first one. Having "cheated the church," as they say, he had to marry her rather hurriedly and belatedly.

Horner advises exhibitors to be alert and attentive and not to engage in conversation with their backs to the judge. I remember one exhibitor who lost best in show because she was bent over the ring ropes, talking to someone. Rather than lay the ribbon on her bottom, the judge turned away and gave it to another dog. I once defeated the greatest dachshund of its day and won the hound group with a whippet. I shouldn't have. But the judge was insulted by the actions of the dachshund exhibitor, who was slightly tipsy.

Horner has plenty of good advice for stewards, and that goes for stewards in any country. Poor stewarding can cost an hour of the judge's time. And that wasted time is time the judge may have needed to give each exhibitor careful consideration.

Horner also warns judges to keep careful records of upcoming assignments or, as he puts it, "appointments." This is something of a nightmare to many judges, who are afraid they'll forget an assignment or go to the wrong show or to the wrong location.

Once I showed up with two dogs to show and heard myself being paged. A judge couldn't be located. I took his assignment, scratching my own dogs. The judge arrived at the building the next day.

Horner has his own ideas on such things as light eyes, and I agree with him. Poor judges defeat dogs because of visible minor faults instead of trying to find the dog with the best overall balance of conformation, type, and movement.

I think he is sound, too, in his ideas of gait. Some standards call for single tracking rather than parallel movement. And this is all too often merely an excuse for dogs that are out at elbows and cross over front and rear.

So I repeat, Horner has written a wise book, one that every judge and exhibitor will gain from reading.

BENCH SHOWS

Clark C. Thompson, on the eve of his retirement as an owner-handler of cocker spaniels and as a leading show judge, commented on changes in the sport during his career.

"When I started, the shows were all benched. You remained all day and, from speaking to handlers, judges, and other exhibitors, learned a great deal.

"Most of the one-or-two-dog owners did their own handling and went to a dozen shows a year. It was a hobby. Now it tends to be a business."

The Great Bench Show

Reports of the first Westminster Kennel Club event at the New York Hippodrome in 1877.

The steamship *Nevada* arrived at the wharf about 3:30 o'clock yesterday afternoon. Among her passengers were Gen. Tom Thumb and Mr. G. de Landre Macdona, Cheshire, England, father of Rev. Mr. Macdona, the great English dog breeder. Mr. Macdona brought with him two celebrated English setters, two magnificent St. Bernard dogs, a black retriever, a red-and-white Irish setter puppy, a fox terrier puppy, a black Skye terrier. There were also on board five superb mastiffs belonging to Mr. A. A. Brown, of Liverpool, and the celebrated pointer, Snapshot, the property of R. J. Lloyd Price, of North Wales. The dogs were all under the forward hatch and were a splendid sight. The mastiffs alone were worth the journey to look at. Immense, broad-chested, fierce-looking brutes, few other animals would seemingly have much odds against them in a struggle.

The show, on the whole, promises to be a success. It is under the patronage of people of standing, who have been careful to eliminate from it any suggestion of the dogfighting element. An exhibition of blooded animals will be provided such as has never before been seen in this country.

The great dog show is astonishing its promoters with its success. They hesitated a long time, when the project was first thought of, whether to undertake the responsibility of the expense involved. The hire of the Hippodrome for three days cost fifteen hundred dollars, and the other outlays for advertising, printing, help, carpenter work, etc., aggregated fully six thousand dollars before the show was opened. Tuesday's receipts at the box office footed up over six thousand dollars, and yesterday's nearly ten thousand dollars in cash. The show will remain open today and tomorrow—the Hippodrome having been hired yesterday until Friday midnight—and it is safe to say that the attendance will increase rather than diminish.

All day long yesterday the Hippodrome was crowded to excess with elegantly dressed ladies and gentlemen. The dogs are getting accustomed to their quarters and to the crowd, and are measurably less noisy than on the first two days of the show. The prize St. Bernard dog, Lion, bit two persons yesterday. He is a vicious brute and should be given a wide berth.

Mr. Macdona's setter bitch, Magnet, was sold yesterday to a gentleman from Pittsburgh for three hundred and fifty dollars, gold. On Friday morning a grand auction sale of over one hundred and fifty dogs will be held in the Hippodrome. The sale will be without reserve, and excellent bargains may be had.

Edited and reprinted from The New York Times, *May 6 to 10, 1877.*

Westminster Kennel Club show at Madison Square Garden in 1977. Out of sight is the benching area, the *Westminster being one of the few remaining bench shows still held in the United States.*

The Fox Hunt That Almost Was—the Second Westminster

It begins "An exhibitor of several fine dogs had a tame red fox with him . . ."

An exhibitor of several fine dogs had a tame red fox with him, which he brought into the Garden. He placed the fox in the middle of the arena, and the foxhounds were brought out chained and held at a safe distance from the pretty animal. The moment the hounds caught sight of their natural prey, they struggled madly to get at him, howling so that it seemed as though pandemonium had broken loose. The fox sat looking at them, entirely unconcerned. Subsequently it was determined to shut the doors, let both fox and hounds loose, and have a grand fox hunt, but although the exhibitor was willing, he had meantime traded the fox for a harrier pup, and its new owner had taken it away.

Subsequently it was determined to shut the doors, let both fox and hounds loose, and have a grand fox hunt . . .

In the afternoon a field trial was improvised. Two live quail with clipped wings were brought in and turned loose in the judging ring, where several bundles of straw had previously been thrown by way of "cover." The quail quickly hid themselves, one under one bunch and one under another. A number of crack setters and pointers were then let singly into the ring. Unfortunately for the success of the experiment, the ring had neither been cleaned nor disinfected during the morning, and the straw used was some on which dogs had been lying for four days. The odor was consequently so powerful that it quite overbore the "scent" from the quail, and one animal after another was retired in disgrace.

If unable to point by scent, the dogs showed no lack of ability to do so by sight. The poor little quail squatted down in the dirt watched by a circle of rigid, quivering dogs, every head thrust forward, every eye bulging with eagerness, every muscle set, and every tail rigid. A prettier sight could not be imagined. A hundred spectators surrounded the ring gazing breathlessly at the picture, every countenance glistening with delight.

Edited and reprinted from The New York Times, *May 17, 1878.*

More Borzois By Far in U.S.A. Than in U.S.S.R.

White-Russian wolfhounds come to America.

When Constantine Kuzminsky, a Russian refugee poet, arrived at Kennedy International Airport in 1976 with a borzoi, he rather gloatingly reported that he had managed to slip the dog out of Russia, against regulations, because customs officials didn't know he was lying when the dog was listed as a mixed breed.

Perhaps the officials could be forgiven their ignorance, since the borzoi is now rare in its homeland—in fact it hasn't been much seen there since the breakup of the great estates in the late eighteen hundreds.

According to Dr. Alfred W. Edlin in *Your Borzoi* (Fairfax: Denlinger's, 1976), a borzoi bred in Russia finished (achieved the necessary points to be designated "Champion") at Indianapolis and Westminster in 1893. The dog's owner, Charles Steadman, imported borzois from the kennels of the Grand Duke Peter Nicholas, Prince Boris Galitzin, and Colonel von Dietz, establishing the breed in the United States.

Howard Pitkin, writing in the April 1907 issue of *Country Life in America*, credits Joseph B. Thomas, Jr., with popularizing borzois in America.

> He began breeding the dog while still a student at Yale. . . . So the first thing he did after graduating was to go to Russia and visit all the famous kennels. [Thomas purchased] the best dogs in the empire, and the striking appearances and sweeping successes of these at bench shows are largely responsible for the favor with which the borzoi is now regarded as an ornamental and useful dog for the country home.

In the mid-1970's more than fifteen hundred borzois a year were newly registered with the American Kennel Club.

HOW TO BECOME AN OBEDIENCE JUDGE

Submit an application for examination to the Board of Directors of the American Kennel Club.

An applicant should have owned several dogs with obedience titles, be able to demonstrate an avid exhibitor interest, and have substantial experience in training dogs—one's own, those of others, or of dogs in regularly organized AKC classes.

Winning Points—the AKC Way to Championship

Exhibitors have been known to show dogs for years without understanding the system. Here it is, simplified. Just remember, there could be 244 winners at a show.

—A dog that has accumulated fifteen points in conformation (breed standard) competition is designated a champion.

—From one to five points may be earned by a dog at any one show.

—Only one male and one female of *each* breed can win points at any one show. At a major all-breed show that could be 244 dogs. (There are 122 AKC-recognized breeds.)

—Dogs seeking points toward the championship are entered in one of five competitive "classes"—puppy, six-to-nine months; puppy, nine-to-twelve months; novice; bred-by-exhibitor; American bred; open.

—The number-one dogs of a breed from each class are judged against each other to select a Winners Dog. The same pattern is followed for females to select a Winners Bitch. Thus two of each breed are the only ones to receive points at a show.

—The number of points that may be earned by a Winners Dog and a Winners Bitch at any given show is determined by the AKC, based on the total registrations of the winner's breed in that show and upon geographic location of the show.

—Shows that carry three or more points for a particular breed are termed "majors." A champion's fifteen-point total must include two "majors" won under different judges.

(A reserve Winners Dog and reserve Winners Bitch are designated so that if AKC later disqualifies either winner, the points for the show go to the reserve dog.)

—Next comes Best of Breed Class, in which the Winners Dogs and Winners Bitches compete against champions of record in their breeds.

—Either Winners Dog or Winners Bitch is chosen as Best of Winners.

—Best of Breed is designated, along with Best of Breed, opposite sex.

—Best of Breed competes in its appropriate group (see AKC groups), and then the six group winners compete for Best in Show.

Dogs being judged in conformation classes are not so much competing against each other, or being compared to each other by the judge, as they are being compared to the official breed standard, which a judge must continually visualize in his mind's eye while working toward a decision.

The official publication of the American Kennel Club, The Complete Dog Book *($7.95; New York: Howell Book House, 15th edition, 1975), contains a photograph, history, and official standard of every breed admitted to AKC registration.*

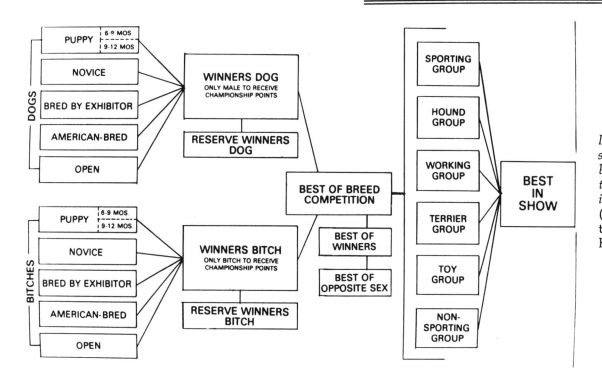

Progressive steps in an all-breed event toward Best in Show. (Courtesy of the American Kennel Club)

The United Kennel Club

U.S. dog registries plus . . .

The United Kennel Club (321 West Cedar Street, Kalamazoo, MI 49006) was founded in 1898 and is the second oldest and second largest registration office of purebred dogs in the United States. UKC now registers purebred dogs from all over the world.

UKC was the original registrar of the American black-and-tan coonhound, American Eskimo, American pit bull terrier, American fox and coonhound, American toy terrier, American water spaniel, Arctic husky, bluetick coonhound, English coonhound, English foxhound, miniature boxer, Columbian collie, Plott hound, English shepherd, redbone coonhound, toy fox terrier, and treeing Walker.

UKC also registers the following breeds: bassett hound, bloodhound, chihuahua, dachshund (short hair), dachshund (long hair), English beagle, German shepherd, Irish setter, Maltese, Pekingese, Pomeranian, poodle, Saint Bernard, Shetland sheepdog.

The United Kennel Club is the largest registrar of coonhounds. Currently there are over one thousand coonhound clubs recognized by UKC, which licenses over three thousand coonhound events each year in forty states of the U.S. and most provinces of Canada.

UKC licenses bench shows for nine breeds of dogs and also licenses water races, field trials, and "nite" hunts for coonhounds. UKC sponsors two large coonhound events a year; Autumn Oaks, which annually attracts a crowd of well over ten thousand and has an entry of almost one thousand dogs in the "nite" hunts and bench show, and the UKC world's championship, which is an elimination competition with regional qualifying events and a four-day final event.

The highest pedigree record achievable under UKC registration is the Purple Ribbon Pedigree. To earn a Purple Ribbon (PR) a dog must have six generations of known ancestors, and all of the dogs within the last three generations must be registered with UKC. Over three-fourths of the dogs UKC now registers have earned the Purple Ribbon Pedigree. UKC offers a certified six- or seven-generation pedigree. A six-generation pedigree contains 126 ancestors. If a seven-generation pedigree with 254 ancestors is desired, both parents must be Purple Ribbon holders.

Some of the breeds are able to work toward UKC Champion and Grand Champion show degrees.

UKC also awards championship degrees for "nite" hunts, field trials, and water races for coonhounds. In each of these a dog competes in an event that simulates the work for which he and his ancestors were bred. In none of these events is there any taking of game.

Some other U.S. registries are:
Field Dog Stud Book
222 West Adams Street
Chicago, IL 60606
International Fox Hunters' Stud Book
Box 577
Lexington, KY 41001
National Greyhound Association
Box 543
Abilene, KA 67410
Animal Research Foundation
Post Office
Quinlan, TX 75474
(see index)

HOW TO BECOME AN AKC JUDGE

If you have owned several dogs of the breed you want to judge, have had breeding experience, stewarded at shows, judged sanctioned matches, sweepstakes, or futurities, compiled a record of exhibiting at dog shows—and if you have a strong background in the sport of dogs, such as club memberships—you may qualify to become a judge. Also, a personal interview will probably be required.

No one deriving a major portion of income from dog commerce—kennel managing, training, food processing, product sales or manufacture, etc.—will be considered.

After preliminary review, applications are considered by the AKC Board of Directors. The names of provisional judging applicants are published in *The Gazette*, the AKC magazine, to elicit comment from the fancy at large. After three judging assignments are completed, a candidate is evaluated again by the directors for regular judging status.

"One of the most important continuing jobs for the kennel club is the approval of judges," William B. Stiffel, AKC chief executive, has said. In an attempt to better measure what he describes as a "very elusive quality," the club's interview program is being expanded and there will be more objective testing—both oral and written—than in the past. "No one of these things alone would be sufficient basis for approving someone as a judge," Stiffel said.

There are some twenty-four hundred AKC judges.

Quick-Study Quiz

1. Where did the Great Dane originate?

2. What breed of dog is called the "little captain"?

3. What dog's name indicates that the breed was once mostly black?

4. What is the modern name of the "round headed bull and terrier dog"?

5. What work does the briard do for French farmers?

6. By what name is the German bulldog generally known?

7. What two breeds of sheepdogs are identical except for size?

8. What is the official top speed record of the greyhound?

9. Which fox terrier was first exhibited in the show ring?

10. Are the miniature and Doberman pinschers two varieties of the same breed?

11. Waterside, working, and Bingley terrier are the former names of which modern breed?

12. The pug occurs in the ancestry of what dog?

13. What breed is England's number-one dog export?

14. Bobtail is the nickname of what breed?

15. What is the modern name of the Rothbury terrier?

16. What is the oldest of the breeds classified as a retriever?

17. What dog is known as the gray ghost?

18. What is the lion dog?

19. The Russian tracker is the ancestor of what modern breed?

20. What is the German shepherd called in England?

---

1. *In Germany where the breed is called the* Deutsche dogge *(German mastiff).*

2. *Schipperkes have a long history as guardians of the barges that travel the canals and waterways of Belgium. In Flemish* schipperke *means "little captain."*

3. *The collie, first called "coalie" by Scots and Englishmen.*

4. *The Boston terrier.*

5. *It works as a draft animal and as a sheepdog.*

6. *The boxer.*

7. *The collie and the Shetland sheepdog.*

8. *The fastest of dogs has been clocked at 41.11 miles an hour.*

9. *The smooth, some twenty years before the wire fox terrier.*

10. *No. The miniature pinscher is a breed many centuries old. Louis Doberman created his pinscher about 1890.*

11. *The Airedale terrier.*

12. *The brabancan, or smooth Brussels griffon.*

13. *The Yorkshire terrier.*

14. *The old English sheepdog.*

15. *The Bedlington terrier.*

16. *The curly-coated retriever has existed as a true breeding strain since 1855.*

17. *The Weimaraner.*

18. *Revered in China centuries ago as a sacred symbol of the Buddha lion, the Pekingese were once called lion dogs.*

19. *The large, taffy-colored Caucasian sheepdog, a sometime circus performer, selectively bred with a dash of bloodhound, produced today's golden retriever.*

20. *The Alsatian. Because of anti-German sentiment during World War I the breed came to be called the Alsatian wolfdog, even though there weren't many of them in Alsace. It was shortened to Alsatian in the 1930s.*

Edited from All About Dogs, *a Gaines Dog Research Center bimonthly sent to the press.*

Judging

Book Reviews

To what idealized and magnificent creature should a judge compare the dogs in competition in his show ring? *Dog Visualizations, Dog Lover's Complete Guide* ($8.95; New York: Arco, 1975), edited by Dennis B. Sprung, shows the ideal in diagrammed black-and-white photographs. There is also the complete AKC standard for, and a color photo of, an exemplary individual of each recognized breed.

Your Show Dog (Garden City: Doubleday, 1968), by Maxwell Riddle, covers in detail a show judge's role and function. There is information on how to become a judge, a code of conduct for judges, record-keeping, weighing, measuring and color determination, how to deal with problems of temperament in dogs, and more.

Greyhounds, as everyone knows, are raced for the money. In recent years more than fifteen million fans bet more than a billion dollars annually at forty-three tracks in twelve states. (Photo courtesy of Greyhound Publications)

8

HUNTING, RACING, FIGHTING

TRAINING THE GOLDEN RETRIEVER

   by Edward P. Cohen

GONE HUNTING

TRAINING DOGS FOR TRIALS
   AND THE REAL THING
   Book Reviews

TIMID DOGS
   by Joseph A. Graham

THE SPORTING LIFE
   by Harold Herrick, Jr.

SLED DOG RACING—AN
   INTERNATIONAL SPORT

EXCLUSIVE: IDITAROD WINNER
   TELLS HOW
   by R. A. Swenson

"I BLEW THE WHOLE THING AT
   GOLOVIN"
   Book Reviews

RACING: GREYHOUNDS,
   WHIPPETS, FOXHOUNDS,
   AND COONHOUNDS, TOO—
   Notes

NOT FOR SALE
   by Williams Haynes

DOGFIGHTING REPORT

Training the Golden Retriever

by Edward P. Cohen

How one man's life, and his wife's, changed for the better when he acquired a dog and read James Lamb Free's book.

"Bang!" It is my wife, Toba, shouting.

"Baaang!"—voice rising somewhat this time, more urgent, a second shout.

Sitting at heel beside me is my golden retriever, Max, an eighteen-month-old russet-colored male, really nice to look at. Hearing Toba's shout, playfulness ends. He suddenly becomes all business, concentrating on her as she stands about a city block away in a field of trees and low-growing weeds.

At this moment Toba throws, in a graceful arch, a retriever training dummy—a soft, cork-filled, oblong, canvas-covered object, rather like a small boat bumper, which mimics in size a duck or pheasant. It lands in a clump of tall grass not far from her. On my command, "Back," Max leaps forward, running at top speed toward the fallen dummy. He finds it quickly, gives Toba, who is now standing quite still, a quick glance, mouths it gently, and brings it back, slower now—trotting with a positively jaunty air, tail wagging vigorously.

"Good dog," I say, meaning it as he sits and "hands" the dummy to me from his mouth.

"We" are in training for a retriever trial over the weekend. About one hundred dogs of the several retriever breeds—Labradors mostly, with goldens and an occasional Chesapeake—are brought together and divided into classes according to age, prior success in trials held elsewhere, and whether or not they have been trained by amateurs like us or professionals. (There are surprisingly large numbers of professionals who train dogs for field trials, and many owners who purchase dogs for this purpose only.) The dogs compete against each other for inscribed cups, trophies, and ribbons. The dog is judged upon the facility with which he finds, and returns, the fallen "bird"; his eagerness; steadiness; and responsiveness to commands, both by voice and, for dogs in advanced training, by hand signal.

Our dog, trained entirely by Toba and me, has done modestly well in the "Derby" group—retrievers between one and two years. This particular weekend we were not to be "winners," receiving no place, but we did take home a ribbon for an "award of merit." Max had searched too long before finding the last "bird."

Max makes us look good. He learns easily and has a

natural intelligence and eagerness to please that leads him to more difficult training exercises. This, along with good strength and a well-muscled body, make him a joy to own. We have never punished him with more than "bad dog!"

This all began about two years before, when we decided to buy a retriever puppy—a ball of fluff with two dark eyes. We had had prior dog experience and knew to buy from an established breeder. We chose a golden because of its reputation for gentleness, moderate size, and spectacular beauty; we rejected other breeds as excessively noisy or overly aggressive. Both Toba and I had gone bird-shooting, ducks and pheasant, when we lived in Colorado. I must add that we had no. prior field trial experience, nor was it our intention to train and enter Max for this.

That began when I purchased James Lamb Free's fine book, *Training Your Retriever*. Only half the book is devoted to such mundane subjects as house training or how to build a kennel. It's the second half that really gets interesting. "How to steady him on the line," "doubles" (two dummies are thrown in quick succession; the dog retrieves the first, remembers where the second fell, and retrieves that one, too), and even "triples."

"Boy did he learn—not only retrieving, but 'sit,' 'stay,' 'don't bark,' 'bark,' 'lie down,' 'come,' and 'go.'"

I followed directions and, shortly after we had the dog home, playfully threw a rag doll to the other end of the living room. "Ball of fluff," with no urging from me, took off like a shot, tripped over his feet only once, and happily—happily, mind you—brought it back to me. Here was a natural, I thought. I was hooked.

Well, it turns out that for rigorous training only one master is allowed. Toba took some convincing. I suggested that it would be temporary (a year or so) and that he'd be a better pet for it. She agreed rather reluctantly and with much misgiving, and while it worked as promised, I don't believe I have quite been forgiven yet. All of this meant he had to have a kennel. We built an A-frame doghouse, complete with cedar-shake shingles and elevated floor, and bought a chain-link fence to place on our newly poured concrete slab. No one was to feed him except me, and he *learned*. Boy did he learn—not only retrieving, but "sit," "stay," "don't bark," "bark," "lie down," "come," and "go"—all according to instructions from Free's book. It really worked. The dog is a marvel.

Dr. Edward P. Cohen is associate professor in the departments of medicine and microbiology and the division of biological sciences at the University of Chicago.

Gone Hunting

Here's an organization designed to foster the sporting interest.

The National Shooting Sports Foundation, which is supported by ninety firms involved in all aspects of the shooting industry and by seven hundred dealers, "exists to promote an active future for everyone whose business or recreational bent relates to the legitimate use of sporting firearms."

The NSSF sponsors a National Hunting and Fishing Day, holds workshops for the Outdoor Writers Association of America, promotes inanimate (target) shooting with an award program for youngsters, and publishes a directory of shooting preserves in the U.S. and Canada, which says in its introduction:

Where else can you spend a crisp autumn morning with a stylish bird dog on point and suddenly a big, flashy ringneck pheasant comes cackling up out of the cover in front of you? There are plenty more where that one came from, too.

This type of action is common on a good hunting club, with its well-managed cover and trained gun dogs. The cost is much more reasonable than you probably imagine. Some preserves charge for the number of birds bagged, others for birds released in your fields that day and still others for a sporting chance to bag some birds when accompanied by a guide. Get set for some of the best hunting you have ever experienced.

A good shooting preserve has quality and variety and follows these minimum standards of the North American Game Breeders and Shooting Preserve Operators Association:

1. The area should look like good hunting country, with a blend of natural and cultivated cover.
2. Pheasants, quail, and chukars should be full-plumaged, more than sixteen weeks old, and of the same color and conformation as birds in the wild.
3. Mallards should be similar in weight and plumage to free-ranging mallards, and capable of strong flight between release sites and rest ponds.
4. Well-trained dogs should be available for the guests, and to reduce crippling losses of game.

In addition to well-trained dogs, flighty birds, and plenty of action, a shooting preserve has some special things to offer. The open season in many states is six months long, with good hunting long after the regular seasons have closed. For nonresident hunters, a shooting preserve license may cost only a fraction of a regular nonresident hunting license. Best of all, a good shooting preserve is an ideal place to take a young hunter, with plenty of action and professional gunners to give a novice the right start in hunting safety and wing shooting.

For a catalog of publications and information contact The National Shooting Sports Foundation, 1075 Post Road, Riverside, CT 06878.

Selected books for training dogs—for both field trials and the real thing.

Training Dogs for Trials and the Real Thing

Book Reviews

Field trials, as recreational activity, have become increasingly popular in the past twenty-five years.

Besides getting its human devotees outdoors, sometimes onto horseback, the trials are the proving grounds of a dog's breeding and bloodlines, testing individual qualities of speed, range, bird-finding ability, trainability, and stamina.

Field trials are conducted on recognized upland game birds, wild or released—quail, pheasant, grouse, prairie chicken, woodcock, and chukar. Dogs that excel at trials are said to be hereditarily the most proficient and contributors of the finest progeny to actual gunning.

Field trials may be compared to the major golf tours, where leading players compete, following the sun from Canada to Florida in autumn and winter, swinging through the midwest and central states in spring.

For information about field trials, bird hunting, and how to acquire a good hunting dog see *Field Trials—History, Management, and Judging Standards* ($12.00;

S. Brunswick, NJ: A. S. Barnes, 1977), by William F. Brown, who is editor of *The American Field*, the oldest sportsman's publication in the U.S. His *How to Train Hunting Dogs* ($7.95; S. Brunswick, NJ: A. S. Barnes, 1942), considered a standard classic, is illustrated with the work of noted photographer W. Eugene Smith.

Other books of interest:

Training Setters and Pointers for Field Trials ($5.95; New York: Arco, 1974), by John M. Beazly, Alfred K. Manners and Arnold C. White-Robinson, explains with diagrams how to do it.

Training the Mind of Your Gun Dog ($9.75; London: Pelham Books, 1977; distributed in the U.S. by Transatlantic Arts), by J. A. Kersley and F. Haworth, an English physician and a field trial judge, respectively, takes a somewhat biological, psychological approach. For instance, we are told that neurosis "is brought about by presenting a dog with a problem that he cannot solve"; scenting is not so much a question of a dog's "good nose" as of an ability to concentrate. In passing, this comment is made: "A dog can differentiate into its several components that mess of potage we call a dog's dinner . . . and perhaps the dog-meat manufacturers are after all correct when they label the tin of their product which consists of cereal and reconstituted offal 'Liver and Chicken Supreme.'"

Coleridge is quoted:

> In Koln a town of monks and bones,
> And pavements fanged with murderous stones,
> And rags and hags and hideous wenches
> I counted two and seventy stenches . . .

In *Retriever Training the Modern Way* ($9.95; North Pomfret, VT: David and Charles, 1976), by Susan Scales, a noted, winning trainer (primarily of Labradors), emphasizes the similarity between training puppies and bringing up children. Some chapter titles—Early Upbringing (playgroup stage), Something a Little More Difficult (primary school), The Great Day (university)—make the point. Illustrated with photographs.

Spaniel Training for Modern Shooters ($8.95; North Pomfret, VT: David and Charles, 1974), by Maurice Hopper, deals with the ancient sport of hunting with spaniels which, "before the muzzle-loaders . . . sprang game for falconers and drove ducks and waders into fowlers' nets. They were certainly doing this in the reigns of the Norman kings and possibly during the Roman occupation," according to the book's introduction. The author, who has for many years run a school for spaniels and retrievers at Cranborne Chase in Dorset, England, has an international reputation as a professional gun-dog trainer.

A book devoted to just one spaniel, the Brittany, is Ralph B. and Robert D. Hammond's *Training and Hunting the Brittany Spaniel* ($7.95; Cranbury, NJ: A. S. Barnes, 1971). The point is made that "General methods and techniques for a specific phase in the training of a particular breed of bird dog do not differ greatly from trainer to trainer. . . . Latitudes and variations are due primarily to the individualities of both the trainer and the dog." While urging common sense and reason, the Hammonds offer their own philosophy and technique of training to bring out a dog's maximum potential. Brittanies are described as good all-day gun dogs. The authors feel field trials are inappropriate for this breed because of an overemphasis in trials on speed, style, wide ranging, and unmoving staunchness to point. "We do not feel that dogs of field trial training may be the best hunting and shooting dogs . . ." they say. They describe the Brittany with all the superlatives that enthusiasts will use, while cautioning that the breed is emotional and more subject to anxiety and insecurity than some, and so should be handled gently.

The Complete Brittany Spaniel ($10.95; New York: Howell Book House, 1974), by Maxwell Riddle, discusses the breed as field trial, obedience, and conformation show competitor. This is a detailed history and in-depth examination of the Brittany in Europe and America. An authoritative book.

Going from the particular to the more general, *Your Bird Dog and You* ($9.95; S. Brunswick, NJ: A. S. Barnes, 1977), by Field Trial Hall of Fame member Mike Seminatore as told to John M. Rosenberg, covers the pointing breeds: English setter, German shorthaired pointer, Brittany spaniel, Gordon setter, Weimaraner, vizsla, wirehaired pointing Griffon, and Irish setter. This author is obviously a field-trial enthusiast—he has trained about two thousand pointing dogs, and has won three thousand placements in field-trial competitions and twenty-seven championships.

Often described as the bird shooter's bible, James Lamb Free's *Training Your Retriever* ($8.95; New York: Coward, McCann and Geoghegan, 1949) is *the* classic in its field. About training retrievers the author says, "There's nothing to it that a fairly bright moron couldn't figure out for himself, if he had the time. Well, I took the time. . . . Now in this book I'm going to tell you what I've learned about these dogs. Where and how to find yourself a good one . . . a dog worth training. . . . In this book I'm going to tell you how to start right, and do it the easy way." And that's exactly what he does in an engagingly informal, free-flowing style. There's a recently updated section on field trials and an excellent bibliography.

For a nice look at the tracking breeds—hounds—there's *The Practical Hunter's Dog Book* ($8.95; New York: Winchester Press, 1971), by John R. Falk. Included is a history of the beagle, the most popular of hunting dogs, expert at tracking the most sought-after small game, the rabbit.

The basset is described as a descendant, in part, of the old French bloodhound, who "will do a creditable job of tracking virtually any small game species that leaves a ground scent for him to follow . . ." The black-and-tan coonhound, once called the Virginia black-and-tan, is a foxhound turned "raccoon dog supreme." After the black-and-tan, the treeing Walker, redbone, bluetick, and Plott are the best-known hounds in the country. The Plott is a boar and bear dog.

A FABLE OF AESOP— A BREED OF FAINT-HEARTS

A fawn once said to the old deer: "Father, nature has made you bigger and swifter than dogs, and moreover you have marvelous horns to defend yourself with. Why then do you flee from them in such terror?"
"What you say is quite true, my son," replied the deer with a laugh. "I don't know how it is; but I do know that the moment I hear the baying of a hound I feel an irresistible impulse to run away."

If a man is born a coward, no amount of exhortation can put a stout heart into him.

Timid Dogs

by Joseph A. Graham

Philosophical background to the training of dogs, "hounds as well as shooting breeds," plus practical advice from 1906.

It is pretty nearly a general rule that a shooting dog that begins active work with a fearless disregard of the gun, the whip, and other alarming circumstances is humdrum and commonplace all his life. It takes a degree of sensitiveness to make high intelligence. As for ginger and keenness, that quality can scarcely exist without a nervous responsiveness, which in youth often looks like timidity.

If the best dogs, hounds as well as shooting breeds, are likely to be endowed with dispositions that stupid handlers would construe as shyness, a little lecture on the treatment of such animals will do some good.

Patience is necessary to the trainers of all animals. And yet a certain application of force is also necessary.

A dog cannot be permitted to do as he pleases. The handler, even if he is a professional, cannot devote his time wholly to waiting for his pupil to grow into excellence. Force and patience must be applied. Success comes to the trainer who can mix these qualities with discrimination.

A man buys a ten-month-old puppy. Perhaps he has been raised in a kennel, has never known but one person, has been acquainted with but one narrow scene. He is crated and shipped—scared out of his wits from beginning to end of the journey. Everything is strange and alarming. He arrives at a new residence and is pulled about by new people. When his owner tries to be friendly, the dog is wild-eyed, crying, ready to run away. Often it happens that he has never worn a collar and never felt the coercion of a chain or lead.

. . . the trainer should be absolutely certain that the dog connects the exact error with the punishment . . .

If the owner has not had much experience, he may think that he has bought a worthless idiot. But he should try a short period of unmixed kindness. First, he should feed the pup himself. At that age chronic hunger is the strongest feeling the dog knows. He will quickly place confidence in the man who feeds him twice a day. Feed him at the kennel where he is supposed to dwell. In a day he will follow the person whom he associates with food, and he will be pretty sure to find his way back to the kennel even if he gets lost in his panics and bewilderments. If he won't lead, put a collar on him and snap in a lead invariably before letting him eat. If you are in the country, or where you can take the chance of not

Photograph by Daniel O'Toole

losing him, have him follow you for short distances before you try to lead him. Still better, take an old dog out with him. No matter how shy he is, he will hang around another dog.

It should not be necessary to say that a gun should never be fired near him until he is easy in his new surroundings; then let the first shooting experiments be made at a distance from him.

Maybe a strange dog will run at him and send him scurrying away in fright. Don't chase him or let anybody else raise a hue and cry. Unless you are in a city, with its labyrinth of streets, the dog is almost sure to reach home before you do. It is a good thing to take him out again at once, over the same route. But that may not be convenient. Give him a bite to eat, make his homecoming happy, and let him alone. While his verdancy lasts, the first consideration is to make him have faith in you, whatever other imaginary enemies excite his apprehension. Make him believe that you are a safe refuge, able and willing to protect him from all troubles.

One introduction to severity may be made early without detriment to his future. It will come up when he howls and scratches at being left alone. That is such a nuisance to neighbors and annoyance to you that compulsory cessation is desirable. If, as you turn away from the kennel, he sets up a howl and begins to bite at the wire or boards of his enclosure, turn back at once and speak sharply, slapping the kennel loudly with a stick. If he doesn't see the point, go into the kennel, whip him a little, and use the sharp tone so that he connects it with the whipping. If he cuts up again when you leave, turn back and administer the same treatment. Usually a few days' persistence on this line settles most of his kennel distress.

It is wise to make this point the first use of force for a reason aside from your own and your neighbors' comfort. The connection cannot be misunderstood by the dog. It cannot teach him bad habits or prevent the acquisiton of good ones. Without injury to his qualities of work, he discovers that when you speak in a certain tone, he must pay attention or suffer disagreeable consequences. You have control of him while the punishment is going on, and that is of the first importance. Be chary of whipping a young dog in the field. All whipping in the early stages of training should occur in the yard or when the dog is on a lead or check cord. When at work in the open, the trainer should be absolutely certain that the dog connects the exact error with the punishment; otherwise he can in a few minutes produce a confirmed blinker or potterer.

I have been describing an extreme instance of apparent timidity. Few young ones are quite so provoking. But I have seen such cases, and have seen some of them turn out to be fine animals a few months later. Once you get the dog to believe that you are the source of all blessings—blessings to a dog meaning victuals and refuge from danger—he will believe that you are the greatest and wisest and bravest of mankind. Then he will take his whipping along with other vicissitudes and trust you none the less.

Quiet behavior in the yard or kennel brings to mind another proclivity which, like unseemly and untimely noise, produces so much friction with other people that it is often a more serious matter than bad behavior in the field. Any young dog whose hunting instinct is specially developed is prone to the pursuit and slaughter of poultry, cats, sheep, and other fleeing creatures. In early America, where most dogs were raised on farms or at large in small towns, this fault was corrected early and speedily. Nowadays your valuable dog grows up in a kennel, and the chicken has all the enticing attributes of game. Your dog may kill enough Wyandottes worth ten dollars apiece to make your investment in him come to more than he will ever be worth.

If he is trained to stop to command, you may control him at once when he starts after a chicken and give him a reproof that will be lasting. Some owners find that the best way is to not wait for the chance fowl, but to buy a cheap one and give a special course of lessons before an evil day produces a feud with humans. Tie the chicken outside the kennel for a few minutes and let the young dog or dogs show an interest. Then bring out the dog. Speak to him sharply if he pulls on the lead and tries to reach his supposed game. Take the chicken by the legs, strike the dog lightly about the face with it, rub it roughly against his nose, and in general give him to understand that chickens are to be avoided. The treatment is nearly always effectual.

Many trainers follow this plan to break up rabbit chasing. After a shooting dog has been thumped with a dead rabbit and compelled to endure the indignity of having it rubbed in his face, he remembers that to catch that kind of animal breeds shame and distress. I have seen a trainer fasten a rabbit's body around a dog's neck and force him to carry it for half a day. I never tried it myself, but can understand that a dog so treated might hate rabbits to the end of his life.

Any of these devices may possibly make a young dog timid on game. But the chance must be taken. You cannot afford to let your dog become a nuisance.

If the experiment spoils the dog's value on game, it doesn't cost much to give him away and get another. In fact, most people are too slow about getting rid of low-grade dogs. It is all right to give the dog a square deal and not expect too much at first, but certain weaknesses soon become apparent. If they are of a vital kind, there should be no hesitation in changing dogs. Life is too short to waste over thirty days in deciding on the wisdom of persisting with any one animal.

Edited and reprinted from The Outing Magazine, *September 1906.*

TO CATCH A FOX

The Masters of Foxhounds Association (of England) stud book dates back only to 1800, but there are records of the true modern English foxhound's arrival in the U.S. as early as 1738, when they were imported by Lord Fairfax. Even before that hunting hounds of various varieties made their way to America—probably first with DeSoto in the early 1500s. Foxhounds seem to have arrived with Robert Brooke, who brought his pack with him from England in 1650. A pack was also imported by Thomas Walker in 1742 (its progeny, today called the Walker Hound, is much admired), and George Washington had an English pack delivered in 1770. In 1785 Washington received a gift of French hounds from Lafayette. The interbreeding of the offspring of these founding packs with later importations of others from England, Ireland, and France resulted in the American hounds—which now include the formally designated American foxhound.

There are four distinct types of American foxhounds. They differ in appearance and, except in one instance, in function from the English foxhound. In the U.S. there are pack hounds used in the traditional manner by American hunt clubs. The "traditional" manner is the well-known sport of a fox chased by a pack of dogs followed by mounted riders dressed "in the pink."

A similar activity involves trail or drag hounds. The dogs follow a prelaid, fox-scented path, and they, too, are pursued by mounted "hunters." The object here is speed, to finish first, because there is no fox to catch.

A lone fox hunter on foot with a gun and a single hound uses another variety of the dog, one that trails slowly and sings boisterously.

The fourth type of American foxhound is the one developed particularly for field trial competition. These hounds look the same but have different skills.

There is a unique Southern American fox hunt. A group of good ole boys takes to the woods with dogs and jugs. While enjoying each others' company round a fire, they listen to their hounds chase the fox through the darkness. Sensitive to the most subtle inflections of their hounds' voices, the "hunters" vicariously enjoy every detail and nuance of the chase without ever leaving the comfort of the fire and good company. In this sort of hunt the fox usually goes to ground (into its burrow), and the dogs are recalled by the horn. MacKinlay Kantor describes such a hunt in *The Voice of Bugle Ann* (New York: Coward, McCann, 1935).

The Sporting Life

by Harold Herrick, Jr.

About fifteen years ago the author, an insurance broker and an enthusiast of hunting with dogs, put both activities together.

My early gunning days started in the Lawrence, Long Island, marshes and tidal creeks. It was here my forefathers enjoyed shorebird, rail bird, and duck shooting. The shorebird carvings (decoys) of the eminent Bill Bowman were used by the sportsmen on this marsh. While duck shooting provided good bags at times, the loss of crippled birds in the marsh grass presented a real problem because my early days in the marsh were without a retriever.

Later I met a young lady, Anne Fowler, who had just bred a golden retriever from the bloodlines of Stilrovin Superspeed· There were ten puppies chasing around in the pen. It was from this litter that my great companion and retriever, Penny, was picked.

Never having been to a dog show, field trial, or obedience training class, I was told to purchase James Lamb Free's *Training Your Retriever* [New York: Coward, McCann and Geoghegan, rev. ed., 1974; see index for review]. In addition, I bought every book and publication dealing with retrievers and their bloodlines. Then, after many months of amateur training with pigeons and ducks, the fall season opened. Penny was eager, alert, and not gun-shy. For the next fourteen years, afield and in the marsh, from Long Island to the Canadian border, this retriever and I shared the great out-of-doors experience.

A hunting dog, whatever the breed, is a faithful companion and a pleasure to be with in fall hunting days.

Many good field dogs have been a part of our household. The large male golden, Dusty, that my son trained and hunts with today performed excellently for Nelson Bryant, an outdoor columnist for *The New York Times.*

Mr. Bryant came for ducks, but the sunny, windless day meant that waterfowl would settle on open water, far from land and hunters. We decided to go for woodcock despite the lack of a pointer. I assured Mr. Bryant that Dusty would perform well even though hunting grouse, quail, or woodcock with a retriever doesn't offer the sportsman the same chance to prepare for a shot that he has when hunting with a pointer. We put up seven woodcock that day and took three.

A retriever that has earned the coveted title of Field Trial Champion has beaten some stiff competition. Many hours of training are necessary for making the retriever steady on the line and to have him respond to hand signals. The training extends also to the dog owner or handler. I have seen many instances where the owner couldn't handle a retriever that had been sent away to be trained—either at a trial or at a shoot for driven birds.

As my interest in golden retriever activities grew with exposures to dog shows and field trials, I met a great many people and learned of the responsibilities that are placed on nonprofit dog clubs. One of the primary concerns was the securing of proper and adequate liability insurance, since in many instances with "shoot-to-kill trials" live shotgun ammunition is used. As an insurance broker I had developed a plan of liability coverage for horse shows. So I developed a similar comprehensive plan for dog clubs.

For information contact Harold E. Herrick, Jr., Box 43, Clayton, NY 13624.

AKC FIELD TRIAL CATEGORIES

The AKC licenses four separate categories of field trials designed to test a dog's ability to perform the work for which it was originally bred. Because the type of activity varies, rules are different for each of the following groups.

Hounds in packs or in pairs pursue rabbits and hares.

The pointing breeds stop and point, allowing the hunter to flush game birds.

Retrievers fetch, from water and land, game that has been shot.

Spaniels flush game birds for hunters and also retrieve.

For information contact the American Kennel Club (see index).

Sled Dog Racing— an International Sport

For seventy years there have been formal sled dog races. Here's how they work.

The records of formal sled dog racing date back to 1908, year of the first All-Alaskan Sweepstakes, a race of 408 miles from Nome to Candle and back. The winning time was 119 hours, 15 minutes, 12 seconds. In 1910 the record for the same trail was reduced to 74 hours, 14 minutes, 37 seconds.

In 1925, when dog sledding was still vital to the North, a relay of native and mail teams was organized to carry lifesaving serum from Anchorage to the diphtheria-stricken village of Nome. Now the dog team as a means of transportation has all but disappeared—replaced by the aircraft and snowmobile.

Sled dog racing has, however, developed into a popular international winter sport. Significant races are held throughout Alaska, Canada, and the northern United States as well as in Scandinavia, Switzerland, and Germany.

So-called Northern breeds are used for racing: Alaskan malamute, Siberian husky, Alaskan husky, Samoyed, and Eskimo dog.

Dogs of northern breed type stand about twenty-four inches at the shoulder and weigh fifty to sixty pounds. They have a full, protective coat of fur, but not

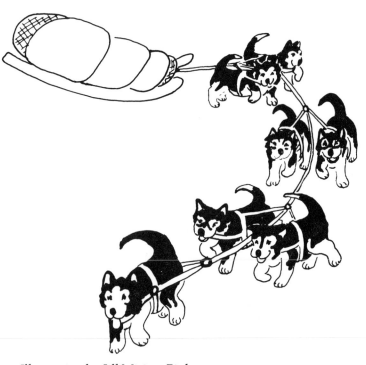

Illustration by Jill Miriam Pinkwater

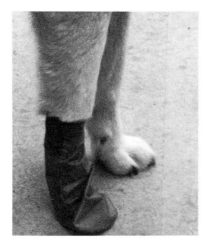

Tun-Dra's dog boot of red cordova nylon is available in three pad width sizes.

Sled dog training tri-mobile weighs 170 pounds.
(Photographs courtesy Tun-Dra Kennels and Outfitters)

Hand-made ash racing sled with poly runners and bows is able to withstand temperatures as low as −70°F. Tun-Dra has it in child, junior, and adult sizes. The largest weighs thirty-seven pounds.

excessively long so as to trap snow. A strong, slightly roached back, straight shoulders, and compact, tough feet are dominant features. A deep chest and large lung capacity, coupled with tremendous heart and stamina, are prerequisites. The dogs are gentle and reliable; a dog that is difficult to handle does not make a suitable "team" and racing dog.

Also used are the English pointer, Irish setter, Dalmatian, and American coon- and foxhounds.

The modern dog race takes place on a closed course—a prepared trail fifteen to thirty miles in length, with the start and finish at the same location. The race is run in one, two, or three daily heats, with the best overall time determining the winner. The teams draw for position on the first day and race against the clock, leaving the start line at two- to three-minute intervals. A top team will average sixteen miles an hour over a twenty-mile trail.

The dogs are marked to prevent substitution, and all dogs that start a given heat must complete the course. Any dog that becomes tired or injured must ride home in the sled basket. A team overtaking another team on the trail has the right of way; the overtaken team must give way to provide a clean pass.

In 1973 long-distance events were reintroduced with the 1,049-mile race run over the Iditarod Trail in Alaska, from Anchorage to Nome.

The sport is growing for novices as well as experts, and most clubs provide a class to suit local requirements. Juniors run from one to seven dogs. (A seven-dog team can give a 170-pound adult a very exciting ride over a ten- to fifteen-mile trail.) Limited classes vary from three to seven dogs, running over trails suitable to the drivers and the size of the teams.

Ten to fourteen dogs comprise the usual unlimited-class racing team. They are hitched to the sled in pairs by means of the Alaskan racing hitch or gang-line. The harness is usually made of light nylon webbing and is custom fitted to each dog.

The racing sleds are eight feet long and weigh under forty pounds. They are usually fabricated from white ash, lashed together for flexibility and maneuverability.

Edited and reprinted from a pamphlet published by International Sled Dog Racing Association. For more information contact J. Malcolm McDougall, P.O. Box 5, Ste. Agathe Des Monts. P.Q., Canada.

For a comprehensive treatment with a good appendix that lists equipment makers, periodicals, and books see *The World of Sled Dogs: From Siberia to Sport Racing* ($12.95; New York: Howell Book House, 1977), by Lorna Coppinger and the International Sled Dog Racing Association.

Exclusive: Iditarod Winner Tells How

by R. A. Swenson

Men and their dogs race in dead of winter over mountains and sea ice for more than one thousand miles from Anchorage to Nome. Here is the 1977 winner's first-person account.

I got interested in dog mushing while living near Ely, Minnesota, in 1971. The following year I drove borrowed dogs and became addicted to the sport. During that winter I did some beaver trapping with an ex-dog musher who gave me very good advice. He said, "If you want to have dogs, go to Alaska, where they have lots of winter and good dogs."

I immediately started planning my move to Alaska and made it that fall. I moved near a deserted gold mining town, Livengood, which is north of Fairbanks. That winter I met a man who has become one of Alaska's most famous dog mushers and race promoters. He is in fact the Father of the Iditarod—Mr. Joe Redington, Sr. When I first met him, I was lucky to buy a young female dog from him. Nugget has been the mother of a good portion of my team. Her breeding is approximately one-half Siberian, one-quarter Belgian sheepdog, and one-quarter Indian dog. She is the only dog I still have that was in my original team five years ago.

My only regret when I get to Nome is that I can't just keep on going.

Ever since I started driving dogs, I dreamed of the time I would run the Iditarod Trail Race. At first it was merely a dream because I knew very little about dog mushing and nothing about racing. After I became more familiar with the race, I knew that someday I must run in it. To me the Iditarod is the ultimate test of what a man and his dog team can do when working together. It is a race that stretches across almost the entire state of Alaska. It covers a distance of 1,049 miles, crossing three mountain ranges and miles and miles of Alaska's vast interior. It starts in Anchorage the first Saturday in March and ends in Nome. It has done more to rekindle interest in dog mushing than any other race. Before the first Iditarod in 1973 dog mushing was dying in Alaska due to the popularity of the snowmachine. Since then literally thousands of teams have been started.

The record time for the running of the Iditarod is fourteen days, fourteen hours, which figures out to be approximately eighty miles per day. Last year I covered that distance in sixteen days, sixteen hours.

Training for the Iditarod is a very long process. It usually starts a good year or two in advance of the actual running of the race. Each musher must carefully select only the toughest sled dogs. Some of the criteria upon which toughness is based are eager attitude, desire to travel, good appetite, good feet, endurance, and good trotting ability. I personally also limit my selection to males, as females tend to come in heat, thus causing problems in the team that must live and work together for up to three weeks.

My own personal training is a year-round chore. In the summer I try to run the dogs enough with a three-wheeled cart to prevent them from getting soft. In September I start to train on a regular basis, trying to establish a fast trotting pace. I like to have all of my dogs trotting at approximately twelve miles per hour. When we get snow in October, I switch to a sled and continue to increase to a ten-mile run by the first of November. That is when I start to use my dogs for basic transportation. I drive them wherever I want to go because by then the roads in Manley, which is where I now live, are no longer driveable. From November until the end of December I sort out the dogs for the Knik 120, which is a one-hundred-and-twenty-mile race run in two sixty-mile heats. The record time for that race was set in 1975 by Joe Redington, Sr., who covered the one hundred and twenty miles in ten and one-half hours. After that race I start driving my dogs long distances of up to sixty miles a day. By the first of February I cut back on the mileage to let the dogs build up their attitude and their tired bodies. By this time they are so tough that the actual race itself is like a picnic.

While training I also prepare supplies and equipment. Supplies are shipped out ahead of the team to twenty-four checkpoints. Each musher is required to carry snowshoes, sleeping bag, axe, dog boots, dog food (twenty-one pounds per dog), and personal food. The placement of supplies can be critical. The gear for the race must be of the highest caliber; your life may depend upon it. In 1974 a chill factor of −130 degrees F. was recorded, and −50 is common. I personally test each item I carry a long time before I decide it is reliable enough to depend on 100 percent.

Dog food for this race varies from musher to musher, but one thing is universal. No commercial dog food is good enough by itself to meet the extreme energy demands of the Iditarod. I personally use Iams Plus dry ration mixed fifty-fifty with beaver or horse meat. To this I add lard and liver. This has given me very satisfactory results. I feed my dogs three to four times per day while on the race. This seems outrageous, but it is necessary for prolonged performance. I figure each dog consumes about six thousand calories per day. My own food for the race consists of steak, unsalted crackers, and butter along with lots of tea, honey, and Tang. Most of these meals are cooked over an open fire or a Coleman gas stove that is carried for use in areas where there are no trees.

On a day-to-day basis the race is long, beautiful, boring, and tiring all at once. What makes the race bearable are the wonderful people along the route and the gorgeous scenery. I personally attempt to maintain a schedule whereby I do most of my traveling at night. I usually drive for about four hours, then stop and make camp. While stopped the first thing I do is build a fire and attend to the dogs' needs. After they have been fed and watered, I feed myself. Care of the dogs is of the utmost importance because they are the ones that will get me to Nome. After a three- or four-hour rest, I start driving again for about four more hours. This is the ideal schedule. Weather, checkpoints, and many other things can alter this, but a four-hour-on and four-off schedule is ideal.

Once on the race, my objective is to reach the village of Unalakleet, about eight hundred miles from Anchorage, with as many of my dogs in as good a shape as possible. From Unalakleet it is two hundred and forty miles to Nome, and that is where the real push starts. It took me fifty-five hours from Unalakleet to Nome. My average speed between checkpoints last year was seven and three-tenths miles per hour. That included stops for feeding. I covered the last one hundred and forty miles in twenty hours. When I arrived in Nome, my dogs were still frisky and eager.

I usually keep about fifteen grown dogs to train for the race. In addition I like to have four to six pups to start training for future use. These dogs weigh fifty-three to fifty-five pounds and are twenty-three inches tall. They are extremely compact, well muscled, and

Rick Swenson, a trapper and pipeline worker from Manley Hot Springs, Alaska, just moments before he crossed the finish line first at Nome (temperature −21°F, time 1:27 A.M.) in the Iditarod Trail Sled Dog Race. "I had stopped short of the finish line even though the next musher was a mere four minutes behind to show my dogs the affection they deserved after such a long, hard race."

About one thousand people stayed up on the morning of March 22, 1977, to cheer the winner and his eleven-dog team in Alaska's biggest sporting event. Swenson's time for the 1,049-mile race from Anchorage to the Bering Sea community of Nome was 16 days, 16 hours, and 27 minutes. The race cost him $16,000; first-prize money is $10,000. Forty-seven mushers started the race; thirty-three finished.

129

agile. A nice dense hair coat is important, but it must not be long and bushy. This will cause heat-dissipation problems and therefore cause snow balls to form on their feet, which in turn mean blisters and cuts that reduce effectiveness. I never keep a dog that has any foot trouble. Some people claim black pads on the foot indicates toughness, but I don't think this is necessarily so. I have some dogs four years old with predominantly pink pads that have never had foot trouble. No matter what color the foot, it must be a tight, compact, Siberian-type foot.

In training I try to gain complete control of the dogs. By race time I like to have them so tuned to my commands that they will do exactly what I say. This requires hours and hours of training. The main dogs are the leaders; my two best leaders are half-brothers out of Nugget. They are very close to each other and to me. The three of us almost think as one. They are a real pleasure to drive.

I buy all my harnesses from Zima Products in Montana. The harnesses that I am using now are at least three years old and have been to Nome twice. Except for a few patches from chewing, they are like new. All the rest of my dogs' gear is homemade by me. I also make my own sleds out of native birch, rawhide, plastic, and hickory. Most of my clothing is also homemade, except for underwear and insulated coveralls. I follow native design. I have yet to use any commercial parka. They are usually too warm and bulky and have poorly designed hoods. They also rely too heavily upon zippers, which can either fail to close or freeze shut, either of which could prove fatal.

The biggest problem with racing the Iditarod is money. It costs approximately sixteen thousand dollars to keep fifteen to twenty-five dogs the year round. Not only must they be fed, but they also need regular worming, shots, and general care. It is really a full-time job. I feel that if we could gain more publicity for the race, big companies would become interested in using it as a testing ground for their products. I can think of no expedition or race where everything (dogs, feed, gear) gets put to as harsh a test as the Iditarod. One friend took a razor that went to the moon on the race. He figured if it could get to the moon and shave astronauts, it ought to be able to go to Nome. No such luck; he never got one shave from it due to the cold. In previous years he had used an electric rechargeable; it never failed to shave him every day without even one recharging.

Once a musher gets to Nome, he can really be proud of himself and his dogs. Rarely in this day and age does anyone have an opportunity to see some of the world's most unspoiled scenery and at the same time prove that he can take care of himself. My only regret when I get to Nome is that I can't just keep on going.

It is really unfortunate that more people can't enjoy the uniqueness of this race through television or a first-rate movie. We hope that someday it will happen.

"I Blew the Whole Thing at Golovin"

Book Reviews

"Trail Talk," a column in a recent issue of *The Iditarod Runner*, has this note: "There is talk amongst the mushers of possibly putting together a clinic on arctic survival for all new entrants in the Iditarod. In the past people coming up from the lower forty-eight have not always been prepared for the harsh conditions we have here."

Whether or not Jack Hooker was sufficiently prepared is a question that he struggles with, but in his sixteen-page booklet, *An "Outsider's" Iditarod* ($3.50; White Tail Ranch, Ovando, MT 59854), he leaves no doubt that the "insiders" were not only not helpful, they were downright rude. But, then, the mushers were going for big stakes, with first prize in the race approaching ten thousand dollars, and even more important, a huge measure of fame.

As it turned out, first-time-entrant Hooker did all right—he finished nineteenth (three hundred dollars

prize money), and he would have done a lot better if . . . if he hadn't overslept within less than one hundred miles of the finish line. Here is his account of the episode, given, as is his style, in the third person:

"He went into a house, which was very hot, and ate a big meal. After feeding the dogs, he sat down in a chair. Barely asleep, a woman woke him; he'd been there only two hours. But since she'd awakened him, he decided to go on anyway, and went outside. For a period of time he couldn't *find* the dogs; he'd forgotten where he left them. Eventually he stumbled across the dogs and attempted to get them up, but they stayed curled and wouldn't respond. He lifted them up one by one, shaking them back and forth, and eventually they would open an eye, let down a leg, and appear ready to stand. But when he set them down, they curled up again immediately. Jack picked up the towline and threw it back and forth, rolling the dogs over and over. Each time they curled up again.

"He gave up and went back into the house, and the woman suggested that he lie down on the sofa. Jack had an alarm watch which he set, to be sure to wake up in another couple of hours.

"When he did wake up, it was bright daylight, and eleven hours later. 'I blew the whole thing at Golovin,' said Jack."

The entire report is just as ingenuously appealing. Of how he got interested . . . of his trials and tribulations in acquiring a team . . . of how he equipped for the race . . . of the mistakes he made—he is careful to fully list and explain (but not to excuse) his errors.

"After it was clear" that feeding dry food to his dogs and then giving them water "wouldn't work, he began mixing the food with heated water like everyone else— but the dogs then came down with diarrhea. Treatment [Darbazine] finally controlled the diarrhea, but when the dogs were off the medication, it came back."

One of the most poignant parts of Hooker's account concerns the attitude of the insiders to the new man:

"There was a banquet before the race, for all the mushers. Jack said it was a nice dinner—but he had expected a briefing on the trail, or some kind of information. There was nothing of the kind, not even a map. The people there expect the entrants to know what they're doing, and many or most of the competitors, living in Alaska, seem to have an idea what's going on. An outsider is not expected to be any kind of threat, and is sort of ignored."

Anyhow, Hooker started off, overcame beginner's shock ("Yes, I thought of quitting"), won the respect of his fellow competitors at the race's midpoint ("They seemed to be friendlier now that I'd made it that far. A lot of them came over to shake hands and say howdy"), and he thrilled in the finish ("There are cars all along the bank with their lights on, people honking and hollering. The sirens go off, and people run out. It's the greatest time of your life").

The next year the "outsider" from Montana went back to run the Iditarod again. He finished tenth.

Following are two other how-to books and a list of outfitters and periodicals.

Racing Alaskan Sled Dogs ($7.95; Anchorage: Alaska Northwest Publishing Company, 1976) is a handsome, excitingly illustrated account of the subject by twenty-three experts. Editor is the late Bill Vaudrin, who competed twice in the Iditarod. Vaudrin, an "outside" (of Alaska) Indian (his father is a Chippewa of the White Earth reservation in Minnesota), died in 1976 when his car hit a moose on the George Parks Highway near Nenana.

George Attla, an "inside" Indian from Huslia, Alaska, wrote *Everything I Know About Training and Racing Sled Dogs* with Bella Levorsen ($9.95; Rome, NY: Arner Publications, 1974). Attla was North American Champion three times and World Champion four.

Outfitters:

Nelson Sled Dog Racing Equipment
Box 208, Hudson
Que., Canada J0P 1H0

Nordkyn Outfitters
Box 1118
Moses Lake, WA 98837

*Tun-Dra
Nunica, MI 49448

Zima
Kila, MT 55920

Periodicals on the subject:

Alaska Magazine
Box 4-EEE
Anchorage, AK 99509

Info:

International Sled Dog Racing Assoc.
Box 11
Bakers Mills, NY 12811

Northern Dog News
Box 310
Snohomish, WA 98290

Team and Trail
Center Harbor, NH 03226

Tug Line
Bemidji, MN 56601

* Besides mushing equipment, Deane and Roma Cheadle of Tun-Dra Kennels also offer posters, greeting cards, and lapel buttons—among the latter, "HUG A HUSKY."

Racing: Greyhounds, Whippets, Foxhounds, and Coonhounds, Too

New West (August 30, 1976) carried an article felicitously titled "Whippet Cream," in which we learn a thing or two about whippets and also that the North California Whippet Fanciers sponsor a race not only for whippets but also for Afghans, borzois, Irish wolfhounds, and greyhounds.

The article doesn't say which breed is favored in such a contest, but according to our authorities it should be the greyhound, which can run at about thirty-seven miles per hour; the whippet gets up to thirty-four miles per hour.

Whippets were first bred in the early nineteenth century by British miners who crossed greyhounds and terriers; later Italian greyhounds were introduced. The whippet, which should stand at twenty-two inches at the withers, has a short, smooth coat. Whippets make good pets. They are not raced for money but for sport.

Greyhounds, as everyone knows, are raced for the money. In recent years more than fifteen million fans bet more than a billion dollars annually at forty-three tracks in twelve states (Alabama, Arizona, Arkansas, Colorado, Connecticut, Florida, Massachusetts, New Hampshire, Oregon, South Dakota, Vermont, and West Virginia). At a greyhound track eight dogs are run in each race; there are ten to twelve races a night and one hundred or so nights a season.

At weaning, a greyhound is priced at from two hundred to four hundred dollars, while racing greyhounds sell from five hundred to more than five thousand.

For a basic guide on how to get into the business of greyhound racing, for a list of tracks around the country, and for a subscription to the sport's newspaper write Greyhound Publications, P.O. Box 520217, Miami.

In a foxhound race a scent is dragged along a ten-mile course and then as many as a hundred dogs are let loose in pursuit. First dog to the finish line wins. Foxhound racing is both a British and American sport.

Then there is the variation on the old coonhound-coon contest. The World Championship Coonhound Water Races are held annually at Lake Hartwell, South Carolina. Six dogs at a time are let loose from a raft about a hundred yards from shore. The hounds frantically swim after a coon that has been pulled before them—the coon being in a wire cage in a boat. The winner is the first dog over the finish line to bark, as in "treeing a coon."

In the old days none of this was so civilized. A coon was chained to a log in the water and the hounds went forth to do bloody battle.

Racing greyhound Boyd Cole with groomer Stephanie Herold. (Photograph by Mike Serlick)

Not for Sale
by Williams Haynes

Only the rich race horses, but even a working-man can keep, train, and race a dog. A pre-World War I episode.

I was in Manchester, England, and one afternoon my friend William Barker suggested that we go to Oldham to see the world-famous mills.

He told me how whole families work in the mills for pitiful wages, and that one of their main pleasures is in whippet racing. Here I was on familiar ground, for I knew whippets and had seen whippet races. A whippet is a dog somewhat bigger than a fox terrier but built like a greyhound—not by any means those shivering, toy Italian greyhounds, but a strong, lively, not very sweet-tempered dog. They are trained to race over a course two hundred yards long in around ten seconds, about twice as fast as a human sprinter. My friend told me how the millhands breed and train their whippets with all the care given a racehorse. They hold race meetings with cash prizes and handicaps and bookmakers. He said that often a family would bet their whole week's income on their dog, that a whippet in training will often eat chicken while the children have only black bread.

I was inclined to put salt on this information, but when we reached Oldham, I saw for myself. On a side street we met a mill operative and his wife with a brace of whippets on leads. Both were shabbily dressed. The man had on a rusty black suit, a blue soft shirt, and a dirty cap. His wife wore a patched cotton dress and a man's straw hat, quite innocent of trimmings. The dogs, however, had on leather box muzzles and plaid blankets bound in leather, all of the finest material and workmanship. I began to believe that my friend might not have been drawing very heavily on his imagination, but I decided to make a test.

"That's a nice brace of dogs," I said to their owner as we came up.

"Aye. They'll be fair 'uns."

"Can we see them with their blankets off?"

He was delighted and showed them off, telling us all about their breeding and the races they had won.

"I'll give you five pounds for the fawn-and-white," I said when he stopped to draw breath. He shook his head.

"Ten pounds for the two?"

Again he shook his head.

"Twelve?"

He swallowed hard and looked sheepishly at his "missus," but was firm in his refusal, though I had offered him more than he and his wife together earned in a month.

"Make it twelve guineas?"

"Don't ye offer no more, sir. I don't want to sell 'em."

[And that is the point where one man stops trying to buy another.]

Edited and reprinted from Country Life in America, *February 1913.*

Dogfighting Report

The New York Times *campaign against dogfighting, the law that resulted, notes about the way it was long ago, and an indication of how to find out more about what is happening now.*

In May 1976 a federal law was enacted that makes it illegal to transport animals across state lines for such activities as dogfights. That there is such a law must be attributed to the sensitivities of *The New York Times* and the vigor of reporter Wayne King, two years earlier.

Here we have a classic case of the power of the press. Until King's investigation *Times'* editors showed little interest in recent decades in dogfighting. That is with one exception—an emotionally neutral report by Robert Trumbull from Kochi, Japan, about Japanese dogfighting. That reporter, after noting that the sport was legal everywhere in Japan except Tokyo and Kanagawa, likened the activity to sumo wrestling in its ritual and discipline. He stated that as many as two thousand fans watch fights, which are stopped before serious injury occurs, and that no death has ever resulted. Further, he said: "The fighting dogs of Japan go into combat without making a sound. The best of them never let go, once they have a hold on an opponent, until forced. The first dog that growls, whines or barks is the loser, and the fight is stopped instantly."

Readers had to be shocked, and the *Times* **and King kept them so.**

On August 15, 1974, *The New York Times* found conditions quite different at home. A headline proclaimed "Dog Fighting: Illegal, Brutal, Growing." In a special dispatch from Chicago, King told how he infiltrated a group of fans and attended a dogfight. He was the guest of a peculiarly talkative man, Pat Podzianowski: ". . . a construction worker by trade, a burly, ponderous man about 40 years old, with a great stomach." King went on to portray a blue-collar ugly: "His bare upper body, across the chest and back and over the arms, is covered with tattoos."

Podzianowski was a breeder of fighting dogs, Staffordshire terriers. He was reckoned to be one of fifty such known breeders; they, and possibly as many as five thousand others, "meet clandestinely at locations across the country to take part in an illegal and apparently growing activity: pitting one dog against another and betting on fights that last up to several hours and often leave one or both dogs dying or dead."

This initial outraged report went on to estimate one thousand matches a year (at which there is heavy betting) of dogs trained to go for the kill after being taunted by paws of live kittens scratching at them through onion bags, of dogs fed dozens of cats or puppies to hone blood instincts, of drugs and cattle prods and prostitutes at the matches, and of a Podzianowski, insensitive to the pain suffered by animals and overly admiring of violence. Here is King quoting the tattooed breeder on the way he sent a fighting bitch into her final triumph:

> Her front leg was broke and sticking through the skin at two places. It would jab holes in the canvas when she walked. . . . The dog didn't know what was wrong, she tried to run at the other dog and that stub of a leg would hit the floor and she'd tumble. . . . You tell me that dog didn't have heart?

Readers had to be shocked, and the *Times* and King kept them so.

August 18, 1974: "Dogfight Reports in Chicago Set Off Inquiries by Police."

August 22: "Jury to Investigate Betting on Dogfights in the Chicago Area."

August 29: "Law Officers Are Found to Be Usually Unaware of Dogfighting."

September 3: "Congress Plans Hearings on Dogfighting."

September 16 (King has gone to Dallas): "Texas a Major U.S. Center for Illegal Dogfighting and Gambling."

October 1: "A Federal Law to Curb Dogfighting Is Urged at a Congressional Hearing."

More hearings were held, a law was passed, arrests made, fines levied.

It was almost as if the editors and reporter King had been looking over century-old issues of their paper. On December 21, 1876, an item had appeared:

A Brutal Dog-Fight. Skip, of Long Island, and Jack, of New York, Fight for $1,200—Both Dogs Die in the Pit with Their Fangs in Each Other's Throats. Early yesterday morning about two hundred roughs assembled at a dog-pit near Laurel Hill, Long Island, to witness a dogfight, undoubtedly the most brutal one on record, between Jack, of New York, and Skip, of Long Island. The fight was for $1,200 and the conditions were that each dog should not weigh over twenty-six pounds. After the usual preliminaries on such occasions, a well-known New York sport was selected referee and the fight announced. Upon time being called, both dogs sprang from the arms of their respective handlers and with a ferocious snarl rushed at each other. Odds of $100 to $60 were freely offered on Skip, with few takers. Skip succeeded in fastening his fangs into his opponent's jaw and dragged him to the ground. Blood once drawn, the brutes became more ferocious, and began devouring one another in the most approved style. They had fought for nearly an hour when they had so lacerated one another as to be almost unrecognizable. The scene became so disgusting that a number of the spectators were obliged to retire. After an hour and ten minutes' fighting, both dogs showed signs of weakening, and it was plain that they could not continue much longer. Urged by the cries of their respective backers, they tore each other's flesh. At last Skip seized his opponent by the throat and shook him as a terrier would a rat. Jack returned the compliment but was again seized by Skip. At this juncture the excitement became intense, and the crowd began to force themselves into the pit. The handlers seized their dogs and attempted to loosen their grip but not until life was extinct in both. The referee decided the fight a draw, when a cry of foul was raised, and in an incredibly short time a general fight ensued, during which knives were freely used. One of the roughs residing in this City was stabbed in the abdomen, and it has since been ascertained that the wound is likely to prove fatal. He was taken to his home by friends.

Mastiffs, vicious fighting dogs, were brought to Great Britain by Phoenician traders from Greece around 6 B.C. Gratius Talicus in 8 A.D. wrote of the "Pugnaces of Britain." The snubnosed animals were then taken to Italy by the Romans to fight wild animals and armed men—a popular spectator sport.

Mastiffs weighed from one hundred to one hundred and twenty pounds with bulldogs—bred short—lighter at eighty to ninety pounds.

Bull-baiting was practically England's national sport from the days of the Norman Conquest. There were French mastiffs, but they were used primarily on the Continent as watchdogs rather than fighting dogs.

Bull-baiting was a lower-class English activity in the thirteenth century. A hundred years later, however, Earl Warren, Lord of Stamford, was enjoying the spectacle of a large bull being attacked by fierce dogs.

Both the Tudors and the early Stuart kings were fond of bear-baiting and bull-baiting. On the Sunday Queen Mary met her sister, the future Elizabeth I, they went to Mass and later to a bear-bait. Typically, four or five dogs were loosed on a bear at once. Usually one or two were killed immediately. The battle lasted until the bear was maimed or dead or there were no more dogs left alive. Bears were toured around the country on a fighting circuit. When the Puritans overthrew the monarchy and beheaded Charles I in 1649, they abolished bear- and bull-baits, not because the fights were immoral, but because they brought an immoral degree of pleasure. When the monarchy was restored in 1660, so were the baits. Incidentally, for a long time it was thought that the meat of a bull baited by dogs was more tender.

There are many references to baiting in Shakespeare—it is known that the bard's home was very close to the "Bear Garden" in London, and he probably attended.

Elizabeth enjoyed the sport so much she would rarely entertain foreign dignitaries with anything else. The Queen's baits were not only for royalty and members of the gentry, but for commoners as well. A typical Sunday's entertainment would include five dogs versus a bear, an ape and a horse at play, and a bear being brutally whipped. After Elizabeth, legislation was enacted that restricted the spectators for baiting to the aristocracy.

James I had a lions' den in the Tower of London, and the royal family and various courtiers frequently watched lions baited by dogs, bears, and bulls. Some fierce mastiffs could stand up to a lion and hurt it. One particular dog that attacked a lion and survived (maimed, of course) was visited personally by the king, who commented on the animal's bravery, saying that it would never fight a lower animal again, since he had hurt the king of beasts.

The court had an official dog pound for James's fighting dogs—the "Great English Bulldogs"—and masters for the Bear Garden. The crown had the power to seize any dog in England.

The History of the British Dog notes that in 1623 a white bear was thrown into the Thames and baited by several swimming dogs to entertain the Spanish ambassador, who reportedly loved the spectacle.

English dogs became quite renowned for their viciousness, and mastiffs were in demand among monarchs of other nations. The King of Poland had English mastiffs for baiting and hunting. In 1615 mastiffs were exported to India, where they were actually used as executioners. In Persia English dogs killed tigers and leopards and were said to have disgraced Persian dogs in boar fights.

Bull-baiting remained popular, but by 1800 it was once again only a poor man's sport. In 1802 there was an attempt in Parliament to abolish the activity as inhumane. However, the French Revolution had recently occurred, and the English were fearful that this might be part of a Jacobin plot against the traditional institutions of Britain. In 1835 the Humane Act was finally passed, which abolished bull-baitings but not the fighting of dogs with dogs. (Illegal bull-baits were reported as late as 1853.)

After the 1835 prohibition against bull-baiting, dogfighting became even more popular, with the chief places of action being the Westminster Pit in London and various pits in South Staffordshire and the mining areas. Fighting dogs' careers were followed by the public. An outstanding fighter was Lord Cameford's Trusty, bought for eighty-four guineas, who won fifty fights and killed three other dogs.

The pits consisted of a circular area with a "scratch line" that the dogs had to cross in order to win. The matches lasted until one or both dogs died or an owner threw in the towel. Before any fight a man had to actually lick the entire body of each dog to make sure no illegal dressings had been applied. The dogs were usually eager to fight, but many people, especially hunters who loved dogs, thought the sport was barbaric. One rule was that when the dogs released their grip on one another, a handler could end a round by picking up his dog. The fights often lasted over an hour, and many a dog, who had an insensitive or cruel owner, died the next day (even if it had "won") from exhaustion that would cause lung collapse.

It was soon discovered that the best fighting breed was not a pure bulldog—courageous but slow—but a cross between a bulldog and a speedy terrier—the Staffordshire bull terrier.

There were several fighting techniques. The best way of winning was attacking and breaking the opposing dog's stifle joint, which corresponds to the human knee. This robbed the dog of his pushing power.

For contemporary information about dogfighting there are said to be at least three publications, obtainable only on the recommendation of others already on their mailing lists. Reportedly they are *Pit Dogs*, published in Starke, Florida; *Sporting Dog Journal*, Flushing, New York; and *Pit Dog Report*, Dallas, Texas.

ILLEGAL ANIMAL-FIGHTING VENTURES

The cruelty and slow death that typify animal-fighting ventures are banned by federal law. Part of the Animal Welfare Act Amendments of 1976 prohibits any event involving "a fight between at least two animals that is conducted for the purposes of sport, wagering or entertainment." All dogfighting exhibitions, bear-baiting, and battles between dog and raccoons plus cockfights —except where permitted by state law— are banned.

Before passing the law, congressmen heard debate dealing extensively with dogfighting. Witnesses detailed drawn-out, bloody, mauling contests and said that three out of four dogs usually die during the fight.

Testimony also showed that about a thousand dogfights had been sponsored annually in the United States, with between two and ten dogs matched per event. About five thousand persons are said to take direct or indirect part in such events. Attendance at a typical fight was said to range from ten to four hundred persons, with up to a hundred thousand dollars wagered.

Some thirty-eight states plus the District of Columbia already had laws against dogfights and other animal fighting ventures when the federal law was debated in Congress. Some other states had considered such fights a violation of their general anticruelty statutes. Even so, from 1969 to 1974, only eight cases of dogfighting were prosecuted. Penalties generally were light, with fines no higher than twenty-five dollars in some states.

Congress passed a strong federal law. Violations are a criminal offense prosecuted in federal court, with penalties ranging up to five thousand dollars in fines, one year in prison, or both. Provisions of the law also allow authorities to issue search warrants for fighting animals and to confiscate animals for their own welfare and as evidence.

Australian shepherd working stock. Owner is Debra Pardridge. (Photograph by Dick Daniels)

9

WORKING— THEY DON'T DO IT FOR THE MONEY

ARF—AND IT'S NOT FROM ORPHAN ANNIE

TRAINING A HERD DOG

A PASTORAL TRAGEDY
by Thomas Hardy

THE AUSSIE EXPERIENCE
by Jerry Robinson

GUIDE DOGS

SNIFFING AND STANDING GUARD

DOG POLICE
by William G. Fitz-Gerald

FOR SPORT, FOR WAR
Book Reviews

FOLLOWING HIS NOSE

ARF—and It's Not from Orphan Annie

The name is Stodghill and the game is genealogy of dogs—non-AKC types such as Texas heelers and Catahoulas.

Tom Drum Stodghill, editor of the Animal Research Magazine, *with his English shepherd. Carol Lee Alberts writing in the magazine says the breed is a "natural born heel driving dog . . . first brought over to America from England by Henry Clay, who at the time was also bringing the first boat load of registered Hereford cattle."*

Mr. Stodghill's letterhead ("phone 214/356-2267 . . . Post Office—Quinlan, Texas 75474") is a document to study and wonder at. Besides laying claim to the Brahma hog, there is a line that states "Improved Texas Long Horn Cattle." And then there is a column: "ARF Registry. We register all leading breeds stockdogs, new breeds, rare breeds cattle, horses, hogs, pygmy goats, etc." And: "Breeders of Brahma hogs, bred sows, service boars, pigs, unrelated pairs." Further, there is this list: "Advanced black-tan English shepherds . . . border collies . . . kelpies . . . Texas heelers . . . Australian cattledogs (Queenland heelers) . . . Australian shepherds . . . trained Catahoula leopard cowdogs, and wild hog dogs, pups, unrelated pairs." Finally, the printed part of the letterhead ends with: "ARF Stockdog Trials every year since 1965, last Saturday in October. Future plans cowdog trials last Saturday and Sunday in October each

137

When this Catahoula leopard cowdog grows up, it will be capable of herding cattle. But at six weeks of age it tries its instincts on a Florida lobster. The puppy named

Ugly is owned by veterinarian Dr. Jesse R. White. (Photograph by Donna Currie)

year. Also help sponsor cowdog school, Texas A. & M. University. Office on Highway 34, between Terrell and Greenville, 40 miles east of Dallas."

Although copy editors of traditional publishing houses would be disapproving of, if not appalled by, Mr. Stodghill's style and nonchalant manner concerning typographical errors, there is no question that he puts out a magazine packed—veritably jammed—with gusto and deep commitment.

"Office on Highway 34, between Terrell and Greenville, 40 miles east of Dallas."

Mr. Stodghill prints notices, readers' letters, and his own comments such as: "Tom, the 50% French Catahoula bayed over 20 wild hogs by himself and carried them near the house and Claude Lively's friend took his gun and killed three fat hogs and drug them to the house . . ."

According to the writer the French Catahoula is also known variously as the Louisiana hawg dawg, Louisiana Leopard, East Texas cowdog, Calcutter cur, black mouth cur, and swamp dog. But regardless of names used for the creature, it is said to be the "leading cowdog and wild hogdog in the nation."

Besides colorful down-home phrases and enthusiasm the magazine includes practical wisdom of interest to those who breed and train working dogs. To wit, from an article "Starting Blue Heelers" by Charles Hodges:

. . . packing is a practice used where two dogs work together. Usually this is used to show a young dog how to work by working him with an older dog. It can be used where two young dogs give each other courage or confidence by working together. [But] it can have bad results. After dogs work together they develop a pecking order when two or more are there. One will be the boss dog, and if you are not careful only one dog will listen to you, the other will listen to the boss dog. That may be OK until the boss dog gets hurt, sick or killed. Then you may be completely without a dog to work.

Training a Herd Dog

For seriously inclined men and women with time, money, and perseverance, training sheepdogs is becoming an increasingly popular avocation.

A dog must be taught to drive animals in a given direction. A narrow fenced road, so that animals cannot scatter, is a good training ground. No sheep or cattle should be used that might turn on the pup and scare it.

Commands are given with voice and motion of the left arm. In bad or stormy weather motion may be the only way a command can be given. Well-trained dogs can often get commands given from as far away as three or four hundred yards. The command "Hup em," "Drive on" (meaning the sheep), or any such are supplemented by an arm pointed horizontally. A staff, stick, or white cloth in the left hand will be helpful to the dog in observing the motion. The dog should be urged to drive on the flock, but if it is too aggressive, it may have to be kept leashed for the first lesson or two. Later a long cord may be used to restrain it from driving the cattle or sheep too fast. The command "Slow" is given, and the dog is checked with leash or cord. To stop the dog the

The old English sheepdog isn't all that old when compared to breeds traceable back to antiquity. The earliest reference, a 1771 Gainsborough painting, gives the old English sheepdog a history of little more than two hundred years. They were used as drovers to drive sheep and cattle to markets. Sheepdogs do different work than shepherds, which herd, guard, and protect rather than drive cattle. (Photograph by Daniel O'Toole for the FDA)

command "Stop" or "Down" is given, accompanied by the left hand held high. It usually requires about twenty to thirty days to teach a dog to drive a flock in the direction indicated and to make it listen to and watch the trainer.

To teach a dog to encircle and bring a flock in, the trainer gives the command "Around," pointing with a circling motion in the direction and advancing a few steps.

Scatter about a dozen sheep. Then encourage the dog to head them back into the flock. Do this several times, sometimes catching one of the sheep to help the dog understand that the idea is to bring the animals in. Repeat this operation until the dog learns to hold the flock up against the fence.

A dog should be able to walk steadily up to a stubborn sheep until it turns and retreats.

Next the sheep should be driven into the center of a large, open paddock. Order the dog down, and then encourage it to run around the flock and bring the flock to you. As the dog circles in one direction, advance along the opposite side of the flock. When the dog is halfway around (at the head of the flock), give the "Come" command, and the dog will circle around and meet you.

Should the dog attempt to come around in front of the sheep (between you and the flock), give the command "Drop" and start over again. As you increase the distance that you send the dog to bring sheep, you will have to cast wider. If the dog shows a preference for always running out on the one hand (side), let it do so for the time being, as it can be taught later to circle from whichever side is indicated.

To teach a dog to take direction, place it between you and the sheep. If you wish the dog to circle to the right, step to the right with the right hand extended, saying "This way" and giving the fetch command. Do just the opposite to get the dog to go to the left side. When casting efficiently and working steadily at all distances, the dog can then be sent to fetch sheep that are out of sight.

To train the dog to bring sheep from a distant point to the trainer or to a pen, take it with you to a point fairly near the flock. Give the fetch command and walk part of the distance. When the dog has circled the flock halfway, turn and walk toward the pen, commanding "Drive on." Repeat daily, gradually increasing the distance from the flock at which the fetch command is given.

To bring stray animals to the flock, point to the strays and command "This way." When the dog reaches the strays, make a sweeping gesture toward the main body of the flock and give the command "Fetch them," at the same time taking a few steps in the direction of the flock. To gather up sheep that have been left behind command "Go back."

When animals are being driven along a road, the dog must be taught to prevent them from turning off into a side road. The dog is urged to the front of the flock, then stopped at the turnoff and told to "Stay," thereby, heading off animals that show an inclination to run up the side path.

Some dogs have what is known as "style" and "eye"—the two qualities generally go together. Style is the crouching approach a herd dog makes when nearing the flock; it is much admired in trial and exhibition dogs. Eye is a fixed gaze when approaching sheep. No sheep can endure having a dog stare at it. A dog should be able to walk steadily up to a stubborn sheep until it turns and retreats. Sheep should not be rushed or frightened, and biting can only be tolerated if a sheep charges.

Further information on training, trials, and breeders can be obtained from Bernard L. Minton, secretary of the North American Sheep Dog Society, 210 East Main Street, McLeansboro, IL 62859.

Edited and reprinted from a Gaines Dog Research Center booklet.

Registered Catahoula leopard stock dog named Dallas Alice. (Photograph by C. L. Rawlings)

A Pastoral Tragedy

by Thomas Hardy

Doing a good job is not necessarily a simple, natural matter for dogs any more than it is for people. Here is a case of a dog who went wrong and caused his owner financial ruin.

Gabriel had two dogs. George, the elder, exhibited an ebony-tipped nose, surrounded by a narrow margin of pink flesh, and a coat marked in random splotches approximating in color to white and slaty gray; but the gray, after years of sun and rain, had been scorched and washed out of the more prominent locks, leaving them of a reddish-brown, as if the blue component of the gray had faded, like the indigo from the same kind of color in Turner's pictures. In substance it had originally been hair, but long contact with sheep seemed to be turning it by degrees into wool of a poor quality and staple. . . .

The young dog, George's son, might possibly have been the image of his mother, for there was not much resemblance between him and George. He was learning the sheep-keeping business, so as to follow on at the flock when the other should die, but had got no further than the rudiments as yet—still finding an insuperable difficulty in distinguishing between doing a thing well enough and doing it too well. So earnest and yet so wrong-headed was this young dog (he had no name in particular, and answered with perfect readiness to any pleasant interjection) that if sent behind the flock to help them on he did it so thoroughly that he would have chased them across the whole county with the greatest pleasure if not called off, or reminded when to stop by the example of old George. . . .

To the shepherd, the note of the sheep-bell, like the ticking of the clock to other people, is a chronic sound that only makes itself noticed by ceasing or altering in some unusual manner from the well-known idle tinkle which signifies to the accustomed ear, however distant, that all is well in the fold. In the solemn calm of the awakening morn that note was heard by Gabriel, beat-

Illustration by Babette Cole from Now That You Own a Puppy *by Joan Tate, New York: Frederick Fell, 1976.* (Used with the permission of the publisher)

ing with unusual violence and rapidity. . . .

He jumped out of bed, dressed, tore down the lane through a foggy dawn, and ascended the hill. . . . Gabriel called at the top of his voice the shepherd's call: "Ovey, ovey, ovey!"

Not a single bleat. . . . He called again: the valleys and furthest hills resounded as when the sailors invoked the lost Hylas on the Mysian shore; but no sheep. . . .

A horrible conviction darted through Oak. With a sensation of bodily faintness he advanced: at one point the rails were broken through, and there he saw the footprints of his ewes. The dog came up, licked his hand, and made signs implying that he expected some great reward for signal services rendered. Oak looked over the precipice. The ewes lay dead and dying at its foot—a heap of two hundred mangled carcasses, representing in their condition just now at least two hundred more. . . .

As far as could be learnt it appeared that the poor young dog, still under the impression that since he was kept for running after sheep, the more he ran after them the better, had . . . collected all the ewes into a corner, driven the timid creatures through the hedge, across the upper field, and by main force of worrying had given them momentum enough to break down a portion of the rotten railing, and so hurled them over the edge.

George's son had done his work so thoroughly that he was considered too good a workman to live, and was, in fact, taken and tragically shot at twelve o'clock that same day—another instance of the untoward fate which so often attends dogs and other philosophers who follow out a train of reasoning to its logical conclusion and attempt perfectly consistent conduct in a world made up so largely of compromise.

Edited and condensed from Thomas Hardy's novel Far From the Madding Crowd.

SHOOTING QUAIL IN GEORGIA

The Georgia quail plantations provide room and meals, guides and dogs, ample land, and a big population of birds. Depending on the bag taken, prices per day range from one hundred and fifty to two hundred and fifty dollars.

For the money a sportsman is assured of dogs that work beautifully and quail (pen-raised) that hold well and don't flush too soon.

By comparison, wild birds in the same general geographic location have taken to thick briar patches and heavy woods and tend to flush fast and wild.

THE BREED BOOKS

Many companies publish a series of breed books, each volume of which is devoted exclusively to a specific breed of dog. The books usually have such titles as *The Complete _____, The New Complete _____, Your _____, Know Your _____* and contain a history of the breed back to antiquity and a tracing of outstanding examples and breeding kennels in the U.S. Dog care information, which is quite similar from breed to breed, is also quite similar from book to book. Howell Book House and Denlinger's publish excellent volumes of this type. Exceptional breed books include:

The Welsh Springer Spaniel, History, Selection, Training and Care ($12.00; S. Brunswick, N.J.: A. S. Barnes, 1977), by William Pferd. Spaniels from prehistory to modern times are discussed, with physical descriptions of archaeological sites and references to fiction.

"Pwyll Prince of Dyfeld," a Welsh story of the second half of the eleventh century preserved in the *Red Book of Hergest and the Mabinogion*, is quoted, and so is Caius' sixteenth-century *Of Englishe Dogges* and Edmund Bert's *Treatise on Hawks and Hawking* of 1619.

Besides color reproductions of eighteenth- and nineteenth-century paintings, there are photographs of Welsh springer champions of the last seventy-five years. A Welsh language dog-naming vocabulary is included.

The German Shepherd Today ($14.95; New York: Macmillan Publishing Co., Inc., 1974), by Winifred Gibson Strickland and James A. Moses. If you've decided that a German shepherd is the dog for you, so is this book. It covers everything from how the breed originated and how to read a pedigree, to raising, training and judging. The definitive book about the third most popular breed in America.

Meisen Poodle Manual ($8.95; Fairfax, Va.: Denlinger's, 1974), by Hilda Meisenzahl. The author has, since 1941, bred more than five hundred litters of poodles, the number-one dog in the U.S. In addition to apricot poodles, her specialty, she has produced countless winning poodles of other colors.

Breed books from two major specialty houses: left, Howell Book House, 730 Fifth Avenue, New York, NY 10019; and right, Denlinger's Publishers, Box 189, Fairfax, VA 22030.

The Aussie Experience

by Jerry Robinson

A rare-breed enthusiast tells his story.

Owning a dog as a pet was always a part of my boyhood life, though I never got much involved with a specific breed. A childhood dream to be a veterinarian never came to pass. Instead I attended the U.S. Naval Academy in the sixties. Now I am an engineer—ministering to modern technology rather than to animal miseries.

While attending postgraduate school in Monterey in 1970 my wife, Kathy, and I "discovered" the Australian shepherd. We acquired a puppy from the local SPCA. It was of mixed parentage but boasted a superior temperament. Next we bought a purebred Aussie.

My love for the breed would have remained at the family pet level but for a chance meeting with a man who became a lifelong friend. Phil Wildhagen owned the most magnificent Aussie I had seen. Dusty was the first champion of the breed, the first Aussie to win an all-breed match, and the first Aussie to be recognized internationally. Phil did three things that changed my life significantly: he inspired me with the Aussie "cause"; he took me to a dog show, introducing me to the sport of competition; and he sold me Dusty's son, Yankee.

From 1972 Kathy and I spent long hours and traveled countless miles to compete in obedience and conformation events. Then, in 1977, Yankee, in his prime, tragically died.

I was prepared to quit the breed after we lost him, but with the help and encouragement of friends managed to start rebuilding our kennel breeding from Yankee's progeny. Our goal is to recreate the natural balance, rhythm, and intelligence that he exemplified.

These days Kathy and I try to attend most matches within a reasonable area to support the breed, limiting

Georjian Goldman and her Australian shepherd after winning Best of Breed and Novice Obedience at rare *breed match.* (Photograph by Spida Grean)

our travel only by the time available in a weekend. I bought a special vehicle that I have equipped for dogs and often drive it hundreds of miles for a match. Most other hobbies have been sacrificed.

As an engineer, I employ my professional training to help organize things at our Aussie club, and I publish the club newsletter at a personal expense of about two hundred and fifty dollars a year.

I am not involved with Australian shepherd dogs for profit. Consequently our kennel breeds only in a limited way—generally by providing studs, which are always chosen for their working instinct. We want, most of all, to preserve that aspect of their heritage.

Jerry and Kathy Robinson breed Australian shepherds at their Downeast Kennels, P.O. Box 148, West Kingston, RI 02892.

Editor's note: The Australian shepherd, a "rare breed" (that is, one not recognized by the American Kennel Club), is a sheepherding dog of moderate size (up to twenty-three inches at the withers) with a smooth, easy, ground-covering stride. The breed originated in the Basque country of France and Spain, accompanied flocks of Merino sheep to Australia and then, in the late 1800s, from Australia to California—hence the name, Australian shepherd. A pretty dog to watch.

For more information write The Australian Shepherd Club of America, Box 843, Meridian, ID 83642.

Gerald Robinson points out the fine points of Australian shepherds to writer Claire Romanof. (Photograph by Don Myrus)

144

A GREAT WAY TO GET
THE GROCERIES HOME

Dog carting, like packing, has a long history. Today the activity is enjoying a revival as a leisure-time sport. The National Newfoundland Club of America features a carting class at its annual specialty. Besides the traditional draft breeds—Newfoundland, Briard, etc.—any large dog, experts say, can enjoy the sport, and when the competition is over, it's a great way to get the groceries home.

Custom carts and harnesses are available from Pearson's Town and Country Carts, 2260 N. Walnut Street, Muncie, IN 47305 and Harry Russ, 123 Yeager Avenue, Forty Fort, PA 18704. For plans and directions for making your own cart, contact Jim McLaughlin, Cart Chairman, Newfoundland Club of America, 14140 South Turner Road, DeWitt, MI 48820.

Paul and His Little Big Dog *by Kathy Darling (Champaign: Garrard Publishing, 1977) is a simply told and charming story of an Irish wolfhound pup that grows* up to become an able carter. The book won Dog Writers' best children's book award of 1977. (Used with permission of the Garrard Publishing Company)

Guide Dogs

A short description of a program in which dogs show their greatest usefulness.

Different breeds are used as seeing-eye dogs—golden retriever, Labrador retriever, and German shepherd.

Puppies are placed with selected families at the age of six to eight weeks, then returned to the training center when mature. The foster home program provides home education and exposure to all types of outside activity. It has proved invaluable in producing an animal better prepared for use as a guide. Golden and Labrador retrievers are bred by the Guide Dog Foundation of New York, German shepherds by the Fidelco Foundation of Connecticut.

The applicant must also be able to provide adequate housing and care for the dog. Dogs are not given to mendicants.

Adult dogs between the ages of ten months to two years are donated by the general public. Female dogs are preferred, although a placid male will be considered for training. There is a minimum height requirement of twenty-two inches, measured from the floor to the shoulder, and the animal should have a short coat in order to facilitate easy grooming. The dog must have a sound temperament and a friendly disposition and be in good physical health. In checking for soundness of temperament the dog should not be shy of people (including children), traffic, and other loud noises. Conversely, it should not be a confirmed dogfighter or animal chaser; it should not be boisterous.

As for instructors, it takes a minimum of three years before an apprentice trainer can qualify.

Each instructor runs a string of six to eight dogs, each worked individually. The dog is taught to sit, lie down, stay, come when called, and fetch any article that the trainer may drop. Then, in town, the dog is taught to walk a straight line in the center of the sidewalk, stop at all intersections, and respond to the forward, right, left, and halt commands. The dog is also taught to disregard cats, squirrels, pigeons, stray dogs, and any other distractions it may encounter while working.

Then the dog is fitted with a harness and is trained to allow adequate clearance when negotiating pedestrians, obstacles, and other hazards. The dog is also taught to be cautious in traffic and, if necessary, to disobey its master's command to go forward if danger threatens. Guide dogs must be able to tolerate loud city noises, such as elevated trains, subways, whistles, horns, and pedestrian traffic.

The dog is taught that once the harness is removed, it is allowed to relax.

With a guide dog a person is able to go shopping in the same manner as a sighted person. The dog has been taught not to sniff food and packages or to jump up on counters, but to make its way safely through narrow aisles and to avoid contact with breakable merchandise.

Training takes a minimum of three months.

Not every blind person can use a guide dog. Aptitudes and abilities—not only disability—determine qualifications. Since a dog always needs more than an average amount of exercise, an owner must be in good physical health.

An owner must be totally blind or have serious visual limitations and must need the dog for constructive purposes. This includes the student who attends school, the housewife who shops for the family, the person engaged in a rehabilitation program, and the wage earner who must travel to and from a job. There is a minimum age requirement of sixteen years, but no maximum limit. The applicant must also be able to provide adequate housing and care for the dog. Dogs are not given to mendicants.

From the time of arrival at the training center the student is under the close supervision of the instructor. The training of student and dog together takes approximately four weeks.

One such student, the great jazz drummer Joe Morello, said of the program, "I was surprised to find that everything at the Smithtown Center was free. The four weeks of training was free, and the dog was given to me without charge. I sent a check anyway. But after I'd been training there for two or three weeks and realized the dedication of the people who work there, I offered to do a concert as partial repayment for what they had done for me. They can always use money."

Mr. Morello's vision had been poor since birth and had worsened until his sight, after thirty-two operations, was almost gone. He shunned the trappings of blindness, carrying an ebony stick instead of the usual white one. He never considered a dog until he discussed the matter with George Shearing, the pianist who has been blind since birth. That discussion led Joe Morello to the Guide Dog Foundation for the Blind and to his appreciation.

The Guide Dog Foundation for the Blind has administrative offices at 109–19 72nd Ave., Forest Hills, NY 11375, and a training center at 371 Jericho Tpke., Smithtown, NY 11787. For information about other guide dog centers write either the *Guide Dog News*, P.O. Box 1200, San Rafael, CA 94902 or *The Seeing Eye Guide*, Morristown, NJ 07960.

Snowdancer Siberian husky models a heavy-duty pack sold by Nordkyn Outfitters.

Jim Mitchell and Snowdancer Siberian huskies illustrate an unusual sport—the dog-pulled bicycle. Gear for bike dogs is available from Nordkyn Outfitters. (Photograph courtesy Nordkyn Outfitters)

Sniffing and Standing Guard

How dogs are trained by the government to protect property and detect dope.

Reward conditioning—vocal and petting praise and sometimes play with a ball—is the major technique used at Lackland Air Force Base, Texas, where all military dogs are trained. In some instances, however, avoidance training must be used too; specifically, if the dog bites his handler or attempts to attack another dog.

Avoidance training teaches the dog it can avoid the emotional pain of a reproving "No!" or a jerk on the choke chain by not making the undesired response. No other physical correction is tolerated.

Avoidance training differs from punishment. Correction is on a one-to-one ratio for incorrect responses; that is, if a dog attempts to attack another dog, correction is only for the specific attempt. Vocal correction is always used first, and only if it proves insufficient is physical correction applied.

With punishment, correction is administered in greater than a one-to-one ratio. A dog receives several jerks on the choke chain for one incorrect response. Punishment is an ineffective training technique because the dog cannot associate more than one reprimand with one specific incorrect response.

Tests have proved that while the odor of heroin is significantly weaker than that of marijuana, dogs can be trained to identify and locate it.

Avoidance training also reinforces correct behavior. The dog learns that by avoiding the incorrect response, it not only avoids a correction, but it is rewarded for correctly completing an assigned task. With punishment, a dog becomes confused and responds to subsequent training efforts out of fear of physical or emotional pain rather than the desire to work positively for a reward.

A dog is a social animal, and primary satisfaction for correctly performing a task comes in praise from the handler.

The only time that problems arise in the reward technique is when the handler relinquishes physical control of the dog—when the dog is released by the handler and ordered to attack. Then the primary reward is the bite itself. In the case of a standoff—where the dog is released and then called off the attack—the dog must be trained to accept a secondary reward and to avoid the actual bite. Acceptance of a reward other than the bite

in an attack standoff is the most difficult thing to teach.

Some dogs complete a whole series of tasks for a simple pat on the chest and a "Good boy!" from the handler. Others require lavish praise after just one or two correct responses.

Repetition, consistency, and patience are the keys to succesful training. Some dogs will be able to perform all but one task correctly. For example, an otherwise qualified dog repeatedly fails to hold the sit position for the required length of time. In this instance a handler employs successive approximation. The task is broken down into components. To teach a dog to hold a sit position for five minutes, the handler first teaches the dog to sit and at once gives a reward. The dog is then required to sit for fifteen seconds before receiving the reward, and so on.

Successive approximation can be used in every task a dog has difficulty in mastering. To some extent it is used throughout the training process as a means of teaching dogs more complex tasks that require multiple responses.

Training dogs to locate concealed drugs and explosives is not as difficult as the uninitiated observer might imagine—it is a rather simple matter for a dog to identify a specific odor. A dog's olfactory system is one of the keenest in the animal kingdom.

In its initial stages the drug-detection program concentrated on training dogs to locate marijuana and hashish. With its pungent vegetable odor marijuana is easy for dogs to locate, even when elaborately concealed or masked with other odors. Hashish, a derivative of marijuana, is equally easy to find.

In the field drug-detector dogs are able to find marijuana hidden in vehicle gas tank nozzles, hollowed-out bars of soap, cans of paint thinner, and bathroom deodorant cakes. They have even located marijuana that has been sprayed with chemicals designed specifically to repel dogs.

Tests have proved that while the odor of heroin is significantly weaker than that of marijuana, dogs can be trained to identify and locate it. A dog has to be closer to heroin in order to positively locate it because its odor dissipates rapidly in air. For this reason, if heroin is the object of a particular search, the search itself is longer and more thorough.

Because of several important differences in techniques, dogs trained to detect drugs are not trained to detect explosives. Though the requirements are the same—energetic, inquisitive patrol dogs with a strong desire to retrieve—the nature of the substances being sought dictates a slightly different approach.

Upon making a find, drug-detector dogs bite or scratch at containers holding the drugs. Some explosive devices have antidisturbance mechanisms or motion-activated detonators, so explosive-detector dogs have to be trained to give a passive alert signal. The sit position is an ideal passive alert and can be easily taught.

Explosive-detector dogs are taught to alert on the four major explosive odors: C-4 plastic, dynamite, TNT, and smokeless powder. In tests conducted by the Los Angeles Police Department Bomb Squad, mechanical sensing devices were able to detect the presence of explosives' odors to a level of five parts per billion in air. Lackland-trained dogs, however, have alerted on one to two parts per billion odor presence and, in some cases, on quantities so small that they could not be measured with equipment.

It is also possible to teach dogs to work alone—in closed warehouses, for example—and to push a danger signal pedal at the first scent of smoke or sight of flame or at the sound of breaking glass or hammering.

At Lackland Air Force Base small dog breeds are being checked out for use in detecting drugs and explosives. Miniature schnauzers, cairn terriers, fox terriers, and beagles are involved. Should they prove adept at locating drugs, they would be able to search for contraband in confined areas inaccessible to German shepherds, currently the military's active-duty breed.

Dog Police
by William G. Fitz-Gerald

A marvelous account from the early 1900s of dogs at work in Belgium and France.

That a policeman on night duty in a great city would be more respected by criminals if accompanied by a powerful and sagacious dog is a reasonable supposition; yet it remained for little Belgium to carry out this innovation.

The chief of police laid before the burgomaster **an** idea he had long entertained of employing Belgian sheepdogs as assistants or colleagues of the night patrols. He pointed out the splendid work of the dogs at the Hospice of St. Bernard and of those employed in the German army, declaring he was certain that the canine

A World War I dog hero is decorated. From Life, *1917.*
(Picture Collection, New York Public Library)

recruits would save the city tens of thousands of francs every year, besides reducing burglaries and night crimes.

Soon there were thirty big, powerful dog policemen on duty, and working with surprising efficiency. They would take a new man over his night beat with a zeal, a thoroughness, and a relentless, systematic ardor that would kill a lazy constable. They knew their work, and could and did correct many a man who was a stranger to the beat.

The animals are given every care. They have swimming baths once a week, and the kennels are disinfected regularly and are periodically whitewashed. For the first fifteen days new recruits are kept in the kennels, and are merely taught obedience. Military brevity, combined with unvarying kindliness, marks all orders. In due time certain night guards come and take out the recruits with the veteran dogs when the night bell sounds. The dog police go on duty at ten o'clock at night and finish work at six in the morning. They never go out in the daytime, and on no account allowed to become acquainted with the ordinary public. Twice during the day, however, they are mustered in the paddock of the bureau for an hour's exercise and fresh air.

They are fed twice a day, at seven in the morning and again at seven at night. During the night each dog receives a large slice of bread, and so carefully are their needs and capacities studied that the animals never appear tired or spiritless on returning to the kennels after the long and often dangerous night watch.

When on duty, each carries a leather collar bearing a tin medal with its name, birth date, and the word "Police." There is also a cloak for stormy weather, which covers the body from neck to tail. It is leather-mounted and waterproof. The dogs also wear muzzles while on duty, for their whole training makes them regard the civilian as an enemy, and a muzzle is necessary for the protection of peaceable citizens.

This muzzle is of a special kind. It is a tin cup, perforated for respiration, which prevents the dog from eating any food it may find in the road at night. An elastic arrangement, however, permits the unmuzzling of the animal in an instant; then the muzzle swings from the collar, ready to be replaced when the emergency has passed.

The entire education of the newly arrived dogs is undertaken by the brigadiers-controleurs, or officers in authority over the night patrol. When coaching the dogs, the brigadier-controleur is always in civil dress, and often he simulates the appearance of a tramp or suspicious character. He goes through the pantomime of assaulting the night guards, runs away, slouches along with suspicious bundles, leaps into ditches filled with deep water, scales high walls, and generally runs the whole gamut of a rascal caught in the act.

When a new recruit begins to show aptitude under training, the night guard to whom it is assigned comes to the kennel and leads it forth when the patrols with the older dogs are assembled for duty. The men are provided with bones or scraps of meat for the newcomer, and in this way stress is laid on the lesson it is sought to teach—namely, that only men in police uniform may be trusted. All others are to be eyed with suspicion, if not with positive ferocity. Later on the night patrol leads out the beginner, to familiarize it with every nook and corner of the beat. For one month this work goes on three or four hours a night in all weather, the hours of duty being gradually increased to the standard eight.

If the animal is slow to understand the object-lessons, he is frequently teased and irritated by a brigadier-controleur. In extreme cases a slow-witted recruit is maltreated and even kicked and beaten a little by the official actor. Simultaneously every policeman in the station caresses the dog and gives it dainties. It is no wonder, then, that the dog at the end of its training is at once eager to obey the commands of the police and more than eager to attack a suspicious-looking person in civil clothes.

Cunning ruffians had often contrived to outwit the solitary patrol, but when a policeman was accompanied by these big, swift, silent-footed, and sagacious sheepdogs, the most desperate evildoers were inspired with terror.

But there is as wide diversity in the intelligence of dogs as there is in that of human beings, and tact and skill are required not to overdo the irritating and violence, lest the dog be cowed and rendered timid. Thoughtless violence may make a dog worse than useless—dangerous, even, to his human colleague.

When an officer arrives on his beat, he releases his dog with the laconic command, "Cherché!" Instantly the dog passes swiftly into and around farms and outhouses beyond the city boundary. Woe to characters of suspicious mien or to people carrying suspicious-looking bundles! The dog does more scouting in ten minutes than its well-paid human comrade could do in an hour.

One of the first foreign police officers to inquire into and adopt the dogs was the police prefect of Paris. It occurred to him that among the great crowds visiting the city during the exposition some would surely fall into the Seine. He therefore organized a body of special police whom he named the *agents plongeurs*, or "diving police." Each of these was a fast and powerful swimmer and a man of ready wit and presence of mind, and each was accompanied by an intelligent Newfoundland dog, trained with no less care than the police dogs of Belgium.

The training of the young Newfoundlands is one of the sights of Paris. It takes place in the headquarters of the *agents plongeurs*, a small building on the quayside not far from the Cathedral of Notre Dame. Dogs and men enter into the exercise with zest, and there is usually a crowd of onlookers. Only dummy figures are used, but the "rescue" is, nevertheless, a very realistic affair. The big dogs know perfectly well what the exercise means, and they wait with comic enthusiasm until the dummy is thrown into the water and an *agent plongeur* rushes out on hearing the splash and the outcry of spectators. While the men are busy with lines and life buoys, the dog plunges into the water, swims to the dummy, watches with rare intelligence for an opportunity, gets an advantageous hold, and then either swims ashore or waits for its master, who brings to the rescue long poles, cork belts, and the like. The more experienced dogs, however, will easily effect a rescue from first to last without human assistance; it is an inspiring sight to watch them looking for a foothold on the slippery sides of the riverbank and pulling the heavy dummy to safety.

It takes about four months to train the dogs efficiently. They are also charged with the protection of their masters when attacked by the desperate ruffians who sleep under the arches of the bridge in summer. Thus in Paris also the police dogs are a proved success.

Edited and reprinted from The Century Magazine, *October 1906.*

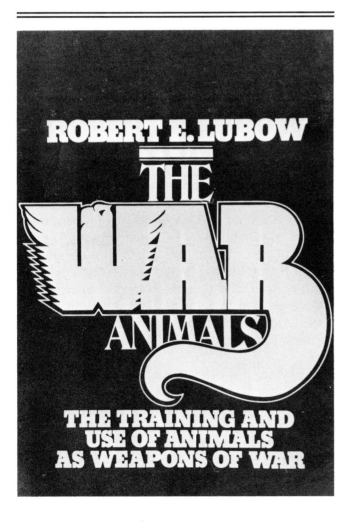

For Sport, for War

Book Reviews

American and European ferrets differ. The black-footed ferret of the U.S. is a rather rare weasel whose natural prey is the prairie dog. The Old World ferret is a semi-domesticated form of the polecat, often albino with red eyes, used at least since Roman times to hunt rats, mice, and rabbits. In some states of the U.S. ferreting is illegal, but not so in England.

Englishman Phil Drabble in *Of Pedigree Unknown* ($8.75; London: Michael Joseph, 1964, distributed by Transatlantic Arts) explains that he became a ratter because of Hairy Kelly and a dog named Mick. Mick was a working fox terrier/Staffordshire bull terrier mix that had his dam's sensitivity to earthy things and his sire's tenacity and courage. Hairy Kelly was the district professional ratcatcher who was hired by local farmers for a per-rat fee to clear the pests from field, hedge, hayrick, and henhouse.

Kelly's technique was to place himself strategically and let three or four ferrets into a rodent den. As the rats fled from razor-sharp ferret teeth, Kelly snatched them up by hand and popped them into his shirt, until all the action was over and the prey could be properly bagged.

The ratcatcher was paid by the farmer to remove rats and was paid again when he sold the live rats to rat-pit operators (terriers and rats were often pitted at the pubs) and to boys like young Drabble to use for the training of pet terrier dogs.

By the time he was seventeen and leaving school, Drabble wanted more than anything else a bull terrier (Stafford, of course) and a racing whippet, neither of which were recognized by The Kennel Club then. Fighting dogs and cocks, racing whippets and pigeons, were kept for sport by the coal miners and ironworkers of Staffordshire, where, in the author's view, the best bull terrier *ever* was developed for the pit.

Drabble has this to say about the bull-baiters of an earlier era, who were the antecedents of all bull terriers.

> At one time, bull-baiting had been a lawful, even compulsory, pastime with a strictly utilitarian objective. Men have long believed—and I think correctly—that meat from an animal which has died after recent exertion is more tender than it would otherwise be. A hare that has been coursed is always deemed superior to flesh from a shot hare. . . . So a bull that has died defending himself . . . was thought to be less tough than he would have been without the enforced exercise.

Drabble describes the training and pitting of fighting dogs, the "rag racing" of whippets that were lifted off the ground and literally flung forward in full stride by the trainer at the "go" signal toward a bit of cloth waved by the "ragman" two hundred yards away. The ragman's tumultuous shouting and whistling urged the dog on. Also described and explained are how the terrier man works with the local hunt and how a fox terrier actually pursues a fox underground and "bolts" it, or stays and "speaks" to keep it from digging further in.

> My dogs earn their place on the hearth by deeds, not looks. . . . Some might despise my dogs because they are "no better than mongrels," but a mongrel is the product of chance, and my dogs have been produced by carefully mixing the blood of different breeds for a specific purpose.

The author is talking about his favorite dog, the lurcher, first bred by gypsies from greyhound and various types of sheepdog crosses and often used for poaching, a "sport" he has also tried. Mostly, though, he and his lurchers hunt hares and leverets and rabbits.

This is a marvelous book about the tough, gutsy dogs and the men who bred and worked them outside the show world and even, sometimes, outside the law.

The Vietcong tactics in using hidden mines, booby traps, and spiked pits caused many American casualties. To combat the enemy's ways Robert E. Lubow describes in *The War Animals* ($7.95; Garden City, NY: Doubleday, 1977) how he trained German shepherds.

That in extremity fighting men turned to help from dogs is an old story. A frieze from the Pergamon, carved about 280 B.C., shows large Assyrian attack dogs with huge teeth and pricked ears taking part in battle. Herodotus, discussing a battle, wrote: "Man was matched against man, horse against horse, and dog against dog."

And the big dogs—mastiff and wolfhound—were trained to impail enemy soldiers on spiked dog collars or, as Bartolome de las Casas put it: "to tare out the bellies."

Warrior dogs were very valuable but did not last long, so when Henry VIII sent four hundred mastiffs to Spain to aid his ally in a battle against France, Charles V was extraordinarily grateful.

The ever-resourceful Benjamin Franklin suggested to his frontier countrymen that dogs would provide good protection against stealthily raiding Indians.

During World War I the French and Belgians began using dogs in trench warfare to pull supply sleds, search for wounded, and carry messages. By the end of the war some ten thousand dogs were in active service, and their duties had expanded to include guarding prisoners and acting as sentinels at the edge of no-man's land.

During World War II the army was not organized to procure or train dogs and had to rely on Dogs for Defense, a volunteer group of dog enthusiasts. Since then, all government dog training has been centralized at Lackland Air Force base in Texas.

In Vietnam, we learn rather poignantly from *The War Animals*, Lubow trained his German shepherds to track guerrillas back to their bases by following the scent of Nuoc Mam fish sauce, which the Vietcong, he says, always carried.

DOG POWER AS AN AUXILIARY IN WHEELING

From time immemorial man has sought to utilize the dog as a beast of burden. This has been accomplished in various ways. Sometimes the dog is put into shafts and made to pull small carts or sledges; this is a daily sight in many of the countries of Europe. The dog has proved useful for this purpose, where other animals have proved worthless. Ever since the days of the old velocipede, inventors have also sought for some kind of motor for bicycles and tricycles that would obviate the fatigue resulting from working the pedals; steam, compressed air, springs, electricity and many of the hydrocarbons have had their turn. Now, in the last decade of the nineteenth century, the dog has been adopted to this means of locomotion.

The dog is hitched behind the tricycle to the end of an adjustable harness rod and is chained to a point under the saddle. An appropriate harness is provided for the dog.

We are indebted for our report to Mr. Joseph Becker of Washington, D.C., who says: "The first impulse is to pity this good little doggie and to blame his big heavy master for working him so. But this is soon forgotten when you have seen this sturdy little fellow at his task, tugging and clawing with the greatest earnestness, apparently delighted with his task."

Possibly so, but even though he might have to work hard when the tricycle was going slowly, still, when the speed is increased, the opportunities for "soldiering" [resting on the job] would be limitless.

Edited and reprinted from Scientific American, *May 16, 1896.*

Following His Nose

Scent and the Scenting Dog (Rome, NY: Arner Publications, 1972), by William G. Syrotuck, is a complete and fascinating explanation of tracking, trailing, and air scenting by dogs. About an eighth of a dog's brain and half its nose are committed to olfaction. Human equipment for smelling can't compare.

There is discussion and comparison of the origin and use of the sense smell by humans and dogs and a survey of the current modern theories—thirty different ones— of the exact molecular nature of odor.

The human body as a highly complex scent source is examined—heredity, diet, emotion, environment, experience, and bacteria are variable and, in combination with soaps, perfumes, clothing materials, etc., account for the individuality of human odors.

Conditions affecting the transmission of odors are air temperature, wind, humidity, geography, snow (or lack of it), and foliage.

The book's final chapter deals with such often-asked questions as: Is scent perceptible upwind? Can dogs find a person who has crossed a stream? How can you remove scent from an object? Can marijuana be masked from detection by a dog?

In *Tracking Dog, Theory and Methods* (Rome, NY: Arner Publications, 1975), by Glen R. Johnson, a very successful Canadian trainer, explains how his program earned a TDX (Tracking Dog Excellent) for a thirteen-month-old.

TRACKING DOG
theory & methods

by GLEN R. JOHNSON

THE BLOODHOUND EXPLAINED

The bloodhound is neither bloodthirsty nor does it track by following droplets dripped by wounded, escaping scoundrels. The name comes down from the Middle Ages, when the ancestors of the breed were owned only by the aristocracy, or nobles of royal blood —thus, the designation bloodhound.

Since *The Hound of the Baskervilles* (which was only part bloodhound) engaged the attention of Sherlock Holmes, the breed has been depicted as terrifying—baying packs, thirsty for human blood, tracking and killing their human quarry.

Bloodhounds actually work singly or at most in pairs, usually silently and always leashed. More often than they are used for police work, bloodhounds engage in rescue operations. They do not follow footprints but catch scent particles from the air.

The bloodhound has enthusiastic champions among rescue workers, law-enforcement people, and dog fanciers. As a house pet, the breed may present drawbacks for some. The overly fastidious, or even the average casual housekeeper, may be appalled to find that the folds of skin around a bloodhound's mouth and its ears are entirely caked with food after every meal and must be washed. Some bloodhounds drool and shake their heads a lot, spraying spittle on floors, furniture, and clothing. Also, they bay, sometimes at night, which could be a problem in urban or suburban environments.

As with any breed, one should know exactly what to expect *before* becoming involved. A reputable breeder will make a prospective owner aware of difficulties to anticipate as well as pleasures.

"Human kindness was like a sun shining upon him, and he flourished like a flower planted in good soil . . . but still there was about him a suggestion of lurking feroc- ity, as though the Wild still lingered in him and the wolf in him merely slept."—White Fang by Jack London. (Photograph by Peter Simon)

10
FANTASY

DOG
  by Lawrence Ferlinghetti

THE DOG AS A BIOGRAPHER'S
  BEST FRIEND

ELEGY ON A YOUNG AIREDALE
  BITCH LOST SOME YEARS
  SINCE IN THE SALT MARSH
  by Yvor Winters

L.A. REPORT—HOLLYWOOD
  CANINES
  by Vincent Tajiri

WHAT MAKES TOBY BARK?
  by Marc Kristal

AS FILMLAND HAS ITS OSCAR,
  SO DOES DOGDOM HAVE
  ITS FIDO

WHERE TO GET YOUR OWN
  PERFORMING DOG

JACK, A BIOGRAPHY OF
  JACK LONDON

THE DOG AS DEMON—THEN

THE DOG AS DEMON—NOW
  by Sarah Hawkes

GOOD OLD DOG—LOYAL,
  MAGICAL, HEALING, HOLY

IT'S THE DOG THAT WAGS THE
  TALE
  by Hal Borland

BOY WITHOUT A DOG—GIRL
  WITHOUT A DOG

BOYS & GIRLS & DOGS
  by Claire Romanof

QUIZ

Dog

by Lawrence Ferlinghetti

One of the seven "oral messages" written for jazz accompaniment and part of the very successful book of poems A Coney Island of the Mind.

The dog trots freely in the street
and sees reality
and the things he sees
are bigger than himself
and the things he sees
are his reality
Drunks in doorways
Moons on trees
The dog trots freely thru the street
and the things he sees
are smaller than himself
Fish on newsprint
Ants in holes
Chickens in Chinatown windows
their heads a block away
The dog trots freely in the street
and the things he smells
smell something like himself
The dog trots freely in the street
past puddles and babies
cats and cigars
poolrooms and policemen
He doesn't hate cops
He merely has no use for them
and he goes past them
and past the dead cows hung up whole
in front of the San Francisco Meat Market
He would rather eat a tender cow
than a tough policeman
though either might do
And he goes past the Romeo Ravioli Factory
and past Coit's Tower
and past Congressman Doyle
He's afraid of Coit's Tower
but he's not afraid of Congressman Doyle

although what he hears is very discouraging
very depressing
very absurd
to a sad young dog like himself
to a serious dog like himself
But he has his own free world to live in
His own fleas to eat
He will not be muzzled
Congressman Doyle is just another
fire hydrant
to him
The dog trots freely in the street
and has his own dog's life to live
and to think about
and to reflect upon
touching and tasting and testing everything
investigating everything
without benefit of perjury
a real realist
with a real tale to tell
and a real tail to tell it with
a real live
   barking
    democratic dog
engaged in real
    free enterprise
with something to say
    about ontology
something to say
   about reality
    and how to see it
     and how to hear it
with his head cocked sideways
    at streetcorners
as if he is just about to have
    his picture taken
     for Victor Records
   listening for
    His Master's Voice
  and looking
    like a living questionmark
     into the
     great gramophone
     of puzzling existence
with its wondrous hollow horn
   which always seems
   just about to spout forth
    some Victorious answer
    to everything

Diane the huntress and her dog on the grounds of the Mallory Company at Tarrytown, New York. (Photograph by Spida Grean)

From A Coney Island of the Mind © *1958 by Lawrence Ferlinghetti. Reprinted by permission of New Directions Publishing Corporation.*

The Dog as a Biographer's Best Friend

A leisurely review of Virginia Woolf's Flush, *the superb biography of Elizabeth Barrett Browning and her cocker spaniel.*

Most peoples' lives lack the variety to keep an extended account of their day-to-day affairs interesting, which is why the gossip columnist's snippet is usually more readily consumed than the scholar's "full-length" biography.

Writers as a group are no more interesting than others. Those—from Byron to Hemingway—who indulge in scandalous activities or who occasionally foray into violence (Greek revolutions, bullfights) can be exceptions. But to an observer the actual work of writing must seem even less exciting than filling teeth.

How then is a writer to be portrayed who is neither a madwoman nor a courtesan but a sickly and withdrawn Victorian lady living in a world of words? How is such a subject to be made worthy of a whole book, especially if she has been shut up a good part of the time in a big, airless London townhouse where servants and other residents seem always to be going about as if on cats' paws?

Virginia Woolf, British novelist and essayist, solved the problem of describing the life of poet Elizabeth Barret Browning by writing mostly about a dog—a cocker spaniel named Flush. This novel approach was made possible by the poet herself recording so much of her thoughts about the dog in journals and letters.

The result is a book ($2.45; *Flush*—New York: Harcourt Brace Jovanovich, 1961) that offers powerful insights not only about a literary tradition, but also about the aristocratic class of nineteenth-century England. The delight, though, is that Elizabeth Barrett Browning, her family, and her husband are purely secondary. Flush is the hero, and it is really his story that is told.

And what delights there are in the telling!

We learn about spaniels. That perhaps the name derives from *span*, which in the Carthaginian meant rabbit, the spaniel's traditional prey. (Thus the place name España, for Rabbitland.) Being the elegant writer she is, Virginia Woolf, suggests, among several possibilities, that "just as a lover calls his mistress monster or monkey, so the Spaniards called their favorite dogs crooked or cragged (the word *españa* can be made to take these meanings) . . ." However, she finds this "too fanciful a conjecture to be seriously entertained." Fanciful, perhaps, but charming, as she well knew.

These are phrases Woolf used to describe the young Flush: a particular shade of dark brown that in sunshine flashes "all over into gold," and having "startled eyes of hazel bland" and "tasselled" ears and slender feet "canopied in fringes."

We learn that "the first months of his life were passed at Three Mile Cross, a working man's cottage near Reading" and that his owner, Miss Mary Russell Mitford, a writer herself, had fallen upon hard times. However,

to sell Flush was unthinkable. He was of the rare order of objects that cannot be associated with money. Was he not of the still rarer kind that, because they typify what is spiritual, what is beyond price . . . may be offered . . . to a friend who lies secluded all through the summer months in a back bedroom in Wimpole Street, London, to a friend who is no other than England's foremost poetess, the brilliant, the doomed, the adored Elizabeth Barrett herself?

From chasing rabbits in the field ("the earth, here hard, here soft, here hot, here cold, stung, teased and tickled the soft pads of his feet") to lying in the dark, ornate bedroom heavy with perfume—a depressing change.

" 'Flushie,' wrote Miss Barrett, 'is my friend—my companion—and loves me better than he loves the sunshine without.' She could not go out. [She was chained, in her mind, to the sofa.] And Flush, to whom the whole world was free, chose to forfeit all the smells of Wimpole Street in order to lie by her side.' " He would rush back from brief outings on Wimpole Street to be with his mistress.

A salient point is raised: A dog, even one of the sporting breed, can sublimate instinct, can adjust to radical conditions (a boudoir smelling of *eau de cologne*, really) if there are two vital ingredients—food and affection. Elizabeth Barrett *needed* Flush, *loved* Flush, *cared* for him.

Four years passed, 1842 to 1845, "and still Miss Barrett lay on her sofa in Wimpole Street and still Flush lay on the sofa at her feet." Then, amazingly, letters began arriving from another great English poet of the time, Robert Browning.

There is nothing sentimental about this account of the years of indisposition, of courtship, of marriage, and of the Brownings' life together in Italy. Through Flush we begin to comprehend a complex woman who overcame her psychological limitations, who escaped her father's Victorian home, who allowed herself to be courted and wooed largely by written word. And through Flush we learn of Robert Browning's dashing style, masculinity, and determination.

When Robert Browning finally arrives for a short visit, Flush, furious with jealousy, bites him, but is simply, quietly, shaken off. "Completely foiled, worsted, without a shaft left in his sheath, Flush sank back on his cushions panting with rage and disappointment."

The dog is relegated for the first time to a secondary

role in his mistress's affections. The previously doting woman, now in love with a man, enraptured with his assertiveness and brilliance, became stronger, less self-indulgent, less indulgent, too, of her pet's weaknesses. When, after hurting his paw, Flush "cried piteously," instead of being engulfed in sympathy as before, he is accused of shamming. Virginia Woolf quotes Miss Barrett sarcastically writing: "Flush always makes the most of his misfortunes—he is of the Byronic school—*il se pose en victime.*" Poor Flush had adapted well to Miss Barrett's need to see him as she had seen herself—a victim, weak and fragile.

Flush knew, though, that he must occupy second place. He accepted Browning finally, and had then *both* master and mistress. All would have lived happily ever after except that, even in Victorian England, even for the rich, life could be difficult. The poor, then as now, have a way of lashing out, of taking that which they have no other means of getting. ". . . when suddenly, without a word of warning, in the midst of civilization, security and friendship—he was in a shop in Vere Street with Miss Barrett and her sister: it was the morning of Tuesday the 1st of September—Flush was tumbled head over heels into darkness. The doors of a dungeon shut upon him. He was stolen."

Virginia Woolf, as all great artists, in creating a work of art borrowed ideas and descriptions, or whatever else she felt appropriate, where she could find them. Since Thomas Beames had taken on the task—taxing "all the resources of the English language"—of describing the degradation "not a stone's throw from Wimpole Street," Virginia Woolf paraphrased him and, using Flush again—placing the dog among the thugs of London—drew the moral: "The terms upon which Wimpole Street lived cheek by jowl with St. Giles's were laid down. St. Giles's stole what St. Giles's could; Wimpole Street paid what Wimpole Street must."

Elizabeth Barrett paid, and no nonsense. "I must have my Flush, you know," she wrote to Mr. Browning, who had different ideas on the matter. "If Miss Barrett gave way," he wrote, "she was giving way to tyranny; she was giving way to blackmailers; she was increasing the power of evil over right, of wickedness over innocence." Her future husband was a man of principle, as was her austere father.

But humans and their dogs have a bond of loyalty—or should have. Elizabeth Barrett persisted and paid.

(Dognapping, not surprisingly, continues to this day. Even now, in New York City, it is calculated from ASPCA and Humane Society data that about one thousand dogs are stolen annually. Ransoms range from fifty to five hundred dollars. Irving West, the founder of Petfinders [see index], says, "It's like preying on widows; the same grief situation. The pedigree doesn't matter, the age doesn't matter. The value of the dog is the emotional attachment, and people will pay a lot for the chance to get their pet back.")

Just one of the delightful aspects of Virginia Woolf's book are its notes. Concerning the stealing she says: "As a matter of fact, Flush was stolen three times; but the unities seem to require that the three stealings be compressed into one. The total sum paid by Miss Barrett to the dog-stealers was twenty pounds."

For the most part, after Flush's return and the Brownings' removal with him to Italy, the three did live happily.

The most serious episode in Flush's later years was an infestation by fleas.

Fleas leapt to life in every corner of the Florentine houses; they skipped and hopped out of every cranny of the old stone; out of every fold of old tapestry; out of every cloak, hat and blanket. They nested in Flush's fur. They bit their way into the thickest of his coat. He scratched and tore. His health suffered; he became morose, thin and feverish. The Brownings, trying various means—powders and scouring—finally had to clip him all over into "the likeness of a lion."

In his great antidote to superstition and "common sense," *The Natural History of Nonsense,* Bergen Evans makes this observation: "Man's consciousness is predominantly visual—'seeing is believing,' we say—and few people are able to imagine what an olfactory consciousness might be like." Then he notes that the "gifted" Virginia Woolf tried it in *Flush.* Indeed she did, and with the following success:

He nosed his way from smell to smell; the rough, the smooth, the dark, the golden. He went in and out, up and down, where they beat brass, where they bake bread, where the women sit combing their hair, where the birdcages are piled high on the causeway, where the wine spills itself in dark red stains on the pavement, where leather smells and harness and garlic, where cloth is beaten, where vine leaves tremble, where men sit and drink and spit and dice—he ran in and out, always with his nose to the ground, drinking in the essence; or with his nose in the air vibrating with the aroma. He slept in this hot patch of sun—how sun made the stone reek! he sought that tunnel of shade—how acid shade made the stone smell! He devoured whole bunches of grapes largely because of their purple smell; he chewed and spat out whatever tough relic of goat or macaroni the Italian housewife had thrown from the balcony—goat and macaroni were raucous smells, crimson smells. He followed the swooning sweetness of incense into the violet intricacies of dark cathedrals; and, sniffing, tried to lap the gold on the window-stained tomb.

It is the artist's role to imagine the unknowable. In *Flush* we learn about a dog and his bond to people and his unique perceptions. It is poetic knowledge.

Elegy on a Young Airedale Bitch Lost Some Years Since in the Salt Marsh

by Yvor Winters

From Collected Poems

Low to the water's edge
You plunged; the tangled herb
Locked feet and mouth, a curb
Tough with the salty sedge.

Half dog and half a child,
Sprung from that roaming bitch,
You flung through dike and ditch,
Betrayed by what is wild.

The old dogs now are dead,
Tired with the hunt and cold,
Sunk in the earth and old.
But your bewildered head,

Led by what heron cry,
Lies by what tidal stream?—
Drenched with ancestral dream,
And cast ashore to dry.

L.A. Report— Hollywood Canines

by Vincent Tajiri

In the tradition of Nathanael West, author/ photographer Tajiri surveys the dogs' life in the fading fantasy land.

Los Angeles. A city born into an era of automobiles and easy obsolescence, whose initial population spurt came from an industry involved in the manufacture of flickering, ephemeral images. Impermanence marks its frail, uninspired structures (influenced, perhaps, by the one-sided buildings that line the backlots of its studios?) and seeps into the life of its inhabitants. "City of the One-Night Stands," it has been called—a community of the transitory.

L.A. can boast of 50 percent more dog-grooming establishments than New York, and it can more than match that city in count of dog kennels, pet shops, and veterinarians. From birth to death the Angeleno's pet can be assured of facilities for pampering.

In such a society there is a desperate need for something to cling to—some sturdy rock, dependable and faithful, upon which emotions can be stored. It may be this that is the underlying reason for Los Angeles' high ratio of dog ownership. After all, where is there a companion as subservient, faithful, and dependable as a dog?

In turn, the Angeleno rewards devotion with devotion. There are more services here that can tend to a dog's every need than there are elsewhere. L.A. can boast of 50 percent more dog-grooming establishments than New York, and it can more than match that city in a count of dog kennels, pet shops, and veterinarians. From birth to death the Angeleno's pet can be assured of facilities for pampering.

And even after death.

A dozen or more miles west of the Hollywood sign—at the tip of an off-ramp marked "Parkway Calabasas" on the Ventura Freeway—there is another sign, similar in structure and appearance. This one is anchored along the slope of one of twin peaks that—with brush seared brown from a long, dry summer—suggest the humps on a camel's back. It reads, cryptically and ambiguously, "L.A. PET PARK."

Black marble burial stone in Los Angeles Pet Park is inscribed: "Man little knows what love is nor hath God made him wise who hath not power to need or see love in a dog's deep eyes." (Photograph by Vincent Tajiri)

This is no natural refuge for the romp of domesticated animals. Nor, as more than one wag has suggested, is it an area set aside for the dalliance of young lovers. The name is a modern-day euphemism, for this is, plain and clear, a cemetery of which the principal occupants are dogs.

Here are thirty-five acres of valuable Southern California real estate of which—after almost a half-century —only five acres are now occupied. Dogs, it can be observed, take considerably less space than people. It was inaugurated in 1929 with the burial of Kabar, the faithful Doberman of Rudolph Valentino. Among those that followed, many were the pets of celebrities: William Randolph Hearst, Sr., John Gilbert, Gloria Swanson, Dolores Del Rio, Lionel Barrymore, Edward G. Robinson, Humphrey Bogart, Mae West, and, to a more cur-

rent time, Tony Orlando and Diana Ross, to name but a few.

In 1973 the L.A. SPCA purchased the park, and a short while ago William Etinger was appointed to the post of supervisor. As befits the role, Etinger is a slim, graying, quiet-spoken man. New to the job, he is uncertain as to how many animals lie buried here. "Without making a count from the records, it's impossible to know. A real rough estimate would be somewhere over thirteen thousand. Right now our average burial of dogs is around forty-five a month."

The cemetery is not restricted to the famed or the affluent. "We have elderly couples come here and pay for burials out of their Social Security checks." Nor is showing grief over the loss of a pet the exclusive privilege of the female. "I've seen many men—big six-footers—with tears streaming down their faces," Etinger says as he looks out from his office window at a middle-aged couple standing over a gravesite.

The devotion of pet owners is evident in the well-tended gravesites—bedecked, as many are, with flowers and plastic toy propellers that whirl gaily and incongruously against the serene, grassy hillside. It is verbalized on tombstones—some of majestic proportions—with inscriptions like: "Man little knows what love is. Nor hath God made him wise. Who hath not the power to need or see—love in a dog's deep eyes." Or, in a more personal vein, "Gather you a dream and rest awhile. Chase rainbows across the skies. And I will come for you when forever is ours."

Attesting that the term "a member of the family" is no mere cliché are familial references to "Our Baby" and "Son," that appear with regularity, as does the annexation of the family's surname to that of the pet. Still, it may often take a moment to realize that "Ginger Jones" was never an ecdysiast but always a Pekingese; that "Mugsy Kamer" was not a street tough but a mastiff better known for its growl than its bite.

For those who live toward the southern edge of this far-spread city, there is another place like this. It is called Pet-Haven. And midpoint between these sites—not too far from City Hall—a firm known as Johnson Professional Mortuary Service offers funeral services for pets.

Are there many other cities in the world that can provide a dog such dignity upon its death? . . . Or the prospects of greater longevity?

"Given proper care and treatment, dogs will generally live longer here than elsewhere," says kennel owner Doris Hall, a hearty woman of goodly proportions who spends her weekends judging dog shows. "You'll find this especially true in great Danes. As you know, Danes have a short life expectancy. By the time they're seven, they're getting old, and a ten-year-old Dane has really accomplished something. Out here I know of several Danes who are eleven and twelve and still going strong."

Asked if there might be other regional differences, Hall pauses before answering. "The coats on the long-haired breeds will not be as good because of the mild climate. I've seen old English sheepdogs from back East with beautiful, profuse coats and borzois with their coats dripping on the ground. However, you'll find that in most breeds the western dog will be slightly larger in stature and—as most judges will tell you—they have better movement and rear ends."

While the poodle is the most popular breed here, as elsewhere, most Southern Californians prefer larger animals. "I think that I'm safe in saying that there are more German shepherds, Dobermans, and Danes out here than in any of the other big cities," Hall observes.

Undoubtedly the L.A. lifestyle is ideal for large dog ownership. Here single-family homes with spacious backyards predominate, and the climate is blessed year-round. Animals requiring exercise need minimal supervision. Then, within an hour's drive there are wooded mountains and the seashore. Although dogs are prohibited on public beaches, savvy owners know the isolated strips along the Pacific that are seldom patrolled. Here they gather with almost scheduled regularity for "canine klatches," basking in the sun and small-talking while their pets chase each other merrily, albeit illicitly, along the surf.

While the Department of Animal Regulation may exercise tolerance at some of its beaches, it has been efficient in its control over surplus dog population, and its antirabies program has effectively checked that disease. Jim McNamara, p.r. officer for the organization, is quick to point out that there hasn't been a single case of rabies in the county since 1962. AR also maintains six animal shelters in the city through which an average of about seventy thousand dogs are processed each year. Consistent with Hollywood's "rags-to-riches" stories, several of the dogs that found fame in the movies have come from animal shelters.

The first dog to find stardom in the movies was Jean, who appeared in several Vitagraph films back in 1911, the days of the two-reelers. Paid a handsome salary of twenty-five dollars a week, Jean was followed, in the years to come, by such stalwarts as Pete (of Our Gang Comedy fame), Strongheart, Rin Tin Tin, Lassie, and most recently, the favorite of Disney Studios, Benji.

Originally known as Higgins during his stint in TV's *Petticoat Junction*, Benji was discovered in a Burbank animal shelter by Frank Inn, one of the best-known animal trainers. When asked about Benji's ancestry (it's part cocker spaniel and part poodle, a combination that has brought into being the term "cockapoo"), Inn is said to have replied, "'I'd call him a cross between Hollywood and Burbank."

Others retrieved from the fate that awaits in animal shelters were Jip, who appeared with Rex Harrison in *Dr. Doolittle*; Bernardo Barkalotte, featured with Tony Curtis in *Wild and Woolly*; and Spot, who starred in an Errol Flynn movie back in 1950.

And, if one is inclined toward tales, one of the better ones involves dog trainer Rudd Weatherwax, who laid claim to a pedigreed male collie named Pal in settlement for a ten-dollar debt. Renamed for a movie role, Pal became the screen's first Lassie. If the story is true, the payment for a ten-dollar debt has turned into a lifetime annuity for Weatherwax, who just starred the seventh generation of "Lassies," a male as have been all predecessors, in producer Bonita Granville's film, *Lassie, My Lassie*.

Weatherwax's explanation for what some may call chauvinistic casting is, "Like all animal species, the male is more beautiful than the female. His coat photographs better, he doesn't shed as much, and besides, he's bigger."

One reason for the success of strays in films might be that they are, more often than not, of mixed breed. According to Bob Blair, trainer of the majority of animals seen in TV commercials, "Mixed breeds are easier to work with. I find that purebred dogs are usually too temperamental."

Still, as most dog trainers for movies will agree, it is not so much a matter of breeding as it is the individual dog's intelligence and receptivity to long, arduous hours of training. The needs of a TV or movie role go far beyond the prescribed routine of obedience training, and only a handful of dog trainers are recognized within the industry as skilled in this highly specialized field. Among these are Inn, Weatherwax, Blair, Karl Miller, and Carl Spitz. All are loath to reveal secrets about their training methods.

"A lot of hard work and special tricks go into each performance you see," Blair says. "If you're working with sound to be dubbed in later, you can give verbal commands. Otherwise the dog has to perform specific actions in response to visual signals. There are times when we'll use several dogs that look alike in a film, since one dog may be better at a piece of action or may look better from a certain camera angle."

In L.A. a dog need not be a movie star to be accorded celebrity treatment. While milady will have to hie herself off to her favorite beauty salon for a wash and set, a mere phone call will bring one of Mr. Groomer's mobile vans directly to her home to provide all necessary beauty treatments for her pet. If Fido's preference is for the local grooming establishment, or if it has an appointment with the vet and there is no one around to provide transportation, another call will bring a dog taxi.

The taxi service for pets, known as *On the Go*, is the brainchild of Herb Zoolman, who keeps two cabs on the street around the clock. While the majority of his calls

"Photograph of Folly and some of her litter of fifteen puppies, born in 1943 in Beverly Hills, California. The father was Buzz, a liver-spotted Dalmatian. Although The Hundred and One Dalmatians *was not written until long afterwards, the overwhelming birth of the fifteen puppies was largely responsible for my writing the book. This photograph, taken by my husband, Alec Beesley, has always been known to us as 'Folly's Milk Bar'." Dodie Smith in a note from Finchingfield, Essex, England, December 1977. (Photograph courtesy of The Viking Press, publisher of* The Hundred and One Dalmatians.)

are for short runs—around a ten-dollar base plus mileage—he also makes frequent runs to the airport when pets are to be shipped. Longest fare? A dog that had to be driven to San Diego—over one hundred and twenty-five miles.

Then there is the Pet Hotel, operated by Al Thomas. Conceived by Thomas in 1962, the hotel provides dogs (and cats, too) with facilities and accommodations a cut above those of the usual boarding kennel. Here each dog has its own "apartment," complete with private patio. All facilities are indoors (unique in this area), the air is purified through filters, the temperature is thermostatically controlled, and music is piped in. The weekly fee—from around $35, depending upon size of dog and length of coat—includes breakfast and dinner, cookies served at lunch, several play periods, and daily brushing and grooming. Special diets and medications come at an extra charge. Manager Vickie Copeland, who has had to prepare many a steak *precisely* medium rare," is used to exotic requests. "We had one dog who would have chicken cacciatore one evening and spaghetti and meat balls the next."

Innovations are the key to the hotel concept. Most popular is the report card that accompanies each dog upon its return. Using the standard A (for excellent) to F (for failure) system, each dog is graded daily on such things as personality, deportment, and eating and toilet habits. Another specialty is the penthouse (with a personal valet) for those who desire super deluxe accommodations. For dogs a bit long in the tooth there is the Senior Citizens' Home and a Rejuvenation Club. The latter, inspired by the Elizabeth Arden Farm, offers special treatments for reducing, hair health and conditioning, and scaly skin and dandruff care.

For dogs with more serious problems the L.A. area abounds with veterinarians and veterinary hospitals. Among these the practice of Dr. Richard Glassberg of Anaheim is beyond the norm. He specializes in acupuncture for animals, having opened the first clinic offering this service in 1973. "I believe that animals respond better to acupuncture treatments than do people," he states.

Aging pets and elderly people desiring the companionship of dogs are among the concern of two groups in particular: Petfinders in Studio City and Actors and Others for Animals in Beverly Hills.

The latter, using the acronym A&O for brevity's sake, was founded in 1971 by people in the entertainment field. Under the leadership of its current president, actor Earl Holliman of *Police Woman* fame, the organization is active in pet adoptions, assistance referrals, emergency aid, control over surplus pet population, and the humane treatment of animals in movies and television.

The Board of Governors of A&O is a veritable Who's Who of Hollywood celebrities. A partial listing includes Paul Newman and Joanne Woodward, the Fred McMurrays, Carroll O'Connors, and James Brolins, Burt Reynolds, Jack Klugman, Zsa Zsa Gabor, Carol Burnett, and Steve Lawrence and Eydie Gorme.

Until recently Petfinders, an independent nonprofit group organized in 1969, was singularly involved in bringing lost pets back together with their owners. In mid-1977 the group began enlarging its area of activity by introducing its own ID tag and animal registry tied into a twenty-four-hour hotline phone number as a means of expediting the return of pets.

According to Paul King, director, the organization is now working on a plan to provide senior citizens with dogs at no cost to the recipient. More idealistic is another proposal for a "retirement home" for aging pets. "The site has already been donated to us," says King. "What we need now is the funding."

In the meantime, Petfinders continues to handle anywhere from three hundred to five hundred calls a week regarding lost pets. Callers are advised as to the various actions that can be taken to aid in the recovery of a pet. Of those calling, those wishing to retain Petfinders' services (approximately 20 percent do) can do so for an overall fee of twenty-five dollars. According to King, "Our records, going back to the day we began, indicate a recovery rate of sixty-eight percent. Now, in a county the size of L.A., that's really remarkable."

Adding a touch of humor to a dash of flamboyance, another in this field is a former insurance salesman named John Keane, who calls himself Sherlock Bones, tracer of missing dogs. Using a technique reminiscent of earlier-day Western sheriffs, Keane recruits bounty hunters by printing up large "REWARD" posters bearing a picture of the missing dog along with a detailed description, "Short hair, grayish black, cropped tail, approximately thirty lbs.," which he affixes to poles and trees and passes out to anyone interested.

Dognappings are apparently a rising problem in this land of sunshine, since dogs are usually accessible. "They'll come right in your backyard to steal them," says Nina Culver, owner of a grooming parlor called Nina's Party Poodle. "They sell them to someone else, to a medical lab, or else they'll wait for a reward."

Rewards can often be substantial. While the average would probably be around one hundred and twenty-five dollars, amounts as high as five hundred dollars are not uncommon. While only care will prevent dogs from straying or being stolen, a method used by many Angelenos as an aid in retrieving their lost pets is that of having the animal tattooed. Culver, who has been tattooing dogs for over ten years, believes it to be the only permanent and positive means of identification. The tattoo, consisting of coded numbers, is usually placed on the inside flank of the animal, and the numbers are registered with one of the national pet identification services. Another groomer providing tattooing services in this area is Royal Pets.

Finally, for the pampered pooches fortunate enough to be born under the sign of Hollywood, there are the fripperies that make life worthwhile. In nearby Colton Dog Show Specialties manufactures and wholesales everything from plastic fireplugs to specially formulated toothpastes and deodorants for dogs. "The most popular items in our cosmetic line," says George Stinson, president, "seem to be nail polishes and colognes. In nail polishes people prefer the higher shades—Orange, Turquoise and Hot Pink. Among the colognes we have one that uses Chanel No. 5 as a base that's very popular."

Then, for women favoring a chichi look while walking their dogs, Stinson makes a twenty-two-carat gold-plated choke chain. As a companion piece the lady can also pick out a matching twenty-two-carat gold brooch or necklace charm bearing an effigy of her pet. These are available in a choice of one hundred and twenty-eight breeds.

Those preferring a more casual look can select from one of the many T-shirts, sweatshirts, and windbreakers made by Western Design in Simi Valley. These come with likenesses of over one hundred and thirty different breeds along with a choice of epigrams. There is one appropriate for the dog owner whose pet—despite all the love lavished upon it—still expresses occasional discontent. It reads: "Bitch! Bitch! Bitch!"

Vincent Tajiri is a writer—among whose works is a recent biography of Valentino—and a professional photographer and editor. He was for many years head of the photography department of Playboy.

THE THIN MAN GOES HOME

WELCOME

What Makes Toby Bark?

by Marc Kristal

A spoof on What Makes Sammy Run? *turns out to be a bittersweet piece.*

Arms folded, I stood beside the dentist's chair and watched as the delicate cap Toby had lost in a Dunhill chew bone the night before was replaced. His handsome shih tzu's face jerked, and I grimaced—not from pain so much as the notion that the beautiful smile that melted the hearts of the matinee set was strictly manufactured. I beat my brains together. *What makes Toby bark?*

The surgery at an end, the little bib removed, Toby jumped to the floor, shaking himself. (Endless hours of exercise had given him an athlete's grace.) Hair flew around the room; Toby shuddered: like all actors he was a vain old dog, and baldness was one of the spectres that haunted his satin-sheeted nights. "Get me an hour with that Swede, the follicle man," he growled.

Sure, I was his flunkie. His best boy. And why not? Being "personal manager" to the hottest four-legged creature in films was, you might say, no more than my avocation. Professionally, I was a full-time Toby-watcher.

You see, back in the old days, when I was keeping Ed Sullivan supplied with party-hatted schnauzers that jumped through flaming hoops, and Toby (once my client) was already snapping at the heels of M-G-M's gate guard—yes, he'd made the trip west, on the Super Chief, as a debutante's lapdog of course, no baggage car for *him*, even if he *was* broke—I got a wire from the coast. My first communiqué from Hollywood, land of dreams—from Toby.

I wondered what he wanted. Just before Toby had gone west, he had begged me to take the trip with him—begged: big, wet olive eyes, much mooning and yodeling, front paws throttling my knee—but I had said no. My animal agency was just hitting stride. Besides, self-abasement means nothing to a dog like Toby: just one

William Powell, Asta, and Myrna Loy in a publicity shot for the film based on Dashiell Hammett's novel in which, incidentally, Asta was not the wirehaired fox terrier shown here, but a schnauzer. (Photograph courtesy of Mark McCrackin)

more irritating flea to be scratched off on the long road Up. I wasn't fooled by his pleading. He knew he wouldn't be able to abuse a big-time agent like he could a star-struck slob from the Apple: Would Swifty Lazar rub his stomach? That was what his act had been about.

So why the cable?

It seems he wanted me to run an errand. "Drop off a grand with my brother," said the Western Union, and gave an address on Rivington Street. "I'll pay you back. And stop with the cold nose treatment—write!"

I did it. After tossing down a few and silently protesting, I shuffled over to the Chase and emptied my account. *Seed money,* I thought of it as—a shot at bringing the *what makes Toby bark?* flower to fruition.

His brother Hymie lived in a store doorway. An awful scraggly little runny-nose with a nervous tick, full of poor pride and self-pity; described himself as "kennel wise but pound foolish." Hymie led Louie the Blind Peddler around the neighborhood four times a week, and Louie kept him in soupbones. New York is full of dogs like this. *Nebbishes:* harmless little good-hearted *nebs* who never bite anyone, whose only crime is in not being rabid enough to snarl and snap and paw their way out of the ghetto.

Hair flew around the room; Toby shuddered: like all actors he was a vain old dog, and baldness was one of the spectres that haunted his satin-sheeted nights.

I bought him a hamburger patty and he gave me the family history. A familiar tale. The father brought the old-country customs over with him and tried to keep them afloat. A good dog; a pious dog. Friday nights would find him, long-whiskered and impressive, Hymie at his side, hunched over a silver dish—his sole possession, smuggled out of China in a giant rubber mouse—and growling religiously. The neighborhood animals sought his advice in many matters—cats, too; and when there was a question experience had not given him the answer to, the old dog would don his best collar, make the long walk to Lohmann's Pets on Thirty-fourth, and sneak back to the Care and Feeding Manuals display for a peek at the Text.

Toby, of course, resented him—thought him foolish for clinging to the old ways. Toby was the type of pup who would bite people in crowds, then pretend to be admiring a fire hydrant. His best friend was a psychotic beagle, Ben (sometimes called "Bugsy" Beagle, though never to his face), who successfully altered his incriminating pawprints by running in front of a bus. Toby romanced pooches of different breeds, which the old man could not abide; they fought unceasingly. When the father lost his tail and a hind leg in a pushcart accident, Toby ran out on him, leaving poor *neb* Hymie to take care of the crippled sage. And never looked back.

What makes Toby bark? seemed a lot closer to being answered that day.

Needless to say, Hymie wouldn't take the money. I let him see me slip it under the stoop, then went back to my midtown office to follow the Toby story as it grew. Toby ran well: ran from Wilson's column to the Lyons Den and back again, week after week, month after month. It was all there in black-and-white: Toby howling for better terms at the Animals' Guild meeting, and getting the presidency in the bargain; Toby breaking his contract with Metro—despite L. B. Mayer's threat that he'd be chasing fire trucks in a week—and negotiating a three-picture deal with Paramount; Toby as social animal, on the leg of every starlet in town, yapping to Louella that he'd work with Dietrich anytime, but never again with Von Sternberg; Toby angling for artistic control; Toby nosing out Rin Tin Tin for the job of Mr. Woofies, and the resulting appearance of his face on billboards and biscuit boxes across the American landscape; Toby and the cute young shelty of Fox's production head taking over Ronald Colman's Bel Air palace. I saw a picture of them together in *Modern Screen* with the headline: "Will a Shocked Hollywood Let 'Sleeping' Dogs Lie?"

When he finally called me again—sending a month's supply of Woofies and the note, "Friends?"—I grabbed it. Hell, I'd have been a fool not to. I was getting tired of housebreaking vain poodles with stage mothers, Toby was the hottest thing on both coasts—and besides, I sensed that things were coming to a head. Toby was running too fast, even for Toby. I wanted to be there when he came to the end of his leash.

I was there, all right. I gave him the lowdown as we left the dentist's, as he was putting his teeth marks in some thrilled child's autograph book. "It doesn't look good, kid," I said, strolling along Wilshire in Beverly Hills. *I Detected Land Mines for Hitler* is in trouble with the Hays Office, and the Woofies brass are thinking of dropping you in favor of a new kid named Lassie. You're broke, of course; might have lived off your earnings if you hadn't blown them on the homeless chippies you pick up outside the SPCA." I stopped, just long enough to hand him the *coup de grâce.* "And tomorrow Hedda's dropping a bomb: about your not being a shih tzu at all, but a lhasa apso with a pretty conk."

He didn't take it very well. Toby put on quite a scene in front of the Beverly Wilshire Hotel—I had to stop a policeman from shooting him—and a lucky boy from a tabloid caught the whole performance with his Brownie. I hustled him away from there and suggested—perhaps cruelly—that Suzanne the shelty might throw him a bone, so to speak. Just then, for the first time in the eternity of our relationship, Toby surprised me. He *cried.*

"That bitch! Handing out engraved collars to every four-flushing poodle with a line! Waking up in strange kennels, never knowing how she got there . . ." He grabbed my pantleg and dragged me into an alley. Shamelessly he clutched my calf and slobbered up at me, his eyes running. "She mocks me! She tells me I'm no good anymore!"

"Is it true?"

He whined horribly. "I got nailed by the pound a while back. I—I was drunk—coked to the gills—couldn't find my ID tag." He could barely get the sounds out. "I tried to tell them who I was, but the vet just laughed. He says to me, 'Sure you're Toby, pal. And *I'm* Francis the Talking Mule!' Can't you see what I'm trying to say? They *fixed* me, damn you! I'm a neuter!"

Well, well. This *was* news. I kicked Toby off my new twill slacks and clasped my hands in silent prayer. *Thank you, Lord, for revealing the secret!* The poor slob. It was *Love* that made Toby bark.

"I loved her," he squeaked, "God, how I loved her." I noticed for the first time that his voice was higher. Ruined for sound film—a canine John Gilbert.

"Okay, Toby. Okay. Okay." My question answered —my life fulfilled by a castrated dog—I felt nothing but pity. "Come on, kid. Let's go have a drink." I tried to take him into the Beverly Hills Derby, but when your stock falls in Movieland, brother, it drops straight off the board. Pierre stopped us at the revolving doors with that cold look his family of headwaiters had been cultivating for generations, like Beaujolais grapes.

"A table for *you*, monsieur," he said, "but no dogs allowed."

Marc Kristal says of himself that when he finally gives up the last stages of childhood he will stop being a writer and start going to law school. He also lays claim to a sense of the absurd that is not large enough to accommodate living in California.

The Gaines Fido is awarded annually to outstanding achievers in the dog fancy.

As Filmland Has Its Oscar, So Does Dogdom Have Its Fido

The annual award of the Gaines statuette to individuals who have made "significant contributions to the world of dogs."

Each year the Gaines Dog Research Center recognizes individuals who have made significant contributions to the world of dogs. The company presents Fido awards as a special part of the Dog Fanciers Club luncheon held in New York City the day after the Westminster Kennel Club Dog Show. This annual event is attended by leading figures in the dog fancy.

On the basis of their outstanding endeavors in behalf of dogs, a Fido is awarded to winners in each of the following categories: man of the year, woman of the year, writer of the year, and handler of the year.

To select the recipients, nominations in each category are made by people active in the dog fancy. After these nominations are tabulated, the top three nominees in each category are then listed on a final selection ballot. The person receiving the greatest number of votes in each category then receives a Fido at the luncheon.

The award itself—the industry's Oscar, so to speak—was modeled after an early Egyptian statue on exhibit at the Metropolitan Museum of Art. Mounted on an ebony base, the gold-plated figure is six inches high by nine inches long. Each award carries an engraved plate attached to the base bearing the recipient's name, the award category, and the year awarded.

To participate in the nominating process write Gaines Dog Research Center, 250 North Street, White Plains, NY 10625.

Where to Get Your Own Performing Dog

Dog stardom is not just the province of the major studios: you, too, can hire a talented beast for a minimum of money. The major animal agencies are on the west coast, among them:

Frank Inn Inc.
12265 Branford Street
Sun Valley, CA 91352

Lou Schumacher
P.O. Box 642
Baldwin Park, CA 91706

If the prospect of bringing a dog and his trainer from California to the east seems excessive, try:

Matthew Margolis
11 E. 68th Street
New York, NY 10022

Dawn Animal Agency
160 W. 46th Street
New York, NY 10036

The cost of renting an animal varies, based on the nature of the role and your own financial limitations. If all you require is an "extra"—a background dog to stand around and provide atmosphere—one can be obtained for fifty to one hundred dollars a day. (Many agencies and kennels will give you a financial break if you genuinely need it.) Then there are the more expensive "hero" dogs, animals that will perform almost any trick that you can imagine for them; their prices, on the average, range from one hundred to one hundred and fifty dollars a day. Frank Inn Inc., the outfit that represents the famous Benji, has in its catalog a Doberman that can open a car door and a puli that faints on cue. Benji, no slouch he, can walk a tightrope blindfolded.

When figuring your expenses, don't forget to include the cost of a trainer, who must accompany any dog doing film work. Trainers, who work with an eight-hour minimum prerequisite, get approximately $100 for their minimum (that figure fluctuates according to union scale: trainers are unionized). A trainer may strike one as a needless expense, but wait until the mutt you're directing walks up and whines: "What's my motivation?"

There was the German shepherd, Rin Tin Tin, back then and now there is this dog—a mutt that was saved from destruction at the Newton, Connecticut, Humane Society Animal Shelter—trained and then starred as Sandy in the Broadway musical Annie. *Shown with him are costars Andrea McArdle as Annie and Reid Shelton as Daddy Warbucks. Sandy's owner-trainer is actor William Berloni, who also now owns Sandy's understudy, Arf. After paying an eight-dollar adoption fee, Berloni reports, "My biggest task at that point was restoring the dog's faith in humans." (Photograph by Martha Swope)*

Jack, a Biography of Jack London

Book Review

Jack ($12.95; New York: Harper and Row, 1977), by Andrew Sinclair, describes the first American macho novelist—hard-drinking, big-spending, self-dramatizing.

Sinclair complains that London has been too long relegated to the ranks of dog writer and juvenile author. London was a Social Darwinist (and therefore a racist) and a socialist. He also was the predecessor of Dos Passos, Hemingway, Steinbeck, Kerouac, and Mailer in that he went "on the road" first, wrote sparse prose before them, and pioneered the boxing novel.

That London was not just a dog writer is true, but his dog stories are among the best of their genre because his wolf-dog relationships are very effective metaphors of the human condition. London's magnificent dog Buck in *The Call of the Wild* (considered his masterpiece) moves away from humanity into the primeval, desolate wastes of the far north. *White Fang* (the other great work) is a wolf-dog that comes in from out of the cold of that terrifying wilderness to the comfort of civilization.

The dichotomy in humans of the cerebral, civilized, and gentle being and the predatory, primitive savage fascinated London as he experienced it in himself and sensed it in others, and his descriptive vocabulary reflects this particular preoccupation. Of San Francisco, for instance, he said, "Nob Hill arose, like any medieval castle from the ruck of common life that denned and laired at its base."

Jack London was born in 1876 in one of those San Francisco dens. By 1913 he was the highest-paid, best-known, and most popular writer in the world. He had already been an oyster pirate, merchant seaman, tramp, and gold prospector in Alaska. He possessed amazing energy and vitality that took him to the Far East as a war correspondent and across the Pacific again with his second wife, as skipper of his own ketch.

Teddy Roosevelt once characterized London as a nature faker because a bulldog overcomes the wolf-dog in a fight in *White Fang*. London was concerned that his writing be true to nature and was able to answer the President that ". . . it was a matter of opinion whether a bulldog could whip a wolf-dog or not."

Attacked also on the biological grounds that "animals could not reason," London responded, "Let us be very humble. . . . We who are so very human are very animal. . . . You must not deny your relatives, the other animals. Their history is your history and if you kick them to the bottom of the abyss, to the bottom of the abyss you go yourself."

Sinclair sees Jack London as the forerunner of the modern sociobiologists—Lorenz, Ardrey, and Morris—who have increasingly emphasized "the behavioral similarities between animals and human beings." London was also thinking along some of the lines of modern linguistics before its founders Lévi-Straus and Chomsky had been heard of.

Jack London was a man of sensibility and intelligence. And he had a wonderfully unique ability to tell a dog story. He died of a drug overdose in his fortieth year, leaving fifty novels—many still in print throughout the world.

A FABLE OF AESOP— THE WAGES OF TREACHERY

The wolves once said to the dogs: "Since you are exactly like us, why do you not come to a brotherly understanding with us? There is no difference between us except in our ways of thinking. We live in freedom. You cringe like slaves to men, letting them beat you and put collars on you, and guarding their flocks for them; and when they eat, they only throw the bones to you. Take our advice. Hand over all the flocks to us; then we will share them between us and gorge ourselves." The dogs listened to this proposal. But as soon as the wolves got inside the fold, they started by killing the dogs.

Such is the reward of traitors to their own country.

The Dog as Demon— Then

The dog in myth—sometimes a frightening notion.

In Egyptian myth the god of death was Anubis, the jackal. It later transmuted to Hermanibus, the dog always present when a carcass decayed.

For Hindus it was the Rakshases, demons of great hostility to men, who haunted cemeteries as dogs causing disease and madness.

Hecate was known as "Our Lady of the Hounds" and "she who rejoices in the barking of dogs." Every night she led a swarm of ghosts through the Greek underworld accompanied by demonic barking dogs. The children of Hecate, the Empusaie, often took the form of bitches. Scylla, Hecate's daughter, was called the "Sea-Bitch," and the name of Scylla means "puppy." It was Scylla who devoured six of Odysseus' crew.

In ancient Britain Gwynn ab Nudd, the god of the underworld, hunted the souls of the dying with a pack of dogs.

Out of the myths of dogs chasing souls developed dogs as guardians of hell. In *God Had a Dog* Maria Leach writes that Cerberus was "the three-headed hound who guarded the entrance to Hades, the Greek underworld and land of the dead." Yet the form Cerberus takes is different in almost every account. Homer speaks only of the dog of Hades and mentions no heads, while Hesiod described him as a loud-voiced monster with fifty heads. In the *Aeneid* Virgil gives the monstrous hound only three heads.

. . . Judas Iscariot was possessed by the Devil, and after he had kissed Jesus, Satan went out of the traitor in the form of a dog.

In Hindu myth the kingdom of the dead is guarded both by day and night—the task being given to the sun-dogs and moon-dogs of Yama, the god of death.

In the *Avesta*—sacred book of the ancient Persians—there is a yellow-eared dog that guards the rainbow bridge spanning the gap between the land of the living and the land of the dead. The *Koran* also contains a legend of a dog guard.

Garm, the great wolf-dog of Norse mythology, is chained to the infernal regions. It is said that on the day of doom, when the watchdog broke free, the way out of hell gaped wide open.

Among North American Indians the dog that guards the entrance to the other world is found in the mythologies of the Iroquois, Huron, Massachusetts, Ojibwa, Menominee, and Seminole Indians, and in those of the Eskimos.

The entrance to Peni' nelau, the underworld of the Koryaks of Siberia, is guarded by dogs. A fiery dog also stands watch over the gate to the land of the dead in the mythology of North Borneo, and all pass by safely except virgins.

The mythological dog as guardian of hell evolved through the ages into the demonic black dog of Mohammedan tradition, while in the folklore of China tailless black dogs called p'eng hen are usually thought to be demons.

According to an Apocryphal gospel Judas Iscariot was possessed by the Devil, and after he had kissed Jesus, Satan went out of the traitor in the form of a dog.

In *Lore of the Dog* Patricia Dale-Green finds another early-Christian mention of the devil in which Simon Magnus, the sorcerer of the Apocrypha, sent to Peter the Apostle "certaine devils in the likeness of dogges to devoure him."

The Devil is said to have appeared to St. Stanislaus Kostka in the form of a terrifying black dog that seized him by the neck and tried to strangle him three times. He drove it away with the sign of the cross.

Throughout the Middle Ages the dog was the Devil, the hound of hell. This concept appears in *The Witch of Edmonton*, the 1658 play written by Rowley, Dekker and Ford. The Devil appears to Mother Sawyer in the form of a big black dog and says his name is Tom.

In a seventeenth-century pamphlet, *The Discovery of a London Monster called the Blacke Dogg of New-gate*, a dog troubles "blacke conditioned people" and lives in the "bosom of traytors, murtherers, theives, cut-purses, cunny-catchers and the like."

Then there was the infamous Salem witch panic, in which one of the accused had a dog "who was the Devil."

CYNOPHOBIA

Satan may have been a dog once, but such views are no longer widely held except perhaps by those who are petrified of dogs—the cynophobics. Suffering from a phobia, their fear is by definition heightened to the point of being illogical, irrational, and, perhaps, of such intensity as to be disabling. The cynophobic fixes on dogs as a means of protecting the ego from anxiety generated by his or her own repressed aggressive drive to strike out.

The Dog as Demon— Now

by Sarah Hawkes

The style has changed but the horrific tone hardly at all. An essay covering three books: A Friend in Deed, Best Friend, and The Dogs.

The demon dog stalks us still, a devilish creature possessed of powers beyond human comprehension or control. The fear of dogs, extending for some to phobic intensity (see index for cynophobia), like fear of the dark, of the sea, of heights, exists because the dog is a corporeal link with a natural, simple, but uncivilized existence. In the dog—the shape of the jaw, the prominence of tooth, the lope, the coat—the wolf lurks yet, and there's always a shade of the unpredictable. Meeting a strange dog alone on a quiet street or deserted road often gives one pause. Just as the wolf is admired because it is so wonderfully doglike, so too can the wolf, as marauding predator, be seen or sensed, perhaps subconsciously, in even the most civilized of dogs. The characterizations of dogs in several recent novels demonstrate that we are quite ready still (or again) to suspend disbelief and find a satanic cast.

The characterizations of dogs in several recent novels demonstrate that we are quite ready still (or again) to suspend disbelief and find a satanic cast.

A Friend Indeed ($7.95; New York: W. W. Norton, 1977), by Robert Jagoda, has obedience-class graduate Friend, a standard poodle, directed by his master's voice on a miniaturized tape recorder hidden in the dog's collar actually commit a murder by triggering an incredible Rube Goldberg device that fires a gun. This is a relatively innocuous tale because the dog here is just the instrument of a man—accommodating, maleable, and obedient.

In *Best Friend* ($7.95; New York: E. P. Dutton, 1977), by Pat Feeley, the dog character is possessed of an intelligence and determination very undoglike and far beyond what could be considered normal. He is so extraordinarily attuned to his mistress—a middle-aged woman in the throes of empty-nest syndrome—that he earns novice through the most advanced obedience titles in a

snap. With guile, cunning, and calculated deception, but without human direction or aid, the dog executes a perfect murder—all for the love of his lady. The qualities of loyalty and devotion, though distorted and grotesque, are still recognizably canine.

The Dogs ($7.95; New York: Delacorte, 1976), by Robert Calder, comes closest of these three stories to touching a nerve of real fear because even though the central dog character isn't well motivated to commit his first act of violence, those that follow—bloody attacks and slaughters—are within the realm of possibility.

A laboratory-bred and -reared pup (there's a suggestion of some unholy meddling with nature, of a Frankensteinlike tampering with life) is lost by a retarded lab attendant. The dog is very cool in its feelings for people except for the professor who finds him, adopts him, and names him Orph (short for orphan). The dog, without believable motivation, attacks and maims one of his master's small sons, then takes to the woods in shame and fear. Orph becomes leader of a pack of strays—destitute and deserted dogs that terrorize the surrounding countryside until they are hunted and destroyed in a massive military maneuver.

While the blood and gore run thick through detailed descriptions of violence, the author makes one salient point—dogs are often shamefully mistreated by humans who are careless or cruel or stupid. Particularly ensanguined are descriptions of an illegal dogfight and then of the hideous rending slaughter of the fight promoter by the wild pack. But the dogs in this book are simply the tools the author uses—instead of sharks, for instance—to let blood flow and bones crack.

BUCKRAM BEAGLES BUNGLE BARKING

Dressed appropriately in black velvet caps, white stocks, forester green tunics, and white duck trousers, the master of beagles and his three assistants led twenty-two beagles across the stage of Philharmonic Hall as the Festival Orchestra of New York performed Leopold Mozart's *Hunting Symphony*. It was "the comedy smash of the season," according to critics. Beagle discipline gradually broke down during repeated cross-stage trips, and howls of laughter drowned out the music.

The senior Mozart's score calls for the sounds of dogs, but even in response to the hunting calls of four French horns, the Buckram Beagles, a real hunting pack, never barked once.

Good Old Dog—
Loyal, Magical,
Healing, Holy

Categories include undying faithfulness, dogs and saints together, and the curing dog.

Except for sexual pleasure and perhaps bourbon there is nothing on earth so agreeable to human comfort as the dog. In her book *My Literary Zoo* ($12.25; New York: Arno facsimile of an 1896 work) Kate Sanborn gives the following description of canine character:

> He defends his master, saves from drowning, warns of danger, serves faithfully in poverty and distress, leads the blind. When spoken to, does his best to hold conversation by tail, eyes, ears; drives cattle to and from pasture, keeps herds and flocks within bounds, points out game, brings shot birds, turns a spit, draws provision carts and sledges, likes or abhors music, detecting false notes instantly; announces strangers, sounds a note of warning in danger, is the last to for-

sake the grave of a friend, sympathizes and rejoices with every mood of his master.

Not much has changed over the millennia. Men and women have cherished their dogs and used them, and when pressed by unseen, overpowering forces, have often in desperation turned to dogs for comfort—even for miraculous cures. This is as true today as it was in pre-Homeric times.

In *Lore of the Dog* by Patricia Dale-Green, the lap dog of a Greek harp-player throws itself on its master's coffin and is buried with him.

And then there is the most classic of all dog stories. In the *Odyssey* the faithful hound Argus greets the twenty-year-absent Odysseus. Book XVII: "There the dog Argus lay in the dung, all covered with dog ticks. Now, as he perceived that Odysseus had come close to him, he wagged his tail, and laid both his ears back."

Then the poor old dog did one last service: he died, thereby saving the disguised Odysseus from premature discovery by the mercenary suitors besetting his wife, Penelope.

Brass rubbings of Crusaders' graves often show dogs underfoot, thus symbolizing man's humility and faithfulness to the Christ as dogs are humble before, and faithful to, their masters.

Photograph by Peter Simon

The most celebrated invocation of the faithful dog occurred in Johnson County, Missouri, 1870, at the summation of the trial of *Charles Burden, Respondent vs. Leonidas Hornsby, Appellant.* At issue was the shotgun slaying of Burden's black-and-tan hound, Old Drum.

In Irish and Welsh folklore fairies sometimes come among mortals in the form of a dog to mend broken hearts.

The text of lawyer George Graham Vest's plea appears on the walls of kennels and dog clubs throughout America, and it is cut into marble on a monument standing on the present Johnson County courthouse lawn.

Although no courthouse stenographer was present at the trial, the well-remembered words were soon after written down. It is now de rigueur to acknowledge at least part of the plea. Here is the peroration, which is said to have caused the jurors to weep and to award fifty dollars in damages to Burden:

> If fortune drives the master forth an outcast in the world, friendless and homeless, the faithful dog asks no higher privilege than that of accompanying him to guard against danger, to fight against his enemies, and when the last scene of all comes, and death takes the master in its embrace and his body is laid away in the cold ground, no matter if all other friends pursue their way, there by his graveside will the noble dog be found, his head between his paws, his eyes sad but open in alert watchfulness, faithful and true even to death.

In March 1925 *The New York Times* reported that the dog of a deceased Mr. Farmer kept vigil on his master's grave for six months until expiring. Four years later the *Times* noted another heartbreak: "Cheerful Billy, an English champion greyhound hurdler, dies of grief because of death of trainer."

In the thirteenth century, when the plague had spread throughout Europe, St. Roch traveled with his dog, caring for those who were stricken. Infected himself, he crawled out of the city to die in the woods. But his faithful dog licked his sores and brought food to him day after day until recovery.

According to legend the mother of Saint Bernard dreamt she had a whelp "all white and red upon the back," barking in her belly. Her son founded the hospice of St. Bernard around 1000 A.D. Great white dogs with red patches on their backs were said to have saved lost travelers.

The twin themes of dog as servant of God and as a healer of the sick came together in an early Christian cult. St. Christopher, represented as dog-headed, gave protection to the faithful from sudden death and from the plague.

In Irish and Welsh folklore fairies sometimes come among mortals in the form of a dog to mend broken hearts. A case in point is the tale of Tristan and Isolt, in which the fairy-dog Petticru had such magical powers. It is said that when Petticru shook himself, a chain of gold bells tinkled, causing Tristan to listen and to forget his sorrow.

Dogs are still thought to be beneficial in their roles of experimental animals for medical research. And they are regularly reported to function as therapists for the disabled or disturbed.

In a reversal of the usual situation—man walks dog—the United Press International reported in 1967 a case in which a dog walked a woman, much to her benefit. A California woman, stricken with cerebral palsy, attributed her recovery to the fact that her dog, a German shepherd, pulled her around until her legs were strengthened enough for her to walk alone. The United Press did not report any medical comment.

There have been, however, a number of doctors who claim the dog to be very important in the psychological improvement of seriously troubled humans—even to the point of dogs being more effective as therapists than people. Dr. Samuel A. Corson of Ohio State reported in 1974 that he had supervised twenty "feeling-heart" dogs in the care of mentally ill patients. One patient, a catatonic schizophrenic—withdrawn, frozen, and almost mute—did not respond to twenty-five electric shock sessions, but after being given a dog as a companion, recovered enough to leave the hospital.

On a more prosaic level, just about everybody on intimate terms with a dog knows the blues can be a lot less blue when the pooch is around.

Photograph by Joanne Dolgow

173

It's the Dog That Wags the Tale

by Hal Borland

Courage, loyalty, separation, and reunion go back to the beginning and constantly recur in good dog stories now.

Long before I read *The Odyssey* I knew the story of Odysseus and his faithful dog, Argus. I heard it from my grandmother, whose brother was in the Civil War. "Charley," she would say, "was gone four years, and we didn't know whether he was living or dead. Then the war ended and one day this tramp came down the road, limping on a stick he'd cut in the woods, and nobody knew him till old Bell, Charley's dog, went and smelled him and licked his hands and cried like a baby."

Grandmother always wiped a tear from her own eyes before she finished the story. "Poor old Bell didn't last the week out. He'd just been waiting for Charley to come back before he lay down and died. Charley planted a wild rose beside Bell's grave and said he wished he could afford a stone. That rose was still growing, the last I knew."

And there was another story I discovered later. In the fragments of old Greek poetry is an epitaph which begins, "Laugh not, I pray thee; though this is a dog's grave, tears fell for me."

I am sure that is one reason the dog story is such an enduring part of our literature. Even when it is banal or downright lachrymose, there is a recognizable grain of truth somewhere in it; and when it is properly told it is classic, as fundamental as the love story or the story of man's valiant struggle with fate. At its best it is a tale of fidelity; often it is a tale of heroism; and the hero is at the heart of the legends by which man preserves his own dreams of greatness and nobility.

From time to time someone tries to tell me that the man-dog relationship is that of master and slave, that the dog, as a species, forfeited its birthright when it submitted to man's taming. I doubt this, as I doubt any broad statement applied to dogs, which are as various as human beings. Growing up, as any rural or small-town boy does, with an assortment of dogs all over the place, I knew that there were all kinds of dogs. Mine, of course, were always heroes. But the town preacher had a vile-tempered, quarrelsome dog that, any small boy could tell, swore like a trooper. The town drunk's dog waited outside the saloon to pilot his master safely home. And the town's slightly addled character (who sometimes insisted that he was Daniel Boone) had a dog that was a star witness in a murder trial.

There was bad blood between an irascible farmer and a young man who liked to hunt quail in his cornfield. One fall the young hunter was found shot to death in the field. There were no witnesses, it seemed. Then addled old Dan said he had been in the woods nearby when it happened, and he was summoned to court. In the midst of his rambling story he said he saw the farmer and the hunter in the field and heard the fatal shot. "But I didn't look. I turned my back and told my dog not to look neither." And the prosecutor, playing a hunch, ordered the dog brought into court. Every dog in town hated the accused farmer, and old Dan's dog bristled and growled at him. That turned the trick. The farmer confessed the murder.

I doubt that the prosecutor had read Andrew Lang's "The Dog of Montargis," but when I read it years later I knew that the same story had been played out, with slight variations, in the courtroom of the small Nebraska town where I was born. [*Editor's note:* In the late thirteen-hundreds a French courtier was murdered near Montargis. His dog incriminated one Macaire, who was then ordered to do battle with the dog. The dog won; Macaire confessed and was hanged for the crime.]

Or take the classic sheepdog story. It, too, has many variations, but Alfred Ollivant's *Bob, Son of Battle* set a durable modern pattern in 1898. It is a story as old as the flock-tenders who roamed prehistoric hills. A sheepherder, twenty miles from the home ranch, was bitten by a rattlesnake and died a miserable, lonely death. His two dogs not only held the flock together till the supply man arrived four days later and discovered the tragedy, but they fought off the coyotes and protected their dead master's body.

It must be admitted, of course, that not all dogs are heroes. Like the human tribe, the canine tribe has its share of cowards, thieves, and scoundrels. But I have yet to know a sadistic dog. Bullies, yes, and even killers—but they are renegades. I once had a dog that would rather fight than eat, but even he finally met his match in a better fighter. And the fate of the renegade dog somehow satisfies the persistent hope for ultimate justice and has its place in the lore and the legends.

The problem in any dog story arises from the fact that dogs are dogs, not people—anthropomorphism is a trap second only to sentimentality. From long association the dog thinks, up to a point, as man thinks. Beyond that point, however, the dog is a dog, now and forever. It is that fine line between dog thinking and man thinking that has betrayed so many writers.

Jack London's *The Call of the Wild* has a degree of nature faking in it and leans on incidents that could never happen—and yet, because Buck, the dog in London's novel, is truly a dog, not a projection of Jack London, it is both a rousing adventure story and a persuasive story of a dog. One of the best examples of truth and falsehood can be seen in Eric Knight's classic, *Lassie Come Home*, and in the television serial called *Lassie*, ostensibly based on that book. The story Knight wrote is beautiful. The TV version is utter nonsense, a clutter of clichés.

Eric Knight knew and loved and understood dogs. So do such writers as Mackinlay Kantor, Farley Mowat, and Fred Gipson, who have given us other memorable dog stories. I have a hound, now very old and baffled by the way his nose betrays him, who in his heyday might have run with Kantor's Bugle Ann if he had been trained to foxes rather than rabbits. I once had an utterly worthless pup whose sole virtue was a sense of humor and of the ridiculous that could match that of Mowat's mutt— "The Dog That Wouldn't Be"—one of the most charming and still credible bumblers in all dog literature. And I knew perhaps half a dozen dogs in my frontier youth that would have been fit companions if not quite equals to Gipson's early Texas dogs, Old Yeller and Savage Sam.

And there, I suspect, is another of the reasons that the dog story persists. We read of Perites, Alexander the Great's dog, and we appreciate their friendship. We read that King Arthur rode with a mythical pack of hunting dogs on moonlit nights in medieval Wales, and we can hear the baying of those great hounds. We read Aesop's fables about greedy and backbiting dogs, and we know that they, too, are true, for we have known such dogs.

We are glad when Shakespeare, particularly in *King Lear*, speaks of bobtail tike and trundle-tail, of mongrel grim and hound and spaniel and when he mentions three dogs by name, Tray and Blanche and Sweetheart. Shakespeare grew up a small-town boy. He, too, grew up with dogs.

Those who have written the really good dog stories, those that become our classics, make us remember and recognize dogs we knew or owned—heroic dogs, one way or another, the memory of which makes us proud to have been their companions. The really memorable dogs are not slaves or servants, but companions, fellow creatures we try to understand, try to know without asserting a human superiority which is always debatable. Yes, I know we all glibly say we "own" a dog: but the dogs that really matter own us, don't they? And that, I suspect, is the gist of the whole matter.

© 1962 by The New York Times Company. Reprinted with permission.

Hal Borland, a naturalist and author, wrote the nature editorials for The New York Times *until his death in 1978.*

MARK TWAIN'S DEVIL DOG— HARBINGER OF DEATH!

(Tom Sawyer and Huckleberry Finn have fled from the graveyard and signed an oath in blood never to speak of what was seen.)

They continued to whisper for some little time. Presently a dog set up a long, lugubrious howl just outside—within ten feet of them. The boys clasped each other suddenly, in an agony of fright.

"Which of us does he mean?" gasped Huckleberry.

"I dono—peep through the crack. Quick!"

"No, *you*, Tom!"

"I can't—I can't *do* it, Huck!"

"Please, Tom. There 'tis again!"

"Oh, lordy, I'm thankful!" whispered Tom. "I know his voice. It's Bull Harbison."

"Oh, that's good—I tell you, Tom, I was most scared to death; I'd 'a' bet anything it was a *stray* dog."

The dog howled again. The boys' hearts sank once more.

"Oh, my! that ain't no Bull Harbison!" whispered Huckleberry. "*Do*, Tom!"

Tom, quaking with fear, yielded, and put his eye to the crack. His whisper was hardly audible when he said:

"Oh, Huck, it's a stray dog!"

"Quick, Tom, quick! Who does he mean?"

"Huck, he must mean us both—we're right together."

"Oh, Tom, I reckon we're goners. I reckon there ain't no mistake 'bout where *I'll* go to. I been so wicked."

Excerpted from the *Adventures of Tom Sawyer* by Mark Twain (New York: Harper & Row, 1920).

Boy Without a Dog— Girl Without a Dog

Remembrances of a dogless childhood.

Boy

For the longest time I often pretended that I was a dog. I had a laundry hamper that I filled with blankets, and in I would creep. My name was Kiki the Dog. All of the chairs in the living room were part of my canine existence, and the hamper was my kennel. These revelations were not easily shared. I would never let my mother know that the laundry hamper had another reason for existing besides dirty laundry.

I couldn't understand why my mother didn't realize that that's what my father wanted more than anything else.

I always wanted to get my father a dog for his birthday. Every summer my mother and I would go to find my father a birthday present. Usually I would end up giving a tie, and my mother a fishing reel or a new rod . . . but never a dog. I couldn't understand why my mother didn't realize that that's what my father wanted more than anything else. No amount of explanations could sway her. I knew that he wanted to walk the dog every morning . . . and furthermore, that I would love to go with him when he did . . . and we could all be together. So much for the dog, and so much for the walks that never occurred with my father.

Henry Felt is a film producer whose own family now includes a dog.

GIRL

Growing up, she always wanted a dog but couldn't have one, so she set up a file on neighborhood dogs, saved money for dog biscuits, and fed them all on her "dog route" to and from school. She and her friends also used to play "dog" (taking turns walking each other, etc.), and often in bed at night she would chant words of magic, trying in vain to cast a spell that would turn her sister into a dog.

From Feminist Press notes on Bobbi Katz, who is author of Nothing but a Dog.

"My Protector." (*The Harry T. Peters "America on Stone Lithography Collection, Smithsonian Institution*)

Boys & Girls & Dogs

by Claire Romanof

Drawing heavily on juvenile literature the writer describes the special, almost mystical bond between dogs and children.

There is something almost mystical between children and dogs. This is especially so of children and puppies who are in some ways quite alike. A. A. Milne knew.

I met a Puppy as I went walking;
We got talking,
Puppy and I.
"Where are you going this nice fine day?"
(I said to the Puppy as he went by).
"Up in the hills to roll and play."
"I'll come with you, Puppy," said I.*

* A stanza of "Puppy and I" from *When We Were Very Young* by A. A. Milne ($4.50; New York: E. P. Dutton, 1924). Used with permission of E. P. Dutton and Methuen Children's Books, Ltd.

Many children identify with dogs. Both are relatively powerless in an adult-ordered world. Little girls often have distinctly maternal feelings about puppies. Konrad Lorenz, speculating on the first domestication of the dog in *Man Meets Dog* (see index), said:

> It is quite conceivable that . . . a little girl playing dolls brought up an orphaned puppy in the family circle. The soft, round, wooly bundle no doubt elicited in that small daughter of the early stone age the desire to cuddle it and carry it round interminably, just like the little daughters of our times; for the maternal instincts which give rise to such behavior are age-old.

The following is a selection of lovely books about little girls and dogs and their very special relationship.

A Wolf of My Own ($4.95; New York: The Macmillan Company, 1969), by Jan Wahl, is illustrated by Lillian Hoban with delicate, impressionistic drawings of a child and her puppy who becomes in fantasy her wild wolf companion. "I would sing you a wolf song without any words when it rained and we crowded under bushes. The other animals would run like fire when we approached them."

Ludwig Bemelmans' thoroughly independent heroine—"She was not afraid of mice—She loved winter, snow, and ice"—is saved from a watery death in the Seine by a dog in *Madeline's Rescue* ($1.95; New York: Viking Press, 1953). Taken home to Miss Clavel's school for young ladies, the dog, Genevieve, precipitates a fight when each little girl cries "Genevieve is *mine* tonight!" Conveniently, Genevieve whelps and ". . . suddenly, there was enough hound/to go all around."

Nothing But a Dog ($2.75; Old Westbury: The Feminist Press, 1972), by Bobbi Katz with pictures by Esther Gilman, communicates most perfectly and poignantly a little girl's desire to mother a pup. "Once it starts—the longing for a dog—there is no cure for it." Not even a whole series of wonderful activities—double-jumping at checkers, skating perfect figure-eights, getting a new tool bench, playing the trumpet—can ease "that sad, achey feeling of if you only had a dog."

A boy and his dog is a pervasive theme in fantasy. In Bartlett's *Familiar Quotations* we learn that Eugene Field said, "I wouldn't give much for the boy 'at grows up/With no friendship subsisten' 'tween him and a pup," and Berton Braley, "Give a boy a dog and you've furnished him a playmate."

In the following books the orphaned, deserted, abused, confused, and lonely boys rely on their dogs for more than play:

Never Is a Long Time ($5.95; Nashville: Thomas Nelson, 1976), by Dick Cate. A boy copes with family life, the chain of generations, birth, and old age.

A Dog for Joey ($1.25; New York: Harper & Row, 1967), by Nan Gilbert. A family moves, and a lonely boy finds solace in a dog.

Silas and Con ($5.95; New York: Atheneum, 1977), by A. C. Stewart. Deserted by uncaring, abusive parents, this boy and his dog wander together through the south of Scotland and start a new life.

The Mills of God ($4.95; Garden City, NY: Doubleday, 1973), by William Armstrong. A story by the author of *Sounder* about an impoverished rural American family and a bluetick hound that brings a measure of hope to their desolation.

And the following deal simply and delightfully with situations that very little children and puppies might experience.

I Am a Puppy ($2.95; New York: Golden Press, 1970), by Olé Risom. Puppy explores the great outdoors,

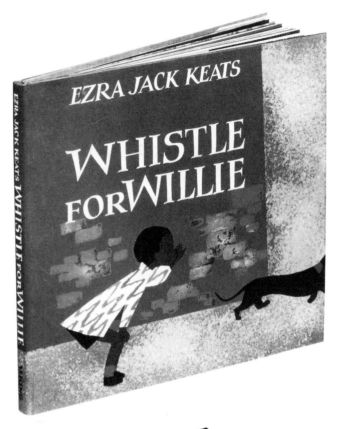

which is sometimes a bit intimidating. Large color illustrations by Jan Pfloog.

Pudding and Pie ($3.64; New York: Coward, McCann and Geoghegan, 1968), by Martha McKean Welch. Endearing black-and-white photos of two tiny cairn terriers taking the house apart while "mother" is out.

Angus and the Cat; *Angus and the Ducks*; *Angus Lost* ($4.95 each; Garden City, NY: Doubleday, 1931, 1930, 1932), by Marjorie Flack. Classics about a fiesty Scottish terrier who, despite his cute but stubborn nosing about, always comes out well in the end.

Harry the Dirty Dog and *No Roses for Harry* ($1.95 each; New York: Harper & Row, 1956, 1958), by Gene Zion, deal with the heavy subjects of taking baths and losing things.

The Little Duster ($5.59; New York: Macmillan, 1967), by Bill Charmantz, is a remarkably inventive, illustrated account of a dog whose master is an apartment-living bachelor.

Dogs in these old favorites cope successfully with identity problems:

Nothing at All ($3.99; New York: Coward, McCann and Geoghegan, 1941), by Wanda Ga'g.

The Dog Who Thought He Was a Boy ($6.95; Boston: Houghton Mifflin, 1965), by Cora Annett.

Pretzel ($6.89; New York: Harper & Row, 1944), by Margaret Rey.

Well-told adventure novels for young adults in which dogs and people are true to life are:

Hound-dog Man and *Savage Sam* ($8.95 and $1.25; New York: Harper & Row, 1947, 1962), by Fred Gipson.

178

In the first book boys and dogs take part in a coon hunt with a notorious hound-dog man. The second, an historical novel set in 1870, is dedicated to ". . . every hog-dog, cowdog, trailhound and flea-infested kitchen-robbing potlicker mongrel" that helped to make a big adventure of the author's childhood. Fred Gipson is well known as the author of *Old Yeller.*

Wilderness Champion ($6.95; Philadelphia: J. B. Lippincott, 1944), by Joseph Wharton Lippincott, ranges from the forests of Canada to field trials in Florida.

Adam of the Road ($1.50; New York: Viking Press, 1942), by Elizabeth Janet Grey, is the masterfully written story of a boy in thirteenth-century England on the road with his old English spaniel.

Some doggy science fiction:
Jagger the Dog from Elsewhere ($6.95; Philadelphia: Westminster Press, 1976), by Alexander Key.
Star Dog ($5.72; New York: McGraw-Hill, 1973), by A. M. Lightner.

A selection of the most artfully illustrated juvenile dog books:
Tales of a Seadog Family ($1.50; New York: Viking Press, 1974), by Joe Lasker. Bold, humorous drawings in color of great moments in seafaring history. The crew of anthropomorphized dogs includes Christopher Collie and Admiral Byrd-dog. Call me Fishmeal, indeed! A very funny book.
Hark! Hark! The Dogs Do Bark and other rhymes about dogs chosen by Lenore Blegvad, illustrated by Erik Blegvad ($5.95; New York: Atheneum, 1975).

Timeless, engaging full-color and line drawings illustrate old nursery rhymes about dogs and puppies—Bingo, Tom Tinker's dog, his highness's dog at Kew, and others less well known are included.

The Pie and the Patty Pan ($2.50; New York: Frederick Warne, 1905 and 1933), by Beatrix Potter. Duchess, a dog, and Ribby, a cat, go to tea amidst birds and flowers and fabrics all done to painterly perfection. A slightly over-palm-sized format.

Corgiville Fair ($4.95; New York: Thomas Y. Crowell, 1971), by Tasha Tudor. One of the very best illustrators peoples a New England village with smiling corgis who all go to the colorful, Corgiville fair.

Whistle for Willie ($1.25; New York: Viking Press, 1964), by Ezra Jack Keats. A realistic story, with superb paintings, of a boy who learns to whistle for his dog.

The Trouble with Alaric ($4.95; New York: Farrar, Straus and Giroux, 1975), by Jan Williamson. Childlike black-and-white drawings that really are subtly sophisticated. The dog of the story gets sent to work at an office because he insists he's a person. He travels by subway and decides he'd rather be a dog.

Muffin ($4.95; New York: Abelard-Schuman, 1972), by Judith Gwyn Browne. These black-and-white, detailed illustrations are old-fashioned in content and detail but impressionistic in overall effect. A charming story of a shy puli pup.

A Flea Story ($5.95; New York: Pantheon, 1977), by Leo Lionni. Robust illustrations in vibrant colors of everything but the pair of fleas that argue incessantly from beginning to end. You never see them.

Quiz

1. What kind of dog inspired the Woki in *Star Wars*?

2. What was the name of Rin Tin Tin's contemporary, a "police" dog who starred in *Silent Call, Brawn of the North*, and other films?

3. What rock singer wrote a song about his dog Martha?

4. What famous New Year's event began as a hunt club exhibition?

5. In what book does a character called Mother Russia keep a dog named Trot under her desk?

6. Who were the mustard and pepper dogs?

7. What Greek tragedian is said to have been killed by a pack of hunting dogs?

8. Which manufacturing companies are associated with the dogs Bingo, Mack, Beans, and Tige?

9. What happened to a show dog named Vickie?

10. Where does Queenie receive a gift of a good gnawable beef bone?

11. What group of islands in the Atlantic are named for dogs?

12. What long famous cowboy star is associated with Australian shepherds and German shepherds?

13. What were the names of the dogs in *Peter Pan, The Wizard of Oz*, and *Oliver Twist*?

14. What was the name of Rip Van Winkle's dog?

15. Who had a mythical moosehound named Elmer?

16. What was one of King Arthur's hounds called?

17. In what story do the Alsatians Jock and Wild Bill hang out together?

18. In what book does Karana tame and love the wild dog she calls Rontu, fox eyes?

19. In Dorothy Parker's story "Mr. Durant" what is the title character's objection to the mongrel dog his children bring home and beg to be allowed to keep?

20. What are the dog days, and why are they called that?

21. Who was mountie Sgt. Preston's dog?

22. What is the meaning of three-dog night?

23. What was the name of the dog that played a ghost in the television show "Topper"?

1. *Film director George Lucas's Alaskan malamute.*

2. *Strongheart.*

3. *Paul McCartney.*

4. *On January 1, 1890, the Valley Hunt Club of Pasadena, California, first paraded hounds, horses, and rose-bedecked carriages through the streets of the city. Five years later the hunt club withdrew as sponsor, but the event, growing ever larger and more elaborate, continued and is known today as the Tournament of the Roses Parade.*

5. *In John Le Carré's* The Honourable Schoolboy *Connie Sachs, British Secret Service Sovietologist, brings Trot to the office.*

6. *The terriers owned by Dandie Dinmont in Sir Walter Scott's* Guy Mannering, *from which the name of the Dandie Dinmont terrier derives.*

7. *Euripides.*

8. *Bingo appears on the Cracker Jacks box; Mack, a bulldog, on trucks of the same name; Beans used to be Campbell's pet; and Tige is the Buster Brown shoe dog.*

9. *She is the dognap victim in Joseph Wambaugh's novel* The Black Marble.

10. *In Truman Capote's story "A Christmas Memory."*

11. *The Canary Islands were named by the Spanish Islas Canarias, literally dog islands, for the wild canines found there once, and the little yellow finch named after the islands.*

12. *Roy Rogers*

13. *Nana, Toto, and Bull's Eye, respectively.*

14. *Wolf.*

15. *Paul Bunyan.*

16. *Cabal.*

17. *In Doris Lessing's "The Story of Two Dogs" from the collection* African Stories.

18. *In Scott O'Dell's* Island of the Blue Dolphins *the dog, which had earlier killed her brother, is the girl's only companion.*

19. *It is a female.*

20. *The time between July and September, the hottest part of the summer, when the dog star Sirius is visible in the sky, are the dog days. The phrase is used to describe any sluggish, slow, uneventful stretch of time.*

21. *King.*

22. *It is a term used to describe a night so cold that it takes three dogs (as blankets) to keep a person warm. It is the name of a rock group, too.*

23. *Neil, a martini-drinking St. Bernard.*

Photograph by Peter Simon

11
ART WORK

THE ALL-AMERICAN DOG:
  Man's Best Friend in Folk Art

A NICE WAY TO MAKE A LIVING

GALLERY OF PHOTOGRAPHERS:
  Gary Krueger, Peter Simon,
  and Vincent Tajiri

AFTER PRETTY GIRLS, IT'S DOGS
  THAT SELL A PRODUCT BEST
  —AND A COMBINATION IS
  SUREFIRE

ANIMALS AND MEN

CRESTS, WALL ART, STATUES,
  FIGURINES, AND STUFF:
  The Ubiquitous Image of the Dog

THE ILLUSTRATIONS OF
  BABETTE COLE

PET PORTRAITISTS: Pat Elkins
  and Paula Wright

WIREHAIRED FOX TERRIER
  MEMORABILIA
  by Mark McCrackin

HAIR OF THE DOG
  by Sara Lee Futterman

Pet Dog, pencil on paper, late nineteenth century. (Courtesy of Mr. and Mrs. Robert Hallock)

The All-American Dog:
Man's Best Friend in Folk Art

The plentitude and significance of dogs in American life and history was delightfully dramatized by an exhibit, "The All-American Dog—Man's Best Friend in Folk Art," held at the Museum of American Folk Art in 1977–78. On display were paintings, sculptures, pottery, textiles, weathervanes. Also a scrimshaw tooth on a stand, a buffalo skinning knife with bone handle, and woolwork on canvas. The exhibition catalog (New York: Avon, 1977), besides having black-and-white and color photographs, quotes anecdotes, folktales, and wise sayings—for example, "A dog is loved by old and young/He wags his tail and not his tongue." Here are selections from the exhibit.

Terrier and Pups Ninepin Pulltoy, papier-mâché, polychrome, gesso, early twentieth century. From the collection of Ms. Molly Epstein, New York City. (Photograph by Joshua Schreier)

"Earl Eyman's Dog Act," wood, 1935, Earl Eyman. (Courtesy of America Hurrah, New York City)

Child with Poodle and Roses, oil on canvas, circa 1840. (Courtesy of the New York State Historical Society, Cooperstown)

Miniature spit dogs, hand-forged iron. (Courtesy of Jill of Story Hill, New York City. Photograph by Noel Allum)

"Crook The Amazing Dog," oil on canvas, 1977, Larry Zingale. (Courtesy of America Hurrah, New York City)

Crib quilt, cotton, appliqued and pieced, circa 1910. (Courtesy of Gloria List)

A Nice Way to Make a Living

William P. Gilbert—official dog show photographer

William P. Gilbert has been going to dog shows for thirty years—man and boy. In 1964 he made arrangements with the then preeminent dog photographer, Bill Brown, to assume a number of contracts between AKC clubs and photographer. (It has long been the practice for a show-sponsoring club to contract with a limited number of photographers; these "official" photographers are then the only ones allowed in the show area.)

Now Gilbert attends one hundred and twenty-five shows a year, photographing, at the request of owners or handlers, those dogs who win. His fee for two eight-by-ten color prints mailed to the purchaser's address within a week is $15.50. The pictures are bought largely for purposes of record and to use as advertisements in the various dog fancy periodicals. It is the chief way that kennels offer litters and stud services, and by buying space to show off a particular dog, owners hope to influence judges in the dog's favor—judges being thought to study the fancy magazines.

Gilbert spent a number of years as a handler, following in his father's footsteps. He believes he has a special sense for understanding a dog—that is, for determining various different personality types.

> When photographing a dog I emphasize virtues and de-emphasize faults. I can do this because I know what makes up a dog's good points. Also, I interact differently with a shy dog than I do with a tough one.
>
> And it's true that I communicate with the dogs. I try to teach my assistants how it's done . . . how to make a squeaky toy "talk" in order to get a particular reaction. Some people think I am nuts to talk like this, but believe me it works.

When a judge selects the winners of an event, there isn't much time to get a particular dog in an appropriate place and to take a photograph showing dog, judge, handler, maybe owner, and a sign describing the event and the dog's standing in it: "We have about thirty seconds to a minute and a half to work our wondrous magic, and therefore all the photographic aspects have to be second nature . . . pull, click, snap."

In his thirteen-year career as a dog photographer Gilbert has used various cameras—changing them as photographic technology has changed. Earlier cameras were the 4 x 5 Speed Graphic and the 2¼ x 3¼ roll film Graflex. Now he uses 4.5 x 6-cm Bronica ETR's. He prefers the 4.5 x 6-cm image to the 2¼ x 2¼ image of the Hasselblad because the former can be enlarged to 8 x 10 or 11 x 14 without cropping.

As a professional Gilbert only feels safe when he has back-up units, so he travels with three Bronica ETR bodies and two 75-mm Zenzanon lenses. All his pictures are made with strobe light fill. Because the Bronica has between-the-lens leaf shutters, strobe can be synchronized at any speed. Gilbert shoots at 1/500 second, either at f/8 or f/11.

He says that when photographing a dog, there is a perfect spot to stand and height to shoot from. "I try to have the lens at just the dog's shoulder height."

Until she retired recently, Evelyn M. Shafer was a renowned dog photographer, and Gilbert recalls how they often found themselves trying to fill the same space. "There might be a half-dozen photographers milling about trying to get settled for a shot and there I'd be right up next to Evelyn. Sometimes we were so close I got the edge of her camera in my picture."

Gilbert uses color negative roll film, which he has processed in his own lab in Ringoes, New Jersey. In that way he is able to provide either color or black-and-white, depending on what a customer wants.

He moved to Ringoes so his daughters could ride horses. Now one of the daughters is showing a keen interest in dog photography, and it might well be that a third-generation Gilbert will be professionally involved in the sport.

A FABLE OF AESOP—TRYING TO MAKE A SILK PURSE OUT OF A SOW'S EAR

A shepherd took a newborn wolf cub he had found and brought him up with his dogs till he was full grown. Whenever a sheep was stolen by another wolf, this one joined with the dogs in the pursuit. And if the dogs had to return without catching the marauder, he went on till he overtook him, and then—like the wolf he was—shared the plunder with him. Sometimes, too, when there had been no robbery, he secretly killed a sheep himself and shared it with the dogs, until in the end the shepherd guessed what was going on and hanged him on a tree.

A vicious nature will never make a good man.

Gallery of Photographers:

Gary Krueger, Peter Simon and Vincent Tajiri

Gary Krueger and friend. The photographer says: "Whether I go to San Francisco or Hollywood Boulevard, I like to play tourist. I travel lightly. The less equipment you carry, the less conspicuous you are and the more you can get away with. Most of my photos are strange juxtapositions in everyday life; consequently I'm required to carry my camera wherever I can. My photos are found, not contrived." (Photograph by Kim Nelson)

Photographs by Gary Krueger

189

Peter Simon and his dog. The following photographs were made at a time when the photographer was a member of a commune in New England. The dogs, too, are obviously having a good time.

Photographs by Peter Simon

Vincent Tajiri, writer of the "LA Report—Hollywood Canines," Chapter 10, has been a photographic editor for Playboy magazine as well as the creator of photographic exhibitions. These pictures were taken expressly for the Dog Catalog. (Photograph by Don Myrus)

194

Photographs by Vincent Tajiri

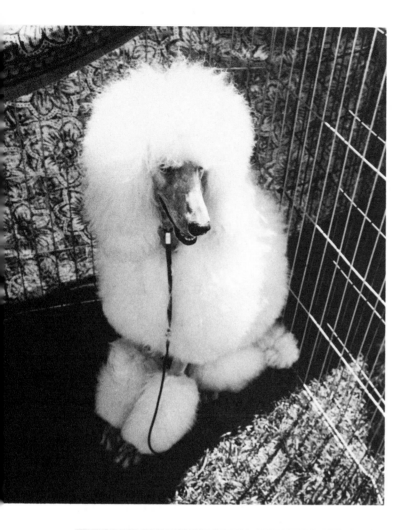

After Pretty Girls, It's Dogs That Sell a Product Best—And a Combination is Surefire

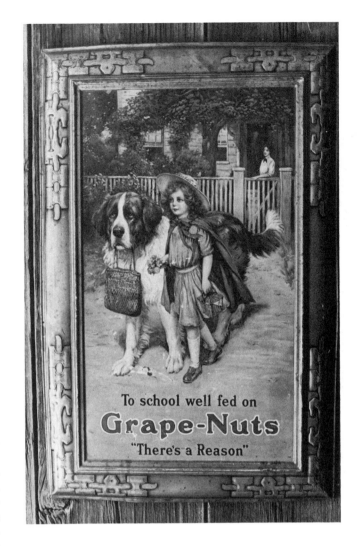

Angelic child, stolid St. Bernard, and confident mother evoke sentiment in favor of Grape-Nuts. (From the collection of Richard Steedman; photograph by Don Myrus)

The most famous commercial dog is Nipper, the RCA Victor trademark, adapted from the late nineteenth-century painting "His Master's Voice" by Francis Barraud. Nipper was the name of the artist's mixed-breed terrier who did actually sit as he is shown, listening attentively to one of the early "talking machines." Nipper's likeness has been reproduced by the millions on records, radios, and Victrolas, but after a seventy-year career the dog was to be replaced on the orders of RCA President David Sarnoff. However, an unused trademark can become part of the public domain, so to protect its image, RCA had to retain and use Nipper. The company announced late in 1977 that Nipper and a sheepdog named Hugo would be starred in a million-dollar TV ad campaign. A tenacious little terrier, that Nipper. (Photograph courtesy of RCA)

Dogs in ads directed at men are usually of the larger sporting types, but these fox terriers capably draw attention to the latest Barney's clothing styles. (Photograph courtesy of Carl Ally Inc.)

Dogs, second perhaps only to elegant ladies and cute babies, are effective attention-getters in advertisements. At left we are advised to listen with the concentration of the two Scotties. At right the distinguished Mrs. T. Markoe Robertson (nee Cordelia D. Biddle) of Guinea Hollow Farm at Old Westbury, New York, is said to prefer her personal car, a Hupmobile, to trains because it is as fleet as her fastest hunter—what looks to be a Dalmatian. (From the collection of Honi Reisman and Sheila Sugarman, purveyors of antique and fine dog items)

Sophisticated-looking lady and her borzoi pose in be-half of clothes from Smartparts. (Courtesy of William Hofstetter, Inc.; photograph by Jerre Burn)

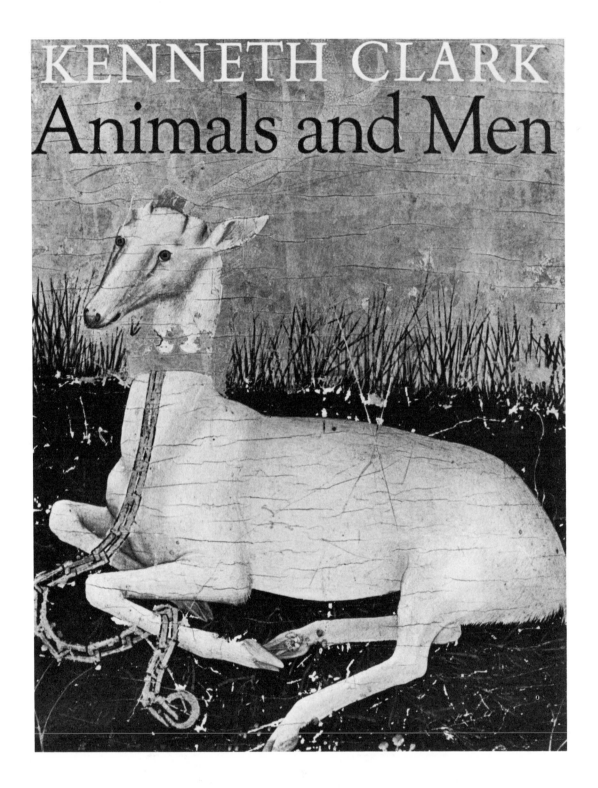

Animals and Men *by Kenneth Clark (New York: William Morrow, 1977)—a fine arts picture book—is arranged to make the author's point that there has always been an ambivalence in man toward animals. Thus there* is a section titled "Animals Beloved," in which many dogs are shown, and another called "Animals Destroyed," in which dogs and men often join to destroy other beasts.

Crests, Wall Art, Statues, Figurines, and Stuff:

The Ubiquitous Image of the Dog

A St. Bernard bronze—one of a hundred different breeds—from the Stone Brothers, Box 5729, Sherman Oaks, CA 91403

Ashod Kassabian created this free-standing photographic screen of a white poodle. He may be contacted through J. L. Anacreon, Suite 4A, 144 W. 76th St., New York, NY 10023.

Dogs in glass and porcelain. (From the collection of Arlene Ward; photographs by Don Myrus)

Cookie jar, white with yellow ribbon, is made by Dor-anne of California, 3201 Bandini Boulevard, Los Angeles, CA 90023.

The Illustrations of
Babette Cole

The line drawings are reprinted from Now That You Own a Puppy *by Joan Tate, New York: Frederick Fell, 1976.* (Reprinted with permission of the publisher)

Pet Portraitists:
Pat Elkins and Paula Wright

Pat Elkins creates portraits of pets from photographs sent to her. She works in both charcoal and pastel. Pat Elkins, 2138 West Moffat Street, Chicago, IL 60647.

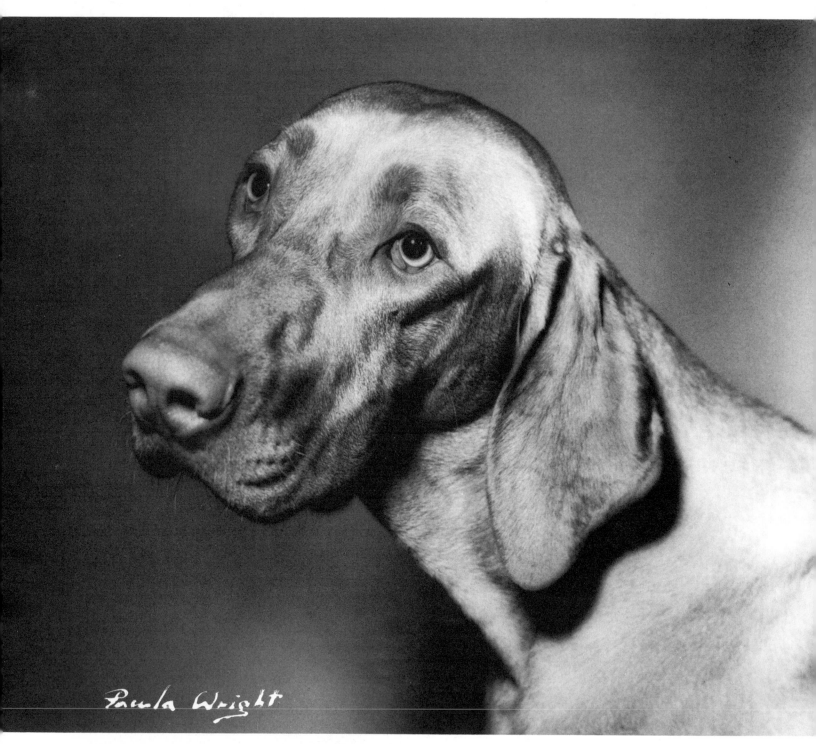

Photographs by Paula Wright, who also works in oil on canvas. Paula Wright, 393 West End Avenue, New York, NY 10024.

Paula Wright

Wirehaired Fox Terrier Memorabilia

by Mark McCrackin

How the writer gathered his unusual collection, and why.

I guess William Powell and Myrna Loy were clever enough in *The Thin Man* films, but for me the real star of those movies was the dog. Since I first saw Asta, I have been in love with fox terriers to the extent that my wife Nanci and I have owned two. The experience is something like harboring a small hurricane in the home.

The affair has created a rather unusual hobby: My wife and I collect fox terrier memorabilia. Objects range from a fox-terrier-shaped lead doorstop to a thin cookie cutter from the twenties, a rhinestone-studded fox terrier broach and an obviously well-loved stuffed pull toy. I proudly wear my fox terrier tie on occasion, use my fox terrier hot pad when cooking, and lean back on three fox terrier sofa pillows in the living room.

In France, where they love fox terriers more than anywhere else, I found terrier decals, publicity photographs of glamorous movie stars with terriers, and dozens of postcards. Great Britain offered a tea cup, a napkin ring, a biscuit box, and children's playing cards each illustrated with terriers. Prerevolutionary China produced a beautifully carved wooden fox terrier that stands on its hind legs and waves. And from America we have good solid stuff such as a fox terrier memo pad holder, a carton of "Duplex Dog Dresser" razor blades, and, best of all, a fox terrier coat rack, lovingly jigsawed, painted, and assembled in a thirties high school shop class. Buttons, a rubber stamp, an ashtray, notepaper (with matching envelopes)—I am never surprised when I discover another medium for fox terrier adoration.

Samples of fox terrier memorabilia from the collection of Mark McCrackin.

210

Collecting anything is a long, time-consuming process. I got my first piece of fox terrier memorabilia—a ceramic figurine—about twenty years ago. My latest acquisition is a deck of silver-and-black playing cards, dated 1926, and decorated with a very proud fox terrier. In between the two I have learned that collecting depends upon three things—patience, a sensitive eye, and friends. Patience is needed to go on looking for half a year without a single find, only to be rewarded by three or four "rare" objects in one afternoon. A sensitive eye helps me to scan my favorite stores for new material in just a few minutes, just as it helps me to spot objects other people would walk right past—even if they were looking. And finally, the hardest to cultivate but the most rewarding aid to collecting is friends. Once you convince your friends that you are not crazy, they will become inexhaustible sources of desirable material.

Fox terriers were extremely popular in the twenties and early thirties. Consequently there is a great deal of material from those years. If you were collecting poodle memorabilia, the late forties and fifties would offer a great many objects. At other times America has also loved cocker spaniels, German shepherds, Irish setters, and Airedales. Also, certain cultures have favorite dogs: go to Germany for the schnauzer, the dachshund, and the boxer, which began as a German bulldog. England prefers hounds, corgis, and spaniels, while the French remain faithful to their old love—*les fox* (terriers.)

I have learned that collecting depends upon three things—patience, a sensitive eye, and friends.

Hard-core collectors of dog memorabilia never forget literary references. "Fox terriers are born with about four times as much original sin in them as other dogs," is from Jerome K. Jerome's hilarious novel of 1889 *Three Men in a Boat* (to say nothing of the dog), which immortalized the impish nature of the breed. F. Scott Fitzgerald, a devotee of fox terriers, mentioned them in his writing several times. Even the mysterious Thomas Pynchon found space for them in his 760-page novel, *Gravity's Rainbow*. One of my favorites is a 1930 children's dictionary from Macmillan with about twenty illustrations of playful fox terriers by Kate Seredy. (It was very disappointing, however, to discover that in the original *Thin Man* book by Dashiell Hammett, Asta is a schnauzer, not a fox terrier.)

I collect fox terrier memorabilia partly because it is an unusual hobby, guaranteed to start conversations and make one more memorable. And it is a challenge and a delight to discover such esoteric objects. But probably I do it because it is just one more way to share the uninhibited spirit of those little dogs—a spirit I wish I could always have for my own.

Mark McCrackin is a Viking Press publicist.

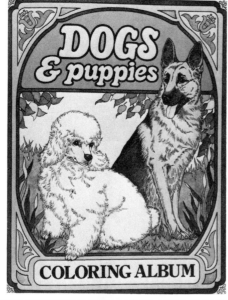

Dogs & Puppies illustrated by Rita Warner (San Francisco: Troubador Press, 1977) is a good book for a patient, artistically inclined child with a fat box of crayons.

A Dog's Book of Birds by Peter Parnall (New York: Charles Scribner's Sons, 1977) is a unique view of birds. In A Dog's Book of Bugs by Elizabeth Griffen (New York: Atheneum, 1967) the same Parnall dog is interested in things that buzz, bumble, leap, and creep. All in all, Parnall has created a distinctive canine persona, something of an intellectual, possessed of the true naturalist's powers of observation, courageous enough to go out on a limb in the relentless pursuit of knowledge.

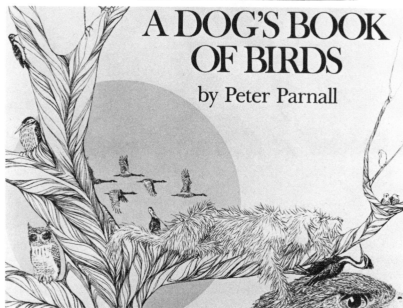

THE CARTOON DOGS OF THURBER, DISNEY, AND SCHULZ

Some of the most famous and best-loved dogs *ever* have taken life and shape on the drawing boards of illustrators. Though canine in form, these cartoon characters are appealing because they are so absolutely undoglike—they think and behave as humans would like to think dogs think and behave.

Thurber dogs, like Thurber people, described by Dorothy Parker as looking like unbaked cookies, are all thoroughly eccentric. Yet the dogs are unlike their masters, being always fundamentally decent and very sensible, and therein lies their extraordinary appeal.

Disney's Pluto is something else entirely—an ingenuous, floppy-eared fool of a dog—clumsy, silly, and often made sport of. Pluto is the essence of the "dumb mutt." Anyone can feel superior to Pluto. He amuses without taxing the intellect.

Schulz's Snoopy, one of the most successful of fantasy dogs, made a real break with cartoon tradition when he came out of the doghouse and climbed up on top of it. He's the first thinking cartoon dog, and under the moon and stars and sun, in heat and cold, his very human imagination and aspirations soar.

212

Hair of the Dog

by Sara Lee Futterman

An appreciation of Nickie Newlon's craft of spinning and weaving.

A baby hair curl has its memories. So can dog hair. Have dog hair spun, just the way sheep's wool is, and then have it woven into almost anything—a tapestry, something soft and cuddly to wear, a sturdy handbag or knapsack.

The Samoyed yields a very soft and silky yarn; the poodle, one that is coarse and bristly.

Many spinners use dog hair occasionally; some use it often. The texture and quality of yarns vary with the breed, and even with the individual dog, so the yarn spun from a dog's hair is a unique, personal product.

The Samoyed yields a very soft and silky yarn; the poodle, one that is coarse and bristly. Shorter hairs may be spun together with wool; long hairs can be spun alone. If you'd like to have your dog's hair spun and woven, write to Nickie Newlon, 44 Wilridge Rd., Georgetown, CT 06829. She's a specialist in working with dog hair—spins it herself and weaves the yarn into pillows, ponchoes, and throws. The hair she spins comes from ordinary brushing or clipping. If you have only a little, it can make enough yarn for a few highlights in the finished piece. If you have a big dog and are patient about collecting the hair, it can be the main yarn in the article you choose to have made. You might want to consult Ms. Newlon before you do too much collecting, just to see what she can do with the hair of your particular dog.

Maria Blanchefleur von Dulon, also known as Nickie Newlon, models her doghair creations. Standing, she wears a woven poncho; sitting at a spinning wheel, she wears a knitted cardigan. The old English sheepdog hair was brushed out, not clipped. She has also spun poodle, Afghan, Samoyed, Lhasa apso, Great Pyrenees, collie, Kerry, and various mixtures. Nickie Newlon, 44 Wilridge Road, Georgetown, CT 06829. (Photographs by Clarence F. Korker)

213

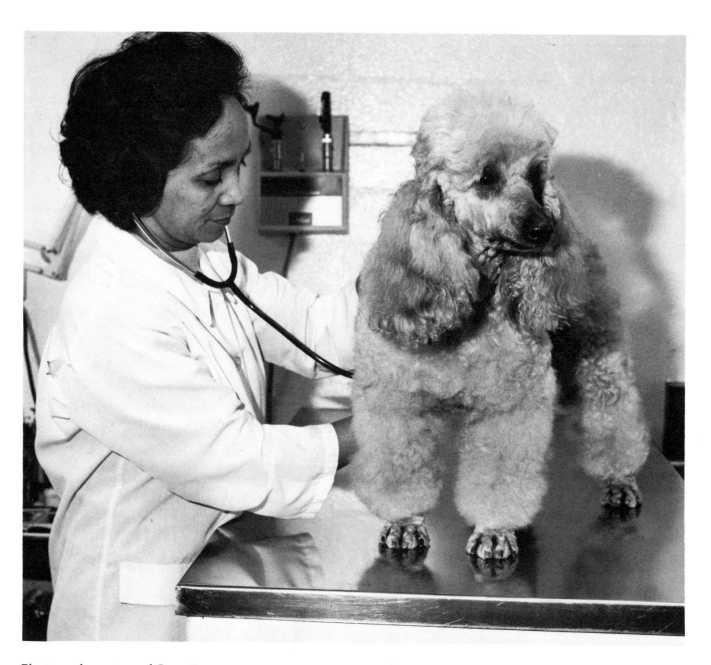

Photograph courtesy of Carnation

12

MY DOG HAS FLEAS AND OTHER MATTERS PHYSICAL, SEXUAL, AND PSYCHOLOGICAL

DOG DOCTOR

PUPPY AND DOG CARE
by Thomas R. Pescod, DVM

CHOOSING A GOOD VETERINARIAN

FLEAS—THE MOST PREVALENT PARASITE

DENTAL CARE OF DOGS

THE DREAD HYDROPHOBIA

DOG AID

BREEDING—A FEW POINTERS

HOW TO SELL DOGS

IMPROVING THE BREED

Dog Doctor

The "business" of being a veterinarian.

The American Dream, in one of its manifestations, encompasses being "your own boss"; in another, "owning your own business"; and in yet a third, being a doctor.

Tom Pescod is a flesh-and-blood embodiment of that dream—just about. He is certainly his own boss, owns the business, and is a doctor of veterinary medicine.* Dr. Pescod, as was Dr. Dolittle himself, is surrounded by animals—mostly dogs and cats, in Dr. Pescod's case, and mostly sick ones, which he generally cures. His is not an abstract world of symbols and paper shuffling but of live creatures who often desperately need him. He's important.

And like everybody else, he's got his problems.

Item: He loves dogs—has his own golden retriever, a beautiful animal that's just a bit overweight. Yet love them or not, he's on guard. Some dogs, especially ailing ones in the strange environment of a clinic, are apt to bite. "Every morning I wonder if this is to be the day. About once every five years I get badly bitten. German shepherds are the worst, and I never trust a St. Bernard male over three years or a female over six."

Item: He went into veterinary medicine because he felt he'd do better not having to spend too much time with people. Now, after a dozen years, he has come to the belief that it is people who are all-important in the treatment of pets. It is the people who must do the talking and the listening if outpatient therapy is to be a success. And people-to-people communication being as complicated as it is, some veterinarians, according to Tom Pescod, don't always hear what the "client" says and vice versa.

Item: "Being your own boss" would seem to connote having at least a measure of freedom. Yet for Tom Pescod—whose clinic hours are nine to five, weekdays; nine to one, Saturdays—his life is his own only when he's out of town on vacation. Otherwise there is an answering service that reaches out to get him by means of the beeper in his pocket. If there is an emergency—say a dog is struck by a car—Dr. Pescod is alerted whether sound asleep, or dining or anything else. He has no peace. He can't hide.

Item: Implicit in the attraction of having your own business is that you get to keep the profits. Dr. Pescod's Hampton Veterinary Hospital makes profits, all right, but only after it takes in about one hundred thousand

---

* The considerable prestige of the veterinary profession was highlighted recently, but in a negative way. Among several professional graduate schools involved in admissions bribery cases was the University of Pennsylvania School of Veterinary Medicine, which, in exchange for support for its requests for state financial aid, allowed a legislator—later convicted of bribery—to place a student in an entering class.

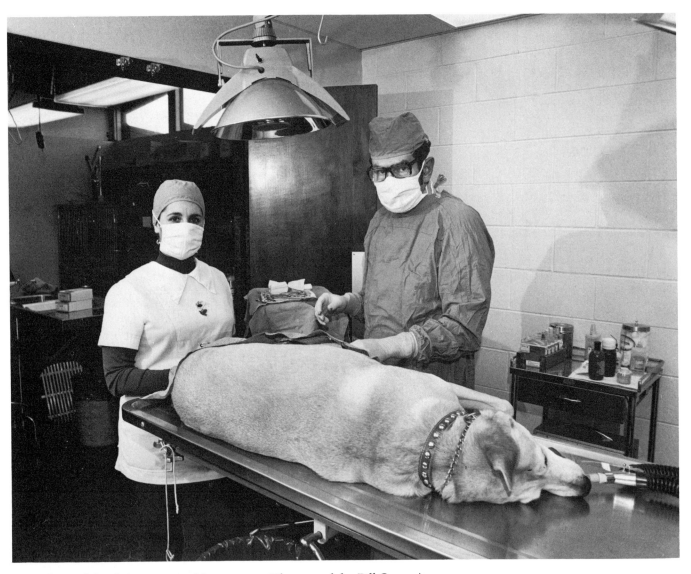

Anesthetized dog being prepared for surgery. (Photograph by Bill Owens)

dollars annually—the "nut," as businessmen put it. Dr. Pescod has discovered, as have countless M.D.s, that the cost of practicing medicine is high not only in dollars but in time. He estimates that perhaps less than half his workday is spent in the actual care of animals. For the rest there is financing and bookkeeping and governmental forms (ad infinitum) and personnel management (his secretary and the kennel keepers) and getting the hospital's grass cut and plumbing unstuck . . . not to mention maintaining the elaborate equipment to test blood, to X-ray, and so forth.

So, the long, intense training, the years of "starting up," the never-ending demands on time. Is it all worth it? Say, thirty or thirty-five thousand dollars a year?

Certainly not for the money alone. But, yes, for the intangible satisfaction of being a key factor in the civilizing process that occurs between people and their pets, especially when the pets are dogs . . . for people with

dogs have something to talk about when they meet. A person with a dog has lived another dimension than would have been the case otherwise. And when these people go to see the vet, there is no end of talk . . . and oftentimes of friendship.

Contact may simply be with an elderly lady seeking somebody to talk to—she already talks to her dog. And to ask advice about all manner of things—investments and so forth. (After all, he *is* a doctor.) Or it may be as complex and long-lasting as Tom Pescod's friendship with Budd Schulberg, the author who rose to fame in the late 1940s with *What Makes Sammy Run?* Schulberg and his late wife created a book about two swans (*Swan Watch* by Budd Schulberg, photographs by Geraldine Brooks; New York: Delacorte Press, 1975). When one of the swans grew ill, Tom Pescod spent countless hours, day and night, hurrying about with Budd to capture the ill swan, to get it to the clinic, to observe it, and to watch over its recovery.

Patients at Dr. Pescod's Hampton Veterinary Hospital are usually seen by appointment, which, happily, makes waiting time brief. After a problem is diagnosed and medication given, patient and owner stop at the inner side of the receptionist's enclave to pay the bill (credit cards accepted), and then leave, not through the waiting room, but through an exit door accessible from the examining room corridor. Dogs and cats coming don't meet others going, which eliminates a possible volatile situation at a tense time. The hospital is neat, clean, odor-free and quiet. There's no residue here of "pet owner paranoia," which can develop over years of unpleasant encounters with veterinarians, many of whom are more huckster than doctor, eager to precipitate panic by interpreting symptoms in the most unfavorable light.

At the Hampton Veterinary Hospital all is not a matter of personality, or organization, or of doctor's manner. Laboratory, dispensary, X-ray, and operating rooms are also impressive—in fact, contain much of the same equipment used for work with humans.

A person with a dog has lived another dimension than would have been the case otherwise.

The same drug companies that supply medication for humans send drug salesmen to veterinarians, too, and the products they bring are often the same, though differently labeled for veterinary use.

Then, too, there is the constant exchange of information and techniques between veterinarians and human doctors—advances in understanding of dehydration in human infants, for instance, were a result of veterinary work with small dogs. And, often, before performing particular surgical procedures on a human patient, a whole team of surgeons, nurses, and anesthetists will practice on a large dog to refine procedures. Disturbing as this may be to some dog lovers, the benefits of such practice to humankind have been incalculable. And besides, the reverse is also true—advances made on humans are then applied to dogs. The use of tiny screws instead of casts to repair broken bones was first developed by surgeons working with human hand fractures.

Animal patients, like human ones, recover more quickly at home, Dr. Pescod feels, and so he tries whenever possible to get his patients back into relaxing and familiar surroundings. For very complex therapy—cranial surgery, for instance—or for specialties like ophthamologic surgery, he refers patients appropriately. "Obviously, if I do a cataract operation every six months and a veterinary ophthalmologist performs the procedure almost daily, the patient will do best with the specialist."

Dr. Pescod's advice on dog care follows.

Puppy and Dog Care
by Thomas R. Pescod, DVM

Our veterinarian discourses, in eight parts, about dogs, people, remedies, and self-help.

1. Dogs and the Healthy Life

I have clients who bring in a dog declaring it to be a child substitute. Sometimes this indicates an unwillingness to have children; sometimes it is a hedge against the possibility of divorce. Sometimes getting a puppy early in marriage is simply a couple's unconscious preparation for having a baby—a lot can be learned about raising children, especially psychologically, when newlyweds take to raising a puppy.

Dogs serve a different purpose for some older people. Mrs. Ryder, who is sixty-eight years old, and her dog are good examples. With her husband Mrs. Ryder lived a full and active life. Following his death, she resisted all attempts by her children to persuade her to live with one of them. As she was resisting them, a friend gave her a miniature poodle puppy.

Mrs. Ryder's first visit to the office was one of trepidation. She stated that she was not going to keep the puppy, but in deference to her friend she would have the puppy examined and vaccinated before finding it a new home. "After all, at almost seventy years of age, I'm too old for this puppy business." Well, one week became a month and then several months and the puppy remained.

Sometimes getting a puppy early in marriage is simply a couple's unconscious preparation for having a baby ...

During this time Mrs. R's personality began to change. She came into the office with stories about Lady Alexander and her antics. Lady had become an enjoyable part of Mrs. R's life.

But even more, she explained, Lady was the reason for turning down her children's offers to live with them and for not having to stay longer than she wished when she did visit—just as the puppy had become her reason for not staying out late with friends when she really didn't want to. These conscious decisions were made in order to keep her independence. She was using Lady as an excuse.

But when a ten-day cruise was proposed by two of her friends, she did not hesitate to pack Lady off to the boarding kennel and to leave herself for fun in the sun.

I find that in other ways, too, a dog can be a dependent that, paradoxically, provides independence—the sort of freedom of action that is possible only when

217

there is routine. For those who otherwise would have meaningless, chaotic lives, a dog requires care. The dog is fed and, almost incidentally, the owner gets into a habit of preparing his or her own food. In this way a dog can foster a healthy life for its owner.

2. Neurotic Dogs and People, Big and Little "Hospitals," and Other Thoughts of a Practicing Veterinarian

The most important attribute of a veterinarian is the ability to listen—not only to what an owner says about the dog, but what the owner says about everything in general. Many problems have an emotional, environmental cause.

Dogs can be emotional sponges, can pick up conflicts that exist within a household. Outwardly the response looks like disease.

Sometimes it's the dog that is badly treated in an emotional way. A puppy once taken everywhere because he was cute has a legitimate complaint when at sixty or seventy pounds he is left at home. A veterinarian must listen and, where appropriate, make the owner aware so that retraining of the dog is undertaken. Otherwise the veterinarian is liable to unsuccessfully treat disease symptoms instead of prescribing social correction. Dogs aren't people, but they sure can be neurotic.

At least a few veterinarians are not much in the way of psychological detectives. They are OK when it comes to hearing classical symptoms and then prescribing with set speeches, "Do this, that, and the next thing." But modern dogs and their owners often require more: individual attention.

Another aspect of modern practice is that its very physical place seems to be changing. Because of high costs the trend now is to move away from the big veterinary hospital. Overhead and clerical work mean that unless there is a big volume of business, the only economical, profitable course is to streamline a practice, to operate out of a storefront in a shopping center, and to treat animals more and more as outpatients. The medicine practiced in this way can be very good—maybe in the long run it is even better. Sending an ill dog home for personal nursing by the owner can be very good for the patient.

There are even some veterinarians who have almost-exclusively mobile practices. That is, they see almost all ill pets on a house-call basis. These veterinarians rent hospital time only for some diagnostic work—X-rays, for example—and surgery.

Veterinary medicine in the past decade has improved immeasurably as far as diagnosis, therapy, and pharmacology. I'd like to see the start up again of animal health insurance to help cover the costs of treatment that the public is demanding. As things stand now, every dollar spent on the treatment of a pet dog or cat is nondeductible from income for tax purposes.

Play postures

Aggressive   Defensive-aggressive

Submissive postures

The outer dog. Body language as illustrated by Jill Miriam Pinkwater.

3. What's Good Enough for a Child Might Be Good Enough for a Dog

Most medications—whether general anesthetics or aspirin or anything that you would use on yourself—are usually OK to use on a dog. Exceptions are Ben Gay and Heat and Absorbine Jr., turpentine and paint thinners, and other chemicals that are applied to the skin. Substances used to create local heat to aid stiffness tend to creat an enormous amount of irritation on the skin surface of dogs and have been known to kill the skin. If a dog gets into paint or tar, just wipe it off with warm water and soap. Tar also apparently can be taken off fairly easily by applying Coppertone, the suntan lotion, before the tar or oil gets too dry.

For vomiting and diarrhea Kaopectate, Pepto-Bismol, Donagel, Maalox can be used. For allergy problems such as hives Contact, Allerest, Dristan, any of the antihistamines, and even some of the low-dose cortisones are effective on dogs as well as people.

With eye and ear problems, what is good for humans is OK for dogs on a short-term, *emergency* basis.

Even cuts don't mean you have to race to a veterinarian. On a general basis, if a wound looks big enough to need stitches, try not to put any ointment on it. No matter how carefully the veterinarian tries to clean it off later, ointment will usually stick to some part of the wound, creating a barrier between the edges of the skin and impeding the healing process. So, in cleaning large wounds, use peroxide or a little soap and water.

For a dog (but not for a cat) there is almost no medication except those mentioned that cannot be used, but sparingly and with common sense.

If a dog is fifty pounds or more, use a normal adult level of medication. For instance, with aspirin or Bufferin (which I prefer), a dog with arthritis would receive a normal dose—one to two tablets, three times a day. Below fifty pounds the dose should be according to weight level—obviously a three-pound toy poodle would not get the same dosage as a thirty-pound miniature poodle. A ten-pound dog, for example, could have two grains (about half an aspirin) three times a day.

If a dog owner would approach the illnesses and the injuries to his dog the way he would approach those to himself or to his children, a lot of unnecessary calls and anxiety can be avoided.

4. Vaccinating

Distemper has nothing to do with a dog's temperament; it is a viral pneumonia afflicting dogs and other carnivores. Besides rabies, canine distemper is the only viral disease in dogs that causes a high percentage of fatalities. Since vaccines have become available, the disease has been well controlled. However, certain wildlife species and unvaccinated animals continue to spread the virus, which makes eradication impossible.

Modified live viral vaccines of chicken embryo or tissue cell culture are recommended. Puppies of unknown immune status that are more than three months of age will usually get two doses of vaccine. If the puppy is younger than three months of age, two or more doses should be administered. The first dose should be given at weaning—six to nine weeks—and the last dose at twelve to sixteen weeks. Annual revaccination is recommended. Pregnant bitches should not be vaccinated because possible side effects of the virus on the fetus are not known. There is a possibility that the virus might cause birth defects in puppies, much as the rubella vaccine has caused human damage. For over ten years now a human measles vaccine also has been used to protect very young dogs against distemper.

When first introduced, measles vaccine was given alone as the first vaccine to puppies four weeks of age or older. Recently a combination canine-distemper and measles vaccine has become available. The manufacturers claim that this combination protects a higher percentage of animals against distemper than measles virus

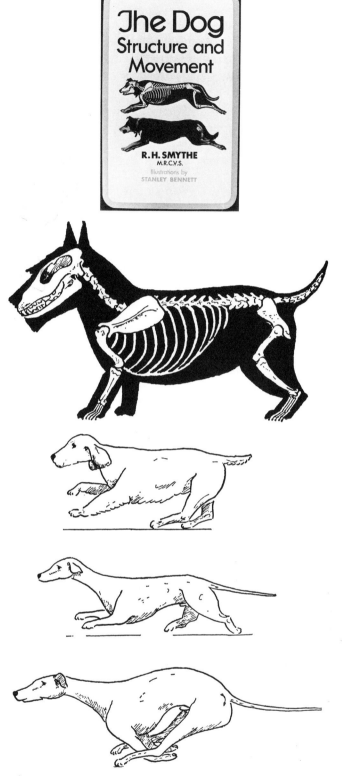

The inner and outer dog. Bone structure and patterns of movement are pictured, diagrammed, and explained in The Dog, Structure and Movement *by R. H. Smythe (New York: Arco, 1970). We learn that the Scottish terrier is an achondroplastic type with large head and stunted limbs. The dogs in a hurry are, from the top, cocker spaniel, dachshund, and greyhound. (Illustrations courtesy of the publisher)*

219

vaccine given alone. Puppies are usually not vaccinated until they are six to eight weeks of age because a great majority have a fairly high level of passive immunity that they receive in the colostrum—the fluid taken orally from the bitch. Usually after the first twenty-four hours the puppies' ability to absorb more antibodies orally ceases—the stomach lining apparently changes.

A dog with canine distemper has symptoms similar to a severe cold—runny nose, runny eyes, and mucous, with temperatures usually rising from the normal of 101–102.2 to 103 or even 104–5. The death rate of puppies with viral pneumonia is about 50 percent. Out of those surviving about one-quarter are left with a central nervous system disorder—convulsions occur because the virus destroys parts of the brain and the spinal cord. Or they may suffer from chorea, which is a constant twitching movement in the muscles of the head, in the pectoral girdle (chest and forelegs), or in the hind legs. It doesn't make any difference whether the afflicted dog is awake or asleep; the only thing that stops the twitching is a general anesthetic. Dogs with chorea have survived and gone on to live fairly normal lives, although they have difficulty walking at times because of the constant twitching.

Vaccination ages for distemper, hepatitis (an inflammation of the liver and gastrointestinal tract that can affect other organs), and leptosporosis (an infectious disease of the liver and kidneys) are the same. Usually the first vaccination is given between six to eight weeks of age, the second one at ten to eleven weeks, and the third beyond thirteen weeks. The length of time varies with the vaccine used and the schedule of the individual veterinarian. Usually it is recommended that a combination distemper, canine-distemper, and measles vaccination be given as early as four to six weeks. Some manufacturers claim that their combination distemper and measles vaccine will effectively immunize 90–95 percent of puppies when vaccinated between four and six weeks. Infectious canine hepatitis, now also called canine adenovirus, can in one form cause corneal edema (blue eye). Most cases correct themselves, but occasionally a case can cause blindness. Another form of canine hepatitis usually occurs during the first few months of a puppy's life. The puppy develops high temperatures and gets very yellow. There is no specific treatment. Therefore, to prevent these diseases, vaccinations are recommended.

Canine leptosporosis is caused by a spirochete. If leptosporosis is endemic or is present in an area, vaccination is recommended at nine weeks of age or older. A second dosage is usually given several weeks later, and a third dose after that. The effective booster range is twelve months.

The most common combination of vaccines given is for canine distemper, hepatitis, and leptosporosis. This single vaccine is called DHL, or three-in-one.

A fourth disease, canine para-influenza virus (ken-

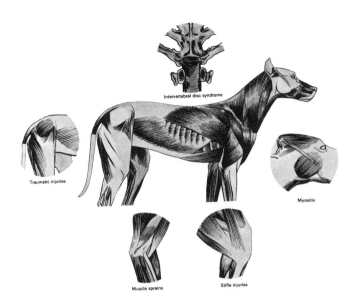

Another view of the inner dog, showing skeletal muscles and certain injuries they are susceptible to. (Photograph courtesy of the Upjohn Company)

nel cough), is often included in a multipurpose vaccine —a DHLP, or four-in-one. The disease involves a persistent, hacking cough—the dog sounds almost like a seal. The disease is most often contracted in kennels, veterinary hospitals, pet shops, and dog pounds.

In rabies-free areas, people ask, Why vaccinate? We haven't had cases in such a long time!

If given a choice between vaccinating a dog for rabies and vaccinating a dog against everything else, I would always vaccinate against rabies and worry about the others as they come along. Why? Because rabies is fatal in all cases. Any dog that contracts it dies; any person that contracts it dies or becomes a vegetable and probably would wish to be dead. Since there are still wild animals that are potential reservoirs for the disease, my belief is that vaccination is insurance that an owner of a dog must take out. I always recommend rabies vaccination for dogs no matter where I am—even in rabies-free Suffolk County, Long Island, in New York State.

A final reason for the rabies vaccination is to provide legal protection for the owner. If your dog bites someone (even in play), the health authorities will often impound the dog for observation if he has not had the vaccination.

Rabies is a viral encephalitis (inflammation of the brain and its coverings) that may strike any warm-blooded animal but is most common in carnivores and in New World bats. In the United States foxes, skunks, and raccoons are the major wild carnivore hosts, while among domestic animals, dogs and cats remain an important source of human exposure.

If a large segment of the dog population is left unvaccinated, rabies can occur and spread—a frightening prospect. Rabies infection usually results from a bite, but it can be airborne—there is evidence of this occurring in bat caves. Once the virus gets into the body, it migrates along nerves and nerve pathways. Entering the nervous system, the brain and spinal cord, it filters into salivary glands. Incubation is influenced by the virus strain and the dose—that is, the number of virus particles that the animal receives in the bite—and the location of the bite. Usually the incubation period is between three and eight weeks, although the Communicable Disease Center in Atlanta states that six months might be a more realistic incubation period; some cases have incubated for two to three years. However, dogs and cats almost invariably develop clinical signs within five days after onset of virus shedding—that is, when the virus reaches the salivary glands. There are two types of symptoms—the excitability and irritability of "furious rabies," and the paralysis of "dumb rabies."

Most animals with rabies do not survive for more than fourteen days. Some, however, last three weeks. The modified, live-viral-rabies vaccine injection should be repeated every two to three years. Some states require vaccination every year.

Remember: vaccinations are recommended annually for distemper, hepatitis, leptosporosis, and para-influenza—all of which are considered puppy diseases because puppies do not have antibodies. Free-roaming older dogs, though not vaccinated, may survive by catching mild forms of the diseases and then by developing "street immunity." It is tragic, however, when a dog of fourteen or so gets distemper and dies after its owner conscientiously had it vaccinated for the first six or seven years and then stopped, thinking that only young dogs are susceptible. It's not so. If your dog does not have a street immunity, has not recently been vaccinated, and does come in contact with the viruses, the outcome can be serious.

5. Heartworm

Heartworm is a parasitic disease caused by the organism *dirofilaria immitis*. The disease, although widely distributed, occurs mostly in coastal areas with high populations of mosquitoes, which do the transmitting. They carry an infective third-stage larva. When a dog is bitten, the mosquito's saliva contains parasites about three hundred microns in length—or about twenty-five red blood cells long. They are about eight microns, or one red blood cell, in diameter. Adults of the parasite grow to about fourteen inches in length and have the total body dimensions of the sort of package string found in bakery shops. Adults wind up in the right ventricle of a dog's heart. From bite to residence in the heart is about nine months.

Blood samples are taken to detect heartworm. However, the number of microfilaria circulating in the blood-stream are no indication of how many adults are present in the heart.

A dog suffering from heartworms becomes quiet and seems to be doing poorly . . . can't run much, tires quickly, lays around, loses weight, coughs, bloats, breathes heavily, and runs a fever. Because the parasites interfere with circulation, the mucous membranes change from light pink to blue as a result of oxygen deficiency. Later the right ventricle of the heart enlarges because the parasites take up space normally reserved for blood.

Controlling heartworm is a matter of breaking its life cycle. Unless the treatment is carefully administered, however, it can be as bad as the disease, and death can result. Therefore, it is better to prevent the disease by giving daily, oral doses (tablet, liquid or powder) of diethylcarbamazine—DEC.

If the mosquito population is seasonal or exposure is limited, treatment should begin about fifteen days prior to possible exposure and extend sixty days after. In temperate climates this means starting treatment in the spring and continuing it for at least two months after consistently cold weather. In some tropical or very warm areas the treatment should be continued all year.

Early detection, before heart enlargement, makes treatment much easier, and it reduces side effects and the possible chance of death from the treatment.

Limitations of treatment depend on the amount of irreparable damage done to major organs from mechanical impairment of blood flow and from toxic products released from the live and dying adult heartworms. Because the young parasites, the microfilaria, are so small, they are able to invade the capillary beds of the liver and kidney. It has been estimated that a dog that has had heartworms for several months and has a fairly good number of adult parasites—fifteen adults, say—may have several million microfilaria circulating through its system. Evaluation of each dog with heartworms must be made, liver and kidney functions checked, chest X-rayed—all before treatment can be instituted.

At present arsenic-containing drugs are used to reduce or eliminate adult heartworms. Treatment consists of twice-daily doses of thiacetarsamide given intravenously for up to three days. Arsenic is a heavy metal and may cause damage to major organs when given in levels sufficient to kill adult heartworms. The liver and kidneys are most severely affected by the drug and also by the parasites, and so they must be closely monitored.

As arsenic-attacked parasites die, they are not eliminated totally from the dog but are swept out of the heart, up the pulmonary arteries, and into the lungs, where their bodies break up. During the two to four weeks after the arsenic treatment if the dog exercises extremely hard, the parasites can be flushed out of the heart and then may hit the lung as a large pulmonary mass, causing death. A dog being treated thus should not be exercised.

Fox terrier skeleton on display at the AKC library in New York City.

A dog in treatment is usually hospitalized two or three days, and then after thirty days microfilaria therapy is begun. The microfilaricides, either dithiazine iodide or levamisole, are given orally, according to weight, for up to twenty-one days.

I recommend taking a blood sample once a year in areas in which the disease is not very heavy and every six months where it is heavy.

Remember, prevention with DEC is a lot easier than treatment.

6. Other Worms

Intestinal parasites—a problem in young puppies—are commonly roundworms, hookworms, and whipworms. They are present in the female when the puppies are born. During the migratory stages of the worms the parasites pass through the uterus. Even puppies taken by Caesarean section and never allowed near a female can have parasites prior to birth.

The cycle starts when a worm egg is ingested by the female. After the egg hatches, the parasite passes through the stomach wall and liver into the lungs, where it stays for several weeks, increasing in size. It's then almost coughed up, but is then swallowed back again into the stomach, where it enlarges to several inches, proceeding with its life cycle.

The larva tend to concentrate in the lactating breast. As puppies nurse, they get a large dose of the parasites. Hence, the paradox of puppies raised in a very clean house passing these three-inch-long roundworms.

Detection of intestinal parasites is accomplished fairly simply by examining a puppy's stool. The eggs are shed in large numbers and are fairly easy to identify.

Roundworms, called ascaris, can be spread to people—especially children under five who haven't developed antibodies—causing an illness called visceral larval migrans. Children usually come in contact with ascaris through ingesting food or water that has been contaminated with fecal material from a dog that has the parasite.

Pinworms, which dogs also get, are something else again. While dogs are often blamed for pinworm infestation in children, the dog is not part of the pinworm life cycle. Pinworms are transferred from person to person, not from dog to person.

Dogs should be checked periodically for intestinal parasites. If the dog is without problems of diarrhea or weight loss, then a stool should be examined every twelve months. The first time a puppy is brought to the veterinarian, the owner should bring along a stool. Medications for parasites are fairly sophisticated, and some may require hospitalization overnight. However, most can be handled on an outpatient basis if the owner is capable of giving medication to the dog.

7. Vomiting

If a dog vomits everything that goes down, don't allow eating and drinking for sixteen hours, particularly if the vomiting persists, say four or five times. By taking away all liquids and solids, irritation of the stomach is lessened.

Watch grass ingestion. Dogs that have mild stomach or intestinal upsets tend to graze and browse. The human reaction often is that all this roughage in the system is either going to stimulate vomiting and thereby get up the source of irritation or it is going to soothe. More often than not, however, the grass just aggravates.

As for medication, owners can treat their dogs, again depending on weight and size, with products they would use on themselves. Pepto-Bismol is a good protectant. Kaopectate, generally used for diarrhea, can be used for vomiting. Donagel, Maalox, and other products that coat the stomach are OK.

It's interesting that while patent medications can be given to dogs fairly easily, many dogs will, within a half hour, vomit back a certain portion. This doesn't mean that the medication isn't any good—just that the stomach was so irritated that it couldn't hold it all down. But a good portion of that medication remains in the stomach, stuck to the wall, coating everything and, over a period of hours, settling it down.

Once vomiting is alleviated, slowly start—but not until eighteen hours later—to introduce clear liquids such as bouillon, broth, water. Try a little at a time, say a tablespoonful. When the dog shows it can hold that down, move to solid food; usually within thirty-six hours the dog will be back on a normal diet.

If vomiting persists beyond twenty-four hours, the dog should be checked by a veterinarian to make sure there isn't a problem of infection or obstruction of the bowels—something that is going to cause the dog serious problems.

222

Coupled with vomiting is often diarrhea. When the two go together, there is a strong suggestion that something in the diet was bad—spoiled meat, for example, or the spoils of a garbage can raid. Vomiting indicates that the dog has taken in something fairly recently. Diarrhea, on the other hand, means the offending food was eaten twelve to twenty-four hours earlier. With diarrhea there is excessive fluid loss through the bowel. So although solid food is stopped, liquid is not. Milk turns into a solid, and so is not allowed. Milk is not recommended as a normal part of a dog's diet anyway because it does tend to predispose to diarrhea.

More often than not, if you stop feeding solids for twenty-four hours and at the same time treat with Kaopectate or Pepto-Bismol, the diarrhea will be gone within thirty-six hours. A long fast in a dog means slowing down hypermotility (excessive movement of the intestines), so that when feeding begins again with a bland diet—a little boiled chop meat, a little boiled rice—there is not likely to be a bowel movement at all after the diarrhea for perhaps two days. Don't feel that the dog has gone from diarrhea to constipation. Relax: Do not give the dog a laxative.

If, however, you notice diarrhea and/or vomiting with blood, then it is not a routine case and should be seen by a veterinarian. Bloody bowel movements, particularly if they have a very foul, almost-dead odor, are usually associated with a condition called hemorrhagic gastroenteritis. This is an acute bacterial infection that irritates the bowel to the point of bleeding. It is an emergency that usually requires immediate treatment with antibiotics, fluids, and occasionally cortisone to prevent shock.

Generally vomiting and diarrhea are induced by unsuitable food. They are problems that can be handled pretty much the way you would handle vomiting and diarrhea in a child.

8. Planned Puppyhood, Sex Education, and Decent Behavior

A wife comes into the hospital objecting to the carryings on of the male dog. She has either had a female dog spayed or would be willing to. Yet when the subject is brought up with her husband about a male dog, the hackles rise as he envisions himself in the same situation. Never mind that the male dog is running off for weeks on end, that he digs holes under the fence, fights, is indeed a nuisance—that he should be altered, castrated. The husband is adamant. He just doesn't want it done.

Often the dog shows up at the hospital with the wife, who explains that her husband is out of town . . . can the dog be put in for surgery and be back with the stitches out before the husband gets home.

It's usually done almost with a smile, and I see her now as she leaves the dog behind . . . the wink and laugh, to herself, as she walks out the door.

The purchase of a dog strictly for the sexual education of children doesn't seem to have any real worth. I think enough things are being done now in schools about sexuality so that children don't have to see an actual dog birth. Surely there is no excuse for increasing the large number of strays just so kids can see how it's done. Buy them a book.

Another thing that we've seen quite a bit of in the office are emotional problems in animals—problems that look very similar to those seen in children.

Animals as well as children are growing up without supervision, without direction, and I think that dogs as well as children need guidelines. Dogs, anyway, have to be brought up with a degree of control. A dog that takes possession of a chair as a puppy is not easily corrected when it's six or eight months old. The owner may try, but it's often too late. Behaviorists call this the Santa Syndrome. The dog grows up totally indulged, without any indication of where the boundaries are, going from

Printed matter provided by drug companies to veterinarians is similar to the abundant, informative, expensive "sell" literature provided to MDs. For every drug used a vet can provide you with a detail sheet describing its characteristics.

pillar to post, looking for some kind of guidance. I have found that a dog enrolled in an obedience course is happier, more emotionally stable, and that problems of biting and chewing and defecation are absent.

It's just so nice to see friendship between an animal and its owner and to know that the woman or the man or the child who is walking a dog is not going to be pulled all over the street.

Choosing a Good Veterinarian

The standards of the Royal College of Veterinary Surgeons are applicable for choosing a veterinary hospital anywhere.

1. The hospital must be clean and in good decorative order, creating an atmosphere of clinical cleanliness and efficiency. All parts of the premises must be kept adequately ventilated, free from offensive odours and in an orderly condition. The buildings should be constructed of brick, stonework, or other permanent materials and the internal walls and floors of such impervious materials as will permit of thorough cleansing and disinfecting. Adequate storage facilities should be provided, and the area immediately surrounding the hospital must be maintained in a clean and tidy state.

2. The staff must also subscribe to this atmosphere by maintaining high standards of dress, cleanliness, and personal appearance.

3. The services of the hospital must be available at all times, and a veterinary surgeon must attend daily.

4. The lay staff must be adequately trained for the efficient performance of their duties, and sufficient numbers of lay staff must be available to ensure adequate care of the animals in the hospital.

5. A waiting room or reception area of adequate size and with good fittings must be provided.

6. There must be a minimum of one examination room.

7. X-ray facilities suitable and adequate for the needs of the hospital must be provided and be readily available. Equipment should be so placed as to constitute no risk to patients, clients, or staff. Adequate safety precautions must be in operation, and standards laid down by the Code of Practice observed.

8. An operating theatre must be provided, apart from the examination rooms and used only for purposes directly related to the conduct of the surgical operations. Such purposes should not include the preoperative preparations of surgical cases, which may not be undertaken in the theatre. The theatre area must be properly equipped with a good supply of instruments and proper

theatre furniture. There must be adequate facilities for sterilization, anaesthesia, and resuscitation, although not all these facilities need necessarily be provided in the theatre itself.

9. An adequate supply of drugs used in the treatment of patients must be available. They must be properly and safely stored with accurate, well-kept stock-lists or other efficient system to ensure that there is no shortage of essentials.

10. Laboratory facilities for all routine diagnostic tests must be available.

11. There must be an area with suitable provision for storage and preparation of food. Feeding equipment should be sterilized or be of the disposable type.

12. Kennels and cages must be of adequate size for the type of animal housed and made of nonpermeable materials with easily disinfected fittings. Heating must be available for use as required. There should be no overcrowding and there should be suitable means of ventilation. Satisfactory arrangements for the disposal of excreta, soiled bedding, and carcasses must be made. A minimum of six kennels or cages must be provided, suitable for long-term hospitalization.

13. Exercise areas must be available, adequate both in number and size for the capacity of the hospital.

14. Facilities should be provided outside the examination or surgical areas for the bathing and grooming of patients admitted for treatment.

15. Office facilities must be provided which will be easily accessible to the staff and to clients as required. Complete medical cards must be maintained for all patients.

16. There must be no boarding kennels at the hospital.

17. Adequate fire-protection equipment must be available.

18. The display of commercial merchandise, or the maintenance of a trimming and clipping business within the hospital premises, shall not be permissible.

Jones's Animal Nursing, *edited by R. S. Pinninger, quoting the Royal College of Veterinary Surgeons hospital standards in England.*

SAND FLEAS
Although fleas found in sandy places often are called "sand fleas," there is no flea by this name. Many kinds of fleas develop in sandy places as a result of being dropped there (as eggs or adults) by flea-infested animals.

Fleas—the Most Prevalent Parasite

Most dogs and, by extension, their owners have been plagued by fleas. Here we learn what fleas are and what to do about them.

It's an old story. There are all kinds of fleas—dog fleas, cat fleas, rat fleas, human fleas, and even a breed called sticktight fleas. The latter prefers poultry but will, if necessary, latch onto a pet or a person and stick tight. The other varieties are more mobile, spending their lives hopping on and off your animal. And the so-called human flea isn't fussy either. It can be found on hogs, dogs, cats, goats, domestic rats, and on wild things like skunks, coyotes, and badgers. In fact, despite their given names, none of these fleas discriminate much. They will take a bite of any warm-blooded, convenient body, and if the body should be nicely furred, feathered, or haired, it's more than likely to become involved in the life cycle of the particular flea that has chosen it.

The life cycle of the flea generally progresses this way: A female flea lays eggs on a dog, which in all likelihood will carry the eggs indoors and drop them into every crevice, rug, and chair of even the most immaculate of homes. (Some dogs, the longer-haired, are so comfy that some fleas never let go.) Eggs hatch into larvae, then proceed to the pupae or cocoon stage from which the adult fleas emerge, sometimes within a few days, sometimes a year or possibly more later, depending on environmental conditions. If you've ever been "flea swarmed" (which is akin to getting mugged by a million little black dots) when returning home after a vacation, you know that fleas can wait a long time for a nibble . . . and you never noticed even one little flea before the trip . . . and how could such a terrible thing happen?

The little black dots that leap about are the males (or the very, very young); females are the reddish-brown lines that creep through fur, depositing about five hundred eggs in the course of a flea lifetime. Most of the eggs hatch, the fleas grow up, mate, and deposit eggs that become larvae, pupae, adults—ad infinitum.

Both male and female fleas live on blood sucked from your dog, or from you, causing anemia in some puppies and older dogs. They can also carry diseases.

Some dogs are highly allergic to fleas. So are some people, who usually begin to itch around the ankles before they even see a flea. These dogs and people will, at the first flea bite, suffer extreme discomfort—itching, swelling, reddening of the skin. Fleas won't take up residence on a person, but oh, the poor dog! Scratching, biting, leaping about, a very agony of eczema that must

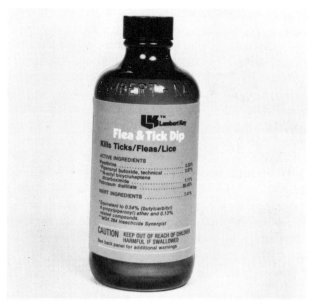

Some of the many products made to fight fleas and other itching external parasites. (Photographs courtesy of Lambert Kay)

be quickly alleviated—and the flea, the cause, persistently, diligently fought.

Fighting fleas is tedious and boring, but there's no getting around it. There are a lot of antiflea products on the market. Special shampoos, sprays, powders, ointments, dips, collars, and medallions for dogs seem to be almost as numerous as fleas. There are sprays, foggers, and dusts for the home or kennel and for the yard or run. The Benz O Matic fogger, for example, comes complete with a propane gas cylinder. It will fog an acre in fifteen minutes and promises to keep it insect-free for several hours.

Some of these products are available in supermarkets, some in pet supply stores, others through veterinarians. We recommend using the mail order pet products suppliers, through whom you can get almost everything you need for about half the veterinarians' prices.

Supermarket products do the job for some, while other pet owners will settle for nothing less than a bath and dip and spray and collaring by a veterinarian. For those who prefer the specialist's touch, a professional exterminator will deflea your house for a fee. If that's the route you choose, be sure to insist on a time guarantee.

Here's how to do it yourself. Bathe the dog. St. Aubrey and Oster make excellent shampoos. A bath won't kill all fleas, but it will rid your dog of flea droppings—those fine brown specks that can be found between the dog's hairs on the skin. Then take the dog outside, away from the house (be sure he's not damp if the weather's chill) and either spray or powder thoroughly. Sect-A-Spray is recommended for dogs not put into a panic by aerosol sounds. Vet-Kem Flea and Tick Powder is effective and not frightening to the nervous dog. Sprays and powders will cause fleas to become very active, then to jump or fall, stunned, to the ground. Be sure to read all product labels to see how long a particular preparation will protect your pet.

In the house vacuum everything possible, then dispose of the dustbag. And spray. For a moderate infestation of fleas a commercial product such as Black Flag should do. Use it on floors, baseboards, rugs, and especially in areas much frequented by the dog. If the place is really jumping, it's best to use a heavy-duty fogger, which you can set and leave to work for several hours in a vacated house.

It may take several repetitions of the whole process to become flea-free—or if the dog should become reinfested, which is not at all unusual.

The Great Flea Collar Controversy involves the following arguments:

The fact is, the pesticide in any flea collar doesn't just seep through the animal's fur as a protective vapor. The active ingredient in the flea collar is absorbed into the dog's blood and metabolized by the liver, affecting the dog's entire system.
Bruce Sessions, *The Dog Owner's Medical Manual* ($5.95; Blue Ridge Summit: Tab Books, 1976)

Organophosphate chemicals act directly on the parasite causing death. Their action in flea collars is *not* due to absorption by the dog and ingestion by the parasite with a blood meal.
Terri McGinnis, *The Well Dog Book* ($10.00; New York and Berkeley: Random House and Bookworks, 1974)

The incidence of flea collar dermatitis is increasing proportionately as more and more collars are worn by animals. Since antiflea collars seem to be effective in controlling infestations and the continued use can be predicted, veterinarians will increasingly be asked to treat cases in which irritation results from the collar. . . . A small number of affected animals may also be hypersensitive to the ingredients of the collar and develop a generalized reaction in addition to the local lesions.
George H. Muller, "Flea Collar Dermatitis," in *Current Veterinary Therapy Small Animal Practice,* edited by Robert W. Kirk ($36.50; Philadelphia: W. B. Saunders, 1971)

Flea collars work safely and well for many when properly used, so be sure to follow directions and to keep an observant eye on your dog for the first few days. When you put on a collar, fleas will leap off in such a rush that the dog will hear a strange popping around its ears and behave accordingly.

To choose your poison follow this U.S. Department of Agriculture guide to contents of premixed flea products for dogs:

Malathion, methoxychlor, rotenone, or pyrethruin (pyrethrins) will kill fleas on dogs. You can buy these insecticides ready for use as flea powders or sprays. Use a powder that contains no more than: 5 percent of Malathion, 5 percent of methoxychlor, 1 percent of rotenone, or 1 percent of pyrethrins. Flea powders sold for dogs often contain several of these insecticides combined—each at a lower concentration than those listed above. Use a spray that has not more than 0.5 percent of malathion or methoxychlor.

For Homes: Sprays that contain methoxychlor, Malathion, or ronnel will destroy fleas in homes. Apply a 5 percent methoxychlor spray or 2 percent Malathion spray to floors and baseboards and to walls to a height of about one foot.

Or mix your own: To prepare sprays for use in homes, mix 6¼ tablespoons of 25 percent methoxychlor emulsifiable concentrate, or 3¾ teaspoons of 50 to 55 percent Malathion emulsifiable concentrate in one pint of water.

If you apply a ronnel spray, see that it is labeled for home use.

Precautions: Pesticides used improperly can be injurious to man, animals, and plants. Follow the directions and heed all precautions.

Store pesticides in original containers—out of reach of children and pets and away from food.

Apply pesticides selectively and carefully. Do not apply a pesticide when there is danger of drift to other areas. Avoid prolonged inhalation of a pesticide spray or dust. When applying a pesticide, it is advisable that you be fully clothed.

After handling a pesticide, do not eat, drink, or smoke until you have washed.

Dispose of empty pesticide containers by wrapping them in several layers of newspaper and placing them in your trashcan.

Dental Care of Dogs

Not much different from the human oral hygiene recommendations, but at least dogs don't have to brush. Photographs of dental equipment for canines.

Dogs have twenty-eight baby teeth and forty-two permanent teeth. The baby teeth start to appear at two to three weeks and begin to be replaced by the permanent teeth at fourteen to sixteen weeks. Dogs seldom have problems with teething, although they tend to chew things, and it is advisable to supply them with rubber toys. All permanent teeth appear by eight months.

Abnormalities of bite are relatively common in dogs. Undershot jaw (lower jaw protrudes beyond the upper jaw) is normal for pugs and bulldogs. Overshot jaw (upper jaw protrudes beyond lower jaw) results in buck teeth. Teeth not normally positioned are said to be maloccluded. Unless the malocclusion is causing a problem, surgery is not necessary.

Dogs may suffer from all the same problems with their teeth that people do: tartar buildup, tooth root abscesses, loose teeth, cavities, gingivitis (gum inflammations), retained baby teeth, extra teeth, and tumors of the gum and teeth. Tartar and gum inflammations are by far the most common problems seen in dogs.

A dog's teeth should be checked yearly when the dog receives booster vaccinations. If this is done and problems are treated routinely, extensive work can be avoided—although sophisticated dental care that includes X-rays, fillings, and root canal is becoming more available. Some owners wipe a dog's teeth daily with saline solution. Dogs will even tolerate daily tooth cleaning using a brush and paste or a Water Pik.

Edited and reprinted from the Nabisco pamphlet Dental Care of Dogs.

Postscript

To keep a dog's teeth in good condition he should be fed something hard every day. A piece of dog biscuit will do, or better still, a hard bone to gnaw which cannot be eaten. This prevents tartar accumulating on the teeth. [Editor's note: Veterinarians no longer unanimously endorse the efficacy of the hard chew.]

Edited and reprinted from Country Life in America, *May 1908.*

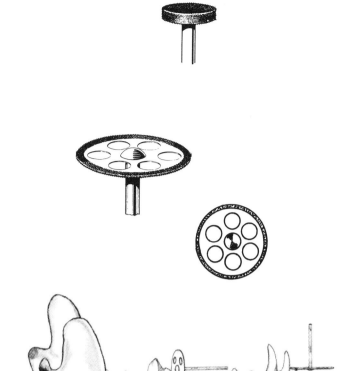

Deepen Enterprises, Box 389, San Mateo, CA 94401, is a supplier of veterinary dental equipment. Deepen's catalog includes instructional diagrams for removing tartar from canine teeth. Diamond grinding wheels and discs with either attached or separate axles are offered for cutting and extraction of problem teeth. Deepen also makes Doggy Dent prophylaxis paste for veterinary use and tubes of Doggy Dent toothpaste for home use by pet owners. (Photographs and drawings courtesy of Deepen Enterprises and its advertising agency, Somers, Gusick & Icardi)

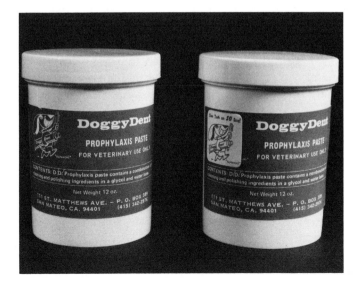

The Dread Hydrophobia

Rabies continues to be a scourge in various parts of the world and a potential threat in the U.S. But there is new hope.

Among the oldest public health problems known to man is rabies—the dread zoonosis hydrophobia—one of more than a hundred diseases that can be passed by dogs (and other animals) to humans. A million people a year around the world, and thirty thousand in the U.S., undergo a painful series of twenty-one injections following an unprovoked animal bite. In most cases this is a precaution because the offending animal escapes and cannot be examined and cleared of suspicion.

Rabies is not an urban problem in the U.S.—it has long been possible to vaccinate domestic animals against the disease—but it has persisted in wildlife, and so for the past sixteen years scientists at the New York State Health Department in Albany and at the National Center for Disease Control in Atlanta have been involved in research to perfect an oral vaccine that would make it possible to eradicate the disease in wildlife worldwide.

In 1977 success was at hand. On the eve of extensive field tests of a time-release capsule containing the first effective oral rabies vaccine, a researcher in Albany contracted the disease. The project was halted until it could be learned how the researcher became infected and until safeguards could be developed.

In the U.S. bats and skunks are the major rabies carriers. In the Caribbean and South Africa it's the mongoose, in South America the vampire bat, in Eastern Europe the wolf, and in Western Europe the fox. Rabies has penetrated even into some European cities.

The disease entered Germany from the east after World War II and spread west and south over the Jura Mountains into Switzerland. It is moving twenty to thirty miles a year toward the west coast of France. It has penetrated the Alpine passes into Italy. Only England and Scandinavia, protected by the sea, and Denmark, where a sanitary line has been created, are free of rabies.

A sanitary line, the only effective means of halting the disease, involves gassing foxes in their dens, thus breaking the chain of disease. This method is opposed by hunters and by conservationists even though the fox population, according to the World Health Organization, recovers rapidly.

In Germany six to eight thousand rabid animals are identified each year and more than six thousand people are treated. It is feared that a great reservoir of the disease may exist among the foxes of the Soviet Arctic.

PERGAMON PRESS

The WHO Center for Rabies Surveillance and Research has been organized at Tübingen, West Germany, to coordinate information. Its efforts, combined with those of U.S. scientists in developing an oral vaccine, could stop the spread of rabies, may even eradicate it completely in the near future. Such efforts did work with smallpox.

THE DOCTOR'S BOOK

If your vet is a little uncertain about a diagnosis and leaves the examining room, only to return moments later beaming and confident, he's probably had a quick look into *Current Veterinary Therapy—Small Animal Practice* ($36.50; Philadelphia: W. B. Saunders, 1977), edited by Robert W. Kirk, an annually updated single volume designed to help the practicing veterinarian stay with it. An expensive, very technical work, but if you have the intellectual ability and the patience, it is an excellent volume to consult both before and after you take your dog to the vet.

Dog Aid

Two fox terriers functioning as paramedics are immortalized in a nineteenth-century painting.

In the board room of King's College Hospital there is a painting that is a replica of one painted by the celebrated dog painter Yates Carrington and exhibited at the Royal Academy since 1888. It represents an event that occurred on August 1, 1887. On that Sunday morning the hospital watchman heard a dog barking at the door; intending to drive him away, he went to the door, but instead of one, he found three dogs there. Two fox terriers ran away as soon as the door was opened, leaving behind them a long-haired black collie with a gaping wound three inches long in his right foreleg, bleeding profusely. The dog was treated as an outpatient, his wound was dressed and bandaged, and eventually he went away.

Mr. Carrington heard of the story and decided to represent it on canvas. A thick path of blood was still on the hospital steps. Starting thence, Mr. Carrington and the secretary traced the blood all around the back of the hospital to Yates Court. In the boarding between the court and the inclosure of the Law Courts there was a hole just large enough to admit the dog. Below the hole was a piece of glass. While the gentlemen were examining the spot, a well-known bookseller came out and informed them that the two terriers which were actors in the drama were his, and he explained their conduct by stating that living constantly so near the hospital, and having during the day the free run of the neighborhood, they must often have seen patients who had met with accidents in the streets taken to the hospital and that they utilized this knowledge for the benefit of their friend the collie, who frequently passed their street.

Edited and reprinted from Scientific American, *November 1897.*

Breeding—a Few Pointers

Manners of breeding.

There is no definite proper age at which to breed a male dog for the first time. Much depends upon the individual dog, his breed and development—the larger the breed, the slower the development. Generally a dog should not be placed at stud until he is at least a year and a half to two years old, although an occasional service may be permitted from about a year on, according to the breed.

The best time to breed a bitch for the first time is during her second or third heat, when her bones are still quite pliant and her strength should be at its maximum. When an immature bitch is allowed to raise a litter too early, the strain on her system may arrest her full growth and development.

The AKC rules for registration regarding breeding age are,

> No dog or litter out of a dam under eight months or over twelve years of age at time of mating, or by a sire under seven months or over twelve years of age at time of mating, will be registered unless the application for registration shall be accompanied by an affidavit or evidence which shall prove the fact to the satisfaction of the American Kennel Club.

The mating of father and daughter, mother and son, or full brother and sister is considered to be inbreeding. When the relationship is farther removed, such as the mating of first or second cousins, it is considered line breeding. If the two dogs involved are selected judiciously, some nice puppies may be obtained as a result of inbreeding. However, the thing to bear in mind in inbreeding and to a lesser extent in line breeding is that faults as well as good points can be intensified. Very careful selection should be employed in the following generation.

As far as AKC registration is concerned, the relationship of the parents does not matter, but both parents must be registered in order for their litter to be eligible for registration.

The usual procedure is for the female to be sent to the male for mating, which is handled by the owner of the male—unless he feels incapable of dealing with the matter and engages a veterinarian or handler to take care of it for him.

Many people make it a practice of servicing a bitch twice with the same stud during a heat, with a day's interval, in an endeavor to be on the safe side. Many others feel one service is sufficient, providing it was done at the proper time and gave evidence of being a successful one.

Questions regarding how often to use a dog for stud service can be touchy. Naturally, the condition of the individual dog, his age, whether he is just being introduced to stud work or is an established stud, must all be considered.

It is not considered good practice to breed a female every time she comes in heat. Once a year is sufficient—or if she is a good healthy brood matron, she possibly could stand being bred two successive heats and then skip one. With dogs six years of age or over that have never been used for breeding or not used fairly recently, the advice of a qualified veterinarian should be sought before mating.

The period of heat in the female lasts from eighteen to twenty-four days. When the external organ swells to three or four times its average size, approximately the tenth to fourteenth day, the bitch is receptive, and it is during this period that she should be bred. The normal gestation period in the bitch is sixty-three days, but the time may vary a day or two either way.

The owner of the stud dog decides what the dog's services are worth based on his show record, background, and so on. A helpful rule of thumb is that the stud fee is often comparable to the price of a weaned puppy of the breed in question. The stud fee is actually for the breeding, but many breeders make a practice of offering a return service at another heat if a mating does not take. Sometimes the owner of the stud dog wishes one or more puppies in lieu of a stud fee. It's best if such an arrangement is fully agreed upon by the owners of both dogs concerned before the dogs are mated. To avoid misunderstandings when the time comes for the puppies to be born, the agreement should be put in writing and signed by both parties. Any particular specifications—such as who gets the pick of the litter, who has sex preference in choosing a puppy, at what age the puppy is to be chosen and at what age taken from the litter, what is to happen if only one puppy is produced (or none), if there is to be a courtesy return service if no puppies are produced as the result of a mating, and so on—should be part of the written agreement.

Edited from AKC Breeding Principles and Practices.

To announce that a bitch is ready to be bred or that a dog is available at stud, one place to advertise is *Pure-Bred Dogs—American Kennel Gazette*.

The Stud Book Register, a monthly periodical, also published by the AKC, contains pedigrees of dogs that have been used at stud and of bitches that have whelped litters for the first time. The register enables one to "search" pedigrees.

CONTROLLING CANINE CONCEPTION

Artificial insemination kits for dogs including tubes, pump, and instructions are available to concerned breeders through pet-product suppliers and catalogs. However, the opposite concern—preventing pregnancies that necessitate the destruction of unwanted dogs—looms far larger.

In current use are intrauterine devices, belts for females, tablets consisting primarily of chlorophyll to neutralize odors that attract male dogs, and anti-mating sprays to mask these odors. None is completely effective and none prevents the onset and cyclic repetition of heat in female dogs. A few hormonal products that do are available, but only through veterinarians who deal with a small and highly responsible segment of the pet-owning population. Tubal ligations and vasectomies are possible.

Mass-market fertility control for dogs has been a concern of several major U.S. drug manufacturers since 1952, when an injectable form of the female hormone progesterone was used to prevent heat (estrus) in females. The need for frequent injections made that early program impractical. Later, as a direct result of the development of human birth control chemicals, other injectable and new oral compounds of both the preventive and "morning after" varieties were tested on dogs and are now used in a limited way, but the formulation of a safe and effective mass-market birth control product for dogs required an increased knowledge of dog reproduction and of canine estrus. Pioneering research in the field done in the early 1900s indicated that female dogs were seasonally monestrus, having two periods of heat each year, usually in the spring and fall. Work done by universities and drug companies in the past dozen or so years has disproven this. In large research colonies bitches were found to breed in all months of the year and factors such as nutrition, temperature, environment, and possibly even light affect breeding.

The process of developing a canine contraceptive for general use is complicated, time consuming, expensive, and important. James H. Sokolowski, head of reproduction and physiology research at Upjohn Pharmaceutical's Agricultural Division, sums up the situation this way:

> Products currently available do not meet the needs for population control in the mass market area.... For maximum control, availability through veterinarians, humane societies and mass market facilities such as grocery and drug stores is essential.

Research continues.

Carnation company laboratory technician at work.

Opposite, Dogsteps *by Rachel Page Elliot explains that gait affects a dog's health and life-span. All dogs do not gait alike. Two good books for the novice breeder are* The Breeding and Rearing of Dogs, *by R. H. Smyth, and the* Meisen Breeding Manual, *by Hilda Meisenzahl. A more specialized book is* The Inheritance of Coat Color in Dogs, *by Clarence C. Little. Information is based on records of the Jackson Laboratory and of thousands of dog breeders.* The Beagle as an Experimental Dog, *edited by Allen C. Andersen, states that the beagle is an ideal lab animal because of its medium size, moderate coat length, excellent disposition, and happy personality.*

How to Sell Dogs

Advertising is one of the chief secrets of success in selling dogs. It is your advertisement that attracts the attention of persons who have never heard of your kennels, or possibly of your stock, and who never would but for your investment in printer's ink.

There is a great difference in advertisements. Too many are like this: "For sale—Litter of Bostons, cheap. Address ———." Such an advertisement is weak because it tells so little about what you have to offer. Note how much better the following one is in this respect: "For Sale—A litter of Bostons, whelped April 12, by Young Guardsman, AKSB 109824 Ex., Bess V, AKSB 86729; two males and three females; mahogany brindle, fine markings, fine heads, and screw tails. Prices $15 to $50. Address ———."

The first advertisement contains no information, while the latter gives the prospective customer an idea of what you are offering. If embellished with a good picture of one of your dogs, it would be still more effective.

The method that will produce the best results is to give as much description in the advertisement as possible without using so much space as to make the advertising bill excessive. If you have good stock and want good prices for it, advertise in magazines that reach the better class of readers. If you value your reputation, never try to get high prices for inferior stock. In answering inquiries give an accurate description and full pedigree. Do not hesitate to mention any defects that the dog may have.

Reprinted from Country Life in America, *April 1912.*

Improving the Breed

Genetic improvement as suggested by an elitist, three-quarters of a century ago.

Europeans notice that both dogs and cats are far tamer, brighter, and more affectionate in the United States than in Europe. It is evident that the average dog which, at the price of a pecuniary sacrifice and of some inconvenience, was carried across the ocean, was more loving and demonstrative than the average dog that was left behind. But all that selection was unconscious and thereby slow.

Let some university found an institution for the intellectual selection of dogs. Let anybody who believes that he has an extraordinarily bright dog write to the institution, state the feats on which he bases his belief, and loan his dog for reproductive purposes. The careful selection of the offspring of such animals, their continual crossbreeding with all other available canine geniuses, would, after a dozen generations, create a race the form and color of which nobody can foresee, but the average intellect of which would probably be superior to that of any dog now living. That such a race would greatly help to solve many psychological problems is probable; that it would, in numberless cases, supply us with faithful servants is certain.

Edited and reprinted from Scientific American, *April 15, 1905.·*

GERIATRIC DOG REJUVENATED

A fifteen-year-old Bolognese dog was brought to the Experimental Sleep Laboratory of the Psychiatric Institute of the Ministry of Health in Moscow in 1951. In the last year of known life for his breed he fatigued quickly, moped, lay in corners, and responded to nothing.

Contending that sleep can restore an old dog's virility and improve his appearance, the Russians treated him to a three-month sleep. His condition reportedly improved, his muscles and limbs strengthened, and down appeared where the fur had fallen out. It was later proved, the Russians said, he had regained his ability to reproduce.

The dog lived six years past his expected lifetime, until he was accidentally killed by a chimpanzee.

SLEEPING DOGS
THAT WON'T BE LET TO DIE

Narcolepsy, a condition characterized by frequent, brief, uncontrollable periods of daytime sleep and also sometimes by loss of voluntary muscle control, is a little-understood disorder that affects about 250,000 Americans. It also affects dogs.

The condition was first noted in canines in 1972 and since then the Stanford Research Center has conducted a nationwide search for dogs so afflicted. Recently a pair of Dobermans produced a litter of pups all of which exhibited signs of the disease. (Other breeds are also susceptible.) Because the condition is genetic, researchers intend to study a narcoleptic canine colony that will be developed from this litter. Hopefully, a better understanding of the condition and a cure for both dogs and humans will result.

Whatever one wishes to do for or with a dog, there's a magazine to help. See bibliography.

13

BEWARE OF DOG AND DOGS BEWARE

THE ORIGINS OF DOG
    DOMESTICATION
by John W. Olsen

A NEW DAY FOR THE WOLF?
by Steven H. Fritts

WOLF FACTS

SERVING BOTH DOG AND MAN

STRAYS
Book Reviews

DOG THIEVES

BEING KIND
by Lorraine Froehlich

THE VOLUNTEERS

THE GREAT LIGHT IN THE
    GREAT CAVE
by Rudyard Kipling

Judas of Ylfanet, a Swinford bandog, and owner-breeder Dayton Grimm. "Bandog" is from the Middle English and refers to a fierce watchdog that has been chained. Edward C. Ash in Dogs: Their History and Development *(New York: Benjamin Blom, 1972), a superb two-volume work, says that the bandog was left chained all day to make it fierce all night. Ash quotes Abraham Fleming, a contemporary of Shakespeare, who described the "mastive" or "bandogge" as "vast, huge, stubborn, eager, of a heavy and burdenous body and therefore but of little swiftness." For information about the breed contact North Jersey Bandog Club, Jefferson Street, Tenafly, NJ 07670. (Photograph by Spida Grean)*

The Origins of Dog Domestication

by John W. Olsen

The latest scientific view.

The effect that animal domestication has had upon human food-procurement strategies cannot be overestimated. Coupled with the development of agricultural techniques, animal domestication contributed to a series of cultural and environmental factors that have led eventually to a more sedentary way of life. This settled life-style, which was necessitated in part by a need to control stock and tend crops, was a major factor that allowed the development of urban civilizations in many parts of the world.

While many animals were involved in the initial processes of domestication by humans, it is generally agreed that the dog was fully domesticated before any of the others. There is ample evidence from many areas of the world—including Japan, the Soviet Union, Europe, and North America—that indicates that as the climate of much of the world changed at the end of the Ice Age, or Pleistocene epoch (about ten to twelve thousand years ago), humans began to expand their geographic distribution in order to exploit newly developing ecological niches. There is also evidence from these areas and others to suggest that as human ranges expanded during this early post-Pleistocene period, the dog may well have accompanied these shifts.

Evidence uncovered at mammoth-hunter encampments such as Afontova-Gora II in Siberia (provisionally dated to 20,900±300 years ago) or Mezin in the Ukraine (dated to ten to twelve thousand years ago), indicates that even at these early dates canids may well have provided invaluable assistance in the tracking and procurement of game. Ritual burials of wolves at Afontova-Gora II suggest that they were held in relatively high regard—perhaps for their hunting prowess and companionship or possibly as totemic symbols.

In the New World early domestic dog remains have been recovered from excavations at Jaguar Cave in Idaho. Recovery of these remains, which are approximately eleven thousand years old, suggests that dogs may well have accompanied humans on their trek across the Bering Land Bridge from Siberia to initially inhabit the North American continent in late-Pleistocene times. In Europe early postglacial settlements such as Star Carr in England yield further evidence that indicates the close association of humans and canids at this time.

The modern Swinford bandog (or American mastiff) was created by the late Dr. John Swinford, an American veterinarian, who crossed the Neapolitan mastiff, the English mastiff, and the American pit bull terrier (UKC version). Dr. Swinford, who is said to have been "philosophically an Adlerian," interested in aspects of aggression, wanted to create a dog that would "fear nothing made of flesh" and yet would not be "sharp." A sharp dog is emotionally unstable and likely to attack unprovoked. For further information about the Swinford bandog write Martin J. Lieberman, 13 Hotchkiss Place, Freeport, NY 11520. (Photograph courtesy of Jean Lepanto)

At present the earliest confirmed domestic dog remains have been recovered from Palegawra Cave, Iraq, and date to about twelve thousand years ago. There are strong indications that continued research in the Soviet Far East, the Mongolian People's Republic, and the People's Republic of China may yield yet earlier evidence for the domestication of the dog.

Noting that archaeological sites all over the world contain remains of early domestic canids, one may be prompted to ask, How did such a worldwide distribution come about? This question is a relevant one, and has been the subject of debate in scientific circles for some time. In the past (and to some extent today) the prevalent theory was that dogs were domesticated in one area, say the Near East, and from there spread with expanding postglacial human populations to encompass the areas of the world where traces of early domestic canids are found.

A second, more recent theory, which seems more plausible based on available archaeological evidence, maintains that the dog was domesticated in *many* regions or centers from which their populations expanded along with their human companions. This is in fact a simple condensation of a very complex archaeological picture. There seems little doubt that dogs were domesticated in more than one region of the world (the anthropological concept of "independent invention" is applied here), but accounting for the time differential between areas for the initial domestication poses perplexing questions. For example, can the New World be considered a center for canid domestication, or does the Jaguar Cave dog, dated to about eleven thousand years ago, represent an appropriate hiatus between the initial domestication of the dog in, say, the Lake Baikal region of Siberia eighteen to twenty thousand years ago and its subsequent *introduction* into the New World by way of the Bering Strait? Because of the circumpolar distribution of the wolf (a *Canis lupus*), it is possible that centers of canid domestication occurred within and adjacent to this zoogeographic range all over the world. The fundamental problem now is to elicit archaeological data that will shed light upon other potential early centers of dog domestication.

. . . wolf pups may have found it just as easy, and perhaps more profitable, to imprint upon dominant human figures rather than upon the appropriate leaders of their own pack.

How did the domestication of the dog take place? It has been often postulated, and recently summarized by Juliet Clutton-Brock (see Suggestions for Further Reading), that the domestication of the dog took place in large part because of the similarity in the social organization of humans and some canids, such as wolves.

Cooperation is a key concept in the hunting behavior of both wolves and humans. Wolves run in packs to bring down game much larger than themselves, which is analogous to the hunting strategies of early humans, who undoubtedly relied upon mass effort to subdue such large game as the woolly mammoth (*Mammuthus primigenius*) and the cave bear (*Ursus spelaeus*), which could not have been taken single-handedly. Anthropological data suggest that many nonindustrial peoples permit wild animals to live in and around their areas of habitation, and in fact often keep them as pets. There is a possibility that a situation such as this could have led to the domestication of the dog through the taming of wolf pups that in time would come to prefer their symbiotic relationship with humans to their natural pack social organization.

Thus the key to the origins of canid domestication may lie in the fact that both wolves and humans utilized similar basic systems of social organization, particularly where hunting subsistence was concerned. It is interesting to note that present archaeological evidence corroborates this view, since strong relationships between canids and humans begin to manifest themselves in the archaeological record at approximately the same time as postglacial climatic shifts allowed human exploitation of more varied resources, rendering a capable hunting companion such as the dog especially valuable. In other words, the human need to adapt to new environments and hence new fauna would have been greatly facilitated by the cooperative hunting behavior of canids.

Whether or not the domestication of the dog was an intentional process from the beginning is a matter of speculation. It would appear that at least in its earlier stages the close association that came to develop between humans and canids arose in response to mutual benefits rather than because of human exploitation of the canids' social characteristics.

Breeding in captivity, which is an essential aspect of domestication, could have been greatly enhanced by the wolf's social tendencies. Becasue of the hierarchical system of dominance characteristic of wolf "families," the wolf pup could extend its regard for the most dominant leader to human beings. With adult wolves this would result in a heightened capacity to breed in captivity. In other words, because of their social background wolf pups may have found it just as easy, and perhaps more profitable, to imprint upon dominant human figures rather than upon the appropriate leaders of their own pack. Assuming that this condition would continue to be strengthened into adulthood, the wolf would come to consider itself part of the human social system, and many of the anxieties that prevent other animals from breeding in captivity would be eliminated.

To summarize, it is apparent on the basis of archaeological and sociobiological evidence that the wolf (*Canis lupus*) and possibly other social canids represent the basal stock from which modern domestic dogs developed. The social compatibility of canids and humans may have formed the key ingredient that made the domestication of the dog possible and, indeed, established its unique position among all of man's domesticates— that of hunting companion, protector, and comrade.

Suggestions for further reading:

"Man-Made Dogs," by Juliet Clutton-Brock. *Science*, September 30, 1977.

The Order of Wolves, by R. Fiennes (New York: Bobbs-Merrill, 1976)

The Wild Canids, ed. by M. W. Fox (New York: Van Nostrand Reinhold, 1975)

"The Chinese Wolf, Ancestor of New World Dogs," by S. J. Olsen and J. W. Olsen. *Science*, August 5, 1977.

John W. Olsen is a candidate for the Ph. D. degree in anthropology at the University of California, Berkeley. His research interests include the origins and dynamics of animal domestication in Asia.

A New Day for the Wolf?

by Steven H. Fritts

A balanced plea for the wild, free, and ever-shrinking numbers of Canis lupus; *photographed in the wilderness of northern Minnesota.*

Sometime in the past—perhaps twelve to twenty thousand years ago—our ancestors brought home a young wolf, and thus began one of man's most successful experiments in animal domestication. Between then and now selective breeding has produced such a myriad of sizes, shapes, and colors of dogs that few breeds closely resemble their lupine ancestors. Whereas the domesticated wolf became man's best friend, our relationship with his wild counterpart has not been so friendly. It is doubtful that any other animal has been the subject of so much misunderstanding and persecution down through the ages as have the wolves. They continued to be viewed with little objectivity and much emotionality.

Man's fascination with *Canis lupus* probably dates back to cave-dwelling days. Our prehistoric ancestors must have been awestruck by these powerful and resourceful killers that howled in chorus, roamed the countryside in packs, and brought down prey animals that ranged up to several times their own size—animals that the spear-wielding hunters wanted themselves. Later the pastoralist probably feared and hated the wolf because of its damage to his flocks.

Perhaps some people prefer to believe that wolves are big, mean, and dangerous because such an image helps keep the pioneer spirit alive within them and enhances the valor of those who dare live and work near such "bloodthirsty" beasts.

Where early man's understanding of the wolf ended, his vivid imagination took over; consequently, much folklore has come to surround this colorful and complex animal. Children's stories such as "Peter and the Wolf," "Little Red Riding Hood," and "The Three Little Pigs" have made no small contribution to perpetuating the bad-guy image of wolves.

When European man unloaded his livestock on the east coast of America, the stage was set for a long and bitter struggle. As early as 1630 wolf bounty laws were adopted in the colonies; by the 1880s the species no longer existed anywhere along the east coast of the U. S. As pioneers pushed farther and farther into the American wilderness, they usurped habitat from the wolf's natural prey. This left the predators little alternative to attacking domestic animals, which brought them into direct conflict with man over large expanses of the continent. In parts of the west wolf predation on livestock was serious enough to cause local stockmen's associations to offer sizable bounties to supplement existing county, state, and federal bounties. There is no question that wolves were a serious economic problem during the seventeenth, eighteenth, and nineteenth centuries. Mainly because of their predation on domestic animals, deliberate efforts to exterminate wolves were carried out by individuals and by state and federal governments.

Wolves have been shot, trapped, snared, and poisoned. Their geographic range has been pushed back to the more remote wilderness areas, where few humans and their livestock are found. Today the gray wolf occupies only about 1 percent of its former range in the lower forty-eight states. This area consists mainly of some thirty thousand square miles in northern Minnesota where approximately twelve hundred wolves are protected by federal law. Between five thousand and fifteen thousand wolves inhabit Alaska. Parts of Mexico and 90 percent of Canada still have wolves, so the species still inhabits about 50 percent of its original

In the wild: a ninety-pound adult male wolf—one of twelve hundred in northern Minnesota. (Photograph by R. Stinchfield)

range on the North American continent and is doing quite well in most of these remaining areas. In the Old World wolves still inhabit parts of Asia and Europe. The similar but smaller red wolf, a separate species, now exists only in parts of coastal Texas and Louisiana, where it is probably doomed to extinction.

Within the past few years the environmental movement has swept the U. S. and Canada. Wolves have captured the sympathy of the public as never before, and their image has improved considerably—at least outside of wolf range. One reason for this change in attitude is a number of scientific studies that have disclosed the role of the wolf in natural ecosystems and proved erroneous some of the misconceptions that have surrounded the species for centuries. Books, magazine and newspaper articles, radio and television documentaries, and commercial recordings have disseminated findings of wolf research to an interested public. It is becoming unusual for movies and television to show attacks by hungry wolves on pioneer families or moun-

On frozen lake: aerial view of male and female eastern timber wolves in transit. (Photograph by Steven Fritts)

239

Steven Fritts, after tranquilizing adult male wolf, attaches a radio collar. (Photograph by R. Stinchfield)

tain men. Some of the more notable books on wolves are *The Wolves of Mount McKinley* by Adolph Murie, *The World of the Wolf* by Russell J. Rutter and Douglas H. Pimlott, *The Wolves of Isle Royale* and *The Wolf: Ecology and Behavior of an Endangered Species* by L. David Mech, and *Wolves and Wilderness* by John B. Theberge.

Some of the basic biological facts about wolves now being publicized are: (1) nonrabid wild wolves seldom, if ever, attack humans; (2) adults usually weigh sixty to one hundred and twenty pounds, much less than many people believe; (3) the number of wolves in a pack is usually less than twenty, and in most cases less than ten; (4) wolves cannot kill every deer, moose, sheep, or caribou they encounter, but prey mainly on immature, old, crippled, or sick individuals because these are most easily captured; (5) the number of wolves in a given area will not increase indefinitely because of intrinsic population control; and (6) wolves exist in low densities, rarely exceeding one wolf per ten square miles of habitat.

There is no question that the public as a whole knows more about and has a more favorable attitude toward wolves than ever before, but this has not removed the species from controversy. In the lower forty-eight states this controversy is centered in Minnesota, where the eastern timber wolf (one of over thirty subspecies) was placed on the U. S. Department of Interior's list of en-

dangered species in 1967, was totally protected in 1974, and since has increased in numbers. People living close to wolves in Minnesota are generally honest, hard-working, independent, and conservatively minded folk who have little use for government intervention in their lives. Most of these people dislike wolves, insist (accurately) that wolves are not presently endangered in Minnesota, and deeply resent being informed by government authorities that they cannot kill a wolf, even to protect their property. The dislike of both wolves and outside control are feelings shared by so many in wolf country that these issues serve as sort of a rallying point. Local politicians exploit these issues to the fullest to win support.

Many, but not all, deer and moose hunters regard the wolf as a competitor, a sort of superkiller with an unfair advantage. Deer are at the top of the list of preferred animals hunted in northern Minnesota, where they appear to represent natural wealth of the land. Some hunters who fail to bring home a deer use wolves as a scapegoat. Each deer killed by wolves is viewed as one less available for the hunter—i.e., wasted—and each wolf killed is supposed to result in the saving of many deer. Many long-time inhabitants of wolf country vehemently deny the findings of modern research programs, which contradict their long-held belief that wolves kill any deer they want whenever they please.

Killing of livestock is another reason for disliking

wolves. Loss of cattle and sheep to timber wolves is not very common in Minnesota (losses from coyotes are more common). Nonetheless, wolves sometimes do kill domestic animals (including dogs) and thus cause considerable financial losses for some farmers. So, predictably, those who make their living by raising livestock near wolf country are not among the wolf's most enthusiastic fans. Their attitude is a normal response to a threat to their economic success.

Another reason for disliking wolves is that they are still perceived as a threat to human life. Just ask any person who fears wolves whether he personally knows anyone who has been attacked, and he will be forced to answer No. Nevertheless, there are still those who keep a rifle handy when working in the woods—just in case!

It is common for humans to believe wolves are larger than they really are. Perhaps some people *prefer* to believe that wolves are big, mean, and dangerous because such an image helps keep the pioneer spirit alive within them and enhances the valor of those who dare live and work near such "bloodthirsty" beasts.

Those who still live close to the land or earn their living from the land seem to have a greater tendency to value natural resources in terms of practical utility (ultimately economic terms). This may be one reason for their low "value rating" of the wolf. Wolves are not good to eat, so in areas where there is no bounty and no legal market for their fur, they are of no apparent worth. Those who do not derive their incomes directly from the land, but view natural processes from a distant urban setting, are more likely to see intrinsic value in wolves and other wild species. In general, then, the perspectives of people living near wolves differ from those of most wolf enthusiasts living in urban areas.

Today the wolf is admired by millions as a symbol of what is still wild and free in an ever-shrinking, man-dominated world. This attitude is encouraging to those interested in the long-range survival of this species. The newfound enthusiasm for protecting wolves must, however, be tempered by discretion in order to remain effective. In some circles the wolf is being viewed as a harmless creature that can do no wrong and that should be left completely alone by man. This attitude is neither objective nor realistic. Wolves cannot live everywhere. If they are to survive in wilderness areas, they must not be permitted to disperse from wild areas to roam uncontrolled in farming country.

The survival of wolves involves complex biological, social, and political problems that ought to be solvable, given a combination of human understanding, habitat preservation, and legal protection.

Steven H. Fritts is a Ph.D. candidate in ecology and behavioral biology at the University of Minnesota in Minneapolis. He has spent five years studying wolves in northwestern Minnesota.

Pack with remains of deer. (Photograph by Steven Fritts)

THE WOLF AND THE BORZOI

Coursing wolves is generally done on horseback, with a brace of dogs of equal speed. When the wolf comes into sight, the hounds are loosed and the chase begins, with the huntsman generally doing his utmost to make his horse keep up with the dogs and the wolf. Little by little the latter is overhauled by the hounds, which run up on it, one on each side, watching for a chance to get a hold. It is rare for a wolf to turn and show fight, as it generally relies on its speed to get rid of its pursuers. The neck hold is the one the wolfhound has learned through centuries of training, and when the opening comes, he makes one jump and catches the wolf behind the ear. His mate gets as good a hold as possible, and the fight is on. It is the neck hold that counts, however, and soon the wolf's throat is caught by those long, powerful jaws, its wind is gradually cut off, and in a few minutes all is over. Of course, the hounds do not always escape scot-free, and a nip through the leg is no uncommon occurrence, but few are ever killed in the fight.
Edited and reprinted from Country Life in America, *1909.*

THE WOLF BOY

Some myths persist. Romulus and Remus were suckled by a wolf, and Rudyard Kipling's wolf-boy Mowgli in *The Jungle Books* was raised by them. In 1977 a TV series about a wolf-boy, Lucan, debuted.
The following is a doctor's description of a supposedly real wolf-boy found near Luchnow, India, in 1954.
His sense of smell was much more strongly developed than that of normal humans.
He was accustomed to eating raw meat and lapping water.
Callouses indicated that he had used both arms and legs for locomotion.
He tried to attack a dog.
He seemed to show affection for wolves he was shown in the zoo.
"All this," said the doctor, "led us to believe that this child has had an animal environment."

Wolf Facts

A fascinating list compiled from numerous sources, including Grizmek's Animal Life Encyclopedia.

—Wolves can be black, all shades of gray, and white. There are great white wolves in Canada's Northwest Territories.
—Adult wolves weigh between sixty and one hundred and twenty pounds.
—Some wolves can take fifteen-foot bounds.
—A wolf consumes five to ten pounds of food a day, can gorge on up to twenty pounds, and can go two weeks without eating.
—The smallest of the wolf's hoofed prey (its primary food) is the deer; the largest, the moose. Wolves eat mice and other smaller animals when necessary.
—When hunting, wolves travel in single file, moving about five miles an hour.
—The wolf's sense of smell is far superior to that of the best-tracking dog's.
—Wolves live in packs that average about ten members and are rarely larger than twenty, though the largest pack on record had thirty-six members.
—Each wolf pack has a territory. The largest pack territory on record is fifty-by-one-hundred miles.
—All wolves love pups. All pack members share in the raising of pups. This establishes pack unity.
—The playfighting of wolf pups establishes the social hierarchy of a pack.
—In large packs there is a separate male and female dominance hierarchy, but the top male is the top wolf.
—A lone wolf may have been a pup too aggressive to show subservient behavior to its parents or the least aggressive pup, picked on by all other pack members. In either case a lone wolf is one that found pack life impossible.

Wolf pups kept as pets will grow up to treat family members like pack members, may try to become dominant in the group, and will attack outsiders.

—Lone wolves survive disease and disaster better than pack wolves. Two lone wolves, a male and a female, will sometimes meet and begin a pack of their own in unoccupied territory.
—There is no documented case of a wolf killing a person in North America. There are, in the literature, cases of wolves killing people in Asia and in Europe. Those wolves are now thought to have been part dog or rabid or both.
—Wolf pups kept as pets will grow up to treat family members like pack members, may try to become dominant in the group, and will attack outsiders.

—Wolves are almost gone from most of Europe. They are on the endangered species list of the Secretary of the Interior of the United States.

For an intimate, endearing account of the affectionate family life of a small wolf pack—observed over a long period of time—see Farley Mowatt's *Never Cry Wolf* ($7.95; Boston: Little, Brown, 1963). It is a book that has attained the status of a classic. Though it shades almost into the mystical, when discussing wolf communication, it describes the three adults and the litter as personalities of dignity, devotion, and gentleness.

What Mowatt did for wolves in North America, Hugo and Jane van Lawich-Goodall (she of chimpanzee fame) do for wild dogs, golden jackals, and spotted hyenas in Africa. Their handsome book, *Innocent Killers* (Boston: Houghton Mifflin, 1971), is profusely illustrated with close-up black-and-white photographs of animals hunting, eating, courting, rearing young, playing, fighting, and resting.

Hyenas, jackals, and Cape hunting dogs (wild dogs) kill by disembowelment—in fact, eat their prey alive—and so have engendered horror and revulsion among men and have been ruthlessly hunted and killed. The authors take pains to make clear that these animals "kill in order to eat and to live in the only way for which evolution has fitted them. . . ." They also state that "they are intelligent animals with a fascinating social life."

A nice book for children by C. B. Colby, *Wild Dogs* ($3.95; New York: Coward, McCann and Geoghegan, 1965), brings together some members of the family canidae—wolves and foxes, dholes and dingos, bush dogs and raccoon dogs, and so on. Facts are presented in a spritely manner, and interesting anecdotes are scattered throughout.

For example, in discussing foxes Mr. Colby says, "The foxes of England and of some southern states, where fox hunting is still considered a sport, are probably some of the smartest canidae in the world, for they have had to be to survive."

He describes the rare maned wolf this way: "Here is an animal which has to be seen to be believed, and even then it is hard to be sure it is real. It appears to be assembled by mistake from assorted parts of other canines, for the legs are far too long, the neck too short,

the ears too big and the fur a sort of hit and miss affair." The maned wolf, the author goes on to say, is thirty inches high, five and a half feet long, and weighs up to twenty-five pounds.

There is a photo of every animal and also drawings of typical footprints, front and rear, of each.

Volume 12 of *Grizmek's Animal Life Encyclopedia* ($34.95; New York: Van Nostrand Reinhold, 1975, 13 Volumes) has a wonderful section on the canids—wolves and dogs among them—illustrated with beautiful color drawings, and photographs, and line drawings. It includes the history, development, folklore, habits, habitats, physiology, and relationship of canids to each other and to man. Examined in fascinating detail are wolves, coyotes, domestic dogs, dingoes, foxes, jackals, fennecs (described as "the smallest, cutest wild canid in the world"), African wild dogs, dholes (found "from Siberia and China to India, Sumatra and Java"), raccoon dogs (the most primitive living wild canid, originally an inhabitant of Siberia, northern China, and Japan, now transplanted to Russia and migrating into eastern, northern and central Europe).

South American canids are grouped separately and include the bush dog, the crab-eating fox, the small-eared dog, the Falkland Island wolf ("the only wild canid species that man has exterminated"), South American foxes, the culpaeo fox, the Paraguayan fox, and the maned wolf, which in spite of its name is not a close relative of true wolves.

Grizmek's Animal Life Encyclopedia is a superb work encompassing in its entirety all of the animal kingdom. Besides four volumes on mammals and three on birds, there is a complete volume on the lower animals—insects, mollusks, fishes, amphibians, and reptiles.

Serving Both Dog and Man

A new view of the dogcatcher.

Dogcatcher. The designation has its pejorative connotations—"he couldn't be elected dogcatcher" represents the nadir of occupational status. Also, a dogcatcher is thought to be the equivalent of a speed-trap cop—the hunter of the helpless.

Recently dogcatchers have become dog wardens, just as janitors have become custodians and garbage men sanitary engineers. Cosmetics only. In this, the third quarter of the twentieth century—an age aspiring to zoological enlightenment—the dogcatcher still does just that. He no longer uses a wire net but now, for recalcitrant cases, a tranquilizer gun, and in some communities he is required by law to hold his prey for at least seven days (twelve, where a license is evident), in others

---

WILD MUSIC

Musician Paul Winter took his saxophone to Wolf Park, a preserve in Indiana, and got a duet going with a howling wolf that, he says, began imitating his melodic phrasing. He taped Ida (his name for the wolf) and others and plans to release "an entire album by wolves in the future," *Rolling Stone* magazine reports.

Dogcatchers on the rue de Bruxelles in 1868. (Picture Collection, New York Public Library)

only forty-eight hours. If and when the time comes for disposal, the victim is sometimes "put to sleep" with an injection. At many dog pounds gas or decompression chambers, not needles, are still used.

In this imperfect world the dogcatcher moderates among the dog-lovers, dog-haters, and the dogs themselves.

No doubt there are dogcatchers who are time-servers —bottom-rung civil servants in jobs now too lowly even for patronage—and no doubt there are sadists among them, the temptations to unaccountable brutality being what they are. For one thing the dogcatcher as an agent of an official humane society has certain privileges of a peace officer, among the foremost being the right to buy and keep a gun.

So a helpless, frightened dog is snatched up by an armed man who incarcerates it, detains it for a week or so, and then destroys it. Not a pretty picture. And yet

Inspector J. E. Eachus, left, of the Royal Society for the Prevention of Cruelty to Animals and formerly of Southampton Township, New York, is a modern, professional animal warden. (Photograph by Don Myrus)

... if the dog had bitten a child, if the dog had been rabid (although there has been no reported case of human rabies from a dog bite in the United States since 1963), if the dog had dug holes on a golf green, if . . . mostly if it and others began to roam in packs (their numbers are increasing) to worry deer, to kill cats, to menace people. What then?

Thus we have the dogcatcher, a personification of society's compromise of conflicting tensions. On the one hand is the seeming inalienable right of every man, woman, child to *own* a dog and to be free with that dog. On the other hand is the group's need for control and for supervision, sanitation, peace, and quiet. The neighborhood cop knows how fierce the antagonism over a controversial dog can become.

In this imperfect world the dogcatcher moderates among the dog-lovers, dog-haters, and the dogs themselves. He tries to see to it (with precious little help from politicians) that all dogs are licensed. There is supposed to be an annual dog census in New York state, but in the township of Southampton there are five thousand dogs licensed but only two thousand reported by the census takers. Peculiar? Yes, especially when the dog population is estimated by dogcatchers there at ten thousand. (Companion animals will be included for the first time in the U.S. Census of 1980.)

Dog licenses, by the way, are probably most beneficial to a dog. Having one, a stray is likely to be returned home, not precipitously killed; if stolen, it is at least dignified to the extent of being listed as a victim of a crime, for a dog is property. Of course, it is property that breathes, which makes it a special case. A dog has certain rights in equity. It should not be mistreated and cannot be legally killed without good reason. Generally it is the dogcatcher who brings these matters to the attention of a prosecuting attorney, and generally the dogcatcher who testifies in behalf of the dog.

Dogcatcher is not a job that pays well, has, as noted, precious little prestige, doesn't take any special training to get, and—what is most remarkable—calls out for conflicting characteristics: The ability to kill frequently (30 percent of all strays) but also the ability to care enough for dogs to protect them from people.

DOGCATCHER ANONYMOUS

In Waukomis, Oklahoma, the identity of the dogcatcher is kept secret because according to the town's mayor, the former holder of the job quit when his life was threatened, and when the town tried to fill the vacancy, potential candidates were threatened and abused.

Strays

Book Reviews

Alan Beck, Director of the New York City Health Department's Bureau of Animal Affairs, worked on his doctorate in 1970 at The Johns Hopkins School of Hygiene and Public Health. His observations of stray and feral dogs in Baltimore led to his Ph.D. and subsequent publication of his thesis, *The Ecology of Stray Dogs* (Baltimore: York Press, 1973). This is the only scientific study to date of free animals in urban and suburban settings.

According to Dr. Beck, the population of free ranging city dogs is made up of released pets that wander but return home every day, escaped pets that jump fences or slip through inadequate gates, pets abandoned by their owners, stolen pets released by dognappers, and the progeny of all of these.

Loose city dogs, which tend to run in small packs of two to five members, have a home range (an area beyond which the pack doesn't venture), rather than a true territory that would be protected from outsiders. The size of the home range is directly affected by the availability of food, sources of which are garbage and, very often, handouts from humans on a regular basis. Some city blocks actually have their own pet strays who are well fed and in one instance, Beck noted, even rescued from destruction by the city shelter after having been collected by dog wardens.

Puddles, drains, dripping air conditioners, car washes, and the like provide an adequate supply of water. Vacant buildings, open garages, construction sites, porch steps, and even dense shrubbery offer shelter for resting, sleeping, and whelping. Making clever use of the urban environment, dogs will sleep under parked cars to avoid the heat of a summer day, rest on tops of cars to escape dampness and cold, and actually warm themselves on warm hoods of newly parked cars.

Stray dogs survive, on the average, only about two and a half to three years, succumbing to disease and injuries from automobiles. They are collected by shelters and sometimes are even attacked by humans. Contrary to expectation, strays almost never die of starvation, cold, or exposure. A particular dog that Beck observed for a period of time was adopted during the course of the study. The dog, referred to as Shag by Beck and said to have been a particularly appealing animal, weighed in at thirty-five pounds, and after almost two months as a well-cared for house pet had gained only one pound.

Dogs in cities create some problems, the management

of strays being one. Each year in the U.S. fourteen million dogs are collected and killed by humane agencies. New York City's Environmental Protection Agency has estimated that dogs, pets and strays, left five to twenty tons of excrement a year on city streets—a health and pollution problem—before the scooper law went into effect in 1978. Bites are another problem. They have increased with the dog population, and victims most often are children between the ages of five and nine. Dog bites are reported to be provoked and unprovoked with equal frequency. German shepherds have the worst bite record.

City dog difficulties aren't dog difficulties at all. Most are man-made (strays) and controllable (wastes). One of Dr. Beck's insightful osbervations is that for some urban dwellers contact with their dogs is a singular, sanity-preserving contact with nature.

Meindert DeJong's *Hurry Home Candy* ($1.50; New York: Harper and Row, 1953), illustrated by Maurice Sendak, is rather an extraordinary book. Directed at preteens, it is free of the saccharine touches that sometimes mar such works. It is in fact realistic and insightful in its description of a well-meaning but thoroughly inept and neurotic family that adopts a puppy, mistreats it, and then loses it because of ignorance and anxiety. The book goes on to tell the sad story of the pup's life as a stray.

DeJong provides a biting, trenchant view of American family life and dramatizes a persistent, often repeated pattern: a child asks, then begs for a puppy; the parents reluctantly agree to getting one, but only if the child will be completely responsible for it. Promises are made, but all too often broken because neither parents nor child understand very much about the physical, psychological, and emotional needs of a puppy.

> The woman made snorting noises. "Yes, yes, I know those promises—good for a day or so, and then it'll be up to me. Believe me, he's going to learn fast, I'll see to that . . ."
> "Can't baby him too much. Start out that way and you'll soon have a dog nobody can do anything with," the father instructed . . . The big sure voice knew all about puppies, and what should be done. ". . . Break their spirit first, then build it up again—your way. That's the way to get a good trained dog."

A long painful time later, the pup finds a real home.

Fitzgo, The Wild Dog of Central Park ($5.95; Philadelphia: J. B. Lippincott, 1973), by Paul Wilkes, is the true story of a lone urban stray that survives the cruelties of nature and man during a winter in New York. Fitzgo is finally adopted, too, by the author and his wife, but only after a long, laborious wooing during which the dog is transformed from a frightened, wild creature to a trusting pet.

Wild Dogs Three ($6.95; New York: Coward, McCann and Geoghegan, 1977), by Michael Fox, is a realistic narrative account, for children, of the lives of three feral city dogs, abandoned by their owners, that find each other in the squalor and deprivation of a slum. The book is based on extensive scientific observation of strays in St. Louis. The author is both a veterinarian and a psychologist who presents facts, often grim ones, and at the same time is able to make the reader privy to the thoughts and feelings of his subjects. This trio is sustained by intelligence and their bond of friendship and loyalty to each other. The book is illustrated with photos of the dogs in parks, on streets, and in the alleys of St. Louis.

No real strays ever so enjoyed an urban winter as those in Harry Cat's Pet Puppy *by George Selden, a captivating fantasy about strays in New York City. Harry Cat's puppy, Huppy, is adopted by a kindly human. The illustrations shown here are by Garth Williams and copyright by him © 1974. The text is copyright © 1974 by George Selden Thompson. The illustrations are reproduced with the permission of Farrar, Straus & Giroux.*

Dog Thieves

The crime is international and at least one hundred years old.

Then

We have here a small journal called *Les Petites Affiches* in which people advertise for servants, for places, houses to let, or offer rewards for objects lost. This has been used of late for a species of industry very common in England—the finding of lost dogs. Recently the number of advertisements in this journal of dogs found, which could be reclaimed by their owners upon payment of a small recompense and the cost of keeping to date, attracted the attention of the police. They saw that a company had been formed for this special business. Last week over fifty dogs were found, and all taken to the same place, where they were reclaimed by their owners upon the payment of money, the sum varying according to the evident value of the animal. Orders were given to the police to look out for the rascals.

Meanwhile the lady was running about in great distress calling for her dog.

Yesterday a lady was passing out of the courts with a magnificent greyhound when a man held out a bit of meat and enticed the animal into the passage. The gendarme on the corner saw the act, but just as he started forward an accomplice of the thief gave a sharp whistle. Meanwhile the lady was running about in great distress calling for her dog. The accomplice continued to whistle, running by the passage, and in a moment the dog came bounding out, followed soon after by an individual who walked away unconcernedly to join the whistler on the corner. The latter decamped when the gendarme laid his hand upon the shoulder of the thief. This individual was a great coward, and revealed the secrets of the band of dog thieves, so that several of them have been arrested. They will be imprisoned not less than six months each, for the Parisians of all classes are very fond of dogs, and they are invariably protected. It seems that the band broken up yesterday had found the business extremely lucrative. Only the other day a prima donna of the opera bouffe gave one hundred dollars for the recovery of a pet poodle, a Havannois, purebreed, and a Russian gave the same sum for a magnificent Levrier.

Reprinted from The New York Times, *November 3, 1876.*

Now

You receive a call late at night from someone who claims to have your pet. They ask you how much of a reward you are offering. You give a reasonable figure, and they hang up. Now you fear for the life of your pet and feel guilty that you did not offer more. The strategy is calculated to encourage anxiety, guilt, and confusion in the pet owner. It is effective!

You may get more than one call, and the conversations may vary. The calls often are from extortionists who have never even seen your pet but have seen your poster or ad. Here's what to do:

Keep your cool. Anyone who has your pet will either hold it until a "deal" is consummated or will set it loose on the street. Destroying and disposing of an animal is no simple matter and, further, is unnecessary, since the pet will not lead the owner back to the petnapper.

Affirm that the caller really has your pet. Is there an unusual mark or scar, visible sutures from an operation, unusual coloration or features (i.e., eyes of two different colors)? We remind you not to rely on variable factors such as behavioral characteristics that will change when the animal is in a strange environment. Keep in mind that a dog that barks on command of the owner will often not respond to the same command given over a telephone.

Decide before your conversation with the petnapper how much you are willing to pay in ransom.

Decide before your conversation with the petnapper how much you are willing to pay in ransom. Offer less and let the individual coax you up to your limit. Bear in mind that an animal napper is not an animal lover and wants to get rid of the pet. As negotiations drag on, the petnapper gets as anxious as you.

Arrange to meet in a public place by day. Pick a square or small park that is well populated and exposed but not overcrowded. Identify what you will be wearing or carrying to expedite the contact. Carry the money in an envelope, and do not turn it over until the animal is in your hands. As soon as the petnapper is out of sight, write down a detailed description of the individual and the license plate of the car or taxi, if used.

If the petnapper does not show up, go home and wait for another call. Point out that you will not be put through this routine again and agree to one more rendezvous.

Edited and reprinted from What to Do When You Lose Your Pet *by Irv West and Freida Chapman. For a copy of the pamphlet send thirty-five cents with a stamped, self-addressed envelope to Petfinders, Post Office Box 205, Planetarium Station, New York, NY 10024.*

Being Kind

by Lorraine Froehlich

The American Humane Association, the Humane Society of the United States, and the ASPCA explained.

Dogs are subject to overt cruelty and to covert neglect. They are speechless and cannot complain or accuse. Because this vulnerable condition can be a constant source of anxiety to those concerned about the general condition of all animals, people have grouped together and formed the humane agencies and organizations, public and private, to help watch and do what can be done on behalf of dogs and other animals.

The first such agency in the U.S., the model for all others, was the ASPCA, the American Society for the Prevention of Cruelty to Animals. Its aims are respected and admired, and its ideals are now generally accepted everywhere. But back in the 1800s animals, as children or even wives, were to many no more than chattel, property to be coldly considered in terms of their usefulness or lack of it and treated accordingly. Cockfights and the mistreatment of circus animals were common, and atrocities of the cattle market went unchecked. Brutally beating a tired, overworked horse to death was taken for granted.

In 1866 Henry Bergh, a rich man's dilettante son, came to grips with life in his mid-fifties and, after much discouragement, founded the ASPCA to fight the cruel and inhumane treatment of animals. Because he demanded a change in the moral conscience of the people, Bergh endured being called a madman and a meddler to achieve his goals. Because of his prestigious social position, some of the first dog shows held in the U.S. were benefits for his new agency.

In the 1970s the family pet has become an indispensable part of millions of people's lives. These pets are cared for and showered with love and affection. It's been over one hundred years since Bergh raised the consciousness of the world and founded the ASPCA. In some ways the problems that concerned him have been amplified. There are still many who horribly mistreat animals. A major problem today is animal overpopulation.

The Society continually works at educating pet owners about their responsibility to animals, including birth control. And they practice what they preach. The ASPCA maintains a low-cost spay/neutering clinic. Every pet adopter must sign a neutering contract and pay for surgery in advance. The cost is fifteen dollars for a male and twenty dollars for a female pet.*

Despite warnings about overpopulation of pet animals, more than ten thousand dogs and cats are born every hour in the United States (four hundred and eighteen human babies are born in the same time). That adds up to a staggering amount in just one day. Who adopts and cares for and loves these animals? What happens to all of them?

Unfortunately, for the most part they become unwanted strays—starving, diseased, often dangerous—and many suffer brutal deaths. These animals are not victims of physical abuse but of professed animal lovers who will not behave responsibly—who don't "believe in" spaying or neutering animals and so perpetuate misery for millions of them. It is far kinder to prevent these animals from being born than to have them face certain death in gas or decompression chambers. Shelters and pounds in the U.S. destroyed almost fourteen million animals in 1977. The ASPCA alone puts over one hundred and twenty thousand pets "to sleep" a year. The cost of doing this exceeds two hundred thousand dollars.

. . . almost every town has some method of animal protection.

The ASPCA provides other services. The first obedience-training classes open to the public in New York City were held under the aegis of the ASPCA in 1944. (Ten lessons for four dollars were taught by Blanche Saunders.) The society still sponsors such classes. The ASPCA dispatches panel trucks with cages to pick up strays and bring them to its shelters, where they are fed and given medical attention. When possible, owners are traced and their dogs returned; others are put up for adoption. Also, the ASPCA licenses New York City dogs.

The humane concerns of the ASPCA have not been limited to dogs and cats and horses. About ten years after its founding, the society was asked by a church worker to help in a child-abuse case that had been refused by the police, the district attorney, and private agencies. The society brought the case to court. As a result, the parents were jailed and the New York SPCC (Society for the Prevention of Cruelty to Children) was founded.

In keeping with the times, it seems, the ASPCA in 1977 came to the aid of an eighty-one-year-old woman and her nine cats who had been evicted from their Brooklyn apartment. A new apartment was found by the ASPCA whose director, Duncan Wright, said, "This

* In the spring of 1978, the ASPCA instituted a free neutering program at its four New York City shelters, to encourage adoptions.

is a classic example of neglect of the elderly. . . . It's incredible that in a city of this size an organization devoted to the welfare of animals has to take care of humans."

The ASPCA has been criticized at times for its inhumanity in the use of decompression chambers to kill unwanted animals and for the passing along of animals to research laboratories.

The ASPCA has inspired the creation of over six hundred SPCAs and individual humane societies throughout the country. They have effected a significant change in attitude about animals, so that almost every town now has some method of animal protection. Most offer basically the same services in varying degrees. Some do not euthanize and therefore sometimes have waiting lists for accepting pets. It can take six months or more. All will gladly accept offers of adoption by responsible, caring people.

The ASPCA (American Society for the Prevention of
   Cruelty to Animals)
441 East 92nd Street
New York, NY 10028

The American Humane Association is a national organization devoted to child and animal welfare through its emergency animal relief program, inspection program, and information services. It was begun in 1877 to fight abuses prevalent in cattle shipping.
American Humane Association
Box 1266
Denver, CO 80201

The Humane Society of the United States is primarily involved in affecting legislative and legal actions to benefit animals and in disseminating information to schools.
Humane Society of the United States
1604 K Street
Washington, DC 20006

The Animal Welfare Encyclopedia series contains legal data on state legislation and higher state court decisions relating to dog welfare, along with a volume of model state laws for animal protection. Available from:
Ford Associates, Inc.
701 South Federal Avenue
Butler, IN 46721

For information about the Federal Animal Welfare Act, legislation relating to the care of laboratory animals, exhibition animals, animals raised for sale to pet shops, and traveling animals, contact:

Animal Care Staff
Animal and Plant Health Inspection Service
770 Federal Building
Hyattsville, MD 20782

The Volunteers

An account of the amazing rescue of Ruffles and a note from the benefactoress Joyce De George. And a statement from the benign propagandist Nicki Meyer.

Working independently of humane institutions, there are thousands of people who, out of a love of animals, perhaps, a sense of duty, or a need to care, donate much of their time and energy to furthering the welfare of dogs.

Some people regularly visit the haunts of city strays, distributing food and water. Some turn their own homes into makeshift shelters and accumulate homeless animals. (All too frequently reports appear in newspapers of eccentric, often older people, whose ten or twenty or even thirty or more dogs, having upset the neighbors, are carted away by authorities to shelters.) There are yet other people who go to great lengths to raise funds to run private shelters from which no needy animal is ever turned away, at which no animal is ever destroyed.

The mystery dog of Ruffle Bar.

The Story of Ruffles

Eighteen-mile-per-hour winds whipped up the waters around a police launch setting out for one of several small, swampy, uninhabited islands of the Jamaica Bay Wild Life Refuge in New York City.

Frequented by gulls and other shorebirds, visited occasionally by boating fishermen or picnickers, traversed many times each day by low-flying jets using New York's airports, Ruffle Bar, the destination of the launch, had mysteriously become the home of a dog, gone feral it seemed, after months, perhaps years alone on a dot of sandy land covered by shoulder-high grass.

In the launch, on a late February day in 1970, were a few policemen, a Coast Guardsman acting as skipper, and two representatives of the ASPCA which, informed of the wild island-dog, undertook its rescue.

The launch waited a hundred yards off shore while the policemen (chilled) and the ASPCA reps (seasick) approached Ruffle Bar in a small outboard-powered rowboat. A police helicopter circled low in an attempt to flush the dog from the tall grass.

"Why don't they leave the dog alone?" a policeman asked.

"The dog is as happy as a pig in a puddle," said another.

"The dog is probably in some nice warm burrow," said yet a third.

After an unsuccessful two-hour wait a trap (described as humane by the ASPCA) was baited and left on the island.

"We'll be back," the ASPCA man said. "Too many people think that we're trying to rob the dog of its freedom. We're just trying to find it a new home. Or maybe we'll make it a mascot."

Tom Murray, a police sailor on the launch, responded. "This dog has been there on the island so long. He has survived summer and winter. He's by himself, away from all the troubles of the world. He must be pretty happy.

"But I guess we'll be going back and forth as long as the ASPCA wants us to."

It took ten days. Then the dog, a German shepherd, was finally caught in the cagelike trap. The dog growled and snapped when first approached, but calmed down to wait with policemen for ASPCA agents to arrive.

Before the trip to the island on what would be the last day of the search, the twenty-second of February, 1970, a policeman was heard to say, "Why should a dog that's probably been living on pheasant want to eat dog food in a trap?" Sea gull perhaps, but pheasant? "We sure hope the dog gets a good home," he said as the animal was led away. "It's earned it."

And that's exactly what happened to the mystery dog of Ruffle Bar. How Ruffles got there (dumped, abandoned, accidentally lost), how long she had been there (a few weeks, a few years), was never learned.

Joyce DeGeorge Writes of Ruffles

I am enclosing a few snapshots of Ruffles. As you can see, she's adapted beautifully to life in our home. I assume you know of her existence on Ruffle Bar and how we came to adopt her seven years ago, so you may like some more recent facts.

She's a very protective dog—not friendly toward anyone outside the immediate family, but for us she's well behaved, very loyal, and a bit of a character.

When we first got her, she was very shy and frightened. She looked up to our other shepherd, Misty, and the two became inseparable. Since then we've added Gypsy (Misty's daughter), a large and varying cat population (two to sixteen), a flock of chickens, and various ducks, peacocks, and pheasants. She gets along with all of them, including the fowl. Since she was supposed to have survived on the island by eating birds and gulls, we feel this is rather interesting.

A few months after we got her, she got sick. We had her to the vet for various tests but couldn't find the problem. Finally he discovered what was one of the first cases of heartworm on Long Island. Since heartworms are spread by mosquitos (and birds), we feel she got it on the island (Ruffle Bar). The treatment was successful and her health has been fine ever since.

We feel she survived the cold on the island by digging a den. Each autumn she would dig a large tunnel near the house, large enough to enter and completely turn herself around. She enjoyed spending time in these tunnels till we filled them in—as we discovered them. We were afraid they would collapse and injure her.

She's showing her age now. She's at least nine, and possibly eleven or twelve. We never found out how she got on the island, but we're delighted we've had these last seven years (and hopefully many more) with her.

Nicki Meyer's One-Woman Educational Effort

Like one born again, the writer rises from the depths of despair, discovers the true way (to raise a dog), and spreads the word.

I was truly a textbook case of the typical well-meaning pet dog owner—full of idealistic love and sentimentality. If there was a mistake to be made, I made it: I patiently endured destructive behavior, agonized and searched for hours when a dog disappeared, and paid untold veterinary bills I could ill afford—all because I believed that a dog needed complete freedom to be happy. But the real sacrifices, I know now, were made by the dogs—two killed, two severely injured on roads, and one put to sleep—because I blindly chose a breed I "fancied" but didn't understand and couldn't control. I did not own my dogs; they owned me. Despite tragedies and heartaches I refused to learn that ignorance, lack of early training, lack of confinement, and lack of control often result in disaster for both dog and owner.

I finally found the right breed for me—the yellow Labrador retriever—and I acquired a bitch puppy of obvious winning potential. Motivated by the promise of blue and purple ribbons, eager to try my hand at basic field training, and anxious to protect the dog from any injury that might hamper her career, I invested in my first crate and a basic step-by-step training book with a section on dog psychology. Everything I read made such good *sense*. When I tried it, it *worked*, and the dog seemed to enjoy every minute. The crate was immediately popular not only with the puppy, but also with my two older dogs, which had never even seen one before. And so, in seemingly no time at all, I had for the first time a well-behaved, well-adjusted, nondestructive, happy, and controllable dog—and it hadn't been that difficult to accomplish. Oh, how could I have been so blind for so long! By thirteen months my lab, Hathaway's Champagne Punch, had earned nine AKC championship points, was a dynamo in the field, a perfectly delightful house pet, and the perfect foundation bitch for establishing my line of Hathaway Labradors. But the results of a routine screen X-ray ended that dream. With obvious grade-three hip dysplasia, Punch was immediately spayed, her promising show and breeding career quickly at an end.

It is said that tragedies occur in threes, and I believe it: Within two months Punch's gentle grandfather mysteriously vanished forever (suspected dog theft), and three weeks later her cherished grandmother, on her sixth birthday, died in my arms after colliding with a tree in a freak accident.

I also believe that everything happens for a reason, so as the tears and self-pity subsided, I knew that there must be another way in which my newfound knowledge and Punch's sparkling desire to perform could be utilized. I vowed to turn tragedy into triumph by helping the average pet dog owner avoid making the many mistakes I had. Having learned the hard way, I felt that I could be helpful to those who were inclined to listen, and perhaps find ways of reaching those who were not.

For the past seven years I have been giving lectures and demonstrations on the school and scout circuit, using Punch as an enthusiastic and popular model, later adding her half-sister Beauty. I put emphasis on the dog as an animal, give an explanation of different breed groups and of basic dog psychology, and my dogs perform. I distribute reading material and answer questions.

For five years *Your Dog and You*, my column in our town's weekly paper, handled such subjects as Deserve to Be Your Dog's Best Friend, The Dog's Sex Drive, and There Is No Such Thing as a Harmless Dog, which won awards from the Dog Writers' Association of America. In early December I write letters to editors of all area newspapers about the Christmas-gift puppy, and I frequently utilize classified ads to call attention to helpful

Photographs by Mitch Dannenberg.

books I donate to the public library.

I became an advocate of the metal dog crate as a training tool as soon as I experienced its "magic." A crate gives the dog security and safety and the owner peace of mind. I have gradually acquired about thirty-five crates of various sizes (puppies always start off in a small one), which I rent out at fifty cents a week after providing careful instruction as to their proper use. Hundreds of pet owners, most of whom pictured the crate as a "cruel cage," have benefited from this rental program, the majority having gone on to purchase adult-size crates of their own.

The obedience-training classes I give for children are now in their sixth year, sponsored by our local Recreation Commission. Over two hundred youngsters have participated, the vast majority of whom would never have sought out an obedience class and whose dogs would never have been exposed to any structured training. A side-benefit, which I had not anticipated, has been that some children have been helped to overcome shyness or to curb impatience in order to gain a pet's successful cooperation.

As I watch all these children struggle, persist, and finally succeed, some with dogs that most adults would despair of ever training, I know that I am making a very real and lasting investment in the future.

When this course is standardized, I hope that other dog/child-oriented adults will teach it in their communities—I know that they will find it among the most rewarding projects they could ever undertake in the field of public education.

(For further information contact The Nicki Meyer Educational Effort, Meadow Ridge, 31 Davis Hill Road, Weston, CT 06883.)

Photograph of Nicki Meyer by Mitch Dannenberg

252

The Great Light in the Great Cave
by Rudyard Kipling

The way it may have been when the first dog came in from out of the cold.

Out in the Wet Wild Woods all the wild animals gathered together where they could see the light of the fire a long way off, and they wondered what it meant.

Then Wild Horse stamped with his wild foot and said, "O my Friends and O my Enemies, why have the Man and the Woman made that great light in that great Cave, and what harm will it do us?"

Wild dog lifted up his wild nose and smelled the smell of roast mutton, and said, "I will go up and see and look, and say; for I think it is good. Cat, come with me."

"Nenni!" said the Cat. "I am the Cat who walks by himself, and all places are alike to me. I will not come."

"Then we can never be friends again," said Wild Dog, and he trotted off to the Cave. But when he had gone a little way the Cat said to himself, "All places are alike to me. Why should I not go too and see and look and come away at my own liking." So he slipped after Wild Dog softly, very softly, and hid himself where he could hear everything.

When Wild Dog reached the mouth of the Cave, he lifted up the dried horse-skin with his nose and sniffed the beautiful smell of the roast mutton, and the Woman, looking at the bladebone, heard him, and laughed, and said, "Here comes the first Wild Thing out of the Wild Woods; what do you want?"

Wild Dog said, "O my Enemy and Wife of my Enemy, what is this that smells so good in the Wild Woods?"

Then the Woman picked up a roasted mutton-bone and threw it to Wild Dog, and said, "Wild Thing out of the Wild Woods, taste and try." Wild Dog gnawed the bone, and it was more delicious than anything he had ever tasted, and he said, "O my Enemy and Wife of my Enemy, give me another."

The Woman said, "Wild Thing out of the Wild Woods, help my Man to hunt through the day and guard this Cave at night, and I will give you as many roast bones as you need."

Edited and reprinted from the Just So Stories *by Rudyard Kipling (1902).*

Opposite photograph by Peter Simon

AKC BREEDS ILLUSTRATED

Sporting. *Breeds that scent, usually with nose held high, in pursuit of game. Many also track. Pointers, retrievers, and flushing dogs (spaniels) are included.*

IRISH SETTER

POINTER

VIZSLA

GERMAN SHORTHAIRED POINTER

IRISH WATER SPANIEL

WIREHAIRED POINTING GRIFFON

LABRADOR RETRIEVER

ENGLISH SPRINGER SPANIEL

FIELD SPANIEL

CLUMBER SPANIEL

AMERICAN WATER SPANIEL

GORDON SETTER

WEIMARANER

ENGLISH SETTER

CHESAPEAKE BAY RETRIEVER

FLAT-COATED RETRIEVER

GERMAN WIREHAIRED POINTER

GOLDEN RETRIEVER

CURLY-COATED RETRIEVER

SUSSEX SPANIEL

BRITTANY SPANIEL

WELSH SPRINGER SPANIEL

ENGLISH COCKER SPANIEL

COCKER SPANIEL

255

Hound. *Tracking hounds follow scent trails and gaze hounds hunt by sight. Gaze hounds are the fleetest of dogs.*

SCOTTISH DEERHOUND

AFGHAN HOUND

RHODESIAN RIDGEBACK

BLACK AND TAN COONHOUND

OTTERHOUND

ENGLISH FOXHOUND

WHIPPET

HARRIER

BEAGLE

BASSET HOUND

LONGHAIRED DACHSHUND

IRISH WOLFHOUND

BORZOI

GREYHOUND

SALUKI

BLOODHOUND

AMERICAN FOXHOUND

NORWEGIAN ELKHOUND

BASENJI

SMOOTH DACHSHUND

WIREHAIRED DACHSHUND

Working. *Dogs that herd, guard, protect, rescue, pull, and carry.*

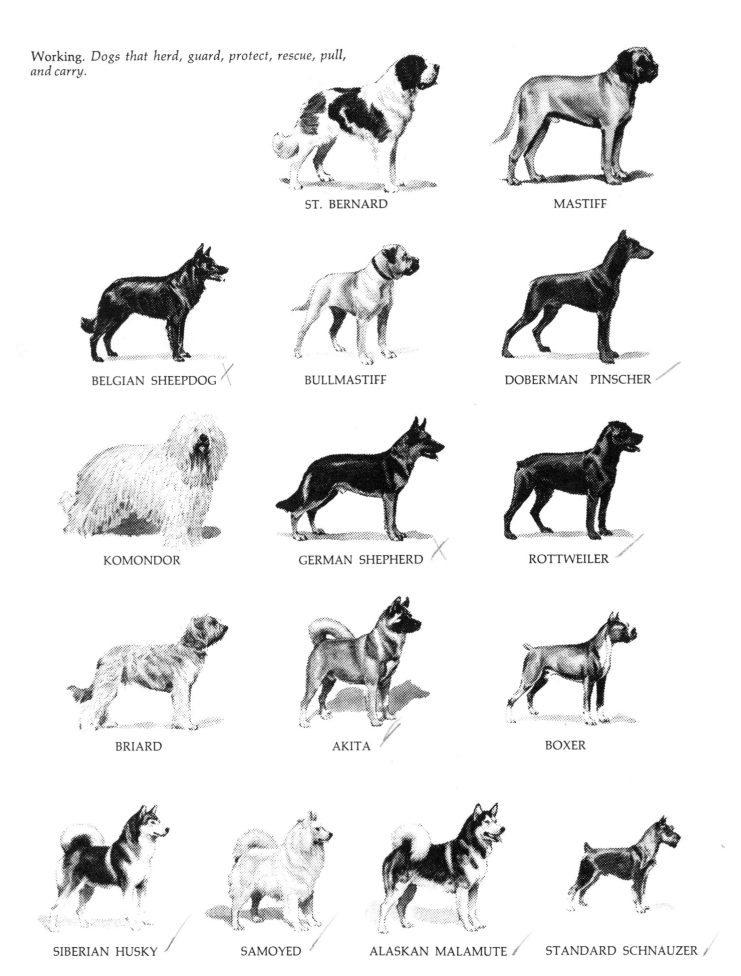

ST. BERNARD   MASTIFF

BELGIAN SHEEPDOG   BULLMASTIFF   DOBERMAN PINSCHER

KOMONDOR   GERMAN SHEPHERD   ROTTWEILER

BRIARD   AKITA   BOXER

SIBERIAN HUSKY   SAMOYED   ALASKAN MALAMUTE   STANDARD SCHNAUZER

GREAT DANE NEWFOUNDLAND GREAT PYRENEES

KUVASZ BOUVIER DES FLANDRES BERNESE MOUNTAIN DOG

COLLIE (ROUGH) COLLIE (SMOOTH) BEARDED COLLIE

GIANT SCHNAUZER OLD ENGLISH SHEEPDOG BELGIAN TERVUREN

PULI SHETLAND SHEEPDOG PEMBROKE WELSH CORGI CARDIGAN WELSH CORGI

259

Terrier. *The word derives from the Latin for earth,* terra. *The fox and the rat are chased into their dens, then flushed out for the hunter to kill in the case of the fox; rats are killed by the dogs.*

AIREDALE TERRIER

BULL TERRIER (WHITE)

AMERICAN STAFFORDSHIRE TERRIER

STAFFORDSHIRE BULL TERRIER

MANCHESTER TERRIER

FOX TERRIER (WIRE)

LAKELAND TERRIER

BORDER TERRIER

DANDIE DINMONT TERRIER

SEALYHAM TERRIER

WEST HIGHLAND WHITE TERRIER

KERRY BLUE TERRIER

IRISH TERRIER

SOFT-COATED WHEATEN TERRIER

FOX TERRIER (SMOOTH)

BEDLINGTON TERRIER

WELSH TERRIER

MINIATURE SCHNAUZER

CAIRN TERRIER

SCOTTISH TERRIER

AUSTRALIAN TERRIER

NORWICH TERRIER

SKYE TERRIER

261

Toy. Most are dwarfed or miniaturized versions of existing larger breeds. Some have been small for so long, however, that it is impossible to identify the parent stock from which they descend.

SHIH TZU   PAPILLON   JAPANESE SPANIEL

ENGLISH TOY SPANIEL   MINIATURE PINSCHER   PEKINGESE

POMERANIAN   YORKSHIRE TERRIER   SILKY TERRIER

BRUSSELS GRIFFON   PUG   ITALIAN GREYHOUND

TOY MANCHESTER TERRIER   AFFENPINSCHER   TOY POODLE

CHIHUAHUA (LONG COAT)   CHIHUAHUA (SMOOTH COAT)   MALTESE

Nonsporting. *Catchall classification for dogs that didn't fit well into one of the other groups because their original purpose in life is obscure or so remote that it's irrelevant.* (Photographically adapted from the Gaines Guide to America's Dogs wall chart with the permission of the Gaines Dog Research Center of General Foods Corp.)

CHOW CHOW

DALMATIAN

KEESHOND

STANDARD POODLE

BOSTON TERRIER

BULLDOG

TIBETAN TERRIER

BICHON FRISE

MINIATURE POODLE

FRENCH BULLDOG

SCHIPPERKE

LHASA APSO

Baron Wolman—writer, photographer, publisher, and dog lover—says: "Old Fritz liked nothing better than to show off his Olympic form by diving into the Russian River on command. And he never asked for a reward, no biscuit, nothing. He was just happy to do his act and bask in the applause and attention." (Photograph by Baron Wolman)

Books

A SELECT BIBLIOGRAPHY

BOOKS
BOOKLETS AND PAMPHLETS
ALL-BREED MAGAZINES
ALL-BREED NEWSPAPERS
CLUB NEWSLETTERS
FOREIGN PERIODICALS
SPORTING BREEDS
HOUND BREEDS
WORKING BREEDS
TERRIER BREEDS
TOY BREEDS
NONSPORTING BREEDS
MISCELLANEOUS BREEDS
DOG TRAINING
HUMANE SOCIETIES

American Kennel Club, *The Complete Dog Book*. Howell Book House, New York, 1975.

Andersen, Allen C., ed., *The Beagle as an Experimental Dog*. Iowa State University Press, Ames, IA, 1970.

Ash, Edward C., *Dogs: Their History and Development*. Benjamin Blom, New York, 1972. First published in London, 1927.

Attla, George, with Bella Levorsen, *Everything I Know About Training and Racing Sled Dogs*. Arner Publications, Rome, NY, 1974.

Beck, Alan, *The Ecology of Strays*. York Press, Baltimore, 1973.

Bishop, Robert, *The All-American Dog—Man's Best Friend in Folk Art*. Avon, New York, 1977.

Braund, Kathryn, *The Uncommon Dog Breeds*. Arco, New York, 1975.

Brown, William F. *How to Train Hunting Dogs*. A. S. Barnes, South Brunswick, NJ, 1942.

Buytendijk, F.J.J., *The Mind of the Dog*. Arno Press, New York, 1973. First published in 1936.

Christoph, Horst-Joachim, *Diseases of the Dog*. Pergamon, Elmsford, NY, 1975.

Clark, Kenneth, *Animals and Men*. William Morrow, New York, 1977.

Davis, Henry P., ed., *Modern Dog Encyclopedia*. Stackpole, Harrisburg, PA, 1956.

Elliot, Rachel Page, *Dogsteps*. Howell Book House, New York, 1973.

Ensminger, M. E., *The Complete Dog Book*. A. S. Barnes, South Brunswick, NJ, 1977.

Falk, John R., *The Practical Hunter's Dog Book*. Winchester, New York, 1971.

Fiennes, Richard, *The Order of Wolves*, Bobbs-Merrill, New York, 1976.

Fiennes, Richard and Alice, *The Natural History of Dogs*. Natural History Press, Garden City, NY, 1970.

Fiorone, Fiorenzo, *The Encyclopedia of Dogs*. Thomas Y. Crowell, New York, 1973.

Fox, Michael, *Understanding Your Dog*. Coward, McCann and Geoghegan, New York, 1972.

———, *The Wild Canids*. Van Nostrand Rheinhold, New York, 1975.

Free, James Lamb, *Training Your Retriever*. Coward, McCann and Geoghegan, New York, 1949.

Fuller, John L., and John Paul Scott, *Dog Behavior, The Genetic Basis*. University of Chicago Press, Chicago, 1965.

Grizmek, Bernard, ed., *Grizmek's Animal Life Encyclopedia*, volume 12. Van Nostrand Reinhold, New York, 1975.

Hooker, Jack, *The "Outsider's" Iditarod*. Ovando, MT, 1976.

Kirk, Robert W., ed., *Current Veterinary Therapy Small Animal Practice*. W. B. Saunders, Philadelphia, 1977.

Leach, Maria, *God Had a Dog*. Rutgers University Press, New Brunswick, NJ, 1961.

Little, Clarence C., *Inheritance of Coat Color in Dogs*. Howell Book House, New York, 1976. First published in 1957.

Lorenz, Konrad Z., *Man Meets Dog*. Penguin, Baltimore, 1953.

McGinnis, Terri, *Dog and Cat Good Food Book*. Taylor and NG, San Francisco, 1977.

Mech, L. David, *The Wolf: Ecology and Behavior of an Endangered Species*. Natural History Press, Garden City, NY, 1970.

Miller, Malcolm E., *Anatomy of The Dog*. W. B. Saunders, Philadelphia, 1964.

Pearsall, Margaret and Milo D., *The Pearsall Guide to Successful Dog Training*. Howell Book House, New York, 1973.

Pinkwater, Jill and D. Manus, *Superpuppy*. Seabury Press, New York, 1977.

Pinninger, R. S., ed., *Jones's Animal Nursing*. Pergamon, Elmsford, NY, 1976.

Riddle, Maxwell, *A Quick Guide to Standards for Show Dogs*. Doubleday, Garden City, NY, 1972.

———, *Your Show Dog*. Doubleday, Garden City, NY, 1968.

Rutter, R. J., and D. H. Pimlott, *The World of the Wolf*. Lippincott, Philadelphia, 1968.

Sinclair, Andrew, *Jack*. Harper & Row, New York, 1977.

Smythe, R. H., *The Breeding and Rearing of Dogs*. Arco, New York, 1969.

———, *The Dog, Structure and Movement*. Arco, New York, 1970.

Syrotuck, William G., *Scent and the Scenting Dog*. Arner, Rome, NY, 1972.

van Lawick-Goodall, Hugo and Jane, *Innocent Killers*.

Houghton Mifflin, Boston, 1970.

Winge, Ojvind, *Inheritance in Dogs*. Comstock, Ithaca, NY, 1950.

Booklets and Pamphlets

American Humane Association, *Catalog of Publications and Materials*

American Kennel Club, *AKC Special Registry Services for Imported and Domestic Dogs, Guide for Bench Show and Obedience Trial Committees in Dealing with Misconduct at Dog Shows and Obedience Trials, Guidelines for Dog Show Judges, Obedience Regulations, Regulations for Junior Showmanship, Rules Applying to Registration and Dog Shows*

American Society for the Prevention of Cruelty to Animals, *Henry Bergh, Founder of the ASPCA*

Federal Register, Department of Agriculture, *Animal Welfare: Definition and Terms*

Gaines and the College of Veterinary Medicine, the Ohio State University, *Papers Presented at the 26th Gaines Veterinary Symposium*

Gaines, *Training a Herd Dog*

Iditarod Racing Committee, *The Iditarod Runner*

International Sled Dog Racing Association, *Sled Dog Racing*

Murie, Adolph, *The Wolves of Mt. McKinley*, United States Department of the Interior, Fauna Series, Number 5

Nabisco, *Dental Care of Dogs*

National Academy of Sciences, *Nutrient Requirements of Dogs, No. 8*

National Shooting Sports Foundation, *Catalog of Publications*

Pet Finders, *What to Do When You Lose Your Pet*

Ralston Purina, *Obedience Trials*

State of New York, Department of Agriculture and Markets, *Circular 930 Relating to Licensing of Dogs and Protection of Domestic Animals Therefrom; Circular 916, Law Relating to Cruelty to Animals*

United States Department of Agriculture, Animal Welfare Enforcement, *Report of the Secretary of Agriculture to the President of the Senate and the Speaker of the House of Representatives*

All-Breed Magazines

Bloodlines
321 West Cedar St.
Kalamazoo, MI 49006

Dogs
257 Park Ave., South
New York, NY 10010

Dogs in Canada (annual)
59 Front St., East
Toronto, Ontario M5E1B3

Dog World
10060 West Roosevelt Rd.
Westchester, IL 50153

Hawaiian Dog Review
P.O. Box 1012
Flagstaff, AZ 86001

Kennel Review
828 N. La Brea Ave.
Hollywood, CA 90038

Pure-bred Dogs—American Kennel Gazette
51 Madison Ave.
New York, NY 10010

Show Dogs
257 Park Ave., South
New York, NY 10010

All-Breed Newspapers

Canine Chronicle
P.O. Box 627
Hartford City, IN 47348

Canine Graphic
P.O. Box 38
Avon-by-the-Sea, NJ 07717

Dogs in Canada
59 Front St., East
Toronto, Ontario M5E1B3

From the Kennels
P.O. Box 1201
Vancouver, WA 98660

LI Dogs
P.O. Box 68
East Northport, NY 11731

The Southern Dog Advertiser
P.O. Box 75
Roswell, GA 30077

Club Newsletters

Barker
463 Wicks Rd.
Brentwood, NY 11717

The Barker
1841 Hotel Rd., RD 4, Box 1
Auburn, ME 04210

Beo News
P.O. Box 1614
Lumberton, NC 28358

The Bow Wow
12558 M 89
Plainwell, MI 49080

Canine Captions
P.O. Box 11659
Philadelphia, PA 19116

Canine Currier
Box 719
Sioux Falls, SD 57101

Dogs of Orange Empire
2623 N. Rosemead Blvd.
So. El Monte, CA 91733

Fondy Flea Flicker
2014 Ct. V, Rt. 3
Fond du Lac, WI

Paw Prints
1420 Antares Dr.
Idaho Falls, ID 83401

Paws for News
P.O. Box 388
Ozark, AL 36360

Puddles & Piles
64 W. Ohio St.
Chicago, IL 60610

Rochester MN Kennel Club Newsletter
3000 36 Ave., SE
Rochester, MN 55901

Sand & Sea Kennel Club Newsletter
285 Clearstream Rd.
Jackson, NJ 08527

S.A.V.K.C. Bulletin
1241 Mc Leod St.
Garden Grove, CA 92640

Scooper
7611 State Highway 69, Rt. 2
Belleville, WI 53508

Tailwaggers
2411 Mockingbird Lane
Baytown, TX 77520

Foreign Periodicals

Australia . . . .

The Australasian Kennel Review and Dog News
2 Dale St.
Brookvale, N.S.W. 2100
Australia

R. A. S. Kennel Control Journal
Showground, Driver Ave.
Paddington, N.S.W. 2021
Australia

The Kennel Control Council Kennel Gazette
Royal Show Grounds,
Epsom Rd.
Ascot Vale, 3032,
Victoria, Australia

Austria. . . . .

Unsere Hunde
1070 Wien 7
Karl-Schweighofer-Gasse 3,
Austria

Belgium . . . .

WOEF
Korte Nieuwstraat 26
2000 Antwerpen, Belgium

Denmark . . . .

Hunden
Parkvej 1, Jersie Strand
2680 Solrød Strand, Denmark

England . . . .

Dog World
32 New St.
Ashford, Kent, England

Kennel Gazette
1 Clarges St., Piccadilly
London, W1Y 8 AB England

Our Dogs
5 Oxford Rd. Station Approach
Manchester M160 ISX, England

Finland . . . .

Koiramme Vara Hundar
Bulevardi 14 00120
Helsinki 12, Finland

France . . . .

Revue Officielle de la Cynophilie Française
215 Rue Saint Denis
75083 Paris, France

Germany . . . .

Unser Rassehund
46 Dortmund 1, Postfach 1390
Mallinckrodstrasse 26,
West Germany

Holland . . . .

De Hondenwereld
Emmalaan 16
Amsterdam-Zuid, Netherlands

India . . . .

Indian Kennel Gazette
Coonoor 1
Dist. Nilgiris, S. India

Italy . . . .

I Nostri Cani
21 Viale Premuda
20129 Milan, Italy

Japan . . . .

The Companion Dog
#1–5, Kanda-Sudacho
Chiyoba-ku, Tokyo, Japan
The Friends of Dog
#5, 1 Chome,
Nishikicho, Kanda
Chiyoba-ku, Tokyo, Japan

Mexico . . . .

*Boletin Club Canofilo de
Jalisco, A.C.*
Av. Vallarta 1835–20
Guadalajara, Jalisco, Mexico

New Zealand . . . .

New Zealand Kennel Gazette
P.O. Box 19101
Wellington, New Zealand

Norway . . . .

Hundesport
Bjorn Farmanns Gate 16
Oslo 2, Norway

Singapore . . . .

Dog Talk
Suite 275-F, 6th Floor
Selegie Complex, Selegie Rd.
Singapore 7

South Africa . . . .

Kennel Union Gazette
P.O. Box 562
Cape Town, South Africa

Sweden . . . .

Hundsport
Box 1308
111 83 Stockholm, Sweden

Switzerland . . . .

Schweizer Hundesport
Wildparkstrasse 253
4656 Wil-Starrkirch,
SO Switzerland

Sporting Breeds

American Field
222 W. Adams St.
Chicago, IL 60606
*The Chase; A Full Cry of
Hunting*
1140 Industry Rd.
Lexington, KY 40505

Pointers (German
shorthaired) . . . .

*German Shorthaired Pointer
News.*
Box 850
St. Paris, OH 43072

Pointers (German
wirehaired) . . . .

Sea-Tac Wire
9713–112 N.E.
Kirkland, WA 98033

Retrievers . . . .

Retriever Field Trial News
4213 S. Howell Ave.
Milwaukee, WI 53207

Retrievers (Chesapeake
Bay) . . . .

*The American Chesapeake Club
Bulletin**
5646 Rotary Rd.
Cherry Valley, IL 61016

Retrievers (Flat-coated) . . . . .

*Flat-Coated Retriever Society of
America Newsletter*
747 West Briarwood Ave.
Littleton, CO 80120

Retrievers (golden) . . . .

Do-Line
770 Alpine Dr.
Hamilton, OH 45013
Golden Gems
4579 Coronado Ave.
San Diego, CA 92107
*The Golden Retriever News**
8918 Westminster Dr.
Indianapolis, IN 46256
Golden Retrievings
6225 S. Old 3C Highway
Westerville, OH 43081
The Link
15 W. Cabot Lane
Westbury, NY 11590

Retrievers (Labrador) . . . .

The Potomac Labrador
606 Vierling Dr.
Silver Spring, MD 20904

English setters . . . .

*English Setter Association of
America Newsletter**
5618 Patrick St., S.W.
Canton, OH 44706

*A Publication of the parent breed club.

Gordon setters . . . .

*Gordon Setter News**
R. 2, Box 83B
Pekin, IL 61554

Irish setters . . . .

*Greater Columbus Irish Setter
Association Newsletter*
314 Delaware Dr.
Westerville, OH 43081

Irish Setter Reflections
8454 Whelan Dr.
San Diego, CA 92119

*Memo to Members**
Roxiticus Rd.
Mendham, NJ 07945

News and Views
13225 E. Old U.S. 12
Chelsea, MI 48118

Red Waggins
12987 Findlay Way
Apple Valley, MN 55124

Tails To Be Red
7574 Honey Ct.
Dublin, CA 94566

The Setter Letter
5868 S. Logan St.
Littleton, CO 80121

The Type-Setter
1325 W. Kimberly
Davenport, IA 52806

Touch O'Blarney
25 E. Magnolia Ave.
Maywood, NJ 07607

Spaniels (Brittany) . . . .

*The American Brittany**
4124 Birchman
Fort Worth, TX 76107

Hound Breeds

Field Advisory News
3378 West Griffin Creek Rd.
Medford, OR 97501
The Gazehound
16258 Lovett Place
Encino, CA 91436
Lure Coursing News
3719 Grove Ave.
Palo Alto, CA 94303

Afghan hounds . . . .

The Newshound
88 Franklin Ave.
Fairview, NJ 07022
*Newsletter of the Finger Lakes
Afghan Hound Club*
33 Trowbridge Tr.
Pittsford, NY 14534

Basenjis . . . .

The Bark
668 Pronto Dr.
San Jose, CA 95123

Spaniels (clumber) . . . .

*Clumber Spaniel Club of
America Bulletin**
6295 Sonoma Hwy.
Santa Rosa, CA 94947

Spaniels (cocker) . . . .

The American Cocker Review
202 South Clovis Ave.
Fresno, CA 93727
Cocker Spaniel Leader
9700 Jersey Mill Rd., NW, Rt. 2
Patashala, OH 43062
Cocker Tales
1638 Heron Dr.
Sunnyvale, CA 94087

Spaniels (English cocker) . . . .

*The ECSCA Review**
P.O. Box 223
Hales Corners, WI 53130

Spaniels (English springer) . . .

Springer Bark
14023 Aurora Dr.
San Leandro, CA 94577

Vizsla . . . .

The Bulletin
2108 Pullman Lane
Redondo Beach, CA 90278
Bulletin
461 W. Forrest Preserve Dr.
Wood Dale, IL 60191
*The Vizsla News**
11031 Aqua Vista St.
North Hollywood, CA 91602

Weimaraners . . . .

*The Weimaraner Magazine**
P.O. Box 6086,
Heatherdowns Sta.
Toledo, OH 43614

The Basenji
935 42nd Ave. North
St. Petersburg, FL 33703

Basset hounds . . . .

The Acorn
1862 Litchfield Tpke.
Woodbridge, CT 06525
Basset Babbler
121 East Francis Ave.
Louisville, KY 40214
Long Eared News
3591 Louis Rd.
Palo Alto, CA 94303
*Tally-Ho**
Rt. 1, Box 59
Roanoke, TX 76262

Beagles . . . .

Beagle Call Rag
23245 Hutchinson Rd.
Los Gatos, CA 95030

Hounds and Hunting
Box 372
Bradford, PA 16701
National Beagling News
P.O. Box 2805
Muncie, IN 47302

Borzoi . . . .
Borzoi Newsletter
37579 Mission Blvd.
Fremont, CA 94536

Coonhounds . . . .
CoonHound Bloodlines
321 West Cedar St.
Kalamazoo, MI 49006
Full Cry
Box 190
Sedalia, MO 65301

Dachshunds . . . .
The American Dachshund
15011 Oak Creek Rd.
El Cajon, CA 92021
*American Miniature Dachshund
Association News**
1215 40th Ave. NE
Columbia Heights, MN 55421
Dachshund Variety
1657 Del Dayo Dr.
Carmichael, CA 95608

Greyhounds . . . .
The Greyhound Racing Record
Box 450130
Miami, Florida 33145

Irish wolfhounds . . . .
*Harp & Hound**
Rte. 2, Box 181
Prospect, KY 40059

The Erin Hound Page
10 S. 216 Springbrook Dr.
Naperville, IL 60540
*Locust Grove Irish Wolfhound
Association Newsletter*
12400 Hobart Rd.
Palos Park, IL 60464

Norwegian elkhounds . . . . . .
Elkhound Paw-Prints
51–24 Garden View Terrace
East Windsor, NJ 08520

Rhodesian ridgebacks . . . . . .
*Rhodesian Ridgeback News**
R.D. #1, Box 520
Dover, NJ 07801

Salukis . . . .
The Oasis
Box 679
Far Hills, NJ 07931
*Saluki Club of America
Newsletter**
R.D. #1, Box 12
Neshanic, NJ 08853

Saluki World
1110 Park Ave.
New York, NY 10028
*American Saluki Association
Newsletter*
P.O. Box 306
Alpaugh, CA 93201

Scottish deerhounds . . . .
*The Deerhound Newsletter**
Deerhound Digs Farms, Reg.
Lincoln, CA 95648

Working Breeds

The World of the Working Dog
P.O. Box 205, 1 Hoffman St.
Spring Valley, NY 10977
Team & Trail
Center Harbor, NH 03266

Akitas . . . .
*Akita Club of America
Magazine**
W. 5418 Garden Springs Rd.
Spokane, WA 99204
*Akita Club of Greater Los
Angeles Newsletter*
1509 W. 213th St.
Torrence, CA 90501
Akita News
285 Clearstream Rd.
Jackson, NJ 08527
The Akita Journal
One Pomegranate Rd.
Rancho Palos Verdes, CA 90274
Cascade Akita Club Newsletter
331 Monroe
Eugene, OR 97402
Dialdo Valley Akita Fanciers
5421 Brookdale Ave.
Oakland, CA 94619

Bearded collies . . . .
*BCCA Newsletter**
Parchment Farm
RR 1, Box 41A
Unionville, IN 47468
Beardie Tales
815 Corona Court
Round Lake Beach, IL 60073
*The Beardie Bulletin**
1526 Massachusetts Ave.
Boxborough, MA 01719

Belgian sheepdogs . . . .
The Blackmail
6325 Emerald St.
Alta Loma, CA 91701
*National Belgian Newsletter**
RR 1
Simpson, IL 62985

Bernese mountain dog . . . . . .
*The Bernese Mountain Dog
Club of America Newsletter**
58 Bellwood Rd.
White Plains, NY 10603

Boxers . . . .
Boxer Banter
1789 Pacific Ave.
Corona, CA 91720
The Boxer Review
8760 Appian Way
Los Angeles, CA 90046
Boxers Incorporated
3074 Trinity Dr.
Costa Mesa, CA 92626
*New Jersey Boxer Club
Newsletter*
R.D. 2, Box 496
Flemington, NJ 08822

Briards . . . .
*The Dew Claw**
3030 Rockwood Dr.
Fort Wayne, IN 46805

Bull mastiffs . . . .
The American Bullmastiff
Box 330
Syracuse, NY 13201
*Bullmastiff Bulletin**
250 Bay Ave.
Huntington, NY 11743
Bullmastiffs West Newsletter
5798 Beach St.
Riverside, CA 95209
The Bullsheet
Nabby Hill
Mohegan Lake, NY 10547

Collies . . . .
Collie Call
3 Aberdeen Rd.
Westbury, NY 11590
Paw Prints
5812-L Royal Ridge Rd.
Springfield, VA 22152
*The Smooth Colliers**
20350 Armada Ridge, MI 48005
The White Collie Club News
C/O Anjo's Collies
30 N. Highway 59
Barrington, IL 60010

Doberman Pinschers . . . .
Dobie Tracks
P.O. Box 3794
Anaheim, CA 92800
Top Dobe
P.O. Box 205
Spring Valley, NY 10977

German shepherd . . . .
*The German Shepherd Dog
Review**
P.O. Box 1221
Lancaster, PA 17604
*The German Shepherd Dog
Gazette*
8532 Vinevalley Dr.
Sun Valley, CA 91352
Kalifornia News
4456 N. Earle Ave.
Rosemead, CA 91770
The Kensington Educator
3915 N. Latson Rd., Rt. 1
Howell, MI 48843

Northwest Shepherd News
11054 S.E. 192nd
Renton, WA 98055
Paw Prints
15921 Smithey Dr.
Haymarket, VA 22069
The Roadrunner
855 S. Sidney
Tucson, AZ 85711
The Shepherd Pad
573 C. Briarwood Ave.
West Islip, NY 11795
Shepherd Speaks
1522 Langlade
Green Bay, WI 54304
Suncoast Shepherd News
1189 Edgeknoll Dr.
Riverview, FL 33569

Giant schnauzers . . . .
*Giant Steps**
735 Lloyd
Madison Heights, MI 48071

Great Danes . . . .
Dane Dispatch
P.O. Box 7759
San Francisco, CA 94120
Dane Tales of San Diego
8264 Wintergardens Blvd.
Lakeside, CA 92040
*Great Dane Club of Hawaii
Newsletter*
1257 Aloheoe Dr.
Kailua, HI 96734
Great Dane International
10022 Melody Park Dr.
Garden Grove, CA 90630
The Great Dane Reporter
803 North Sweetzer Ave.
Los Angeles, CA 90063

Great Pyrenees . . . .
Pyr News and Notes
853 Garland Dr.
Palo Alto, CA 94303

Komodors . . . .
*Komondor Komments**
19900 Hiawatha St.
Chatsworth, CA 91311
Komondor News
102 Russell Rd.
Princeton, NJ 08540

Kuvasz . . . .
*Kuvasz Newsletter**
18 South Terrace Ave.
Mt. Vernon, NY 10550

Mastiffs . . . .
*Mastiff Club of America
Newsletter**
867 Queen Anne Rd.
Teaneck, NJ 07666

Old English sheepdogs . . . . . .
Old English Dispatch
P.O. Box 7759
San Francisco, CA 94120

*Old English Times**
4936 Crownover Dr.
St. Louis, MO 63128
The Shaggy Dogs Bark
2500 Catalina Way
Irving, TX 75061

Puli . . . .

Pulikeynotes
2617 Lakewood Ave.
Los Angeles, CA 90039
*Puli News**
2719 Overland Ave.
Los Angeles, CA 90064
Puli Parade Newsletter
4351 Stonehedge Way
Sacramento, CA 95824

Rottweilers . . . .

*Colonial Rottweiler Club
Newsletter*
Old York Rd., RD #2
Burlington, NJ 08016
*Golden State Rottweiler Club
Newsletter*
P.O. Box 423
Manhattan Beach, CA 90266
*Medallion Rottweiler Club
Newsletter*
2N600 Fair Oaks Rd.
West Chicago, IL 60185
*Orange Coast Rottweiler Club
Newsletter*
1203 N. Groton St.
Anaheim, CA 92803

St. Bernards . . . .

The Desert Saint
P.O. Box 9357
Phoenix, AZ 85068
The Monk's Guide
P.O. Box 78388
Seattle, WA 98178
Pacific Tails
15244 Arnold Dr.
Glen Allen, CA 95442
The Paw Print
9020 Link
Overland, MO 63114
Saintly Affairs
517 Spruce St.
Madison, WI 53715
Saints and Sinners
9725 N.E. 2nd St.
Midwest City, OK 73110
Saints-in-Ati
337 N. Monroe St.
Xenia, OH 45385
Saints of '76
959 Akumu St.
Kailua, Oahu, HI 96734
The Saint's Tale
713 Chinn Chapel Rd.
Lewisville, TX 75067
The Standards
P.O. Box 314
The Woodlands, TX 77373
True Saint
423 Rose Arbor Lane
Houston, TX 77060

Samoyeds . . . .

Howls n' Growls
R. 1, Box 176
Waldo, WI 53093
*Samoyed Club of America
Bulletin**
3969 Weber Rd.
St. Louis, MO 63123

Shetland sheepdogs . . . .

*Bulletin Board**
Rt. 5, Box 1375
Fredericksburg, VA 22401
*Bulletin of the Shetland
Sheepdog Club of
Greater San Diego*
7638 Topaz Lake Ave.
San Diego, CA 92119
The Colorado Sheltie
1749 S. Dallas
Denver, CO 80231
*The Dallas Shetland Sheepdog
Club Newsletter*
5916 Meadowcreek Dr.
Dallas, TX 75243
*The Des Moines Shetland
Sheepdog Club Newsletter*
6892 S.E. Vandalia Rd.
R 2, Runnells, IA 50237
The Pooper Scooper
Rt. 3
Allegan, MI 49010
The Sheltie Special
P.O. Box 2008
Menlo Park, CA 94025
Sheltie Sunshine
11745 Ave. 416
Orosa, CA 93647
Shetland Islander
6 Sutton Place
Ronkonkoma, NY 11779

Siberian Huskies . . . .

*Greater Washington Siberian
Husky Club Newsletter*
1404 California St.
Woodbridge, VA 22191
Lead and Line
473 Chambers St.
Spencerport, NY 14559
*Siberian Husky Club of
America Newsletter**
227 Middle Rd.
West Newbury, MA 01985
Siberian Husky News
P.O. Box 5195
Terre Haute, IN 47805

Standard schnauzers . . . .

*Pepper N Salt**
Rt. 2
Bloomington, IL 61701
The Wiretap
4812 Willet Dr.
Annandale, VA 22003

Cardigan Welsh corgis . . . . .

Cardi Tales
9201 Kenwood Dr.
Spring Valley, CA 92077
*The Cardigan News-Bulletin**
11605 Waples Hill Rd.
Oakton, VA 22124

Terrier Breeds

Terrier Type
Post Office Drawer A
La Honda, CA 94020

American Staffordshire
Terriers . . . .

*American Staffordshire Terrier
Association for Fanciers
Newsletter**
5714 Swiss Ave.
Dallas, TX 75214

Bull terriers . . . .

*Barks**
12885 S.E. Bobby Bruce Lane
Boring, OR 97009
The Bull Terrier Breeder
1010½ Michigan Ave.
Evanston, IL 60202
*The B.T.C.A. Record**
11 Walnut St.
Farmingdale, NJ 07727

Cairn terriers . . . .

Cairn Chatter
116 North Waterman
Arlington Heights, IL 60004

Fox terriers . . . .

*The Newsletter**
2811 Hopkinson House
Philadelphia, PA 19106
Gay Tales
2124 Richmond Ave.
Granite City, IL 62040

Kerry blue terriers . . . .

*Kerry Blueprints**
1021 N. Sierra Vista Dr.
La Habra, CA 90631

Manchester terriers . . . .

*Newsletter of the American
Manchester Club**
1828 E. Orange Grove Bl.
Pasadena, CA 91104

Toy Breeds

Chihuahuas . . . .

Los Chihuahuas
Rt. 2, Box 812
Dover, FL 33527

Pembroke Welsh corgis . . . . . .

*Newsletter of the Golden Gate
Pembroke Welsh Corgi Fanciers*
1255 Hamilton Ave.
San Francisco, CA

Miniature schnauzers . . . . . .

Schnauzer Shorts
P.O. Drawer A
La Honda, CA 94020

Norwich terriers . . . .

*The Norwich Terrier News**
R.F.D. 1, Box 156
Bethlehem, CT 06751

Scottish terriers . . . .

Scottie Talk
2102 Marsh Rd.
Wilmington, DE 19810
Scottie Times
1441 Montak Ave. #2108
Jacksonville, FL 32210

Skye terriers . . . .

*The Bulletin**
8217 Warfield Rd.
Gaithersburg, MD 20760

Soft-coated wheaten
terriers . . . .

*Benchmarks**
511 Church Rd.
Hatfield, PA 19440
Wags & Brags
854 Downing Rd.
Valley Stream, NY 11580

Staffordshire bull terriers . . . .

*Staff Status**
22 Packet Rd.
Rancho Palos Verdes, CA 90274

West Highland white
terriers . . . .

Wags
2606 Crossgates Dr.
Crossgates
Wilmington, DE 19808
West Highland Highlights
1524 N. King George Ct.
Palatine, IL 60067

Italian greyhounds . . . .

The Italian Greyhound
1816 Doric Dr.
Tallahasse, FL 32303

Japanese spaniels . . . .

Chin Chit Chat*
21 Disney Dr.
Toms River, NJ 08753

Maltese . . . .

Lapsitter News
11553 Coral Hills Dr.
Dallas, TX 75229

Papillons . . . .

The Cocoon
Rt. 3, Box 210 C
Algonquin, IL 90102

Pekingese . . . .

Pekingese News
P.O. Box 5195
Terre Haute, IN 47805
Pilgrim Pekingese Fanciers
Newsletter
20 Marshall St.
Brookline, MA 02146

Poodles . . . .

Journal of the Hub Poodle Club
of Orange County
5642 Peabody St.
Long Beach, CA 90808

The Poodle Review
26 Commerce St.
New York, NY 10014
Our Poodle
12003 Kagel Canyon Rd.
San Fernando, CA 91342

Pugs . . . .

Pug Talk
1803 Hillburn Dr.
Dallas, TX 75217

Shih Tzu . . . .

Shih Tzu Bulletin*
385 Solano Prado
Coral Gables, FL 33156
Shih Tzu International
P.O. Box 1654
Tacoma, WA 98401
Shih Tzu News
P.O. Box 5195
Terre Haute, IN 47805

Silky terriers . . . .

Capital Byline
1611 Heather Hts. Rd.
Sykesville, MD 21784
Silky Terrier Club of America
Newsletter*
1605 Carney Ave.
Rockford, IL 61103

Nonsporting Breeds

Bichons Frises . . . .

Bichon Dispatch
P.O. Box 7759
San Francisco, CA 94120
Bichon Frise News
P.O. Box 5195
Terre Haute, IN 47805

Bulldogs . . . .

Bullcraps
3217 West Charleston Blvd.
Las Vegas, NV 89102
The Bulldogger*
45 Carolane Trail
Houston, TX 77024

Chow Chows . . . .

Chow Chatter
P.O. Box 1666
Anthony, NM 88021
The Oriental Express
1807 England Court
Arlington, TX 76013

Dalmatians . . . .
Dal Tales
72 Cypress Ave.
Oceanside, NY 11572
Spot-Lite
402 S. Henderson #11
Bloomington, IN 47401
The Spotter*
N54 W26326 Lisbon Rd.
Sussex, WI 53098

French bulldogs . . . .

The Frenchie Fancier
75417 W 164th Place
Tinley Park, IL 60477

Keeshond . . . .

Kee Topics
14 Cumana St.
Toms River, NJ 08753

Lhasa Apsos . . . .

Dorje
2264 Creston Ave.
New York, NY 10453
Lacogny News
3081 Edwin Ave.
Fort Lee, NJ 07024
The Lhasa Bulletin*
1862 West Maple Ave.
Langhorne, PA 19047
The Lhasa Apso Reporter
4125 La Salle Ave.
Culver City, CA 90230

Tibetan terriers . . . .

The Journal of the Tibetan
Terrier Club of America*
12215 Devilwood Dr.
Potomac, MD 20854
Tibetan Terrier Club of Greater
New York Area Newsletter
6 Yellow Pine
Middletown, CT 06457

Miscellaneous Breeds

Long Island Rare Breed
Association Newsletter
111 New York Ave.
Smithtown, NY 11787
The National Stock Dog
Magazine
Rt. 1
Butler, IN 46721
Stodghill's Animal Research
Magazine
Quinlan, TX 75474
Australian cattle dog . . . .
AuCaDo News
443 Bell St.
E. Palo Alto, CA 94303
Cattle Dog Catalogue
Beaver Island, Box 56
St. James, MI 49782
Border collies . . . .
Border Collie News
R.F.D. #2
Durham, NH 03824
The Canaan dog . . . .
The Canaan Kibitzer*
521 Whispering Pine Court
Naples, FL 33940

Chinese Crested . . . .
The Chinese Crested Courier*
43 Melvin Rd.
Arlington, MA 02174

Ibizan Hounds . . . .
The Third Eye
133 W. Lanvale St.
Baltimore, MD 21217

Pharaoh Hound . . . .
Hieroglyphics*
3 Ivy Place
Huntington, NY 11743
Pharaoh Phancy
23355 Califa St.
Woodland Hills, CA 91364

Swiss mountain dog . . . .
Greater Swiss Mountain Dog
Club of America Newsletter*
Carinthia, Rt. 3 (6210N 700E)
Lafayette, IN 47905

Xoloitzcuintli . . . .
American Hairless Dog Club
Journal
755 Center St.
Hanover, MA 02339

Dog Training

Canine Capers ·
1720 Virginia Court
Lakeland, FL 33803
Canine Post
3611 43rd Ave., W.
Seattle, WA 98199
Council Fires
Southern California Dog
Obedience Council
206 Bellino Dr.
Pacific Palisades, CA 90272
Dog Tales
20 Steeplehill Lane
Ballwin, MO 63011
Dog Tracks
22235 Parthenia St.
Canoga Park, CA 91304
Front and Finish; The Dog
Trainers News
113 S. Arthur Ave.
Galesburg, IL 61401
(Dog Training Newspaper)
"Heel, You Say"
4101 East Michigan St.
Indianapolis, IN 46201
Hotline
2002 Seamist Court
Houston, TX 77008

No Bones
4275 West 188th St.
Country Club Hills, IL 60477
Obichaff
#5 Froude Circle
Cabin John, MD 20731
OCOTC Courier
2412 N.W. 110th
Oklahoma City, OK 73120
Off-Lead
P.O. Box 307, Graves Rd.
Westmoreland, NY 13490
Paw Power
P.O. Box 5502
Oxnard, CA 93030
The Recall
4948 F. Nimtz Rd.
Rockford, IL 61111
Sit 'N' Stay
46 Cooper Lane
Larchmont, NY 10538
Tales
P.O. Box 4932
Walnut Creek, CA 94596
WDA Trainer—
Working Dogs of America
1164 Wall Rd.
Webster, NY 14580

Humane Societies

Animals; the Magazine for
Animal Lovers
350 South Huntington Ave.
Boston, MA 02130

ASPCA Bulletin
441 East 92nd St.
New York, NY 10028

American Humane Magazine
3531 S. Roslyn St.
Englewood, CO 80110

Animal Shelter Shoptalk; the
Trade Magazine for Animal
Care Personnel
P.O. Box 1266
Denver, CO 80201
The National Humane Review
5351 S. Roslyn St.
Englewood, CO 80110
Our Fourfooted Friends
10 Chandler St.
Boston, MA 02116

INDEX

Abruzzo National Park, 84
A Coney Island of the Mind
   (Ferlinghetti), 157
Actors and Others for Animals
   (Beverly Hills), 164
Acupuncture, 164
Adam of the Road (Grey), 179
Adrian, C., photograph by, 87
Adventures of Tom Sawyer (Twain),
   175
Advertising, dogs in, 197–99
Aesop, fables of, 37, 85, 122, 169, 187,
   238
Affenpinscher, illustration of, 262
Afghan hound
   illustration of, 256
   photographs of, 92, 94, 30
   representative of hound group, 30
Afontova-Gora II, 235
Airedale terrier, 117
   illustration of, 260
AKC
   breed groups, illustration, 22
   field trial categories, 126
   literature, photograph of, 21
   obedience trial rules, 33
   recognized breeds, illustrations,
      254–63
   registration with, 17, 18, 23
   sanctioned match shows, 98
   scope and history of, 21–22
Akita, illustration of, 258
Alaska Magazine, 131
Alaskan malamute, illustration of, 258
Alexander (the Great), 175
All About Dogs (Gaines), 117
All About Small Dogs in the Big City
   (Seranne), 26
"All-American Dog—Man's Best
   Friend in Folk Art" (Exhibition),
   illustrations from, 182–86
Allergies, 229
Alpo, 53–54
Alsatian, 117
American Dog Book (Unkelback), 25
American Field, The, 121
American fox hound, 125
   illustration of, 257
American Humane Association, 249
American Indian myth, 13
American Kennel Club. *See* AKC
American pit bull terrier, photograph
   of, 2
American Society for the Prevention
   of Cruelty to Animals. *See* ASPCA
American Staffordshire terrier,
   illustration of, 260
American water spaniel, illustration
   of, 254
Angus books: *Angus and the Cat,
   Angus and the Ducks,
   Angus Lost* (Flock), 178

Animal Care Staff, 249
Animal Research Foundation, 116
Animal Research Magazine, 137
Animals and Men (Clark), 200
Animal Welfare Act, Amendments
   of 1976, 133, 135
Animal Welfare Encyclopedia (Ford),
   249
Annie, 168
Anthropomorphism, 175
Anubis, 170
Apennine wolf, 84
Ardine, Judith K., photograph by, 87
Argus, 172, 174
Arsenic, 221
Arthur (King), 175
Artificial insemination, 231
Ascaris, 222
Ash, definition of in dog food, 59
ASPCA, 248
Asta (fox terrier), 210, 212
   photograph with William Powell
      and Myrna Loy, 165
Australian shepherd, photographs of,
   136, 144
Australian Shepherd Club of America,
   144
Australian terrier, illustration of, 261
Avoidance training, 148
Aylings, Nan, 73

Baines, Art, 98
Barkalotte, Bernardo (film star), 162
Barrett, Elizabeth, 158, 159
Basenji, illustration of, 257
Basset hound, 122
   illustration of, 256
Beagle, 122
   in *Hunting Symphony*, 171
   illustration of, 256
Beagle as an Experimental Dog
   (Andersen), 231
Bearded Collie, illustration of, 259
Bear Garden, 134–35
Beckmann, Ed, director of Problem
   Puppy School
   dog training advice, 38–41
   on dog tricks, 42n
   photographs of, 19, 39
Bedlington terrier, 117
   illustration of, 261
Beds, 61, 66
   instructions to build your own, 66
Beesley, Alec, photograph by, 163
Belgian sheepdogs
   illustration of, 258
   in police work, 149
Belgian tuvuren, illustration of, 259
Bench shows, 112
Benji (film star), 87, 162
Benz-O-Matic fogger, 225
Bergh, Henry, 248
Berloni, William, trainer of Sandy, 168
Bernese mountain dog, illustration of,
   259
Best Friend (Feeley), 171

Best in Show, 115
Best of Breed, 115
Bichon frise, illustration of, 263
Bites, how to avoid, 27
Bivin, Edd Embry (judge), photograph
   of, 110
Black-and-tan coonhound, 122
   illustration of, 256
Blair, Bob (dog trainer), 163
Blenheim spaniels, 85
Bloodhound, 153
   illustration of, 257
Blue eye, 220
Bluetick, 122
Bob, Son of Battle (Ollivant), 174
Bones, Sherlock (John Keane), 164
Boots, for sled dog, from Tun-Dra, 127
Border terrier, illustration of, 260
Borland, Hal, note about, 175
Borzoi, 48–50, 114
   also known as Russian Wolf hound,
      51, 52
   illustration of, 257
   photographs of, 48–50
Boston terrier, 117
   illustration of, 263
Bottles with nipples, from Borden, 64
Bouvier des Flandres, illustration of, 259
Bowls
   from Rubbermaid, 64
   from Toppet, 64
Boxer, 117
   illustration of, 258
   in Japan, 71–72
   photograph of, 35
Brabancan, 117
Breed
   care of, 24
   choice of, 24
   deciding on, 16
Breed clubs, photograph of pamphlets
   and information, 21
Breeding, 229–30
Breeding and Rearing of Dogs (Smyth),
   231
Breeding Principles and Practices
   (AKC), 230
Breeds. *See* AKC; Rare breeds; United
   Kennel Club
Briard, 117
   illustration of, 258
Britanny spaniel, 122
   illustration of, 255
Brown, William, photograph by, 96
Browning, Elizabeth Barrett, 158, 159
Browning, Robert, 158
Brussels griffon, illustration of, 262
Bryant, Nelson, 126
Bull baiting, 135
Bulldog, illustration of, 262
Bullmastiff, illustration of, 258
Bull terrier
   illustration of, 260
   photograph of, representative of
      terrier group, 28
Burn, Jerry, photograph by, 199
Burton, Richard (actor), 84

Butterfly Lions (Godden), 31
Buzzing collar, from Thomas Instruments, 63
Byrd, Richard (Admiral), 3

Cairn terrier, illustration of, 261
Call of the Wild (London), 169, 175
Campaigning, 93
Canaan dog, photograph of, 87
Canine adenovirus, 220
Canis lupus (wolf), 238
Care, pamphlet of the Animal Protection Institute, 60
Carl XVI (king of Sweden), 84
Carnation Farms, 52, 54, 55
    address for pamphlets, 62
    dogs of, photograph, 55
Carrying case, 61
Carswell, Laddie, 95
    photographs of, 96
Carter, Amy, 87
    photograph of, 6–7
Carter, Caryn and Chip, 87
Carting, 145
Castration, 223
Catahoula leopard cowdog, photographs of, 138, 140
Cats and Dogs: getting along together, photographs of, 18
Caucasian sheepdog, 117
Cemeteries: Hartsdale, Bubbling Wells, Bide-A-Wee, 67
Center Laboratories of Port Washington, 229
Cerberus, 170
Chamberlain, Safford, note about, 37
Champion (AKC), 115
Chesapeake Bay retriever, illustration of, 255
Chihuahua, 1
    illustrations of, 262
    photograph of, 1
Child with Poodle and Roses, 185
Chinese Names for Oriental Dogs (Mooney), 26
Chinese shar-pei, 78–79
    photograph of, 78
"Chinese Wolf, Ancestor of New World Dogs" (Olsen), 237
Chow Chow, illustration of, 263
Christopher, Saint, 173
City Dog (Wolters), 39
Clayton, John
    note about, 6
    photograph of, 5
Clayton, Laura, photograph by, 5
Closer Look at Dogs (Cook and Pitt), 27
Clumber spaniel, illustration of, 254
Clyde, Bob, 93
    photograph of, 94
Cocker spaniel
    illustration of, 255
    photograph of, 91
Cohen, Edward P., note about, 120
Cole, Babette, illustrations by, 141, 204–206

Coleridge, Samuel Taylor, 121
Collar, 63
Collected Poems (Winters), 160
Collie, 117
    illustrations of rough and smooth, 259
Cologne of Holiday, 63
Color blind, 42n
Combs, 63
Complete Brittany Spaniel (Riddle), 122
Complete Dog Book (AKC), 25, 115
Complete Poodle Clipping and Grooming Book (Kalstone), 44, 45
Complete Puppy & Dog Book (Johnson), 25
Conformation classes, AKC, 115
Conspicuous consumption, dog as, 2
Contraception, 231
Coonhounds, 116, 132
Corgi. See Welsh Corgi
Corgiville Fair (Tudor), 179
Corneal edema, 220
Corson, Samuel A., 173
Count, Ellen, photograph by, 80
Coursing, 242
Cowdog, 138
Cowdog school, 138
Coyote, public menace in South Pasadena, 37
Crate, 62, 252
Cream rinse of Holiday, 63
Crib quilt, 186
"Crook the Amazing Dog," 186
Cruft's Dog Show, 81, 100
Curly-coated retriever, 117
    illustration of, 255
Current Veterinary Therapy Small Animal Practice (Kirk, ed.), 226, 228
Currie, Donna, photograph by, 138
Cycling, 147, 152
Cynophobia, 170

Dachshund, longhaired, smooth, wirehaired: illustrations of, 256, 257
Dalmation
    illustration of, 263
    photographs of, 88, 163
    photograph of, representative of nonsporting group, 29
Dandie Dinmont terrier, illustration of, 260
Daniels, Dick, photograph by, 136
Dannenberg, Mitch, photographs by, 251, 252
Dawn Animal Agency, 168
Death
    disposal of remains, 67
    of Maxwell Riddle's great Dane, 66
    See also Cemeteries
DEC, 221, 222
Deepen Enterprises, 227
De George, Joyce, 249–50

Dell Encyclopedia of Dogs (Ashworth and Kraft), 25
Denlinger's Publishers, 143
Dental Care of Dogs (Nabisco), 227
Dental equipment, 227
Diane the Huntress, 156
Diarrhea, 223
Diethylcarbamazine (DEC), 221, 222
Discovery of a London Monster Called the Blacke Dogg of New-gate, 170
Disney, Walt, 212
Distemper, 219
Dithiazine iodide, 222
Diving Dog, 80
Doberman pinscher, 117
    of Britain, 83
    illustration of, 258
    photograph of, representative of working group, 28
Dog, Structure and Movement (Smythe), 219
Dog & Cat Good Food Book (McGinnis), 56
Dog Behavior, The Genetic Basis (Scott and Fuller), 24
Dog biscuits, recipe for, 56
Dog by Your Side (Hess), 107
Dogcatcher, 243–45
    illustration of, 244
Dog Days at the White House (Bryant), 85
Dogfights, 133–35
    history of, 134–35
    in Japan, 133
    law prohibiting, 133, 135
Dog food, 52–55, 56–59
    contents of, 58
    digestibility of, 58
    dry, 54
    industry, 52
    moist, 54
    nutrition in, 58, 59
    semimoist, 54, 58
Dog for Joey (Gilbert), 177
Doggie cleanup, 38
Doggie Dooley, 38
Doggy Dent, 227
Dognapping, 159, 247
"Dog of Montargis" (Lang), 174
Dog Owner's Medical Manual (Sessions), 226
Dog photographers, 187
Dog-pulled bicycle, 147
Dogs (Calder), 171
Dogs, Best Breeds for Young People (Bronson), 27
Dogs, Pets of Pedigree (Troy), 25
Dogs, Their History and Development (Ash), 31
Dogs and Puppies (Rockwell), 27
Dogs & Puppies Coloring Album (Warner), 212
Dog's Book of Birds (Parnall), 212
Dog's Book of Bugs (Griffen), 212
Dogs for Defense, 152
Dog Show Specialties, 165

272

Dogsteps (Elliot), 231
Dog trainers
  Ed Beckmann, 38–41
  theatrical, 162–63
Dog Training My Way (Woodhouse), 39
Dog Visualizations, Dog Lover's Complete Guide (Sprung, ed.), 117
Dog Who Thought He Was a Boy (Annett), 178
Dog Writers' Association of America, 81
Dolgow, Joanne, photograph by, 173
Domestication, 235
Door, 61
Doranne of California, 203
Drug detection, 148
Dry skin, 58
Dumbbells, 35

Eachus, J. E., photograph of, 244
"Earl Eyman's Dog Act," 184
Ecology of Stray Dogs (Beck), 245
Elizabeth I (queen), 134
Elkins, Pat, 207
Empusaie, 170
Encyclopedia of Dogs (Fiorone, ed.), 25
English cocker spaniel
  illustration of, 255
  name explained, 23
  photograph of, 91
English foxhound, illustration of, 256
English setter, 110
  illustration of, 255
English shepherd, photograph of and quote about, 137
English springer spaniel
  illustration of, 254
  photograph of, 96
English toy spaniel, illustration of, 262
Ente Nazionale della Cinafilia Italiana, 102 (caption)
Esbilac, milk replacement, from Borden, 64
Especially Dogs . . . Especially at Stillmeadow (Taber), 97–98
Estrus, 231
Euthanasia, 66
Everything I Know About Training and Racing Sled Dogs (Attla), 131
Expenses of dog, photograph and caption, 57
Explosives, detection, 148

Fala (Scottish terrier), 85
Fancy
  definition, 89
  international report, 79–80
Far From the Madding Crowd (Hardy), 141–42
Federal Animal Welfare Act, 135, 249
Fédération Cynologique International, 71

Felt, Henry, note about, 176
Ferrets, 151
Fertility control, 231
Fiber, in dog food, 59
Fidelco Foundation of Connecticut, 146
Field Dog Stud Book, 116
Field spaniel, illustration of, 254
Field trial categories, AKC, 126
Field Trials—History, Management, and Judging Standards (Brown), 121
Fire alert decals, 97
Fitzgo, The Wild Dog of Central Park (Wilkes), 246
Flat-coated retriever, 110
  illustration of, 255
Flea collar, 226
Fleas, 159, 225–26
Flea Story (Lionni), 179
Flush (Woolf), 158, 159
Food, dogs as
  by Aztecs, 2
  in Taiwan, 72
Foxhounds, 125, 132
Fox terrier, 117, 151, 210–12, 229
  illustrations of smooth and wire, 260, 261
  photographs of, 14–20, 46, 112, 165, 278
Franck, Frederick
  note about, 76
  photograph of, 74
Franck, Lukas, photographs by, 74, 75
Franklin, Benjamin, 152
French bulldog, illustration of, 263
Friend Indeed (Jagoda), 171
Fritts, Steven H.
  note about, 241
  photograph of, 240
  photographs by, 239, 241
Futh, Sara, 81

Gaines
  address for pamphlets, 62
  Fido award, 167
Gait, 231
Garm, 170
Gazette, The (AKC), 116, 230
General Foods, 52, 54, 263
German shepherd, 117
  in Germany, 83
  illustration of, 258
  as military dog, 149
  military dog in Vietnam, 152
  photograph of, 249
German Shepherd Today (Strickland and Moses), 142
German shorthaired pointer, illustration of, 254
German wirehaired pointer, illustration of, 255
Gilbert, William P., 187
Gipson, Fred, 175
Glass and porcelain, dogs represented in, 202
Glassberg, Richard (D.V.M.), 164
God Had A Dog (Leach), 170

Golden retriever, 117
  illustration of, 255
  photograph of, representative of sporting group, 29
  training for field trials, 119–20
Good Dog Book (Siegal), 26
Gordon setter, illustration of, 255
Gould, Jack, quotation from, 6
Gravity's Rainbow (Pynchon), 211
Gray, Gary, dumbbells, 35
Grean, Spida, photographs by, 3, 24, 101, 102, 144, 156
Great Dane, 66, 117
  illustration of, 259
  life expectancy of, 162
Greater Swiss mountain dog, photograph of, 87
Great pyrenees
  illustration of, 259
  photograph of, 11
Greyhound, 118, 132
  illustration of, 257
  photograph of, 132
Greyhound Publications, 132
Grits (White House dog), 87
Grizmek's Animal Life Encyclopedia (Grizmek, ed.), 243
Groomers, photographs of, 43–45
Grooming and Showing Toy Dogs (Hogg and Berndt), 44
Grooming tips, 45
Groups (AKC)
  illustrations of, 254–63
  photographically illustrated with owners' comments, 28–31
Guide Dog Foundation for the Blind (of Smithtown, New York), 146
Guide Dog News, 146
Guide Mi Chien, 81
Gwynn ab Nudd, 170

Hair dryer, 63
Hair spray, 98
Hamlyn Guide to Dogs, 25
Hampton Veterinary Hospital, 216–17
Handlers, 93–97
  Baines, Art, 98
  Carswell, Laddie, 95
  Clyde, Bob, 93
  fee structure, 95
  income of, 93
  qualifications of, 93
Hardy, Thomas, 141
Hark! Hark! The Dogs Do Bark (Blegvad), 179
Harnesses, from Zima Products, 130
Harrier, illustration of, 256
Harry books: Harry the Dirty Dog and No Roses for Harry (Zion), 178
Harry Cat's Pet Puppy (Selden), illustration from, 246
Hartsdale, Pet cemetery, 3, 67
Hawkes, Sarah, note about, 3
Hawks and Hawking (Bert), 142
Hayfever, 229

Heartworm, 221, 250
Heat, 230, 231
Hecate, 170
Heinz, 52, 54
Heirs, dogs as, 51
Hemorrhagic gastroenteritis, 223
Hepatitis, 220
Hereditary disorders, 22 (caption)
Hermanibus, 170
Hero
    dog as, 3, 174
    illustration of, 149
History of the British Dog, 135
Holiday: cologne, cream rinse, 63
Horner, Tom (judge), 109, 111–12
Hound-dog Man and *Savage Sam*
    (Gipson), 178
Hound group, 30
    illustrations of, 256–57
Hound of the Baskervilles (Doyle), 153
Housebreaking, 38
Howell Book House, 143
How to Bring Up Your Pet Dog
    (Unkelbach), 26
*How to Raise a Dog in the City and
    in the Suburbs* (Kinney
    and Honneycut), 26
How to Show Your Dog and Win
    (Unkelbach), 107
*How to Train, Groom and Show Your
    Dog* (Saunders), 43
How to Train a Watchdog (Sessions),
    39
How to Train Hunting Dogs (Brown),
    121
How to Train Your Dog in Six Weeks
    (Landesman and Berman), 40
Humane Society of the United States,
    249
Hundred and One Dalmations
    (Smith), 163
Hunting Symphony (Mozart), 171
Hurry Home Candy (DeJong), 246
Hydrophobia (rabies), 2, 81, 162,
    220–21, 228

I Am A Puppy (Risom), 177
Ident-A-Pet, 52
Iditarod race, 128–31
Iditarod Runner, 130
Income tax deduction, dog as, 54
Inheritance of Coat Color in Dogs
    (Little), 231
Inn, Frank (dog trainer), 162, 168
Innocent Killers (van Lawich-
    Goodall), 243
International Fox Hunters' Stud Book,
    116
International news from
    Germany, 73
    Great Britain, 72
    Italy, 72
    Japan, 71
    Monaco, 72
    Northern Ireland, 72
    South Africa, 72

Soviet Union, 73
    Taiwan, 72
International Sled Dog Racing
    Association, 127, 131
Intestinal parasites, 222
Irish setter, illustration of, 254
Irish terrier, illustration of, 261
Irish water spaniel, illustration of, 254
Irish wolfhound
    illustration of, 257
    photograph of, 145
Iscariot, Judas, 170
Italian greyhound, illustration of, 262

Jack (Sinclair), 169
Jagger the Dog from Elsewhere (Key),
    179
Jaguar Cave, 235
Jamison, photographs by, 65
Japanese spaniel, illustration of, 262
Jean (film star), 162
Jip (film star), 162
Johnson, Lyndon Baines, 85
Johnson Professional Mortuary
    Service, 162
Jones's Animal Nursing (Pinniger),
    224
J. P. and Moonlight, address of, 65
Judge (AKC), how to become, 116
Judging (AKC), point system, 110
Junior Showmanship (Boyer), 107
Just So Stories (Kipling), 252

Kantor, Mackinlay, 125, 175
Kassabian, Ashod, 201
Keeshond, illustration of, 263
Kelly, Hairy, 151
Kennel, automated, 67
Kennel cough, 220
Kennel Union of South Africa, 79
Kerry blue terrier, illustration of, 261
King, Paul, 164
King, Wayne, 133
King Lear (Shakespeare), 175
Klein, Stephen, photograph by, 110
Komondor, illustration of, 258
Korker, Clarence, photographs by, 213
Kostka, Saint Stanislaus, 170
Kristal, Marc, note about, 167
Krueger, Gary
    note about, 188
    photographs by, 188–89
Kufeld, Georgia, photograph of, 69
Kuvasz, illustration of, 259

Labrador retriever, 13, 250–52
    illustration of, 254
    photograph of, 252
Lackland Air Force Base, 148, 152
Lakeland terrier, illustration of, 260
L. A. Pet Park, 160
Lassie (film star), 162
Lassie Come Home (Knight), 175

Layne, Abner A., photograph of, 53
Leash laws
    of England, 81
    of South Pasadena, 36–37
Leavitt, David, 86
    photographs by, 86
Leptosporosis, 220
Levamisole, 222
Lhasa apso, illustration of, 263
Liberated Dog (Margolis and
    Grayson), 40
Lieberman, Martin J., 236
Liggett Group, 52, 54
Linn's Chinese shar-pei, 78–79
Linoleic acid, 58
Lion dog, 117
Little Duster (Charmantz), 178
Little lion dog, 103
    photographs of, 92, 103, 104
Long Island Rare Breed Association,
    101
    second annual match of, 91
Lore of the Dog (Dale-Green), 170, 172
Lost and stolen dogs, 247
Love, praise, reward training, 38
Loy, Myrna, 165, 210
Ludwig, Joan, photograph by, 110
Lurcher, 152

McCall, Maggie, note about, 84
McCrackin, Mark, note about, 212
McGinnis, Dr. Terri, 56
Madeline's Rescue (Bemelmans), 177
Magnus, Simon, 170
Magyar dog organization, 80
Mail order, dog supplies, 69
Majors, dog shows, 115
Malathion, 226
Maltese, illustration of, 262
Manchester terrier, illustration of, 260
"Man-Made Dogs" (Clutton-Brock),
    237
Man Meets Dog (Lorenz), 24, 177
    quoted in reference to dog trials, 42n
Margolis, Matthew, 168
Marlborough, Dowager Duchess of
    (née Gladys Deacon), 85
Mars, 52, 54
Marvin, John T., 81
Mastiff, illustration of, 258
Mastino Napolitano, 83. *See also*
    Neapolitan mastiff
Maxey, Charles, photographs by,
    48–50
*Maxwell Riddle's Complete Book of
    Puppy Training*, 26
Medications, 218–19, 220, 221, 222
Meisen Breeding Manual (Meisenzahl),
    231
Meisen Poodle Manual (Meisenzahl),
    142
Methoxychlor, 226
Meyer, Nicki, photograph of, 252
Microfilaria, 221
Milk
    digestibility of, 58

as dog food, 57, 223
for sick dogs, 223
Miller, Karl (dog trainer), 163
Mills of God (Armstrong), 177
Milne, A. A., 176
Mind of the Dog (Buytendijk), 24
Miniature pinscher, illustration of, 262
Miniature spit dogs, 185
Minicozzi, Philip, photograph by, 9
Mixed-breed. *See* Mongrel
Modern Dog Encyclopedia (Davis, ed.), 25
Mongrel, 16, 74–76
George Bernard Shaw quoted, 91
Morello, Joe, 146
Movers: Flying Fur Travel Service, Pet Transportation Service, World Wide Pet Transport, 68
Mowat, Farley, 175, 243
Muffin (Browne), 179
Muzzle, for turn-of-the-century police dogs, 150
My Dog, Your Dog (Low), 27
My Literary Zoo (Sanborn), 172
Myrus, Don
note about, 278
photographs by, 2, 12, 14, 15–20, 28–31, 35, 43–46, 92–95, 101, 108–13, 118, 194, 197, 202, 244, 278

Nail groomer, 63
Narcolepsy, 232
National Center for Disease Control, 228
National Greyhound Association, 116
National Newfoundland Club of America, 145
National Shooting Sports Foundation, 120
Natural History of Nonsense (Evans), 159
Natural Method of Dog Training (Whitney), 40
Neapolitan mastiffs, 102
photographs of, 90, 101, 102
Nelson, Kim, photograph by, 188
Nelson Sled Dog Racing Equipment, 131
Neurosis, 218, 223
Never Cry Wolf (Mowatt), 243
Never Is a Long Time (Cate), 177
New Dog Owners Handbook (Hajas and Sarkany), 26
Newfoundlands
illustration of, 259
trained as life savers, 150
Newlon, Nickie
note about, 213
photographs of, 213
Newton, Donald W., photograph by, 53
Nicki Meyer Educational Effort, 252
Nipper, 197
Nonsporting group, 29
illustrations of, 263

Nordkyn Outfitters, 131, 147
Norsk Kennel Club, 79
North American Sheep Dog Society, 140
Northern Dog News, 131
North Jersey Bandog Club, 235
Norwegian elkhound, illustration of, 257
Norwich terrier, illustration of, 261
No Tangle, of Lambert-Kay, 63
Nothing at All (Ga'g), 178
Nothing But a Dog (Katz), 177
Now That You Own A Puppy (Tate), 26, 141
Nutrient Requirements of Dogs, 59
Nutrition in dog food
animal by-products, bone meal, calcium, canned, dry, grains, legumes, meat, minerals, phosphorous, protein, vitamins, 59
for Iditarod race, 128

Obedience Class Instruction for Dogs (Strickland), 40
Obedience judge, 114
Obedience trials, rules of, 33–35
Odyssey (Homer), 172, 174
Of Englishe Dogges, The Diversities, The Names, The Nature and The Properties (Caius), 31
Of Pedigree Unknown (Drabble), 151
Old Drum, 173
Old English bulldogge, 86
Old English sheepdog, 16, 117, 139
illustration of, 259
photograph of, 139
Old Fritz, photograph of, 264
Old Yeller (Gipson), 179
Olsen, John W., note about, 237
Order of Wolves (Fiennes), 237
Oriental breeds, 27
Oster
hair dryer and nail groomer, 63
shears, photograph of, 60
O'Toole, Daniel, photographs by, 1, 11, 58, 123, 139
Otterhound, illustration of, 256
"Outsiders" Iditarod (Hooker), 130
Owens, Bill, photographs by, 10, 57, 216, 278

Pads, 61
Palegaura Cave, Iraq, 236
Papillon, illustration of, 262
Para-influenza, 220
Pariah dog, 87
Paul and His Little Big Dog (Darling), 145
Paul Loeb's Complete Book of Dog Training (Loeb), 40
Pearsall Guide to Successful Dog Training (Pearsall), 41
Pearson's Town and Country Carts, 145

Pekingese, 117
illustration of, 262
photograph of, representative of toy group, 31
Perites, 175
Pescod, Tom (D.V.M.), 215–17
Pesticides, 226
Pet Dog, 183
Pete (film star), 162
Petfinders
New York, 247
Studio City, 164
Petfood Industry, 59
Pet-Haven, 162
Pet Hotel, 164
Pet Names (Taggart), 27
Pets/Supplies/Marketing, 59
Picone, Raymond, photograph by, 105
Pie and the Patty Pan (Potter), 179
Pinkwater, Jill Miriam, illustrations by, 22, 100, 126, 218
Pinworms, 222
Pit Dog Report, 135
Pit Dogs, 135
Please Don't Call Me Fido (Johnes), 26
Plott hound, 122
Pluto, 212
Poaching, 152
Pocket Encyclopedia of Dogs (Swedrup), 25
Podzianowski, Pat, 133
Pointer, illustration of, 254
Polecat, 151
Polo shirts (for dogs), 65
Poodle
corded, 100
illustrations of miniature, standard, and toy, 262, 263
photograph of miniature, 99
photograph of standard, 32
representative of nonsporting group, 29
Portuguese water dog, description and photograph of, 105
Powell, William, 165, 210
Practical Guide to Dogs (White and Joshua), 26
Practical Hunter's Dog Book (Falk), 122
Prairie dog, 151
Pudding and Pie (Welch), 178
Pug, 117
illustration of, 262
Puli, illustration of, 259
Punishment in military training, 148
Puppies
in bed with, 18
starting off right, 18
Puppy for You, A (Hess), 27
Puppy mills, 16
Pure Bred Dogs—American Kennel Gazette, 116, 230
Purple Ribbon Pedigree, 116
Pyrethruin, 226

Quaker Oaks, 52, 54
Quarantine, England, 81

Quick Guide to Standards for Show Dogs (Riddle), 107

Rabies (hydrophobia), 3, 81, 162, 220–21, 228
Racing
    coonhounds, foxhounds, greyhounds, whippets, 132
    sled dogs, 126–31
Racing Alaskan Sled Dogs (Vaudrin, ed.), 131
Racing sled, from Tun-Dra, 127
Ragman, 152
Rakshases, 170
Ralston Purina, 52, 54
Rare breeds, 101
Rat pits, 151
Rawlings, C. L., photograph by, 140
Rechler, Roger, photograph of, 30
Redbone hound, 122
Redington, Joe, Sr., 128
Retriever Training the Modern Way (Scales), 122
Reward conditioning, 148
Rhodesian ridgeback, illustration of, 256
Riddle, Maxwell, photographs of, 110
Rin Tin Tin (film star), 162, 168
Robinson, Gerald, photograph of, 144
Roch, Saint, 173
Romanof, Claire, note about, 20
Romanof, Richard Benjamin, photographs by, 94, 99
Roomkin, Janice
    note about, 51
    photograph of, 49
Roosevelt, Franklin D., 85
Roosevelt, Teddy, 169
Rotenone, 226
Rothbury terrier, 117
Rottweiler, 3
    illustration of, 258
    photograph of, 3
Roundworm, 222
Royal College of Veterinary Surgeons, England, 224
Ruffle Bar, 250
Ruffles, photograph of, 249
Rufio's T-shirts, 65
Russian tracker, 117
Russian wolfhounds, 51–52

Safari combs, 63
Saint Bernard, illustration of, 258
Saluki, illustration of, 257
Samoyed, illustration of, 258
San-Away, from NBS, 65
Sanctioned Match Shows, AKC, 98
Sand fleas, 224
Sandy (of *Annie*), 87, 168
Sanitary line, 228
Santa Syndrome, 223
Scent and the Scenting Dog (Syrotuck), 153
Schipperke, 117
    illustration of, 263

Schnauzer
    illustration of giant, 259
    illustration of miniature, 261
    illustration of standard, 258
    photograph of, 99
Schulberg, Budd, 216
Schulz, Charles, 212
Schumacher, Lou, 168
Scottish deerhound, illustration of, 256
Scottish terrier, 15, 198
    illustration of, 261
Scylla, 170
Sealyham terrier, 3
    illustration of, 260
Secrets of Dog Show Handling (Migliorini), 107
Sect-A-Spray, 226
Seeing-eye dogs, training of, 146
Seeing Eye Guide, 146
Selecting a breed, *Man Meets Dog* (Lorenz), 20
Sex education, dogs used for, 223
Shafer, Evelyn M., 187
    photograph by, 96
Shakespeare, William, 134, 175
Shar-pei, 78–79
    photograph of, 78
Shaw, George Bernard, quoted about mongrels, 91
Shay, Sunny, photograph of, 30, 94
Shearing, George, 146
Shetland sheepdog, 117
    illustration of, 259
Shih tzu, illustration of, 262
Siberian husky, 16, 23, 73
    illustration of, 258
Siberian Husky Club of America, pamphlet of, 24
Silas and Con (Stewart), 177
Silky terrier, illustration of, 262
Simon, Peter
    note about, 190
    photographs by, 8, 9, 41, 70, 106, 154, 181, 191–93, 253, 264
Skeletal muscles, photograph of, 220
Skeleton (fox terrier), photograph of, 222
Skye terrier, illustration of, 261
Sled dog racing, 126–31
    Alaskan, 128–31
    Iditarod, 128–31
    rules of, 127
Sled dogs, 126–27
Sleep, effect on longevity, 232
Slick Jack, smooth fox terrier, subject of "The Puppy Journal," 14–20
Smith, Red, 98
Smooth Brussels griffon, 117
Smooth fox terrier, 14–20
    photographs of, 14–20, 278
Snoopy, 212
Snowdancer Siberian huskies, photographs of, 147
Société Canine de Monaco, 80
Société Canine Internationale de la Méditerranée, 80
Soft coated wheaten terrier, illustration of, 261

Sokolov's (Raymond A.) dog food flavor test, 56
Sokolowski, James H., 231
Some Swell Pup (Sendak and Margolis), 25
Southern American fox hunt, 125
Soviet dogs, 107
Spaniels, 158
    photographs of, 91
Spaniel Training for Modern Shooters (Hopper), 122
Special Registry Services (AKC), 71
Spitz, Carl (dog trainer), 163
Sporting Dog Journal, 135
Sporting group, 29
    illustrations of, 254–55
Sportsmen's insurance, 125–26
Spot (film star), 162
Staffordshire bull terrier, 151
    illustration of, 260
Standard Book of Dog Grooming (Fenger and Steinle), 43, 45
Star Dog (Lightner), 179
Star quality, 110
Stewards, 112
Stiffel, William B., 116
Stinchfield, R., photograph by, 239
Stinson, George, 165
Stodghill, Tom Drum, photograph of, 137
Stone Brothers, 201
Strays, 2, 245–46, 248
Street immunity, 221
Strongheart (film star), 162
Stud Book (AKC), 87, 107
Stud Book Register (AKC), 230
Stud service, 230
Successive approximation, 148
Sugar, tolerance for, 58
Sulphur dip (old fashioned), 105
Superpuppy (Pinkwater), 26
Sussex spaniel, illustration of, 255
Swenson, Rick, photograph of, 129
Swinford, John (D.V.M.), 236
Swinford bandog, 234
Swope, Martha, photograph by, 168

Tajiri, Vincent
    notes about, 165, 194
    photographs by, 32, 34, 161, 194–96
Take Them Round, Please (Horner), 109
Tales of a Seadog Family (Lasker), 179
Target Group Index, 60
Tattooing, for identification, 52
Taylor, Elizabeth, 84
Team and Trail, 131
Teeth, 227
Temperature of dogs, 220
Terrier and Pups Ninepin Pulltoy, 184
Terrier group, 28
    illustrations of, 260–61
That Hilarious First Year (Boynton), 26
Theory of the Leisure Class, 2